Mothers and Other Clown

Mothers and Other Clowns

The Stories of Alice Munro

Magdalene Redekop

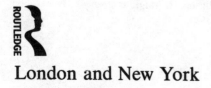

London and New York

First published 1992
by Routledge
11 New Fetter Lane, London EC4P 4EE

Simultaneously published in the USA and Canada
by Routledge
a division of Routledge, Chapman and Hall, Inc.
29 West 35th Street, New York, NY 10001

© 1992 Magdalene Redekop

Typeset in 10/12 Times by
Falcon Typographic Art Ltd, Fife, Scotland
Printed and bound in Great Britain by
Clays Ltd, St Ives plc

British Library Cataloguing-in-Publication Data
Redekop, Magdalene
  Mothers and Other Clowns: Stories of
  Alice Munro
  I. Title
  813.54

Library of Congress Cataloging-in-Publication Data
Redekop, Magdalene.
  Mothers and other clowns: the stories of Alice Munro / Magdalene
  Redekop.
  p. cm.
  Includes bibliographical references (p. 240) and index.
  1. Munro, Alice – Criticism and interpretation. 2. Magic realism
  (Literature) 3. Mothers in literature. I. Title.
  PR9199.3.M8Z87 1992
  813'.54 – dc20 91–33773

ISBN 0–415–01097–7
ISBN 0–415–01098–5 (pbk.)

In memory of
my mother, Elisabeth (Schellenberg) Falk
and of my friends
Doreen Otto
Birgit Baurmeister
and
Inge Pache

Contents

Abbreviations

Dance of the Happy Shades – DHS
Lives of Girls and Women – LGW
Something I've Been Meaning to Tell You – SIB
Who Do You Think You Are? – WDY
The Moons of Jupiter – MJ
The Progress of Love – PL
Friend of My Youth – FY
Oxford English Dictionary – OED

(See bibliography for full details about editions used.)

Preface

This book mimes the circling and apparently repetitive movement of Alice Munro's fiction. What is much harder to capture is the freshness in each of her stories, the way each one ventures daringly into new territory. To impose a master narrative on a writer who has explicitly rejected long narrative forms would be wrong, and yet some kind of ordering was necessary if I was to avoid writing a book which was merely a collection of random samples. Since Munro herself does not write chapters in the usual sense, what should a chapter be in a book about Munro? The shape of this book reflects my response to the dilemma. I have tried to define the concerns and images around which Munro's fiction circles. At the same time, however, I insist on the provisional nature of these definitions. I am not retelling *the* story that Munro is telling. A narrative does, nevertheless, emerge in my book: it is the story that I hear Munro telling *me*.

Mary Jacobus has pointed to a "drift toward narrative in recent works of feminist criticism" (Jacobus, 1986, 29). Munro's fiction suggests some reasons why a woman might resort to storytelling and might rely increasingly on the authority of her own personal experience. I see in Munro's stories a reflection of my own wariness of symbols, metaphors, and myths. I haven't always been so suspicious. After years of teaching my students about the quest pattern – departure/return – I can remember being startled by my own anger. I was sitting with my 2-year-old daughter one day, watching (for the third time) the video of a Muppet Christmas special. There were Ernie and Bert and assorted monsters – male, every one of them – having a marvellous adventure. And there was the only female, Miss Piggy, waiting like Conrad's Intended, absorbed in her own mirror reflection. The first two times I watched, I happily identified with questing Man. The penny dropped while I watched for the third time as Ernie and Bert, Sesame Street buddies, put on a play within a play: "The Night Before Christmas." Bert, coming on in female costume, protests: "Ernie, must you always humiliate me?" to which Ernie replies: "*Somebody* has to play Momma." Indeed! Especially on the night of the birth of Christ. The next time I watched the video (at my children's insistence) I identified not with adventuring Man but with the pig and I felt nausea. I guess I was trapped once too often and now I feel as if the old myths have designs on me and on my daughter.

Such a wariness has, of course, far-reaching implications for my work as a literary critic. I am amazed when people talk about feminism as if it were some kind of easy polemical position to take. It would be much easier to take the line of least resistance. To acknowledge my alienation from these patterns is to court paralysis as a critic. I was much more clear about my job as a critic when I could accept without question Northrop Frye's lucid distinction between ideology and mythology. I can still agree that an ideology is an "applied mythology" (Frye, 1990, 23) but I can no longer get myself to that place where the "ideological function disappears" and the myths become "purely literary" (Frye, 1990, 31). I do not think of myself as one of those critics "less interested in literature than in the relation of literature to some primary ideological interest, religious, historical, radical, feminist or whatever" (Frye, 1990, 27). It is true that literature, for me, is "subordinated to something else which by definition is more important and urgent" (Frye, 1990, 27) but that something else is not an ideology but life. My working assumption is that an ideology is most dangerous when it is most hidden and that our electronic culture works, minute by minute, to conceal the continued power of ancient ideologies to obstruct life itself.

My response to these dilemmas has been to opt for a kind of narrative criticism. The old gentle methods of literary criticism – sorting out themes and allusions, tracing patterns – just don't work with a writer like Munro who repeatedly undermines her own fiction. While there is no master-story finally sanctioned or fixed by Munro, the activity of storytelling is seen in her stories as an aspect of life itself. Munro shows people surviving by means of story; it is what enables them to go on with their lives. I would not have bothered writing this book if I did not consider Munro's stories to be among the finest I have ever read. Her unique strength, however, is intimately bound up with her democratic approach to storytelling. We all exercise power in this way, she seems to say, whether we know it or not, whether we do it well or do it poorly.

The story in this book is simultaneously the story of Munro's developing aesthetic and the story of my developing understanding of that aesthetic. I tell the story as my argument in the first part of this book, then recapitulate it in full in the chapters that deal with *Lives of Girls and Women* and *Who Do You Think You Are?* Those chapters, since they are concerned with Munro's two efforts to construct something like a "novel," form the double hinge of this book. Since Munro kept writing and publishing stories while I was working out this argument, I kept revising my reading of earlier stories in the light of the ones recently published. This is the disconcerting but inevitable consequence of writing on a living author. Paulina Palmer has recently drawn attention to what she sees as a scandalous failure of contemporary feminist theory to deal with contemporary women writers (Palmer, 1989, 3). I think of these contemporary writers as living voices and writing on Munro has made me very conscious of the gap to which Palmer draws attention. Munro has no overt feminist agenda and yet no writer is more devastatingly effective at dismantling the operations of our patriarchal structures. At the same time, however, she is curiously inarticulate when she is interviewed about her writing. She cannot speak the language of literary theory – but then, neither can the women about whom she writes. Like many feminists, I have been disturbed when the battered woman I am trying to help does not speak my language. I am attracted to Munro's writing partly because the language she uses has the potential of speaking to many kinds of women. In trying to account for Munro's achievement, I myself have been helped greatly by the writings of various theorists. The relation between contemporary feminist theory and contemporary storytelling, however, is not simply a matter of finding the vocabulary to explain what the storytellers are doing. I have excavated an aesthetic from Munro's stories because I want to invert this premise and show that Munro's stories have a lot to teach theorists writing today.

I know very well, of course, that Munro herself claims to have no such thing as an aesthetic. That's just because she thinks in images. If you think along with those images – houses, clothing, cameras, eyes, food – a very powerful aesthetic emerges from her fiction. From *Dance of the Happy Shades* to *Friend of My Youth*, I have followed a simple chronological line and selected for attention those stories that offer a distillation of an emerging aesthetic that revolves around mother figures. Substitute mothers are the focus of a struggle to forge a relation between compassion and irony. Women figure prominently in this struggle because of the burden on them to *be* compassionate, to be the caregivers in a patriarchal society. We live in a world that is desperately in need of nurture. "*Somebody* has to play Momma." Like Adrienne Rich, I am a feminist

> because I feel endangered, psychically and physically, by this society, and because I believe . . . that we can no longer afford to keep the female principle – the mother in all women and the woman in many men – straitened within the tight little postindustrial family, or within any male-induced notion of where the female principle is valid and where it is not.
>
> (Rich, 1975, 104–105)

Munro explores female experience as a way of rethinking an old conflict. Meda's withdrawal, in "Meneseteung," is a response to an intense version of a conflict that is of crucial importance to all writers. Munro stages the conflict between compassion and irony as a struggle between "keepers" and "watchers" (PL, 88) and the maternal clown makes it possible to mediate between these two. Mothers who clown for their children have always known this. What I have come to see, eventually, is a new approach to comedy that entails a new way of thinking about autobiographical form.

Munro invokes details from her own life not as a traditional autobiographer would do, but as a clown would do. A clown, for example, might take her own characteristic way of walking or talking and exaggerate it for comic effect. Lucy Ricardo, a clown alluded to in a Munro story (MJ, 18), made use of her own pregnancy in this way on the *I Love Lucy* show. Patricia Mellencamp calls it a "hyperreal pregnancy" (1986, 88). Adapting language used by Munro to describe the minister in "Wild Swans," we might say that Lucy's was a real pregnancy posing as a phantom pregnancy posing as a real pregnancy. Munro's posing of female helplessness, however, is much more dangerous than Lucy's because she dares to pose material from her own mother's life. The mother with Parkinson's Disease is not Munro's mother only, but the helplessness of the face glimpsed in "The Ottawa Valley" forms a thread of referentiality – slender as a spider web but strong enough to become a means of resisting old symbols.

It is by means of this courageous comedy that Munro achieves a new way of making "the progress of love." When Swift used that phrase as a title, he initiated a satiric questioning and Munro pushes further with those questions. Her very refusal to write long narratives reflects her rejection of the old kind of progress. As my title implies, I see her stories, instead, as forming a kind of parade or procession. She writes aspects of the old narratives in slow motion or with exaggerated attention to specific details. The result is a kind of tableau effect, as if old conventions are briefly held still for us so that we may examine their workings. Her collections are like a long float parade, a genre that (according to Francis Sparshott) has been "neglected by aestheticians" although it is a "long-established tradition . . . often associated with annual festivals – Mardi Gras, homecoming week, carnival week" (Sparshott, 1988, 326). Munro's collections resemble the "typical form of these parades": "a procession of wagons decorated and surmounted by fantastically dressed people in tableau, interspersed with bands and accompanied by clowns and tumblers" (Sparshott, 1988, 326). Paul Bouissac's work on circus language has helped me to see that such performances make a kind of poetic space that holds the old narratives still for a moment, allowing us (even as we are entertained) to walk around them and see how they work.

Oddly enough, I had already worked on a similar conjunction of generic transformations when I wrote my doctoral dissertation on James Hogg. Hogg wrote and rewrote his "life" repeatedly. I studied his clownings and self-parodies more than a decade before I ever considered writing about Munro. Imagine my astonishment, then, when I discovered (well into the writing of this book) that Alice Munro (whose maiden name was Alice Laidlaw) traces her ancestry back to the Ettrick Shepherd. Munro confirmed this connection in a letter to me: "Yes. One of Margaret

Laidlaw's brothers (she was James Hogg's mother) was my direct ancestor."
Now I see that Munro's egalitarian approach to storytelling – like Hogg's
– is based on an oral model. Her explorations of the idea of matrilineal
narrative, moreover, seem to me bound up with the fact that she traces her
own lineage back to the woman – Hogg's mother – who helped Sir Walter
Scott compile *Minstrelsy of the Scottish Border*. The Scottish connection is
increasingly pronounced in *Friend of My Youth* and may be something to
look out for in future Munro stories, especially as it enriches her developing
ideas about history.

Adapting a passage from *Lives of Girls and Women*, an honest critic
might admit that "it is a shock, when you have dealt so cunningly,
powerfully, with [Alice Munro's stories], to come back and find [them]
still there" (LGW, 251). I have taken a long time completing this book
because each summer when I came back to the stories, after a year of
teaching, I found them changed, ever more complex, more treacherous,
more rewarding. At the same time, however, each revision of this book
has intensified the focus on maternity. Munro's courageous explorations
of this issue, indeed, have influenced my own writing of family "history"
in dialogue with my sisters. I have written down this story, this story that I
think Munro is telling me, in the hopes that my reading will find or perhaps
help to create a shared community of readers.

When I first began work on Munro, no full-length study of her fiction had
yet been published. Now I have a whole shelf full of books on Munro. Their
cumulative impact supports John Moss's observation about the "continued
refusal" of Munro's fiction "to yield graciously to critical inquiry" (*Globe
and Mail*, 3 February 1990). Other critics have found other ways of
ordering Munro's work. My way begins with the concession that it cannot
be mastered. Readers should not come to this book in search of symbolic
design but rather with a willingness to join in an adventure. I hope the book
that has finally taken shape approximates the spirit of Munro's storytelling.
I hope that my readers will be encouraged to reread Munro and that they
will be made conscious of their contrasting stories and of the communities
which condition the construction of those stories.

Acknowledgements

An acknowledgement – as distinct from knowledge – is an act of faith. The paradox inherent in the convention, however, is that it is somebody else's faith one acknowledges. Let me begin, then, by thanking Alice Munro for having faith in her readers.

Without the support of Linda Hutcheon, this book would never have been written. She not only administered the initial push that got me started, but also offered unfailing support throughout the years of writing and revising. In the meantime, Janice Price did a marvellous imitation of a woman who kept believing in a book that did not exist.

My colleagues here at Victoria College have offered ongoing support and lent me their tolerant ears. I am indebted to all of them but especially to Paul Bouissac, James Carscallen, Eleanor Cook, Michael Laine and Francis Sparshott. My debt to Northrop Frye will be obvious and his personal support and encouragement have meant more to me than I can say. I am especially indebted to Jennifer Levine, not only for her insights about jokes but also for being the first to point out to me that my mock mother is a clown. Jay Macpherson's "Substitutions" sustained me throughout the writing of this book. I abducted her Tadwit at a time of crisis; when I was finished, I put him right back where I found him. Other friends and colleagues have been invaluable, in particular William Aide, Donna Bennett, Russell Brown, Bill Keith, Maggie Kilgour, Mary O'Connor, and Ted Parkinson. I am grateful to Ted Davidson for inviting me to give a paper on Munro at an MLA convention, and to Sam Solecki, for inviting me to present a paper to the Department of English here at the University of Toronto. I thank my friend and colleague Patricia Brückmann for the second-hand rose and for her crucial support during my years at Trinity College. I gratefully acknowledge assistance from Trinity College's Cassidy Fund in the preparation of my manuscript.

I learned a great deal, especially about allusion, from the senior essay on Munro that Clare MacMartin wrote under my supervision. Sydney Shep often startled me out of my settled ways with Renaissance examples; she helped me to clarify my thoughts about imitation and about jokes. Mary

Bertram made invaluable suggestions based on her experience as mother, teacher, and clown. Barbara Ibronyi spent an afternoon talking with me about our shared readings of Munro's stories, and subsequently did the painting of the Egyptian goddess Nūt (pronounced Noot) that adorns the cover of this book. The painting was not done as an illustration of my book or of Munro's fiction, but in an uncanny way it captures what I find most compelling in Munro: her courageous confrontation with something black and the resulting experience of celebration and renewed creation. I cannot find words to express my gratitude to Barbara Ibronyi, but readers can see for themselves how much I have to be thankful for.

The trouble with specific acknowledgements is that one can be certain only of knowing that one is invariably leaving out names. I am most conscious of this with relation to my students. I have already named some former students but it is impossible to give credit to all those who helped.

I have not always been able to take up the space that would be necessary to situate my readings within various theoretical contexts. What this means is that my bibliography should be taken as a list of acknowledgements. Most of the new books on Munro appeared just a little too late to be of much use to me. I have not been able to do justice, either, to my debt (and Munro's debt) to the larger context of Canadian literature. The sheer density of Munro's stories demanded all the space I had, but I was aware at all times that the issues here discussed could be explored also in the fiction of Margaret Atwood, Timothy Findley, Audrey Thomas, Mavis Gallant, Joy Kogawa, and many more Canadian writers who make up the nurturing community within which Munro writes.

The debt that is the most difficult to acknowledge is my debt to members of my own family. I see much of Munro's fiction as an oblique tribute to her parents. This book is also my way of paying tribute to my own parents. As the youngest of twelve children writing a book about surrogate mothers, I express gratitude to the six older sisters who took turns caring for me. Two of my sisters, Elizabeth Falk and Mary Neufeld, now care for me by reading nearly everything I write. I depend on their curiosity and their love, without which I could not write at all.

Still closer to home is the support of my husband, Clarence, keeper of the faith. Above all, I am grateful to my children. Adopting them has brought me intense joy. The satisfaction of mothering them has made it possible for me to separate the *experience* from the *institution* of motherhood. I could add that I am also grateful to the birth mothers of my children, whose courage will be a humbling example to me for the rest of my life. To say this, however, is to move outwards into a blind area that is just outside my line of vision.

Although acknowledgements come to an end, dictated by convention, the debt does not end. The polemical heart of my book is hidden behind the names listed in my dedication. It is one of the things I have learned from Alice Munro: the debt of the living is always to the dead.

The author and publishers are grateful for permission to reprint excerpts from Alice Munro's published works. Quotations from the following are reprinted by arrangement with the Virginia Barber Literary Agency: excerpts from *Dance of the Happy Shades*, copyright © 1968 by Alice Munro; excerpts from *Lives of Girls and Women*, copyright © 1971 by Alice Munro; excerpts from *Something I've Been Meaning To Tell You*, copyright © 1974 by Alice Munro; excerpts from *Who Do You Think You Are?*, copyright © 1978 by Alice Munro; excerpts from *The Moons of Jupiter*, copyright © 1982 by Alice Munro. All rights reserved.
Quotations from *The Progress of Love* and *Friend of My Youth* by Alice Munro are used by permission of the Canadian Publishers, McClelland and Stewart, Toronto.

Part I

The argument

Chapter 1

Paying attention: here come the mothering clowns

The pleasure of reading Alice Munro is, in the first place, a pleasure of recognition. Even readers, for example, who have never been to a place called Miles City, Montana, will experience recognition in "Miles City, Montana":

> No place became real till you got out of the car. Dazed with the heat, with the sun on the blistered houses, the pavement, the burned grass, I walked slowly. I paid attention to a squashed leaf, ground a Popsicle stick under the heel of my sandal, squinted at a trash can strapped to a tree. This is the way you look at the poorest details of the world resurfaced, after you've been driving for a long time – you feel their singleness and precise location and the forlorn coincidence of your being there to see them.
>
> (PL, 99)

Never mind that the word "forlorn" will soon be a bell to toll you back to your sole self and to artifice. Pay attention. For the time being this place becomes "real." The pleasure of these listed details in a "precise location" is like the pleasure described by Barthes as "an excess of precision, a kind of maniacal exactitude of language, a descriptive madness" (1975, 26) Aha, we say to ourselves, and yes, she's got it just right: that is just how "you" feel when you are travelling. When we pay attention, however, to the fact that the details are refuse and that they refuse meaning, then we are returned to a recognition not of the place but of "the way you look" at a place. The pleasure of reading Alice Munro is, in the final analysis, that we catch ourselves in the act of looking.

Munro's fiction offers many examples of what Nancy Miller, in another context, has called a "sudden staging of the hermeneutic act" (Miller, 1986a, 278). I have selected this particular example of a staged reading act because the story so clearly illustrates how "the way you look" is different when the watcher is a mother. When I first set out to write a book on Munro, the issue that commanded my attention – along with her much-admired "magic realism" – was her obsession with mothering. Munro has talked about her "intense relationship" with her mother (who died slowly of

Parkinson's Disease) and she has acknowledged during conversation with Geoff Hancock that "the whole mother–daughter relationship interests me a great deal. It probably obsesses me" (Hancock, 1987, 215). I was fascinated by the stories ("The Peace of Utrecht" and "The Ottawa Valley") in which Munro struggles with the impossibility of picturing her own mother. I was even more interested in the multiplication of surrogate mother figures in her stories. Her stories are peopled with stepmothers, foster mothers, adoptive mothers, child mothers, nurses, old maids mothering their parents, lovers mothering each other, husbands mothering wives, wives mothering husbands, sisters mothering each other, and numerous women and men behaving in ways that could be described as maternal. The gestures of tucking someone in, of rocking and being rocked, and of feeding and being fed, are, for example, recurring ones.

As I read and reread the stories, I began to discern the outlines of a composite figure – a mothering clown that I decided to call a mock mother. The mock mother is constructed as a result of the impossibility of picturing the "real" mother. Often she performs as a kind of trickster who challenges our old ways of looking at the relation between the work of art and the human body. Unlike the spread-eagled male body made famous by Leonardo da Vinci, this body is not static. The belly expands and contracts, sometimes an arm or a leg or a breast is amputated, the iris moves in and out, the blind spot floats over various parts of the body, and the body may be stood on its head or perform acrobatic stunts. What happens if you substitute this figure for the spread-eagled male with the centrally placed penis who is so often seen as an analogy for the work of art? The first thing that surfaces is an awareness of the danger of objectification. If we don't feel this danger when we look at the body of a male it is surely because male consciousness is seen as the peak of our civilization. The first step to take to avoid the trap of turning the maternal body into an object, is to see that the mother is in the act of looking at *herself*, even when she is also looking after her children.

The scene from "Miles City, Montana" is a particularly graphic example of how a woman's act of looking at herself may come into conflict with her act of looking after others – or mothering. The "watcher" and the "keeper" are at odds in her. The story also reflects Munro's concern with the implications of this for the construction of autobiography. The narrator is a woman who is mothering her self – she refers to a "wooing of distant parts" of herself (PL, 88) – as well as mothering her often distant children. Her juggling act will be familiar to those readers who are "real" mothers: "I could be talking to Andrew, talking to the children and looking at whatever they wanted me to look at . . . and pouring lemonade into plastic cups" (PL, 88). For her the details are more than idle pleasure: "a pig on a sign, a pony in a field, a Volkswagen on a revolving stand" are all "bits and pieces . . . flying together" inside her to form an "essential composition"

(PL, 88). Nothing less than the survival of her self is at stake. This process of composition (related, by implication, to the composition of the story) is dramatically at odds with her responsibilities as a mother. She has a dread of turning into one of those mothers who move in a "woolly-smelling, milky-smelling fog, solemn with trivial burdens" (PL, 90). She sees the anxious "attention these mothers paid" as the "cause of colic, bed-wetting, asthma" (PL, 90). By simultaneously paying attention to her children and to the Popsicle stick, however, she is performing a precarious stunt. It leads, as so often happens in a Munro story, to a carefully staged failure.

"Where are the children?" (PL, 99) is the question that triggers the collapse of the composition. When the family act is reconstituted, it is with ironic distance. "What I can't get over," says the husband after they rescue their daughter from drowning, "is how you got the signal. It's got to be some extra sense that mothers have." She, meanwhile, marvels at the sudden mysterious strength that enabled him to scale the fence. Maternal intuition and paternal strength are seen as a kind of circus stunt. The narrator confesses: "Partly I wanted to believe that, to bask in my extra sense. Partly I wanted to warn him – to warn everybody – never to count on it" (PL, 105). Munro's fiction is warning us all never to count on it.

The drama of the near-drowning in "Miles City, Montana" comes from a conflict between two ways of paying attention. Like Rose, many of the women in Munro's stories are tempted to "jolt" their families by yelling the words of Lady Macbeth "into the kitchen": *"Come to my woman's breasts,/ And take my milk for gall, you murdering ministers!"* (WDY, 49). Milk is an image of maternal self-lessness whereas gall is associated with the bitterness of self-interest. When Gerard Manley Hopkins announces "I am gall," it is a way of saying "my taste was me" (Hopkins, 1953, 62). Gall is a recurring image in Munro's fiction, Flo's gallstones being one conspicuous example. In "The Turkey Season," Herb, a homosexual, warns the gutters not to break the gall "'or it will taste the entire turkey'" (MJ, 62). Although the turkey in question has testicles, Herb issues the order "'Knees up, Mother Brown.'" The gender confusion shows how hard it is for a man to be associated with the milk of human kindness and for a woman to have the gall to say "me."

Hélène Cixous has argued that women write in "white ink": "Voice. Inexhaustible milk. Is rediscovered. The lost mother. Eternity: voice mixed with milk" (Cixous, quoted by Stanton, 1986, 167). Cixous's work is part of what Bella Brodzki refers to as a "thriving brand of feminist criticism (call it womb criticism)." It "seeks to replace or subvert phallic criticism" (Brodzki, 1988, 247) but ends up installing, once again, the very essentialized maternity that it aims to shatter (see also Stanton, 1986, 163; Auerbach, 1985, 171). There is an intoxicating power in Cixous's imagery, partly because it is a necessary repudiation of earlier stages of feminist thought which saw the experience of mothering as by definition hostile to feminism itself. Feminists and sexists often conspire to blame the mother, the one seeing her as a "tool of patriarchy" (Palmer, 1989, 96), the other blaming her for not living up to the ideal of maternity constructed *by* that patriarchy. By the same token, feminists and sexists are often indistinguishable when it comes to apotheosizing the mother. Graves, Briffault, Jung and company clearly believe they are doing women a favour when they indulge in this process. I agree with Millicent Fawcett's view that feminists should know better than to "'talk about Woman with a capital W. That we leave to our enemies'" (quoted by Parker, 1984, 4).

Munro's stories are best served by approaches to motherhood that separate (as does Adrienne Rich) the experience and the institution. The yearning for an archaic maternal past is acknowledged by Munro, but it is seen from an ironic, anti-nostalgic distance. Voice mixed with milk will not show up on paper unless there is at least a little gall. Unless the voice uses a little black ink, moreover, the woman will not achieve either identity or fame. In "The Progress of Love" Fame's mother describes how "One drop of hatred in your soul will spread and discolor everything like a drop of black ink in white milk" (PL, 6). Milk is an inherently absurd image to many of the people in Munro's stories. While Fame milks the cows, her visiting aunt wonders aloud if it hurts the cow and adds: "'Think if it was you'" (PL, 16). Fame is "shaken by this indecency," but Munro's own fame is built on just such daring connections. When Jocelyn and Rose are in the maternity ward, they laugh hysterically about "'False tits, false bums, false baby cows!'" (WDY, 102) until the "vacuum-cleaning woman" issues a threat: "She said if they didn't stop the way they carried on they would sour their milk. . . . She asked if they were fit to be mothers" (WDY, 102). Jocelyn wonders if maybe her milk "'*is* sour'" since it is an "'awfully disgusting'" shade of blue, which leads Rose to speculate that "'maybe it's ink!'" (WDY, 102). These conversations undermine the idea that women write with milk and remind us that the same society that etherealizes motherhood places a very low economic value on the act of nurturing. The duplicity is captured by Nicole Brossard: "The milk sours. The Mona Lisa smiles" (1983, 21).

Since milk and cows recur as images in Munro's stories, it is perhaps not surprising that a crucial staging of the reading act takes the cow as a dead metaphor. Looking at the dead cow in "Heirs of the Living Body," Del sees the cow's hide as a map to be read. But this map acts as a guide to no place; it is something non-referential posed by Del *as* referentiality and leading her to an unanswerable question: "Why should the white spots be shaped just the way they were, and never again, not on any cow or creature, shaped in exactly the same way?" (LGW, 44–45). The result of Del's straining is to lead us away from sacred cows and back to the surface of words themselves: "day-ud cow" does not become a symbol of something greater than itself. Del could say, like Gertrude Stein: "and what did I do I caressed completely caressed and addressed a noun" (Stein, 1967, 138).

The "day-ud cow", like Barthes's double sign (*S/Z*), points transparently to the corpse of the cow but at the same time it points at its own opacity and at Del's use of the sign, at the pleasure she takes in that exercise of power: "'Day-ud cow,' I said, expanding the word lusciously. 'Day-ud cow, day-ud cow'" (LGW, 44; see Godard, 1984, 43).

Munro's "magic realism" is a kind of meta-realism. What I notice here is that Del's caressing of the word is an evasion: she is afraid to caress the "real" cow. Munro has described how she sees even "totally commonplace things" as having a "kind of rim around them" (Hancock, 1987, 212), but her stories (like the paintings of Mary Pratt or Alex Colville) are examples of a typically Canadian product: the realistic work that is not realistic. Her popularity among so-called "common readers" seems to be based on their recognition of what is "real" or "natural" and this makes literary critics twitchy. The word "natural" has been treacherous territory at least since people started misreading Wordsworth's "Preface" and realism has become an increasingly vexed issue in recent years. Post-Saussurean work on language questions the concept of realism and representation by emphasizing the arbitrariness of the sign.

The signs in Munro's stories do not pretend to be natural, and this is true for the sign *Mother* just as it is for the dead cow or the Popsicle stick or the "pig on a sign" (PL, 88). The subtlety of her method, however, suggests that you cannot understand the full power of the old traps if you see yourself as standing on some moral high ground, free of old habits. Munro herself is positioned along with her reader, inside the old patterns, breaking them up from within. The word "real" is not an easily dismissed illusion in Munro's story. The word echoes and re-echoes in Munro's fiction as it does in the poetry of Wallace Stevens. It acts as a kind of reproach, like a conscience keeping the artist honest (Grant, 1970, 14). In "The Spanish Lady," for example, the narrator hears a "real cry" which she describes as "coming from outside myself" (SIB, 189), the cry of a man dying. "By that cry" the whole fiction we have just read is "pushed back. What we say and feel no longer rings true, it is slightly beside the point" (SIB, 190).

Munro's gift for "realism," then, leaves us confronting a blind spot made visible. Her stories are like rare presents that are as hard to unpack as the presents brought by now absent family visitors in "Connection." In the house, in the room, in the dresser, is a linen-drawer which contains a chocolate-box which contains, in turn, the "empty chocolate cups of dark, fluted paper." The narrator sometimes goes to "read again the descriptions on the map provided on the inside of the box-top: hazelnut, creamy nougat, Turkish delight, golden toffee, peppermint cream" (MJ, 3). Is there any intrinsic reason why the list could not be altered to read: walnut cream, strawberry delight. . . ? The list, like the salvaged box, waits for some "ceremonial use" that never presents itself and Munro writes against the grain of our desire for symbolic meaning. Tempted by the precise detailing of the fluted rim the greedy reader may try to fill in the missing content. If we do so we destroy the magic and achieve, instead, something resembling the "thought of Cora" in "Privilege": "the sense of a glowing dark spot, a melting center, a smell and taste of burnt chocolate, that [Rose] could never get at" (WDY, 34).

If this failure is felt most intensely when the reader in question is a mother, that is because the mother, in the symbolic order, is transgressing just by *being* a reader. She *is* the Symbol. She *is* the vessel and has no business expressing a hunger for the contents of the cup. Derrida describes the mother as the "faceless figure of a *figurant*, an extra. . . . Everything comes back to her, beginning with her life; everything addresses and destines itself to her. She survives on condition of remaining at bottom" (Derrida, 1985, 38). We are sadly familiar with this erasure now. The idea of the mother's absence has come to form a central part of our notion of narrative, and of language itself. Many have argued that the uncanny presence of the absent mother ensures that what is left out of the container as unrepresentable is, in the end, what is most powerfully represented (see for example Jardine, 1985, 38). The haunting sense of an absence, however, is not the main manifestation of maternity in Munro's stories. I am tempted to say that these are real mothers in her stories but as I say it I become conscious of Lacanian capitals looming over me. In my use of the word *real* (as of the phrase *symbolic order*) I am influenced by Lacan. In the end, however, I untied Munro's women from his capitals, preferring to leave them free to do their levelling stunts. Dancing in front of the erasure, the conspicuous mock-maternal figures do not affirm something inexpressible or sacred. Munro achieves, instead, what Bakhtin has termed a destruction of "epic distance." The entertainments of her mock mothers enable us to walk "disrespectfully" around our idealized images of maternity. With her "comical operation of dismemberment," Munro enables us to see the "back and rear portion" of an object as well as the "innards" (Bakhtin, 1981, 23–24).

The term mock mother is my invention but it is Munro who repeatedly establishes a mocking distance from the very word *Mother*. In "The Progress of Love," for example, Fame confesses to "a childish notion – I knew it was childish – that Mother suited my mother better than it did other mothers" (PL, 9). The mother's story can be told only if the daughter stops calling her Mother and calls her Marietta. The word echoes both Mary, Mother of God, and marionette. To diminish and mock the figure of the mother in this way is to make it possible to deal with the power projected into her. The narrating daughter in "Images," by contrast, cannot get past the block called Mother that is set up by her own "irascible and comforting human mother." That Mother is compared to the "name of Jesus" and is the ghost that haunts many of Munro's stories. She is an

"everlastingly wounded phantom" who brings the daughter "wretchedness
and shame" (DHS, 33). We confront this ghost again in "The Progress
of Love," where Fame imagines beating her head against her mother's
"stomach and breasts . . . demanding to be forgiven," only to have her
mother direct her to God. "But it wasn't God," Fame concludes, "it was
my mother I had to get straight with." The "sickening shame" is like a
cloud or a poison that "you couldn't see through, or get to the end of"
(PL, 13).

How to get straight with the mother? How to celebrate her? How
to get rid of her? How to get to the end of this shame? The mock
mothers are Munro's response to this dilemma. They call "into question
the assumption of an unmediated presence embodied in/by the mother
and an unproblematical relation to the maternal origin" (Brodzki, 1988,
247). Munro often stages the death of the "real" mother with self-conscious
melodrama in order to make room for the mock mothers. A mother is
pictured dying on the kitchen table among the "teacups and ketchup and
jam" (LGW, 77). A mother dies imagining an egg stuck in her chest (WDY,
2). A mother bleeds to death while giving birth to her daughter (PL, 150).
When the mother is dead, killed off spectacularly, or simply rendered
helpless, her role is taken over by surrogates. Caddy, in the *Sound and
the Fury*, substitutes for Mrs Compson and her care of Benjy is echoed in
Patricia's care for the retarded Benny in "The Time of Death."

The behaviour of the mock mothers may be comforting, frightening,
or entertaining but it is always related to an investigation of the power
of the symbolic order in relation to reproduction. The reproduction of
writing may itself become a form of resistance to Rousseau's statement
that "there is no substitute for a mother's love" (quoted by Derrida, 1974,
145). The problems come in distinguishing the regenerative powers of the
supplement as a "substitution of mothers" (Derrida, 1974, 146) from the
dangerous powers of what Derrida describes as the "bad or false mother"
who (like Hattie Milton) gives dictation and who is linked, by a "leash in
the form of an umbilical cord, to the paternal belly of the State" (Derrida,
1985, 35–36). The belly is an old metaphor for the state, a notable example
being the "cormorant belly" in *Coriolanus* (I, ii, 118). In Munro's stories,
the belly is usually maternal and it is (to adapt words used by Robert
Durling in another context) like a "Trojan horse pregnant with disaster"
(Durling, 1981, 73). We glimpse a possible disaster in the spectacular death
of Stump Troy in "Executioners," who burns while a girl called Helena
looks on, rendered helpless by the powers of a one-armed mock mother
called Robina. It is only logical that a woman would find her strength *in*
weakness and that is what Robina and other mock mothers do.

Munro's failure to "*get rid*" (SIB, 246) of the mother signals the depth
of her commitment to her craft – her work with words. One comment by
Mary Jacobus is so apt that it seems to refer to Munro: "Getting rid of

the mother is a way of cleaning up . . . a way of denying the materiality of signs." Jacobus claims that the missing mother "leaves her traces in [the] hysterical pregnancy" of Freud's text. This "phantom pregnancy" discloses "the pre-oedipal whenever it throws up or gives birth to . . . the impropriety which is the material of language" (Jacobus, 1986, 193). Munro makes these phantom pregnancies visible. The body of the mother is often a startling presence in her stories. The mother of Mary Agnes, for example, is surrounded by a "gynecological odour" and seen as a "likely sufferer from varicose veins, hemorrhoids, a dropped womb, cysted ovaries, inflammations, discharges, lumps and stones in various places" (LGW, 40). Far from being an absence, the body of this mother is one of those "heavy, cautiously moving, wrecked survivors of the female life, with stories to tell" (LGW, 40). This heavy body with stories to tell contrasts with Lacan's view that the body of the mother is an absence, a lack, that "drives forward the narrative of our lives, impelling us to pursue substitutes for this lost paradise in an endless metonymic movement of desire" (Eagleton, 1983, 185). Because women have a different relation to the mother, they also have a different, more mocking, relation to this view of the storytelling process as a substitution.

This can be clarified if we take a woman's view of the Freudian game of "fort-da" which is so often used to describe this process. The boy observed by Freud threw away a spool, lamented "fort" (or "gone"), then reeled it back and shouted "da" (or "there it is") (Freud, 1955, 15–16). Freud interpreted this game not only as the boy's way of comforting himself for the mother's absence, but also as an effort to recover power. By repeating the game, the boy escapes the "passive situation" in which he is at the mercy of the mother who comes and goes at will. He becomes active and takes mastery of the situation. If we change the child to a girl, however, then it is easier to see this game as a repeated *failure* to be master. It is useful to imagine the toy, the substitute mother, not as a spool but as a dolly, an effigy of the mother. Gods and idols may be made, as Del's mother reminds her, in the image of man (LGW, 107). Man tends to make dolls, however, in the image of the female and for the use of the female. If a doll is "an image of a human being (commonly of a child or lady) used as a plaything; a girl's toy baby" (*OED*), then the image of a doll is an image of an image. Instead of *fort/da* we may say *I/da* or *Me/da* – the names of two of Munro's most conspicuous mock mothers.

This seems to me the source of Munro's comedy. Bringing the maternal body back into the "scenes of representation" (Stanton, 1986, 163) involves conscious play and parody and Munro often does this with dolls or doll-like women. Since women are introduced to the reproduction of mothering via dolls, is it any wonder that dolls would form a prominent part of this play for a woman writer? Paying attention to Munro's play with dolls offers clues to her strategy of resisting a society that wants to say "Hello Dolly" and use women as playthings. Irigaray's focus on femininity as a masquerade is useful. Miss Marsalles is described as a "character in a masquerade" (DHS, 217) and the word is an important clue to how women look at the production of art in Munro's fiction. Camouflage, after all, is second nature to women. To be all dolled up or to be a real doll may suggest, as it does with some women writers, that women are like robots or mannequins. It may also, however, be a camouflage that can be used to a woman's advantage. When a woman puts on her make-up and wig in "Wigtime" (FY, 265), she does no more than what millions of women do as a routine every day. The often quoted passage from Irigaray is especially useful in the case of Munro:

> There is, in an initial phase, perhaps only one "path," the one historically assigned to the feminine: that of *mimicry*. One must assume the feminine role deliberately. Which means to convert a form of subordination into an affirmation, and thus to begin to thwart it. . . . To play with mimesis is, thus, for a woman, to try to recover the play of her exploitation by discourse, without allowing herself to be simply reduced to it.
>
> (Irigaray, 1985b, 76)

The aim, according to Irigaray, is to "make 'visible' by an effect of playful repetition, what was supposed to remain invisible" (76). What she says about women in general is especially true of Munro, the consummate mimic.

Chapter 2

The madonna and the harlot join the family circus

When Tereseus cut out Philomela's tongue so that she could not tell the story of her rape, she wove that story into her tapestry. This is Munro's territory: familiar, domestic actions are elevated to serve as a powerful means of resistance. Rejecting the defamiliarizing techniques common to many contemporary writers, Munro opts instead for a domestication so radical that we move through the homely to the *unheimlich* or uncanny. As she domesticates the figures of madonna and harlot, they become complex persons. Despite her frequent appearance with a baby in her arms, the madonna is not traditionally considered as a part of ordinary kinship structures. Munro's method operates to destroy the distance that makes her an object of adoration. Robert Graves, whose "White Goddess" is mocked by Rose in *Who Do You Think You Are?*, notes that the Goddess is "anti-domestic" and that the muse often cannot resist the "temptation to commit suicide in simple domesticity" (Graves, 1960, 449). Munro takes up this challenge and demolishes Graves's aesthetic by including both madonna and harlot in her parade of mothering clowns.

As an object of worship, the image of mother and child is so common-place that we do not see it. Like Poe's purloined letter, it is hidden out in the open. Do we see her, for example, when she appears on the label of a bottle of *Liebfraumilch*? Instead of reconstructing the madonna in order to deconstruct her, Munro mimes this invisibility in her stories. She reflects back to us our own ability to domesticate a symbol. The object of idolatry so deeply imbedded in our culture, is deeply imbedded in Munro's fiction. Her method of exposing it consists of a subtle exploitation of the ease with which we reproduce our mental pictures. In "Royal Beatings," for example, the voice of the father speaks nonsense: "Macaroni, pepperoni, Botticelli, beans – " (WDY, 4). While we may respond with the knee-jerk reaction of someone doing an IQ test (What do they have in common? Are they all Italian?) we are also being invaded by the images. Munro is mocking the society that reproduces Botticelli's images as easily as it multiplies macaroni. Botticelli, as it happens, ran a shop for the reproduction of *madonnas* and many of these were forged in the nineteenth century.

The image takes only a split second to reproduce itself in our mind, as long as it takes to read the word *Botticelli*. Distracted by the activities of that splendid mock mother, Flo, we do not even feel it registering, and yet we have judged the wicked stepmother by how far she falls short of the madonna. If we become aware of having done this, it is because of the nonsensical nature of the list, the double signing of each item that makes us do a double-take. In the moment that the invisible madonna is made visible, she also turns into a mock mother who joins a parade that resembles the parade of words in "Spelling" (WDY, 184).

Elizabeth Fisher comments on the way maternal sensuality – the bond between mother and infant – is displaced into adult heterosexuality. She notes that Robert Briffault, in *The Mothers*, "speaks of sex as a nasty business made beautiful by the tenderness and love transferred from the maternal relationship, and 'maternal love is sacrifice'" (Fisher, 1979, 40). Munro's sexual scenes often contain a buried parodic image of the madonna and child. As we alienate the domesticated image, however, we discover that the power projected into the symbol is recovered and exposed in the actions of two people who are using each other. The lover called X in "Bardon Bus" is first seen by us as someone in the act of looking at a scene of maternal tenderness: a woman nursing her baby at a picnic. The narrator's self-representation is parodic. She describes herself as "a nursing mother. Fat and pink on the outside; dark judgements and strenuous ambitions within. Sex," she adds, "had not begun for me, at all" (MJ, 118). The baby she holds becomes invisible, is Xd out, because she describes this scene as the beginning of her affair with X. X is by no means a stereotypical male worshipper and the narrator is no beatific madonna. He offers her a bottle (suggesting that beer will be good for her milk) and this inversion appears to acknowledge that her appetite might coexist with her infant's appetite. There may be some comfort in being reminded that there is sex after mothering, but what follows is profoundly ironic.

A subtle double-take happens at the end of the story when Kay tells the narrator what her new lover did when he first met her: "After dark when we were sitting around the fire he came over to me and just sighed, and laid his head on my lap. I thought it was such a nice simple thing to do. Like a St. Bernard. I've never had anybody do that before" (MJ, 128). Like a magician, Munro uses the St Bernard as a large distracting object while she reproduces her image on another level. She dares us to extract the X from Alex and assume the responsibility of our own recognition. She challenges us to recognize that what we are reproducing is the madonna–child scene. If you block out the St Bernard, you notice that the gesture is not in fact something that nobody ever did before. What you see is a replica of the earlier scene, with the difference that the man is in the place of the infant. What you see, in short, is the Pieta. Since the lover in "Bardon Bus" is called X and is associated at the outset with Jesus Christ, we might well change the phrase "Like a St. Bernard" to "Like Jesus Christ." If we put this peculiar imitation of Christ on top of the earlier picture of mother and child we gain ironic distance. The newborn infant is replaced by a middle-aged man aware (like David in "Lichen") of his own mortality. The part of the madonna is played by a woman in a school-girl's tunic. In the first scene there was milk, and this pre-Oedipal reality undermines the symbolic scene, making it absurdly visible. What we notice at the end of "Bardon Bus" is the silence of the narrator who is struggling to repress her own sexual appetite. Her lust for life competes with her implicit yearning to be in the place described by Kay, the place of the madonna.

What has to be repressed in order for us to see this as a beatitude, however, is left over as the figure of a whore. Unlike the madonna figure, the harlot is spectacularly visible in Munro's stories. No need to excavate her, for example, from "Bardon Bus," where the image confronts us as if in a pornographic centrefold. In the story "Material" the "harlot in residence" lives in the basement. Her name is Dotty which, like Dolly, is an abbreviation of Dorothy. The woman called Dorothy in "Mischief" has a "chipped and battered look" like that of a used doll. "In a city she would have looked whorish" (WDY, 137). While Dorothy is a name that arbitrarily inverts a word meaning gift of God (see Withycombe, 1977, 87), Dolly is associated not only with a "girl's toy-baby" (*OED*) but also with "a drab, slattern, useless woman" (*OED*). In "Mrs. Cross and Mrs. Kidd" we discover that Mrs Cross has a Christian name which only Mrs Kidd remembers: Dolly Grainger (MJ, 161). The suggestion seems to be that in taking her husband's name, with its Christian connotations, Mrs Cross has had to cross out the associations that go with the word "dolly." When the dolly is a whore called Dotty whose material conditions are of the kind pictured in "Material," then we begin to see the whore as the woman who is burdened with the full weight of what is left out of the symbolic order. When the boys shout "Hello hooers" and "Hey where's your fuckhole?" Del feels stripped of freedom and reduced to "what it was they saw, and that, plainly, was enough to make them gag" (LGW, 117). Del's fantasies about being somebody's whore domesticate the harlot. Harlot and madonna, in fact, collapse into a single activity of mock mothering as the little girl, a young lady (or "baby") is used for sexual purposes that require maternal sacrifice. The "fancy, inventive dancer" in "Baptizing" rolls his eyes "in a grotesque way" and calls Del "baby" in a "cold, languishing voice" (LGW, 188).

The image of the adult as baby is recurrent in Munro's fiction, perhaps because the activity of mothering so easily becomes a way of infantilizing people. When male characters are seen as babies, they may be associated (as is Alex Walther at the end of "Bardon Bus") with the baby Jesus Christ who is also King. When Arthur is tucked in (in "Something I've Been Meaning to Tell You"), we have a fleeting image of him as Et's baby king. When female characters are seen as babies, however, they are more likely to be toys. Del's unsatisfactory dance, in fact, is like the "often repeated clown gag in which the clown dances with a large rag-doll dummy of a woman whose feet are attached to his, so that the only life in her is what ripples through from his movements" (Willeford, 1969, 182–183). Del's dance is one way of picturing this kind of dispossession. Munro's stories often revolve around a rape scene in which the object is like a doll. This is made explicit in the case of Callie: "it was as if they had used a doll" (PL, 146).

Those who still doubt that readings are gender conditioned, should consider the difference in how women and men respond to the name "Dolly" and to the political implications surrounding the word. A giant rag-doll was raped some years ago in a mock ceremony that formed part of annual celebrations by members of the Engineering School at the University of Toronto. Now that fourteen female engineering students have been murdered in Montreal by a feminist-hater, we may be spared such a spectacle in future. It is impossible not to feel rage and yet Munro's fiction seems to insist that we must keep calm enough so that we can pay attention. If we are beside ourselves with rage, we will not be able to understand the danger.

The "lady in danger" in circus acts is usually a member of the circus family. When Franny is raped by her brother it is described as "relations performing" and viewed as a freak show. Rose later thinks of Franny whenever she comes across the "figure of an idiotic, saintly whore, in a book or a movie" (WDY, 26) and notes that the "men who made books and movies" cheat by cleaning her up. They also cheat by denying her place in the family. What Rose can see of Franny during the rape is not this "figure" but one leg: "She kept jerking one leg. . . . There was her white leg and bare foot, with muddy toes. . . . That was all of her Rose could see" (WDY, 26–27). The blind spot eliminates the entire woman when she is used as a dolly. Rose saves the situation by seeing the leg, the muddy toes. She acknowledges the reality of Franny by consciously *failing* to represent her, by refusing to reproduce the "figure."

In Munro's stories we glimpse the familiar contrast between the Bride of Christ and the Whore of Babylon but there is no easy resolution in theological paradox. The narrator of "Material," herself "pregnant with Clea" (SIB, 31) reproduces Dotty's litany of complaints. It includes three miscarriages. "My womb," says Dotty, "is in shreds. I use up three packs of Kotex every month" (SIB, 32). Our laughter cannot take away from the reality of Dotty's suffering, the material conditions of her life in "material." The narrator of "Material" tries to write a letter to Hugo about his story. The letter is intercepted by the reader and here is what we read: *"This is not enough, Hugo. You think it is, but it isn't. You are mistaken, Hugo"* (SIB, 44). I see Munro's stories as a response to the challenge issued by that jabbing sentence. It is not enough to see madonna and harlot as all dolled up to join the parade. They must be domesticated by being taken up into the family. How may a woman's reproductions act to resist a mimicry that is simply a burlesque, like Del's rag-doll dance? The question will partly turn itself into a question of how the woman can learn to *be* the clown instead of the rag-doll dummy used by the clown. The answer will lie, once again, in Munro's focus on looking. If the rag-doll is to be brought to life, she must first be given eyes. She must have a past.

Chapter 3

Dilemma: watching through Orphan Annie eyes

A time-honoured way of seeking to avoid being somebody else's Dolly, is to affirm your own ability to construct yourself as a subject, to say "I" and "me." It is an activity sanctioned by the masters: St Augustine, Rousseau, Proust, Wordsworth. The construction of the female subject, however, is obscured by a milky fog. The subtle comedy of Munro's fiction derives in part from her sense of the absurdity surrounding the female subject. The woman does not easily say "me" or "I am" but may, instead, call herself something silly like Ida or Meda. Much of Munro's fiction is concerned with the issue of autobiographical form which, for a woman, comes down to the very survival of identity itself. Bella Brodzki and Celeste Schenck sum up the "case of autobiography" today as "the imperative situating of the female subject in spite of the postmodernist campaign against the sovereign self" (Brodzki and Schenck, 1988, 14). Nancy Miller has confronted some related questions in a problematic essay that deals with how women writers might respond to reports of the death of the Author (Miller, 1986b, 102–120).

Munro dramatizes a woman's dilemma in the "Epilogue" to *Lives of Girls and Women*. It is impossible to read that book as a *Bildungsroman*. There is no single *Bild*, no portrait of the artist as a young woman, let alone as a "sovereign self." There are only the multiplied "Lives", and our own eyes, looking at the white eyes of Caroline who is looking at the eye of the camera, which is hidden under the black cloth. As Elizabeth Bruss demonstrates (1980, 296–320) the eye of the camera makes impossible the construction of a tidy, autonomous I. As the artist points the camera at herself, the picture that results is instantly invaded – constructed out of the conventions and images of the society around her. If the camera eye works by what Benjamin has called "unconscious optics" (1969, 237), then it might be said that Munro's literary mimicry of the camera makes optics conscious.

Autobiographies are not triumphant expressions of autonomous subjectivity but rather expressions of the shared conventions we use to construct our subjectivity. There is nothing inherently new in this; the so-called autonomy of the male subject is very much open to question.

Any competent reading of "In Memoriam" or "The Prelude" will indicate awareness of such conventions. What is notable is Munro's ability to illuminate a woman's position by exposing the way the conventions operate within popular culture. The woman is the object of the camera's gaze and the monster mass culture is often envisioned by theorists as feminine. A woman, even more than a man, may feel dragged along by the mass media, as Del is dragged along by the "fancy, inventive dancer" who calls her "baby." Del complains: "I heard the words but could not figure out the meaning" and she responds with mimicry:

> all I could think of to do was get some idea of this person he thought he was dancing with and pretend to be her – somebody small, snappy, bright, flirtatious. But everything I did, every movement and expression with which I tried to meet him, seemed to be too late; he would have gone on to something else.
>
> (LGW, 188)

Although her timing is off, Del is on the right track. If you are forced to play the part of the dummy rag-doll as you dance with a clown, only this kind of camouflage will allow you to see from behind the disguise. The project is like installing real eyes in a dummy body.

Mary Jacobus refers to the "hysterical doubleness and incompleteness which representation must repress in order to figure as true, unified, and whole – as masculine" (Jacobus, 1986, 203). She notes that the "hysteric's drama is the drama of self-representation, the acting out or doubling which allows us to contemplate, not only our thoughts, but ourselves" (272). The danger for hysterics, however, lies in isolation and resulting madness. Allon White has observed that "carnival debris" appears in the speeches of the "terrified Viennese women in Freud's *Studies on Hysteria.*" White sees these "torn shreds of carnival" as in a state of "phobic alienation" from public festivals. Reduced to "morbid symptoms of private terror," these remnants of carnival can no longer contribute to a robust community life but signal, rather, a progression into private madness (White, 1989, 157). This "private" madness, however, is now acted out within the context of an electronic culture. If the woman cannot escape seeing herself as she is seen, then going through the looking glass must now mean going inside the camera. The inside of the camera is the place of her reproduction.

In "Marrakesh," Jeanette travels to Marrakesh with a camera but returns without one to tell her story. Her storytelling becomes a way of repossessing a power invested in the camera. "'In North Africa I had everything stolen,' said Jeanette. 'I had everything stolen even though the camper was locked'" (SIB, 169). The repetition of the phrase "I had everything stolen" suggests a loss of virginity and of identity. Like Lucy Locket who lost her pocket, Jeanette is emptied, dispossessed of all value. Since she has lost everything in Marrakesh, the Jeanette that she invents for her story and that we see in

"Marrakesh" cannot be the real Jeanette. "'It was in Marrakesh,' Jeanette said, 'I had everything, everything, stolen, lovely things – Moroccan dresses, cloth I had bought for friends, jewelry – as well as my camera naturally and all the stuff I had come with'" (SIB, 169). Two Arab men approach her, one corners her and takes out a knife, demanding: "'well, by this time he was getting very graphic about the whole thing.'"

Jeanette herself refuses to get graphic and her story tells of the potential loss of the *graphic* in *photographic* and in *autobiographic*. Jeanette reports that she said "no, *no*, and refused to look at *any*thing!" Her story has an ambiguity all too familiar to rape scenarios. She confuses the issue by adding that one of the men asked her to marry him: "He said he loved me, naturally." This echoes the earlier phrase "as well as my camera naturally" (see Carscallen, 1983, 128–129). Like Jeanette, we may avert our eyes and say "no, *no*" and refuse to look at "*any*thing" but our vision will be invaded by what is *not* natural, by the *graphic* language of pornography and by the invisible hand of mechanical reproduction. To what extent is Jeanette, the world traveller, in control of her self-representations? This question cannot be asked independently of issues of power, economics, and technology. Who has the purloined camera and whose finger will press the trigger and who will possess the images reproduced by that camera? These questions will be repeated when we confront a Polaroid shot in "Lichen."

The camera is gone. But is "everything" lost? Not quite. Jeanette's conscious act of imaging is a way of "graphing" that refuses to get "graphic." She playfully insists on being her own camera ("it was all like a play") and this is her survival. She never gets back her camera, but the act of telling, of playing it out, so to speak, is a way of re-appropriating what she has lost, of repossessing her own body. There remains something haunting in the story, a sense of permanent emptiness, as if the dispossession is graphed in dust – like Nora's writing on the dusty car in "Walker Brothers Cowboy." This feeling is imaged in Dorothy's final response to the figures that appear, unbidden, on "the underside of her eyelids." They are "chalked-in drawings" – like temporary graffiti – and yet they are "two welded figures, solid and bright" (SIB, 174).

The moment of almost pure horror, of nightmare, is to find yourself fixed in the centre of the pupil itself, engulfed in the black dot. The pupil is so called from the Latin *pupilla*, meaning "female child" because the image seen is miniaturized in the pupil. Socrates notes that "the face of a person looking into the eye of another is reflected as in a mirror; and in the visual organ which is over against him, and which is called pupil [*kore*] there is a sort of image of the person looking" (Plato, *Alcibiades*; quoted by Irigaray, 1985a, 327). As Irigaray observes, however, "this image (of oneself) in a pupil is always dependent upon *Kore*. That is to say upon a *young girl*, a *young virgin*, or even a *doll*. A reduced image, then, which cannot satisfy someone who wishes to have knowledge of the All" (327). Munro is not interested in showing us "All" but she does take us beyond the blind spot of the pupil and captures the act of looking itself. The phrase "iris in – iris out" is not used by Munro but her technique seems to me to be an adaptation of this effect, familiar from silent films. In the story "Connection," the visit of Cousin Iris offers a startling example. A picture has filled the frame but a circle closes in on the picture. It decreases in size until all that is left is a pin-point of light and then blackness. Life is in the eyes – in the movement of the eyes and the "iris in–iris out" pattern of Munro's stories mimes life itself. Caroline, to adapt Iragaray's words, is "a Kore *Dilated to the Whole Field of the Gaze and Mirroring Herself*" (1985a, 327) "*Caroline's eyes were white*" (LGW, 247) because Caroline, in giving herself over to the sinister eye of the photographer, has eliminated her own vision.

The closest we get, in Munro's fiction, to a description of this nightmare is the scene in "Images" during which the narrator watches a man with an axe approaching her father:

> All my life I had known there was a man like this and he was behind doors, around the corner at the dark end of a hall. So now I saw him and just waited, like a child in an old negative, electrified against the dark noon sky, with blazing hair and burned-out Orphan Annie eyes.
>
> (DHS, 38)

Like Caroline's eyes, Orphan Annie's have no pupils. The empty circles that form Orphan Annie's eyes in this story signal the apparent impossibility of self-imaging. As she attempts to reproduce herself, the narrator in fact reproduces an image from American popular culture. Little Orphan Annie, invented by Harold Gray in 1924, owed her immense popularity to a perception of her as a feisty, self-reliant individual. In fact, of course, Orphan Annie was an image at the mercy of Gray's conservative political views. Her eyes, in this crucial passage, act as a graphic image of the dilemma I have been defining. She is the image of the totally paralyzed reader, the reader who has no power to resist the invading forces but who yet, like a woman, responds by dancing to the tune of her creator. This then is the dilemma, exaggerated by an electronic culture. We are all orphans, our burned out eyes invaded by the "dirty old man of the imagination" (Munro's original subtitle for the story "Wild Swans"). This dirty old man has in his hands the camera that represents the technology of reproduction. The image is potent: it is that of the sexually molested little girl, exiled from her family.

Chapter 4

Response: dancing with the puppet Alicia

How does Munro respond to this dilemma? She abdicates. The most visible place of this abdication may be the "Epilogue" to *Lives of Girls and Women*, but the most subtle is in the story "Something I've Been Meaning To Tell You." In this story we meet a lady ventriloquist in Mock Hill who "talked to her dolls – they were named Alphonse and Alicia – as if they were real people, and had them sitting up in bed one on each side of her" (SIB, 9). The echo of an author's name (by convention and by the inevitable vulgar curiosity of the reader) invites us to give more emphasis to the name *Alicia* than to anything else in this passage. If we do a blow up of that name (inflating the lady's doll, so to speak) we find ourselves in the paradoxical position of being forced to acknowledge the diminished role of the author who thus points to her signature even as she deletes it. One does not need to be conscious of the fact that a little girl called Alice was a plaything for Lewis Carroll to be aware of the implications of this diminution in the name *Alice*.

It is like a magician's trick. Munro distracts our eye from the name *Alicia* with various ploys. The narrator comments that "those dolls, who wore evening dress and had sleek hairdos in style of Vernon and Irene Castle, were more clearly remembered than the lady herself" (SIB, 11). This is very distracting indeed. The reader is either busy trying to remember who Vernon and Irene Castle were, or else picturing them dancing in imitation of Fred Astaire and Ginger Rogers. As the names, the characters, and the puppets dance before us, they erase the name of the author. *Alicia* becomes a proper noun locked up in the *Castle* of another proper noun. The marriage of the mock-boy Blaikie to the mock-mother ventriloquist in Mock Hill makes the dolls Alphonse and Alicia into mock children. This puppet show is instructive. Alicia speaks what the lady ventriloquist wishes her to speak. She takes dictation. In the act of recovering her name, we acknowledge the conditioned power of the author who is the "et" in "puppet." The author is not, like Thackeray, the puppet master, but rather a strategically placed puppet, at the site of invasion, "reading the signs of invasion." The author introduces her name fleetingly into her fiction, the better to make her exit, to abdicate her power. The gesture of abdication is anticipated by Munro's ancestor, James Hogg, who appears at the end of his novel – *The Private Memoirs and Confessions of a Justified Sinner* – in the character of a simple shepherd who does not understand his own story (Redekop, 1985, 178). The self-mockings of Alicia (and of the Ettrick Shepherd) demonstrate the folk wisdom that you may gain some measure of freedom from discovering that you are not free.

As she explores the limits of our freedom to create, Alice Munro helps the reader towards a means of resisting the conditioning power of mass culture. She does this by drawing on a repertoire of gestures that go back to medieval folk festivals. Like the medieval fools and clowns, Munro's artist is "real and ideal at the same time" and stands "on the borderline between life and art" (Bakhtin, 1968, 8). The artist in Munro's implicit aesthetics is not someone who achieves completion or vision but rather somebody who is exceptionally good at staging failure. Her stories are like the acts of the famous clown George Carl, a "succession of failures" resulting in a belittling of "artistic status" (Bouissac, 1990a, 424). Like Carl, who is dwarfed in stature when he leaves the ring, Munro shrinks to the puppet Alicia as she exits. Like Carl's, however, Munro's very dwarfing is "considered by the public and [her] peers a masterful achievement" (Bouissac, 1990a, 424).

Munro, however, is a female clown and her staged failures are therefore domesticated. Flo turns her body in the air between two kitchen chairs. When the mother in "Connection" stands on her head or Callie does an aerial walk (PL, 141), the show is almost invisible. The mother in "Miles City, Montana," similarly, is hardly recognizable as a juggler. These domestications, however, are so extreme as to turn into their opposites. As Bouissac notes, "once it is borrowed by the circus the chair loses its unequivocal meaning" (1976, 22). The objects in a Munro story are dislocated in this way from their ordinary spheres of meaning but the act is so skilful that we hardly notice. Language itself is the most unstable element in the circus and this is perhaps most noticeable in Munro's play with proper nouns.

What Munro does, then, is to work from inside domesticity to expose the unstable nature of all human constructs. Rachel Brownstein discusses the traditional assumption that comedy somehow suits women better than tragedy. "The lives of housewives," she observes

> are sequences of disillusioned days in which order is established, then lost, then established and lost again. Even the depressed ones live according to comic, not tragic, plot lines; what is threatened is not the possibility of a supreme meaning, which life proves, Monday to Monday, absurd, but the possibility of effective human artifice.
>
> (Brownstein, 1982, 25)

This absurdity characterizes Munro's comedy. Housekeeping chores are disruptive in a way that challenges the narrative line. Callie blacking the stove while Miss Kernaghan tells the story of her birth (PL, 151) and Flo washing the floor while her quarrel with Rose escalates (WDY, 14) are only two examples of how the earthy business of housekeeping undermines the narrative.

The actions of these mock mothers, whether they are working or entertaining, are striking because they do not move the story ahead. They certainly could not be called static, but neither do they advance the narrative. They contrast to the narrative in the way that the shape of a stunt at a circus contrasts with the shape of the narrative implied in carnival festivities. The rituals of a medieval carnival (alluded to most forcefully in *Who Do You Think You Are?*) are specifically tied to a narrative line that celebrates an archetypal pattern of death and rebirth. The dying mother spread out on the kitchen table is a stunt that does not lend itself to absorption in any such mythical narrative. Munro's stories resemble, in fact, what Bouissac refers to as the "antinomic structure" of the "circus text." The circus has a "narrative structure and a poetic structure. The first is characterized by its information value (the succession of events), the second by its repetitive form (actualization of poetic devices)" (Bouissac, 1976, 102).

The "poetic structure" of the isolated physical performance serves, in a Munro story, to challenge the "succession of events." Del's imitation of a seal for Art Chamberlain is a domesticated parody of a circus animal act that exposes his artifice as a sham. When Richard, at the end of "Connection", gets a pie in the face, his wife compares it to a scene in "an *I Love Lucy* show" (MJ, 18). The analogy is useful. Lucy Ricardo, like the clowns in Munro's stories, performs physical stunts that appropriate a role that the narrative forbids her to take. Patricia Mellencamp sees the *I Love Lucy* show as shifting "between narrative and comic spectacle, the latter being contained within the resolute closure of the former" (1986, 88 and 94). Munro's stories, by contrast, allow the physical performances to prevent closure. The poetic structure is usually dominant, as it is in a circus act (Bouissac, 1976, 102). These poetic stunts have a lasting visual power that overrides the storyline itself. Long after I have finished trying to make out the chronological connections in "Connection," I still see the figure of the mother standing on her head (MJ, 4). Long after I have lost the flow of narrative in *Who Do You Think You Are?*, I can still picture Flo's body turning between the two chairs, like a piece of meat on a spit (WDY, 20).

The relation between circus performances and kinship structures offers a means of understanding Munro's fiction as it relates to the role of the artist as mothering clown. What she offers is an alternative to Freudian family romance. Bouissac notes that "circus acrobatic acts are not purely formal demonstrations" but "are always 'embodied' in cultural categories, firstly regarding kinship" (Bouissac, 1990a, 439). In Munro's family circus, the figure of the mother is prominently placed and the phantom pregnancy is like the biggest circus balloon. The mother often stages a crisis known, in circus language, as the "lady in danger" (Bouissac, 1990a, 433). In traditional carnival, Mother Folly is seen as a misruler of sorts and this allows for the expression of aspects of the feminine that are ordinarily repressed. Munro, however, avoids setting up an alternative matriarchal hierarchy of entertainment. Her mothers are simply in the parade as clowns or doing their stunts. Often it is hard to tell whether the mother is male or female. Milton Homer, for example, rocks newborn babies in mock maternal fashion; his actions are an example of the "ritualistic profanation of the sacred" that "accounts for the stigmatized social status of the clown" (Bouissac, 1990a, 196).

Circus parades, as Willeford notes, often include a clown mother, "usually a transvestite man, with babies in a buggy, often twins or triplets, identical with one another and (despite their difference in size) with her" (Willeford, 1969, 177–178). Munro's picture of such a homogenization of reproduction is so subtle as to be nearly invisible. In "Heirs of the Living Body," as Del lies inside the room that is compared to the inside of an egg, she sees a baby carriage that is full of old *Family Heralds*. This mock baby is the product of the phantom pregnancies that abound in Munro stories. The mother is nowhere in sight but we do notice that if we are stuck inside this egg (to echo the title of a story by Marian Engel) we might as well do some reading.

Chapter 5

Large pink woman reading a joke

The pleasure of reading Alice Munro is, in the last analysis, that we catch ourselves in the act of reading. Like every other human activity in a Munro story, however, the act of reading happens in groups. The narrator of "Images" has eyes without pupils because she behaves like an orphan in her own family. Her pose makes an ironic distance that is crucial to the activity of the "watcher" but an Orphan Annie with working eyes is no longer an orphan. She will be able to begin looking, however, only if she averts her gaze from the "large, fragile and mysterious object" that is her real, pregnant Mother (DHS, 33), her place of origin. She looks instead at the images of her father and the mock mother, the nurse Mary:

> But at present there was a lamp on the table. In its light my father and Mary McQuade threw gigantic shadows, whose heads wagged clumsily with their talk and laughing. I watched the shadows instead of the people. They said, "What are you dreaming about?" but I was not dreaming, I was trying to understand the danger, to read the signs of invasion.

(DHS, 35)

In the act of reading the signs of invasion, little Orphan Annie recovers her pupils and at the same time recovers some of the power that she has projected into the bad man who is always "around the corner."

Charlotte Gilman's "The Yellow Wallpaper" (1989) has been canonized by feminists because of the vivid way it dramatizes the horror, for a woman, of not being allowed to read. The most sinister feature of Margaret Atwood's *The Handmaid's Tale* (1985), similarly, is the fact that the women are not allowed to read and write. Munro's stories offer a multitude of little dramas about women who are at varying stages of learning to be "resisting readers," to use the phrase coined by Judith Fetterley. From Prue in "Prue," where the reader is a kleptomaniac who cannot find meaning in the objects she steals, to Rose in *Who Do You Think You Are?*, where the reader is an actor, the women in the stories represent a tremendous variety of ways of reading. This multiplicity itself is one of the greatest comforts of reading Alice Munro. As the cumulative impact of Munro's many women readers began to grow on me, Orphan Annie not only acquired eyes but also began to put on weight. I imagine the composite figure of the reader in Munro's stories as large and pink, like the "Fat Lady" in pink who does a high-wire act in Margaret Atwood's *Lady Oracle* (1976, 102). The stereotyped view of the female reader is that she secretly consumes candy while she consumes romance and for such a process the swollen pink body is an apt image. Wallace Stevens invented a "Large Red Man Reading" but a more comfortable position for the woman writer and reader is that of the chameleon – taking on the protective colours of the surrounding symbolic order.

This camouflage produces ironic distance, of course, but it works in conjunction with compassion in Munro's stories. Even Sophie, in "White Dump," can just imagine the "'kid's dream'" of a big candy mountain if she pictures marzipan (PL, 306). Munro's compassion works from within the experience of living in an electronic culture that makes consumers of us all. We may squirm when Jocelyn exults in the pleasure: "'We're Consumers! And it's Okay!'" (WDY, 131). Whether we are ironic about it or not, however, we all do our share of consuming. Ironic distance does make it possible, however, to make distinctions among the things that Jocelyn lumps together: paintings, records, books, t.v., hair dryers, waffle irons, heated towel racks, etc. (WDY, 131). The weight of goods is like the "pile of old *Family Heralds*" that Del finds in the baby carriage (LGW, 54). It is difficult, in these circumstances, for the carriage to make progress. The most we can hope for is not a pilgrimage or quest but a circus parade. Munro's fiction makes a small space for us within which to realize the limits of our freedom but also to act within those limits. Even as we gain ironic distance from conscious clichés and dead metaphors, we are encouraged to imitate her compassion towards our fellow creatures who are all caught up within this same machinery.

I use the word "read" in the broad sense that Munro herself uses it: the young girl who reads the map of a chocolate box, the girl who tries to read the skin of a cow as a map, the sister, Et, who tries to "make Char read what [Blaikie] might do again in the light of what he had done before" (SIB, 22). Et's life is itself a reading or misreading of stories she has read: "like some story . . . Romeo and Juliet, she thought later" (SIB, 23). Identity itself *is* a reading – as we see when Addie becomes Princess Ida. No single character goes back to some primal maternal origin but is rather constituted from bits and pieces of earlier characters in a manner consistent with the thinking of Jean Laplanche (1976, 128–129; cited by Brodzki, 1988, 246–247). The name Jerry Storey encapsulates this fact; his reading is limited, so he talks in "a dialect based roughly on the comic strip *Pogo*" (LGW, 204) but he is no less a story for that.

The multiplication of storytellers and readers in Munro's fiction helps us towards an understanding of the conventions according to which we construct (and constrict) our lives. Reading, because it is situated within groups and in time, is an act within a historical context. Awareness of history or time is matched in intensity in a Munro story only by awareness of place (see Weaver, 1988, 381–402). Her sense of the land she loves, of her own region in southern Ontario, informs her most powerful stories. The act of rewriting history, indeed, acts as a kind of comfort to women who confront the myths and symbols that have designs on them. In "Hard-Luck Stories," for example, tourists are on a mock pilgrimage in a country church, where Munro stages one of her many group reading acts. While decoding religious symbols, the narrator thinks she sees, in the needlework of a footstool, a white lily: "No – it was a trillium" (MJ, 197). She is inordinately pleased with her "homely emblem," as if she had "secretly, come upon an unacknowledged spring of hopefulness" (MJ, 197). The trillium is Ontario's provincial flower and grows profusely in the countryside here. Munro's sense of belonging does in fact provide just such a "spring of hopefulness." History and myth form a kind of cross-stitch, like the lily and the trillium, but the greater comfort derives from history.

Since *lily*, like *rose*, is a word often used as a woman's name, this particular image helps to illuminate the relation between language and the construction of the female subject in Munro's fiction. Munro's use of language, to adapt sartorial terminology, could be characterized as "thrift-shop dressing." Kaja Silverman sees this style as a means of providing "the female subject with a more flexible and capacious 'envelope'" than any uniform sartorial system (Silverman, 1986, 150). I am not suggesting, of course, that the characters *in* Munro's fiction dress in "retro" style. Stella, for example, when she comes "bursting out of the female envelope" (PL, 33) seems to have ordered her new clothes from a mail-order catalogue. Dina, in the same story, is dressed in nothing but her pubic hair, which is "like lichen." Munro's fascination with language, however, turns even pubic hair into a thrifty disguise. "The function of figuration," as Mary Jacobus has noted, "is to manage anxiety; any figuration is better than none – even a fungoid growth is more consoling than sheer absence" (Jacobus, 1986, 246).

Faced with the dangers of being turned into a rag-doll with no eyes, Munro adopts a "sartorial strategy" of the kind suggested by Silverman. Her irony is compassionate precisely for this reason and she can walk perilously close to nostalgia because of this strategy. Like "thrift-shop dressing," her images suggest an "affection for objects which were once culturally cherished, but which have since been abandoned" (Silverman, 1986, 150). When Cora appears in a "dull rose crepe" castoff that is "loaded with fringe," (WDY, 30), it is only an exceptionally explicit instance of such dressing. Names like Cora and Flora reflect a "predilection for a tarnished and 'stagey' elegance." The naming of a Rose works to "denaturalize its wearer's specular identity" and puts "quotation marks around the garments it revitalizes" (Silverman, 1986, 150). The title of Munro's most recent collection, *Friend of My Youth*, is the most conspicuous example of her strategy of refashioning the unfashionable.

The subtle clowning of the thrift-shop dresser is most concentrated in Munro's choice of proper nouns. Her names resonate, whether they are common names like Helen and Mary, or uncommon ones like Euphemia and Almeda. Often the names suggest particular books that Munro herself has read. The name Catherine, in "Lichen," for example, has a resonance that makes us rethink *Wuthering Heights*, a book that Munro read so often that her mother "hid it under the mattress in the guest room" (Munro, in Horwood, 1984, 124). The names Prue and Rose, from different stories, suggest the daughters of Mrs Ramsay in *To the Lighthouse* and the name Stella sets up multiplying literary echoes. Names are like sites of invasion, places from which a close reader can trace historical corridors stretching far back in time. Rose, for example, is a dead metaphor that is resuscitated when it is thus historicized. A powerful sense of historical particularity underlies Munro's stories. The names Alphonse and Alicia, for example, resonate if you read that story and *Who Do You Think You Are?* in conjunction with Katherine Burton's biography (1956) of Nathaniel Hawthorne's daughter Rose: *Sorrow Built a Bridge: The Life of Mother Alphonsa*. For every historical echo that I notice (in this case by chance), there are innumerable others that I have missed.

When the puppets Alphonse and Alicia led me to Mother Alphonsa, who had previously been in the blind spot behind Hawthorne, I was conscious of the fact that the pleasure of recovering a lost historical detail is particularly intense when the process unearths a previously silenced woman. Munro's thrift-shop strategy, to use Silverman's terms, "establishes a dialogue between the present-day wearers" and the "original wearers" of a name and "provides a means of salvaging the images that have traditionally sustained female subjectivity, images that have been consigned to the waste-basket not only by fashion, but by 'orthodox' feminism" (Silverman, 1986, 151). The "poetess" in "Meneseteung" is one such unfashionable pose and Munro wears the garment with such aplomb that we *almost* don't notice the ironic distance. The distance is there, however, in the simple fact that the first person of the story is a *reader* of Meda's work. This ironizing is what distinguishes this kind of thrift from that of the Presbyterian aunts in "The Peace of Utrecht." Like them, Munro insists on recycling and exploiting literary fashion's waste. She refuses to discard entirely the old patriarchal images but succeeds, rather, in "recontextualizing" them. In this way she is able to "'reread' them in ways that maximize their radical and transformative potential" (Silverman, 1986, 151).

A yawning gap remains, however, between history as written and history as felt in Munro's stories. "The Peace of Utrecht" is a title that obliquely suggests this gap. The erasure of women's lives in the histories written by men forms an implicit but powerful feature of Munro's fiction. Ultimately Munro represences the absent mothers of the past by insisting on their place in history, on their sheer existence in time. History, in "Meneseteung," is potentially an elegant joke on the woman who becomes a "figure of fun." Munro's strategy seeks for new ways of looking at history, ways that allow a woman to "see the joke" (DHS, 10) rather than to be left out of every "'new in-joke'" (PL, 278). If, like Fern, she is going to end up *being* a joke, then she might as well wear the garment with irony.

Jokes are astonishingly prolific in Munro's fiction. Freud describes jokes as a "special case of condensation" and notes that joking techniques are "dominated by a tendency to compression, or rather to saving . . . . 'Thrift, thrift, Horatio!'" (Freud, 1960, 42). *Thrift* is a word that characterizes Munro's fiction. In a joke, the *"yield of pleasure corresponds to the psychical expenditure that is saved"* (Freud, 1960, 118). Munro offers a thorough exploration of the implications of Freud's point that "laughing at the same jokes is evidence of far-reaching psychical conformity" (151). Since practical jokes exploit someone's credulity (Freud, 1960, 199), they serve as a particularly useful way for Munro to explore the figure of the scapegoat. In Munro's fiction the woman stops *being* a joke when she *reads* a joke.

Jokes within the stories – whether practical jokes or narratives – are like texts set up to be read. Jokes mean nothing at all without a response. When the daughter in "Walker Brothers Cowboy" feels the graffiti on the sidewalk laughing at her mother and when Fern is described as "a joke," we see women's very lives endangered in some way. Even a failure to respond to a joke is a response. Marietta, in "The Progress of Love," refuses to laugh when her sister Beryl tells of their mother's mock hanging as if it were a practical joke. Freud notes that the construction of a joke is not complete until it is communicated (143). The response is conditioned by the particular context of each person who hears the joke: conditioned by class, gender, age, ethnicity, race, etc. Each time a joke is told, it acts as a set-up that exposes the distribution of power. By our own response to the joke we align ourselves with one or another power structure. Each time a joke is told, order is hastily constructed, the walls are thrown up surrounding us and we watch warily to see if we can read the "signs of invasion."

The storyteller, then, is a jokester. Sam and Edgar's rape of Callie (in "The Moon in the Orange Street Skating Rink") is like a practical joke, exploiting her credulity and thus putting her in a "comic situation" (Freud, 1960, 199). She is compared to a doll or a dog. In her countermanipulation of the narrative, however, Callie turns the tables and in the end it is Sam who appears as a stupid-looking doll. Women like Callie understand the conventions and the patterns as only she can understand who lives caught up *in* the pattern, feeling its oppressive power at every turn in her life. This knowledge is often conveyed by Munro in terms of the activity of sewing, crocheting, and knitting. I think, for example, of Et's skill as a dressmaker, of Callie's pride in her sewing, and of the way their skills translate into their activity as readers and storytellers. The women have varying kinds of power – some benign, some sinister. The mimicry of an Et or a Callie duplicates the kind of aggression that characterizes the father in a patriarchal system. Sometimes the mimicry is a *denial* of reading. When Grace and Vera sit in the driveway crocheting tablecloths for as long as they can see (MJ, 207), there is a strong feeling of an oppressive fixed pattern. Munro does not write about woman's handiwork with contempt, but neither is it inherently benign.

In Ebbitt Cutler's *I Once Knew an Indian Woman*, Madame Dey can take an old elaborately knitted sweater and memorize the stitch backwards while she unravels it. "'There's not a thing that woman can't do,'" says the mother of the narrator, "'except read and write'" (Cutler, 1967, 54–55). In Munro's stories, such a total understanding of the pattern *is* a kind of reading skill. Knowing the pattern backwards and forwards, moreover, is a potential source of power. Although such readings are not necessarily resisting, no greater resistance is achieved by the women who occupy a higher economic class. The repetition of a sewing pattern, at the lower class level, is echoed in another kind of repetition on the middle-class level: recitation. Munro uses the old-fashioned parlour game of capping poetry quotations in "The Ottawa Valley" as an example of group readings. Here she thriftily recycles some of the material from the old Ontario readers.

The result of reading Munro's fiction is not to allow the reader – whether male or female – to be comfortable and smug. It is rather to find ourselves caught in the act of smugness – certainly defined as part of a group. This is the most subtle of Munro's many tricks, to make us initially unaware of our participation, to lure us into a position where we settle into our own prejudices and stereotypes – then to follow this up by making us excruciatingly aware of our own self-deceptions. In this final heightened awareness there is a breathtaking, exhilarating surprise as she pushes us beyond our own self-created illusions and as we watch our stereotypes crumbling before our very eyes. The luxurious pleasure of passivity, of revelling in recognition, of wallowing in the delights of shared gossip are accompanied by a deeper kind of recognition which shocks us and has the power to shatter the boundaries of our egos, to fracture our settled ways of seeing.

There remains something about Munro's fiction that is, in the best sense, "culinary" – a word often used to deride woman's fiction. Eating is an old metaphor for the act of reading and it is one that is particularly apt in the case of Munro, a writer who gives much food for thought but who, like any good hostess, also knows that our digestive system works best when we do not work at it. It works best, in fact, when we are simultaneously being entertained. Seneca puts it most lucidly: "What in our bodies we see Nature do without any conscious effort of ours . . . we must perform on those things that nourish the mind. . . . Let us digest it" (Epistle 84, quoted by Durling, 1981, 62). Food is such a frequent metaphor in Munro as to offer a veritable feast. "Half a Grapefruit," "Labor Day Dinner", "White Dump" – these titles label the story itself as an item for consumption. Del is "bloated and giddy" from reading Uncle Benny's papers and not being able to digest them (LGW, 5). Miss Kernaghan's stomach "rumbles, groans, and even whistles" because she is "troubled with indigestion" and does not understand the story she is telling (PL, 149). When the narrator of "Material" and her husband Hugo pretend to be Lady Chatterley and Mellors, he complains of having lost "that little rascal John Thomas." She responds, in "ladylike" fashion: "Frightfully sorry, I think I must have swallowed him" (SIB, 36). We eat to gain strength but do we put on the power of what we read? Has the narrator appropriated some of the power invested in Hugo, the writer? She has, after all, written *this* story: the story "Material." Is the voice of the woman writer powerful only to the extent that it has swallowed and digested the voices of male authors like Lawrence? While puzzling over this, I was startled to come across the following passage in an article by Nina Auerbach entitled "Engorging the Patriarchy": "For me, writing about something is an imperial act: it is my way of claiming power over it. . . . Probably, I share the primitive superstition that by writing about the patriarchy, as by eating it, I engorge its power" (1985, 237). Is the woman writer of "Material" engaged in such an "assertion of power"? Auerbach is right, I think, to describe reading as an "engorgement and appropriation: an intensely read text circulates through our body and mind" (238). I found myself, however, seeing Munro's fiction as a way of qualifying her conclusion that "If we make men our property, we can absorb the patriarchy before it embraces – and abandons – us into invisibility" (238). This kind of appropriation of the male language of imperialism, power, and property, does not seem to be adequate: "*This is not enough, Hugo.*"

Like the woman who is impregnated, the writer does allow herself to be invaded by the patriarchal texts – not in order to be wiped out by them, rendered invisible, but in order to produce something different, something other. Munro herself is obviously a voracious reader with an excellent digestive system. Her stories are, in a sense, oblique but radically revisionist readings of old texts: Mother Goose, Plato, *I Love Lucy*, Freud, Old Mother Hubbard, Dante, Ingmar Bergman, Shakespeare, Gilbert and Sullivan, Tennyson, Yeats, Humpty-Dumpty, Faulkner, the Bible, and many more. I now see all her fiction as a kind of ironic historical quotation, directed with most devastating accuracy at our old notions of autonomous identity, especially as these are celebrated in the figure of the

Artist. The woman writer and storyteller is an intensified instance of the parodic activity described by Linda Hutcheon (1985). In *Lives of Girls and Women* and in *Who Do You Think You Are?*, Munro works this out as a structural parody, the former commenting ironically on texts like *The Portrait of the Artist as a Young Man*, the latter offering a parodic version of *The Romance of the Rose*.

Thrift-shop dressing, as Silverman notes, often works to blur gender distinction. The mother who wears the father's overalls in "Connection" is an explicit image for something that is more broadly true in Munro's stories. As women usurp the part of men, the results range from a duplicating of aggression to an appropriating of the old power of play. The unearthed Chinese soldiers that are put together in "Bardon Bus" are compared by Dennis to X's women, row on row. This image has a subversive potential that is realized by many of Munro's female characters. The woman warrior is clothed in armour borrowed from the patriarchal system. We see this when the mother in "The Ottawa Valley" recites the words of the dying Arthur. There is the suggestion of the warrior, also, in the poppies on Nora's dress in "Walker Brothers Cowboy." The woman warrior is not, however, prepared to go to war. Colour those poppies green. The maternal warrior is a clown who, like the father in "Walker Brothers Cowboy," pretends to be herself. We can see the maternal camouflage best when she pretends to be Mother Earth. We glimpse this "figure of fun," for example, when Ada, like the Chinese warriors, is covered with mud from head to toe on the Jericho Road in "Princess Ida."

How far, though, does this playfulness extend? And how do we prevent the mock mother from becoming a figure turned in upon itself? What is to prevent her from resembling the graffiti in Hodgins's *The Invention of the World*? In the bus shelter there was "a great fat naked woman that grew out of the rolls and creases from around a long iron-shaped knothole. She was humped over, as if she were trying to see back in through the gap that had been knocked out of her body's centre" (Hodgins, 1977, 144–145). What is to prevent the play around the hole in the outhouse (WDY, 23) and around that other hole from becoming endless and pointless and leading to nihilism? Derrida describes Freud's play of the *fort/da* game as having no limit; he is interested in "the play of the *fort/da* infinitely exceeding the limits of the text" (Derrida, 1985, 70–71).

I found that in order to get myself out of this dilemma I had to return to the notion of the real mother *as* a limit. There *is* a reality that is never contained in our constructs and this is just as true of fiction as it is of history. The "squirming facts," as Wallace Stevens put it, "exceed the squamous mind" (Stevens, 1967, 167). The "real" remains other; it remains excluded from the *fort/da* game as did Freud's own daughter Sophie, the mother in the original game. The recognition of the persistent otherness of the body that was our origin, is a means of recognizing, more broadly, the otherness of the reality that can never be reproduced in art. This excluded reality, our confrontation with the fact that it is excluded, is the limit to our playfulness. The other limit, of course, is our own death and the knowledge of our death. "What I have," says Munro to Hancock:

> is people going on. Just as if every day had its own pitfalls and discoveries and it doesn't make much difference whether the heroine ends up married or living in a room by herself. Or how she ends up at all. Because we finally end up dead.
>
> (in Hancock, 1987, 214)

Despite the humour and playfulness of Munro's fiction, there is something black that we experience in relation to the blind spot. The experience of reading and rereading Munro's stories has led me to question our prevailing tendency to celebrate the power of the reader. I find I cannot enter fully into the spirit of the party, into the feeling of intoxication that comes from affirming the activity of the reader who constructs a writerly text (Barthes, 1977). I am struck by the extent to which all our constructions are shaped by what Jacques Ellul terms "integration propaganda" (Ellul, 1965, 71). It is often at just the point where we feel most euphorically free that we are most conditioned, most acting within a particular role. No reader reads as an individual. The sense of euphoria comes from having discovered a convention, from having discovered a community of shared readings. We cannot, by the same token, make a judgement from any safe place. The reader is not a new authority standing outside the patterns of the story and outside the fictional structure. We are all looking for space, for breathing room. The powers of our imagination are severely modified by the power of the machine to reproduce the patterns and images that we create. The machine, however, is only exaggerating an aspect of human nature that is a constant, the fact that we mimic each other, that we pretend to create when we are, in fact, copying. To read the signs of invasion is to make the effort to become a resisting reader. Although Fetterley applies the term to female readers, it is an equally urgent requirement for male readers.

There are ways of testing our play to ensure the honesty and integrity of the tricks and these ways insist on the importance of the excluded "reality" itself. Et's story to Char in "Something I've Been Meaning To Tell You" is a reproduction of a very familiar pattern, with the one difference that she has not proved that it did in fact happen in this case. That does matter. It is not always easy, however, to know how to read without making Et's error. Aristotle's definition of history as what happened and fiction as the kind of thing that happens supplies the ironic texture of "Royal Beatings." There, more explicitly than anywhere else in Munro's fiction, the "real" mother is left out of the story as someone who is utterly impossible to represent. Patrick announces: "Of course she's not your real mother," echoing a line from Jay Macpherson's "What Falada Said": "Those who let these things happen were – believe me – / Foreigners, strangers, none of those who loved you: / Not your true mother" (Macpherson, 1981, 91).

Irigaray notes that a "text that describes the daughter's attempts and failures to free herself from the mother, may be read as a metaphor for the inability to achieve freedom from the body of law" (quoted by Stanton, 1986, 173). Munro's fiction, in my opinion, escapes this bleakly conservative conclusion because her failures are so self-conscious and so spectacular. Like the staged failures of a clown, her clowning mothers reject the goal of a primal maternal origin while, at the same time, exploiting the potential for freedom within the repertoire of tricks that history has to offer the writer. Munro's fiction gains its vitality from an association with a folk tradition and with a maternal line of storytellers. This, however, is no easy nostalgia or primitivism. She is engaged in an activity shared by other women writers, and described by Brodzki as a "relentless self-interrogation . . . of female psychic and moral boundaries." A "matrocentric autobiography necessarily involves guilt and fear of (self) betrayal" (Brodzki, 1988, 248). The guilt of the daughter towards the mother, however, is matched by the betrayal of the mother who is an "unknowing collaborator with male authority" (Brodzki, 1988, 248). The trickster "motherly or grandmotherly" women in "Wild Swans" are imagined by Flo to be offering drugged candy (WDP, 55). They are only one example of how maternal figures are seen to collaborate at the deepest level with the structures of oppressive fiction that are reproduced by popular culture. They are matched in power, however, by the tricks of a Miss Marsalles or a Miss Farris. Munro's own tricks do not stop with the thrill of power or even with the moment of ironic understanding. Her clowning offers comfort because it leads to a *mutual* failure. We read for enlightenment and arrive, repeatedly, at the point of recognized blindness. In this experience, however, we have company: reader and writer share this discovery of mutual foolishness.

Part II

Readings

Chapter 6

Dance of the Happy Shades
Reading the signs of invasion

"WALKER BROTHERS COWBOY": PLAYING "I SPY"

The first story in Alice Munro's first collection of stories begins with a prologue that compares paternal and maternal images of reproduction. A playful tone is set in the first sentence: "After supper my father says, 'Want to go down and see if the Lake's still there?'" The sentence immediately following, however, exposes the dark underside of the mocking surface:

> We leave my mother sewing under the dining-room light, making clothes for me against the opening of school. She has ripped up for this purpose an old suit and an old plaid wool dress of hers, and she has to cut and match very cleverly and also make me stand and turn for endless fittings, sweaty, itching from the hot wool, ungrateful.
>
> (DHS, 1)

The daughter resents being a dressmaker's dummy; like the daughter in "Red Dress – 1946," she is humiliated by the exposure of her body during fittings: "I felt like a great raw lump, clumsy and goose-pimpled" (DHS, 148). If the daughter is like a lump of clay ("with me, her creation;" DHS, 5) the mother in "Walker Brothers Cowboy" is like a parody of the biblical God who fashions Adam out of clay. The mother herself, however, is virtually bodiless. She is nothing but a pair of sewing hands that work on thriftily with patterns and plaids of the past to construct something for the daughter's future.

We remain aware of these caring hands as we listen to the father explaining to his daughter about the origins of the Great Lakes: "Like *that* – and he shows me his hand with his spread fingers pressing the rock-hard ground where we are sitting" (DHS, 3). It is not, in the father's account, a divine hand that made these lakes but rather "fingers of ice" that gouged out the deep places. Unlike those fingers, moreover, the father's hand makes "hardly any impression" since he is working with rock, not with fabric or clay. This gesture, like the mother's sewing, is an absurd and failed miming of the action of the Father in *Genesis*. The difference is that the maternal action requires the body of the daughter. What the father will give his daughter in this story is not totally unlike the mother's reproductions. The difference is that while the mother sews a dress for her, the father shows her, by example, how to construct a mask. Both parents ensure, however, that the daughter's idea of reproduction will be one based on thrift. The father's mask is also made from a borrowed pattern.

Cowboy songs are a product of the American frontier. This Canadianized "cowboy," however, does not make his own laws as he travels but is more obviously bound to the economy of his country. There is no melodrama of the wild west here. The major danger is the boredom that threatens the pedlar's day. The horse, that brute energy or matter which is dominated by the heroic cowboy, is conspicuous by its absence and replaced by the car. Although this machine suggests domination of nature, the proper noun *Walker* mutes that image and the solitary romantic cowboy is acknowledged as part of a company, a male collective of "Brothers."

The father can cheerfully say "I" because he is a member of the company. He knows, from the beginning that "I" is a pose, a disguise. The father's "salesman's spiel" – the mask of the "Walker Brothers Cowboy" – becomes associated, by Munro's choice of title, with the story itself. *Spiel* is the German word for play and the father puts his very identity into this play. The absence of the mother on this field trip thus shows that her identity is not so easily put into play. In the midst of the radical instability of the father's sense of self, there is a paradoxical stability. When they arrive at Nora's yard, Nora does not at first recognize him. When she does, she says: "Oh, my Lord God . . . it's you" (DHS, 10) to which the father responds with typical self-mockery: "It was, the last time I looked in the mirror" (DHS, 10). The father's clowning will offer the daughter a means of survival but his gift to his daughter has a cutting edge; if she adopts his method (and she has no choice if she writes herself into playful existence) then she seems to be denying the mother's world. The daughter who writes will find herself caught, willy-nilly, between the maternal and paternal responses to self-representation. The narrating daughter is embarrassed by the mother's efforts to be more than herself, to be a "lady" and she prefers the father's pose as less than himself – a boy. The mother's idea of self-reproduction is ironically more bound than is the father's, by the patriarchal order. She is trapped inside the sign "lady" which balances the word "Lord" (raised as a fleeting echo by Nora's exclamation). The mother conspires, furthermore, to keep herself there.

When we do become aware of the mother's body in this story it is not her body but the body of a lady: "She walks serenely like a lady shopping, like a *lady* shopping, past the housewives in loose beltless dresses torn under the arms" (DHS, 5). Her voice, the "voice so high, proud and ringing" is the voiceless voice of a lady. The daughter loathes even her own name when this voice speaks it in public. Although Nora later says the names in turn (DHS, 12), they are never inscribed in the story. Ben Jordan, the father, has the power to rename himself, however playfully, while the daughter sees her nameless mother and herself as "objects of universal ridicule. Even the dirty words chalked on the sidewalk are laughing at us" (DHS, 5). They cannot be resisting readers of the text on the sidewalk unless they have some sense of a self that is doing the reading. Mother and daughter will remain as objects of ridicule, unless they can find a way to construct themselves as subjects.

This mother who is confined to the body of a lady has no sense of humour. Her husband's talk of piles and boils hints at the comic protuberances that characterize what Bakhtin calls the "grotesque body." Since the body of the woman is the "major battleground in the hysterical repression of the 'grotesque form'" (White, 1989, 165), the mother's bourgeois response is predictable. The "pedlar's song" is "Not a very funny song, in my mother's opinion" (DHS, 4). "Sometimes," says the daughter, "trying to make my mother laugh he pretends to be himself in a farm kitchen, spreading out his sample case" and the mother does "laugh finally, unwillingly" (DHS, 8). Laughter requires distance and the mother cannot pretend to be herself when she is so firmly encased in the costume of the lady. Like Addie in *Lives*, she has an "innocence," a "way of not knowing when people [are] laughing" (LGW, 81). The narrating daughter yearns to escape the mother, to escape the evidence of the cruelty that her mother does to herself in the name of the Father. The father, in his "salesman's outfit," offers a "rising hope of adventure" (DHS, 6).

The adventure that does occur is a practical joke that acts as the central text within the text of the story, evoking multiple responses that expose the distribution of power. The adventure is less important, in itself, than are the reproductions of that adventure, the responses to the joke. These are played out against a grey background. The children play the game "*I Spy*" but "it is hard to find many colours" (DHS, 9). The daughter's own first hand account is a spare reporting of what her eyes spy while her father waits at the door of the house and someone empties a chamberpot from an upstairs window. The little brother "laughs and laughs" but the daughter is silent. She sees a window "slammed down, the blind drawn" and notes that "we never did see a hand or face." The silence of the father and the menacing hand behind the blind help to distance the daughter from her brother's naive response: "'Pee, pee,' sings my brother ecstatically. 'Somebody dumped down pee!'" To which the father replies: "'Just don't tell your mother that. . . . She isn't liable to see the joke'" (DHS, 10).

"Just don't tell" is a phrase echoed in "Images" where the father instructs the daughter: "'But don't say anything about it at home. Don't mention it to your Momma or Mary, either one'" (DHS, 42). "Walker Brothers Cowboy" is full of "things not to be mentioned" (DHS, 18). In this story (as in "Images") the text of the story itself is an unmentionable joke hidden from the mother, a guilty secret shared with the father. We share the daughter's pain about the mother since she cannot "see the joke," since she cannot read what we are reading. The victim of the practical joke is literally the father but by this silence a substitution takes place and the scapegoat is seen to be the mother, who is the "object of ridicule." We are sensitized to this by the fact that the "other" woman – the father's old flame – usurps the mother's place. The father is a comedian in need of an audience and that is precisely what Nora provides.

The approach to the house and to the character of Nora will be recapitulated in a different form in the later story "Lichen" (PL, 32–55). Like Stella in that story, Nora is overweight. Her "arms are heavy, and every bit of her skin you can see is covered with little dark freckles like measles" (DHS, 12). Like Stella, Nora dresses flamboyantly. The body, rendered highly visible, is matched by the high visibility of the dress which is flowered lavishly. "'It's the first time I knew there was such a thing as green poppies,' my father says, looking at her dress" (DHS, 12). His boyish wonder echoes that of Stephen in *Portrait of the Artist as a Young Man*: "But you could not have a green rose. But perhaps somewhere in the world you could" (Joyce, 1916, 12). Nora's denial is significant: "You would be surprised all the things you never knew. . . . They're not poppies anyway, they're just flowers" (DHS, 12–13). The father here presumes to label the fabric (choosing an image associated with male heroism) and Nora's resistance takes back the acts of fabrication and naming.

Shortly after arrival at Nora's house, the father constructs a narrative joke out of the practical joke:

> But after a while he turns to a familiar incident. He tells about the chamberpot that was emptied out the window. "Picture me there," he says, "hollering my heartiest. *Oh, lady, it's your Walker Brothers man, anybody home?*" He does himself hollering, grinning absurdly, waiting, looking up in pleased expectation and then – oh, ducking covering his head with his arms, looking as if he begged for mercy (when he never did anything like that, I was watching), and Nora laughs, almost as hard as my brother did at the time.
>
> (DHS, 15)

Nora is right when she protests: "That's not a word true!" and yet the exaggeration, the distortion, the mocking self-presentation is a release. Release comes from the multiplication of pictures produced by the father's imperative: "Picture me." What we picture, in fact, is a convention of clowning. The cowboy steps aside to make room for a Charlie Chaplin act.

Francis Sparshott refers to Charlie Chaplin's characterizations as having a "quality of pure mime, an illumination of an action from within" (Sparshott,

1988, 336). This adaptation of the "movement traditions of circus clowns" is one of a "variety of movement arts" that are "neither acting nor dance but belong to this alternative tradition of mime, an enhanced and poeticized presentation, neither of personality nor of body movement, but precisely of action as taking on an exemplary nature of its own" (Sparshott, 1988, 336). At the end of *Lives of Girls and Women*, Bobby Sherriff's gesture will offer another example of Munro's interest in such movements. Like many kinds of body language, such gestures are *"thrown away"* (Sparshott, 1988, 331) and Munro's fiction recovers them. The miming of the father in "Walker Brothers Cowboy" is of particular significance because he claims to be miming or "doing" himself. Miming, however, is not impersonating, as Sparshott notes (1988, 335). The very absurdity of the father's claim serves to draw attention to the mime itself and to his immediate audience and the particulars of this visit. "One can mime oneself walking as one walked on a specific occasion or as one walks in specific circumstances," Sparshott notes, "so long as the occasion or the circumstances do not at present obtain" (1988, 334). The father's act of doing himself shows up the absurdity of our illusions about autonomous identity, exposing the reality that we make ourselves up out of an assortment of conventions. It also makes visible the presence of Nora who, in turn, makes his mime visible by her laughter.

Subsequent stories by Munro will show just how important the father's example of mimicry is to the daughter's work as an artist. When Ralph Gillespie in "Who Do You Think You Are?" does Milton Homer and Rose does Ralph doing Milton Homer we are seeing complex variations on this father doing himself. The problems enter when you consider *doing* the mother who cannot *do* herself. Nora, the mock mother, plays a mediating role in the daughter's response to this problem. The song, "Walker Brothers Cowboy" which, to the mother, was "[n]ot a very funny song" is to Nora hysterically funny: "she laughs so much that in places he has to stop and wait for her to get over laughing so he can go on, because she makes him laugh too" (DHS, 15). Nora is open to comedy. She is a match for the father because she can pretend to be herself *doing* her own mother. We sense the father's need for her nurturing as we enter her maternal space and we remain conscious of the infantilized mother who is the object of her mothering.

Two dead metaphors of the mother are enclosed in Nora's house, like mocking icons set up for Nora to imitate. The first is the body of Nora's own Momma: "Blind! . . . Her eyes are closed, the eyelids sunk away down, showing no shape of the eyeball, just hollows. From one hollow comes a drop of silver liquid, a medicine, or a miraculous tear" (DHS, 12). The blind mother "falls asleep, her head on the side, her mouth open." The open mouth does not speak and the eyes do not see. This maternal blindness is not transcended by paradox. Unlike Milton and Homer, but like Milton

Homer, this mother is no seer. In contrast to this image is the "picture on the wall of Mary, Jesus's mother . . . in shades of bright blue and pink with a spiked band of light around her head" (DHS, 14). This picture, unlike the blind Momma, does make claims to authority. The image of the virgin birth, however, is belied by the multiplicity of phallic spikes.

It is Nora who is able to confront the limits of her own power. When the father invites her to visit and gives directions, "Nora does not repeat these directions." Instead, she writes her own text on the machine, a text which we cannot see: "She touches the fender, making an unintelligible mark in the dust there" (DHS, 17). Don't look to Nora for help. Implicitly she warns us all "never to count on" the extra sense of the mother (PL, 105). In the act of writing her unintelligible mark in the dust, Nora gestures her abdication, her retreat into her house. Like an inversion of Ibsen's Nora, she plans her own exit and writes herself out from inside the story. This exercise of choice, anticipating that of Meda in "Meneseteung," is what gives her potential power. Her very abdication, moreover, makes available to the daughter, as reader in the text, a possibility for resistance. Hope comes not from the "rising hope of adventure," not from desire for some nebulous ideal (a cowboy's futuristic dream) but rather from the opacities themselves, from awareness of the very *act* of imaging. "I was watching" (DHS, 15) is the crucial phrase and "*I Spy*" is the game. I spy something that is green.

The awareness of this act of imaging, however, comes with a sense of the inadequacy of the images. Nora remains other – unabsorbed into the images that surround her – and the landscape left behind "changes into something you will never know" (DHS, 18). This is not the blurry and romantic view seen from a horse but rather the miniaturized and severely framed view seen in the rearview mirror of a car. The concluding image of the story is that of the children facing backwards in the car while the father drives them forwards towards the house in which their mother lies, having her headache. The inversion is complete. We have been turned inside out if we began by assuming that children look to the future and adults look to the past. The narrator, of course, looks in both directions and that is why she is a writer.

At some deep level, the daughter is aware that what they are driving towards and what they are driving away from are the same thing in this sense: both are something that you do not know. Nora began as an ideal reader for the father's text – the text being the song "Walker Brothers Cowboy" which is situated within the story "Walker Brothers Cowboy." By her act of making a mark (an alternative text) that we cannot read, she absents herself from the story. She does not, however, by this gesture become a non-reader. She becomes, rather, the reader of texts that we do not see. The other in "other woman" and the other in mother come together behind a blind spot which cuts the daughter off, painfully, from her endearing father. He – small wonder – is "fresh out of songs" as they return home.

This story demonstrates that any daughter's first person self-representations will be conditioned and invaded by what she has watched her father do – what we all watch our fathers do as they construct the laws of genre. This daughter is blessed with a clowning father whose physical performance undermines those laws. Since the mother refuses to come out and play, the daughter must learn to clown from her father and to dance from the mock mother. The story itself and the "I" that is written is inside the paternal idea of craft, inside a world that is made. The power of the fiction, however, comes from what is excluded by that view of creation. We can begin to glimpse the implications of this for a woman's writing. Nora's writing – her signature, so to speak – is not read by us, but Nora (unlike the narrator and her mother) does have a name. The fact that it is not only her name, that it has been used by Ibsen and others, is a clue to Munro's method. The mock mothers that you meet when you run away from the "real mother" will direct you back to an acknowledgement of the other in mother and of the fact that the female subject, like the male subject, has to be constructed out of recycled fabric.

"IMAGES": DON'T TELL MOMMA

"Images" is what we used to call a seminal story, rich in reflected and refracted images. The pattern of departure and return which was enacted in "Walker Brothers Cowboy" is here repeated with a difference, but this fact will not make us confident of possessing an archetypal pattern if we pay close attention. Catherine Sheldrick Ross uses this story as evidence for a claim that Munro "turns to myths and legends" for her patterns. The details add "texture" but they do not threaten that pattern. In Ross's view the "pattern is deepened with each reworking" but not challenged (Ross, 1983, 113–114). She notes that the structure of "Images" is "the familiar motif of the underground journey" (114). It is true that Munro works with "elements that have become central in the shared storehouse of story-telling conventions" (Ross, 1988, 122). What Ross fails to note, however, is that the details do challenge the pattern. Munro herself has observed (in conversation with Tim Struthers) that she admires a writer's focus on "the way the experience was looked at" and does not like a mythological "framework." She says explicitly, "I wanted to do without this. And that, I think, is my personal bias" (Struthers, 1983, 16).

I don't believe that Munro (or any other writer) can do without the myths or conventions, but I hope to demonstrate that she shows how the major myths do without the body of the mother. It is for this reason that she has to write against the grain of the conventions. The quest pattern in "Images" comes clear only if we turn a blind eye to the women left behind. In "Walker

Brothers Cowboy" the mother was left behind and the substitute mother was the mock goal. In this case both mother and mock mother are left at home while the daughter goes adventuring with her father. As Lorna Irvine notes with relation to *Lives of Girls and Women*, "the women . . . pull against the straightforward development of the plot and will not allow clarification to occur" (Irvine, 1983, 107). The word "plot" here could be replaced with "myth" or "quest."

The most conspicuous presence in "Images" is that of a mock mother who parodies the role played by the "Intended" in Conrad's *Heart of Darkness*. Nowhere are women more firmly and ironically excluded from the quest formula than in *Heart of Darkness*. "'Did I mention a girl?'" asks Marlow.

> "Oh, she is out of it – completely. They – the women I mean – are out of it – should be out of it. We must help them to stay in that beautiful world of their own, lest ours gets worse. Oh, she had to be out of it. You should have heard the disinterred body of Mr. Kurtz saying, 'My Intended.' You would have perceived directly then how completely she was out of it."
>
> (Conrad, 1984, 84)

In *Heart of Darkness*, the "Intended" is in a kind of blind spot, alluded to briefly at crucial points in the narrative. At the end of the narrative she comes towards Marlow "all in black, with a pale head, floating towards [him] in the dusk" (117).

The Intended in "Images" is, by contrast, in the foreground. Mary McQuade is a conspicuous physical presence. The jokes lost on the mother swell her up "like a bullfrog" and make her "red in the face" (DHS, 34). The narrator pretends not to remember Mary's previous visit – the time of her grandfather's death. He lay in "near-darkness all day, with his white hair, new washed and tended and soft as a baby's, and his white nightshirt and pillows, making an island in the room" (DHS, 30). Mary McQuade, "the other island," is in her starched white uniform and sits "mostly not moving" waiting for the grandfather to die. This figure of power is dominant. The patriarch is infantilized by her and thus put on a level with the narrator who is "put to sleep in a crib." "Out in the daylight" Mary turns out (like Nora in "Walker Brothers Cowboy") to be "freckled all over, everywhere you could see, as if she was sprinkled with oatmeal" (DHS, 31).

She is waiting not only for birth and death but also for a lover. As Ben teases her about potential husbands, however, she does not fade into the shadows like Conrad's "Intended." On the contrary, we become increasingly conscious of her body: "Her laughter would come out first in little angry puffs and explosions through her shut lips, while her face grew redder than you would have thought possible and her body twitched and rumbled threateningly in its chair" (DHS, 34). Her ominous presence makes it impossible to give ourselves totally over to the quest pattern which dominates the story. It's astonishing how much power can be invested in one such person, simply a "practical nurse" given to playing practical jokes on members of her family. Her stay-at-home power is set up as a counter to the power of the ancient quest pattern – departure and return / descent and ascent. Munro takes the figure of the "Intended," costumes her in dazzling white, paints her face bright red, and sprinkles her body generously with freckles so that we can see her. This spectacle, in turn, changes the way we look at the body of the pregnant mother. The "large, fragile and mysterious object, difficult to move" (DHS, 33) is transformed, through Mary's mocking eyes, into a kind of circus balloon. The real pregnancy poses as a phantom pregnancy as the mother threatens to "'bob up to the ceiling, just like a big balloon'" (DHS, 33).

Mary's power is associated with the beginnings of life and with the end of life. The first time I read this story I assumed that the mother was dying and many of my students make the same assumption. There is an ambiguity in the story: the mother could as easily be dying as giving birth. Mary cannot control the time of either death or birth. The place where she sits is a place of waiting and what the young girl learns is the limits of power. The mother is reduced to being like an infant, whimpering "childishly" for Mary to rub her back (DHS, 33) and the mother's abdication makes a space for the activities of the mock mother. Although Mary's practical jokes are frightening, they are easier to cope with than is the "everlastingly wounded phantom" called "*Mother*." Her tricks serve to deflect and refract the power of the mother. Swollen with jokes like a bullfrog, her body is a mocking reproduction of the body of the mother, swollen in pregnancy. At the same time, it mimics the male aggression suggested by the word *bull*. Her activities as trickster and clown make the text visible. They give the daughter something to interpret and encourage her to be wary while she reads.

The narrator's father is the victim of Mary McQuade's practical jokes and their pattern of interaction is consistent with what anthropologists know of the relation between permission to joke and kinship structures. A disturbing aggression is thriftily suggested by these jokes: "She gave him a fork with a prong missing, pretending it was by accident. He threw it at her, and missed, but startled me considerably" (DHS, 34). Like "Walker Brothers Cowboy," this story also puts the author herself in the position of a trickster and the quest pattern itself is part of her bag of tricks. The father claims to be the author of a joke on the Intended when he presents the story to Mary on his return: "We found the one for you today, Mary" (DHS, 43) but a double-take highlights the word "we." That "we" includes not only his daughter but also a larger collective – we who want these archetypal patterns and we who reinforce their rigidity. In actual fact (as the humble father knows perfectly well) it is by no means clear who is having the last laugh. Despite his "we found" it is clear that he did not go out hunting for the ideal husband for Mary; he went out to check his trapline for muskrats.

The trapline leads to the body of a muskrat: "the stiff, soaked body, a fact of death" (DHS, 36). The archetypal storyline, similarly, leads to a dead end. The mock mother is called Mary. The man who lives in the underground house is called Joe. The archetypal story, thus turned into a practical joke, leads to a repetition of the father's pattern of teasing. "His teasing of Mary was always about husbands. 'I thought up one for you this morning!' he would say" (DHS, 34). Mary enjoys "all these preposterous matings." This last one is a mating of Joseph and Mary that leads to a dead metaphor. Where is the baby? If we look too closely, the distortions multiply. The mother of the narrator, when she refers to herself "gloomily in the third person" as *Mother* is associated with "the name of Jesus" (DHS, 33). Efforts to fix the archetype, then, produce a mockery of the holy family.

Asked by Hancock if names are a "clue" to her characters, Munro answers (somewhat disingenuously) that she simply chooses names that "sound right" and does not think about why (Hancock, 1987, 213). The names Joe and Mary do "sound right" but not because they are clues leading to the end of a game. They are, however, clues to something that is intimated by the father's description of Joe to Mary: "'I thought up one for you this morning!'" (DHS, 34). The names, in short, are "thought up" – arbitrary fictions. Joe's talk of the Silases who burned his house may echo the biblical Silas but also, perhaps, a literary one. Silas Marner is a surrogate father in a novel by George Eliot alluded to in *Lives of Girls and Women* (LGW, 175). It is not possible to track down these echoes and nail them to the wall, because the narrator eats the nails. Joe Phippen feeds them to her in the form of a "tin of Christmas candies, which seemed to have melted then hardened then melted again, so the coloured stripes had run. They had a taste of nails" (DHS, 41). Eating this candy, the narrator consumes also the archetypal Christmas story about Mary and Joseph and, in so doing, makes it impossible for the holy family to be made up of this Mary and this Joe.

When the old symmetries are burned out, two houses are still left in this story. One is the building which houses the pregnant mother. The other is Joe Phippen's underground house. The trapline and the storyline make up a connecting journey between these two houses, when father invites daughter to "come with me and look at the traps" (DHS, 35). The storyline is riddled with traps for unwary readers and the dream-like atmosphere is itself a trap. The narrator corrects the people who ask "'What are you dreaming about?'" with an explicit "I was not dreaming. I was trying to understand the danger, to read the signs of invasion" (DHS, 35). She can read the signs of danger only if she watches "the shadows instead of the people." The journey leads to Joe Phippen's underground house, to a place of shadows that suggests primordial depths, Plato's cave, and "fairy stories" (DHS, 43). Ultimately, however, it is only a "hole in the ground" (DHS, 39) and we do well to pay heed to the advice that Joe gives to his visitors as they enter: "Mind your head here" (DHS, 39).

The severing of the head is an image already evoked by the stories that the narrator remembers her mother telling, about "a queen getting her head chopped off while a little dog was hiding under her dress" (DHS, 33). With the house destroyed, and the head of the symbolic order chopped off, does it come down to "the horror, the horror"? Our desire to believe in such essentials is what Munro, like Conrad, exposes. The quest pattern tantalizes, evoking our desire to reach a place of origin, perhaps identified with the "hidden place" in the Wawanash River (DHS, 37). This is a failed journey, however, for we do not arrive at a place where it all began. Joseph did not, after all, father Jesus. It's not that there is no quest; it's just that the quest is repeatedly displaced. What they find when they arrive is something made, not something born. The narrator recognizes it in retrospect as "the sort of place I would like to live in myself, like the houses I made under snow drifts" (DHS, 40). This recognition is anticipated by the reversal that takes place when Ben and his daughter encounter the man with the axe. The man threatening her father with an axe is

> the sight that does not surprise you, the thing you have always known was there that comes so naturally, moving delicately and contentedly and in no hurry, as if it was made, in the first place, from a wish of yours, a hope of something final, terrifying.
>
> (DHS, 38)

"Made in the first place" is a crucial phrase in this passage because it underlines the story's focus on human reproduction and on beginnings.

Making and invention intersect with the world in which a grandfather dies and a baby is born. It is possible to dismiss the danger in the story as a fiction. Since Joe Phippen seems obviously paranoic, the narrator's fears of Joe may be similarly imaginary. The axe remains there, however, lying on the table in the underground house. The object of the child's fear may be constructed from a wish of her own but that wish is shared and reproduced not only by her but also by the machinery of popular culture. In her state of paralysis she waits, "like a child in an old negative, electrified against the dark noon sky, with blazing hair and burned-out Orphan Annie eyes" (DHS, 38). We wait with her, hypnotized by the strong circle of the eyes. Like the child, we may escape paralysis by becoming active readers but this will be impossible as long as we project total meaning or essence into the places we cannot see. Our eyes, in that case, will be "burned-out," like Joe's house: "they burned me out, Ben" (DHS, 39). As she watches the surfaces in Joe's house (her father's good manners, Joe's hospitality), the daughter begins to see the underground as a repetition, not a rejection, of the house she left behind.

The return home after the visit is a return with a difference – a difference which draws attention to the act of storytelling and redefines those secret "hidden places." The house left behind and the house to which they journey are both, to adapt Ross's phrase, a "shared storehouse of story-telling conventions" (Ross, 1983, 122). The "hidden places" are not where *the* story hides but are simply what we do not understand. The recognition of this by the narrator makes it possible for her to realize that she is no longer afraid of Mary MacQuade's power (DHS, 43). Power is not embodied in any one figure or house, but dispersed. That does not mean there is no danger, that heads are not chopped off queens or traps snapped on muskrats or cats victimized by crazy men. The narrator learns to see all stories as partial. When her father, for example, tells the story of Joe Phippen to Mary MacQuade, the daughter notes: "He left out the axe but not the whisky and the cat" (DHS, 43).

We are returned to the world of surfaces but, more important still, we have discovered that what appeared to be underground is also made up of surfaces. There is no escape from the Conradian irony that civilization is built on lies and manners. The "hole in the ground" where Joe, our mock father reigns, is no more our place of origin than the belly of our mock mother. The quest is a deliberate failure and we see this when we look at how the father, like the one in "Walker Brothers Cowboy," tells a story to the mock mother. "She served my father his supper and he told her the story of Joe Phippen" (DHS, 43). He makes a joke out of it. The joke is on Mary McQuade. She becomes the scapegoat of the story. The joke is also on Joe, however. Since we have witnessed the father's compassion towards Joe Phippen, it is troubling to see him so cavalierly reproducing Joe for the amusement of Mary. Who, in this version of storytelling, holds the power? We have learned that it is not Mary. It is not she who decides when life begins and ends. If the father in "Walker Brother Cowboy" teaches his daughter to clown, this one gives his daughter a lesson in "humility and good manners." When he was with Joe, he listened to Joe Phippen's story and went along with the idea of the Silases: "'I heard about that,' my father said" (DHS, 39). When he is with Mary, by contrast, he goes along with the fiction that the Silases are a fiction; here, at the supper table, he enters instead into the fiction of her search for an ideal lover.

This insistence on compassion as a motivating force in storytelling will come to fruition in the much later story, "The Progress of Love," where moments made up of compassionate lies are preferred in the end to the "old marriages, where love and grudges could be growing underground" (PL, 30–31). The underground in "Images" is not the place of the perfect story or of ultimate horror. It is the place where stubborn grudges are nurtured, a place of rigid convention and of obsessive and terrified behaviour. The father's world of good manners and playful clowning is a relief from those obsessions but it too is surface. The motive for telling the story – compassion – may be more important than the content of the story. The difference, however, between this compassionate lie and the lie that ends Conrad's *Heart of Darkness* is that this "Intended" is in on the joke and can hold her own with the father. The absence of the mother looms large in the two opening stories of this collection, but what is equally noteworthy is the comforting and solid presence of the father. His playful reproductions, his good manners, and his humility offer an alternative to grandiose quests. Instead of reaffirming the robust, individual male ego, his little acts of compassion and of failed understanding begin "the progress of love."

"THE OFFICE": WRITING ON THE WALL

This story demands attention, however briefly, since it is specifically about mothering and writing. The writer acquires a room of her own, but the walls of the room crumble for the simple reason that the narrator takes her mothering self with her and responds to Mr Malley, her landlord, as if he is a hungry child needing attention. She sees his portrait before she meets Mr Malley, and the "gilded frame" encloses a man in a business suit who looks "pre-eminently prosperous, rosy and agreeable." In person, however, Mr Malley moves "with a sigh, a cushiony settling of flesh, a ponderous matriarchal discomfort" (DHS, 63–64). As this mock matriarch fusses over the writer, bringing her assorted gifts, he begins to seem, however, more like a big fat baby who is "eatin' into" her time (DHS, 66). He seems to her "so wistful, so infantile" and she cannot turn away from his "obsequious hunger" (DHS, 67).

The repeated changes in the image of Mr Malley lead the narrator to see through the image of herself as a nurturer and to a confrontation with herself as a potential murderer. When he charges her with writing filthy things on the walls of the bathroom, she makes a confession: "I really wanted to murder him. I remember how soft and loathsome his face looked" (DHS, 73). Would this be matricide, patricide, or infanticide? The kaleidoscopic reversals expose the patterns of family behaviour as human constructs open to change. What holds the kaleidoscope still for the space of this story is the focus on the act of writing. His activity ("arranging in his mind the bizarre but somehow never quite satisfactory narrative of yet another betrayal of trust," DHS, 74) is seen as a mirror reflection of her activity ("While I arrange words, and think it is my right to be rid of him;" DHS, 74). The filthy writing on the wall in the washroom is yet another practical joke. Like the writing chalked on the sidewalk in "Walker Brothers Cowboy," this writing seems to be laughing at the narrator. The author of the writing on the wall is never identified and this throws the notion of authority into question, in contrast to the writing on the wall in the Bible. The narrator does get her vengeance, of course, by writing this story and thus nurturing him back with a vengeance. We cannot actually see him "in the flesh" so her reproduction is a conscious failure. Knowing this, the narrator cannot help but wonder why his arrangements and stories are obscene and hers are authorized and classified as literary.

We may say (anticipating the ending of "Material") that "this is not enough" and (anticipating the end of "Ottawa Valley") that she will never "be rid of him." This story, like so many of Munro's best stories, is about the failure of story. There is too much left over. The writer, the mother, the house, the office, the children, the husband, the landlord, the very trinkets in the office down to the last detail ("I forgot – a little plastic pencil sharpener") all appear separated, sharpened in their divisions, by this dramatic confrontation. At the beginning of the story the narrator claims to have discovered "the solution to my life." This is a failed solution and the details cannot be dissolved. After all the reproductions are done, the unincorporated flesh returns as a reproach. The self-representation in this little sketch questions any idea of art as final mastery. Nobody has the last laugh. Munro succeeds by a conscious failure and in this way her reproduction stands in sharp contrast to Mr Malley's self-portrait in the "gilded frame." This self-reproduction is that of somebody who watches – she watches herself in the act of watching the landlord watching her.

When the focus is on how we see, then nobody is the lord of the land. The naming of Malley reflects Munro's ironic view of power. The letters *mal* have been prefixed, since the sixteenth century, to many English words to convey the sense of something "ill," "wrong," "improper," – as in the word *malevolent* (*OED*). Since the prefix *mal* also suggests the word *male* it may be tempting to fix blame and see the story as a stereotypical feminist rejection of the male figure of power. I hope my reading, however brief, has been enough to show that Munro does more than this. She shows the male figure to us as her reproduction and by this reversal we see, not his evil power, but her power. The story, after all, is about class as well as about gender. What we have is a diffusion of malevolence and power and a demonstration of the way in which we all live inside the "gilded frame" of the patriarchy.

"THE PEACE OF UTRECHT": BREAKING THE PINK BOWL

"Walker Brothers Cowboy" and "Images" both sketch out ironic retellings of the quest pattern – departure from home and return to home. The mother is left behind as the daughter ventures forth with her father and this exclusion is the source of the irony. In "The Peace of Utrecht," the mother is not left behind. She is dead, and the result of this is that the "quest" is inverted: we begin with the daughter who is returning to the house. Alice Munro has spoken about this story and about her own mother:

> the incurable illness of a parent makes a relationship – its stresses become more evident that way. And so her illness and death and the whole tension between us – she had Parkinson's disease – was very important. The first real story I ever wrote was about her. The first story I think of as a real story was "Peace of Utrecht." It's about the death of a mother.
>
> (in Hancock, 1987, 215)

There is an ambiguity here. The narrator calls herself Helen but we know that Alice Munro is writing about herself; she admits candidly to Hancock that the story is "about" her own mother. The resulting confusion between fiction and reality disturbs our neat assumptions about the autonomy of art. The very awkwardness of the naming points to the transparency and inadequacy of our conspicuous fictions. Although this is probably one of the least funny stories Munro has ever written, it offers the strongest clues to the origins of her comic art. The details of Parkinson's Disease, like a "tasteless sideshow" (DHS, 195), will keep recurring as a signal that Munro refuses to dispense, entirely, with referentiality. This refusal will draw her repeatedly into a blurry area between life and art, an area where self-parody will be the only option.

Munro displaces and contains the situation by using the time of a visit as a framing device. Unlike a quest, a visit is acknowledged to be temporary, offering perhaps a flash of insight but never claiming to arrive at a fixed destination. A visit home, of course, is a contradiction in terms. In this story, Helen is both the girl who was once at home and the woman who is watching that girl. This eerie doubleness makes it possible to explore the issue of identity without collapsing inward into the claustrophobic centre of the story. Her sister Maddy is away when Helen arrives and she has left an absurd note on the door: "VISITORS WELCOME, CHILDREN FREE, RATES TO BE ARRANGED LATER (YOU'LL BE SORRY) WALK IN" (DHS, 197). The sign has the effect of playfully estranging the reality which ought to be home and of drawing attention to itself *as* a sign. It has meaning, of course, but the meaning is self-consciously detached from the gesture of signing and from the person doing the signing. "YOU'LL BE SORRY," for example, shows Maddy in the act of internalizing a pointing finger of blame that later becomes externalized for us. "WALK IN" has an ominous sound, as if the doorway marks the entrance to a family hell. The names of the sisters hint conspicuously at madness and hell.

The denial of the mother's body here precedes her actual death and the image of clothing makes this vivid. In the rare "periods of calm" that are part of the tricks of the disease, the mother employs her daughters in her efforts to be a lady. "She would demand that we rouge her cheeks and fix her hair; sometimes she might even hire a dressmaker to come in and make clothes for her, working in the dining room where she could watch" (DHS, 200). These are dresses that she will never wear "(for why did she need these clothes, where did she wear them?)" (DHS, 200). They are "unnecessary from any practical point of view" and they become like symbols without any symbolic significance, clothes that will never contain a body that can give them shape and meaning. Unlike the Emperor, whose clothes are the product of a shared collective self-deception, the mother's clothing is real but her body (indeed, her very identity) is an illusory construct. We can reproduce her clothes ("'I just got a new coat. I have several coats,'" (DHS, 206)) but we cannot reproduce the mother.

In this story there is no mock mother like Nora or Mary McQuade. The daughters themselves mock the mother with their mimicry. They will not, however, be able to move ahead to construct themselves as active subjects until they have confronted the moral issues raised by their caricatures of the mother. When Helen enters the house upon arrival, she turns and waits, out of force of habit, for her "mother's ruined voice" to call: "Calling, *Who's there?*" (DHS, 198). It is a "cry for help . . . shamefully undisguised" (DHS, 198), but Helen disguises it, frames it. While remembering this cry, she looks into the hall mirror, which contains the reflection of a "habitually watchful woman" who is "recognizably a Young Mother" (DHS, 197–198). The watcher in the woman comes into conflict with the keeper because she opens herself up to this cry for help. "*Who's there?*" Who is really there? Who is in the mirror? Who is calling? Who is called? *Who Do You Think You Are?* These questions spell ruin for the daughter's notion of her own autonomous identity. The frame of the mirror is all we have to contain this ruin, and it contains a reproduction of the "Young Mother." The daughters responded to the call with the words "You go and deal with Mother" but they are never finished dealing with her because they cannot stop the reproduction of mothering. Years later, in the story "The Progress of Love," Munro writes a dramatic version of the other side of this estrangement: a young girl "was howling 'Mama!' she was howling 'Mama!'" (PL, 12). The mother calling "Who's there?" (in "The Peace of Utrecht") and the daughter calling "Mama" (in "The Progress of Love") are divided by the invisible walls of separate stories and cannot answer each other.

What is the cause of this agony and how can the daughter respond to it? Reproduction is at least a place to begin and it is here linked to having the courage to look at what is framed in the mirror. It may be because the phrase "your mother" is a reproduction that it is felt by Helen as a "cunning blow" to her pride: "at those words I felt my whole identity, that pretentious adolescent construction, come crumbling down" (DHS, 194). Now that the mother has died, the town has turned her into one of its "possessions and oddities, its brief legends." She too is a "construction" and the daughters' mimicry is based on that fact. Like many of the women in Munro's later stories, she *is* a joke. "Wild caricatures we did for each other (no, not caricatures, for she was one herself; imitations)" (DHS, 195). The trouble is that their imitations are internalizations of collective perceptions. Before the death, Maddy labels her: "'Our Gothic Mother' . . . 'I play it out now, I let her be. I don't keep trying to make her *human* any more'" (DHS, 195). But letting her be is precisely what the sisters cannot do and when they reproduce her they cannot ignore the town. The act of perception is invasive and invaded by convention. This particular label "Our Gothic Mother" – contains at least two conventions: Gothic fiction and the Lord's prayer.

The conventions are awkward and conspicuous failures. "In the ordinary world it was not possible to re-create her," writes Helen. The picture is never complete: "Our Gothic Mother, with the cold appalling mask of the Shaking Palsy laid across her features, shuffling, weeping, devouring attention wherever she can get it, eyes dead and burning, fixed inward on herself; this is not all" (DHS, 200). This is not all. It is never enough and the face remains hidden by a mask. Success of a kind can, however, be reached by an acknowledgement of failure. In many stories Munro invokes a mock mother to play out that failure. In this story she does it by showing how the past mocks us with its very deadness if we look for an accurate reproduction or copy. Maddy and Helen make Fred Powell a present of nostalgia, "a version of our childhood," says Helen, "which is safely preserved in anecdote, as in a kind of mental cellophane." The "child-selves" in these anecdotes are "beyond recognition incorrigible and gay." The sisters will have to break free of this paralyzing, false kind of safety and tear the cellophane to get to a deeper level of recognition.

Munro gestures the place of this tear when Helen opens the drawer of a washstand and finds pages from a loose-leaf notebook.

"I read: 'The Peace of Utrecht, 1713, brought an end to the War of the Spanish Succession!' It struck me that the handwriting was my own" (DHS, 201). The writing is distanced by time and by the fact that it is written from dictation. The words written and read become oddly irrelevant. They gesture in the direction of authorized historical reality, of wars fought by men and recorded by men. Reading these words, Helen feels her old life lying around her, "waiting to be picked up again" (DHS, 201). She sees the "rudimentary pattern" of the town as "meaningful" and "complete . . . under an immense pale wash of sky" (DHS, 202). This pattern, however, is an epiphany of false historicism as the repetition of the word "wash" suggests. What will stand and what will wash away with time? This question is condensed into the single word that locates this text: *washstand*. The historical "Peace" goes against the idea of a final peacemaking. It was not so much peace as a complicated narrative of temporary arrangements and realignments. The historical complexity points towards a meaning left blank in this story. There are two conflicting threads of referentiality in this story. One leads to Munro's mother, the other to military history. The very title, then, "The Peace of Utrecht," is like a blind spot, like a deliberately failed clue. Like "The Moons of Jupiter," which forms a kind of companion story to this one, the title is a careful mistitle. The "Peace" is an "understood" historical allusion which, by inversion, points to what we do not understand. It is in this sense that it is like the mother who also eludes possession and understanding. By this oddly oblique gesture, Munro claims a place in history for the maternal line.

Paradoxically, Helen reclaims the real mother that has become one of the town's possessions by confronting the fact that the mother *cannot* be claimed at all. Representations or re-creations of the "real mother" keep turning into mock mothers and the act of trying is so painful that it might be described as a recurring feeling of doing matricide. What is potent in this story is the courage to confront this guilt – the guilt of having murdered the real mother to make room for mock mothers. This guilt is brought into focus during the visit within the visit – Helen's visit to see Aunt Annie and Auntie Lou. Aunt Annie forces Helen to confront the absence of the mother's body in her empty clothes. As Helen watches helplessly, Aunt Annie holds up "for inspection" the items in this bodiless fashion show. This, in Aunt Annie's opinion, is the maternal heritage. It is what the daughter can possess. The daughter's revulsion at the very idea is a catalyst leading her in an opposite direction, to a fuller awareness of the mother's absence, her otherness. Guilt is realized in the finger of blame that Aunt Annie figuratively points at Maddy. The emotional climax of Aunt Annie's story is the mother's flight from the hospital. "*The snow, the dressing gown and slippers, the board across the bed* . . . all her life as long as I had known her led up to that flight" (DHS, 208). Helen has a "longing not to be told" about the failure of the flight: "Oh, Helen, when they came after her she tried to run. She tried to *run*" (DHS, 208). Literally, the mother is captured and returned to the hospital. In death, however, she does escape our clutches and this is oddly comforting. Although we may thus pay tribute by acknowledging the failure of our own representations, this does not alter or correct the exclusion of the mother from written history. Munro's choice of title here is an augury of her developing interest in history as it relates to the erasure of the maternal heritage.

With the realization of the silenced and marginalized mother comes also a heightened awareness of the otherness of other characters. Strike out the M in Mother and you see the other in Maddy. It is she, after all, who acted as surrogate mother to her own sick mother and it is she who is the object of the pointing finger of blame. Aunt Annie claims to have said to Maddy, after the funeral, "Maddy, may it never happen like that to you" (DHS, 208). In fact it *is* happening to Maddy like that. She too desires flight. It is in this sense that the flight "concerns everybody." The imprisonment of the real mother is an exaggeration of a brutality that lives at the heart of our society and Maddie too is a victim of it – a castout. Aunt Annie "was afraid of Maddy – through fear, had cast her out for good" (DHS, 209). As nurse and mock mother, Maddy has borne the full burden of the role of sustaining the idea of "mother" and she is most clearly imprisoned. Her reproduction of mothering is visible in her eager nurturing of Fred. With the mother dead, Helen transfers her guilt into an effort to help her sister escape. That sister, however, has her own ideas about the past and her own version of the mother.

The sisters look into "the desert that is between" them that is the product of trying to pin down a claim to the real mother. The dilemma is a product of attempts to make the mother fit into a pattern prescribed by the dressmakers of the symbolic order. Comfort comes, however, as a result of the fact that the sisters have a shared dilemma in the *now*. They have a job to do in this shared present. The ending of "The Peace of Utrecht" finds the sisters in the kitchen. Since Helen has just "got home" from her visit to the aunts, the prevailing emotion is one of relief. In contrast to her initial arrival, we now experience it as a genuine coming home. As the sisters share the chores of food preparation, we also feel the stress taken off any one female figure since both are involved in that act of mutual mothering which characterizes sisterhood at its most comforting. "I got some raspberries for dessert. . . . Do they look all right to you?" asks Maddy and Helen replies with an echo: "They look all right" (DHS, 210). They are in harmony in their actions, in what is understood between them, but their conversations are elliptical and ambiguous.

Since it is Maddy who has been bearing the full burden of the symbolic order, it is fitting that it should be Maddy who comes out of the dining room "carrying a pink cut-glass bowl, for the raspberries." The pink bowl stands in, mockingly, for the female vessel within the symbolic order. It is only when Maddy drops the bowl and it falls as if in dreamlike slow motion, that we notice it. It is "quite a heavy and elaborate old bowl" (DHS, 210). As Maddy picks up the "pieces of broken pink glass" we are dimly aware of the muffled violence in the word "cut-glass" and perhaps even in the colour pink, which could be watered down blood. Like a bowl in a painting by Mary Pratt, this one seems to be surrounded by a magical rim that lifts it out of ordinary reality even as it is in the act of shattering. We sense ourselves approaching, with Maddy, the madness of hysteria as she offers herself the hollow comfort: "It's no loss to me. I've got a whole shelf full of glass bowls. I've got enough glass bowls to do me the rest of my life" (DHS, 210). Arrayed on a shelf like items to be sold, Maddy's pink bowl turns out, after all, to have been a reproduction.

In his reading of this story, W.R. Martin fills the pink bowl up with raspberries. He claims that "Maddy drops and breaks the cut-glass bowl of raspberries" and concludes that "the symbolism is rather heavy and obvious" (Martin, 1987, 44). Perhaps Martin has in mind Henry James or Ecclesiastes and is forgetting that Munro asks us to colour this bowl pink, not gold. Martin's reproduction of Munro's story turns a blind eye to the implications of that shelf full of reproduced bowls. He is ignoring the challenge thus issued to our assumption that an original pink bowl might reproduce some essential metaphor of maternity. Although he does not spell out the symbolism, he seems to assume that it is too obvious to spell out. He assumes (I assume) that the bowl is an image of the mother's womb. Why then, is the bowl (in his mind's eye) full of raspberries?

If I seem to be mocking Professor Martin I do so to challenge my own assumptions and those of the reading masses. The ease with which an industrialized society can reproduce copies of the bowl is repeated in the ease with which both Professor Martin and I can reproduce the archetypal story of the Holy Grail. So obvious is this story, indeed, that he does not need to tell it. Like Ross (1983, 112–126), Martin fails to see that the archetypal level of Munro's stories does not exist in a place that is possible to separate from the reality of a technological society. Just as our reconstructions are shaped by the "understood" ideologies and stories that we live by, reinforced by the powerful apparatus of technology, so the mock bowls follow, down to the last detail of each angle, the pattern of the pink cut-glass bowl.

It is the bowl and not the symbolism that is "heavy and elaborate." The very elaboration is designed, moreover, to lead us to a confrontation with a sign that is emptied of symbolic significance. I do not deny that there is an awkwardness in the story. The clumsiness, however, is deliberate, like the stumbling of a sad clown. The clumsiness itself is a transparent disguise, like the naming of Helen and Maddy, and it is made real in the story when Maddy cannot hold on to the bowl which is itself a clumsily disguised grail. Leaving the raspberries out of the bowl for the moment (as Munro does) let us look at the pink bowl, then, as a metaphor. If we do this we see that the metaphor is as dead as the mother. The cup used to commemorate the death of Jesus Christ and the womb of our mother simply refuse to dissolve into an identity. Cirlot notes that the "loss of the Grail is tantamount to the loss of one's inner adhesions" (1962, 116). The breaking of this pink grail shatters the idea of the autonomous text and of the autonomous subject.

Munro's frequent allusions to Arthurian legend show her taking on the powerful story in order to juggle with it, rearranging, displacing and mocking. She uses old legends and conventions slyly, embodying them in order to question them. Cirlot notes that the "appearance of the Grail in the centre of the Round Table. . . . closely parallels . . . the Chinese image of heaven (Pi), which is shaped like a circle with a hole (analogous with cup or chalice) in the middle" (1962, 116). This circle can be spotted in Munro stories but it is mockingly reproduced. I am thinking, for example, of the "Hole-in-One" doughnut shop in "Providence" (WDY, 136). The grail implies "above all, the quest for the mystic 'Centre'" (Cirlot, 1962,

116), but Munro is writing against the grain of this kind of symbolism. There are no knights at a Round Table here. Just two sisters working in a kitchen. The critic as treasure hunter, looking for a rich centre in the story, is doomed to failure. Such a reader could be compared to the character Arthur in "Something I've Been Meaning to Tell You." Arthur loves "schoolteacher's games" and when he wins a word game he is "immensely delighted. 'You'd think you'd found the Holy Grail,' Char said" (SIB, 3).

It is true that the pink bowl is described as "heavy and elaborate" but that very elaboration and heaviness is designed to lead us, not to symbolism but to a sign devoid of symbolic significance. Adapting the language of Naomi Schor, we might say that the pink bowl, so insistently demanding to be looked at, is a "disproportionately enlarged ornamental detail" which testifies "to the loss of all transcendental signifieds." Far from being full of symbolic significance, heavily laden with raspberries, it is a "parody of the traditional theological detail. It is the detail deserted by God" (Schor, 1987, 61). Like the chocolate cups in "Connection," the bowl waits for a ceremonial use which never presents itself (MJ, 3). These are the kinds of cups you tend to find in a woman's autobiography. Female autobiography is frequently like two sisters playing house while the mother is gone. Unlike the "shattered dishes" in the "children's house of make believe" in Frost's "Directive," however, this shattered bowl does not lead us to a place where we can ever "Drink and be whole again beyond confusion" (Frost, 1963, 253).

All is not lost, however. We do, after all, have the raspberries left over. If we wish to have them for dessert, there's work to be done: "Oh, don't stand there looking at me," says Maddy, "go and get me a broom!" (DHS, 210). This is what happens when a symbol is shattered; it comes back to us as a sign. Symbols are invested and filled up with meaning by the authorities that control the symbolic order. Signs, by contrast, are fractured and defined by context. This is not to say that we do not constantly try to see a symbol in a sign but always we fail and the object is returned to us *as* an object, to be dealt with as we go about our daily mental housekeeping chores.

"DANCE OF THE HAPPY SHADES": WATCHING THE CHILDREN PLAY

The title story of this collection is also the last one and in it Munro anticipates the directions she will take in later collections. She describes this as a "fairly important story" but as one that "backs off quite a bit" from what she calls the "real material" (in Struthers, 1983, 23). It also backs off from the figure of the mother, but only in order to stage her powers on another level where we can observe the interaction of those powers with artistic power. The piano recital staged by Miss Marsalles (she calls it a party) dramatizes the two activities I have isolated as central to the dilemma of the artist: watching and keeping. The proud, bored mother, who watches her performing daughter play, appears as an ironic version of the maternal keeper. The audience of mothers, in fact, exposes an almost total absence of the compassion we associate with maternity. That compassion, instead, is grotesquely exaggerated and projected into the figure of the piano teacher, Miss Marsalles. "The deceits which her spinster's sentimentality had practised on her original good judgment" are viewed as "legendary and colossal" and she speaks of "children's hearts as if they were something holy" (DHS, 213).

Our participation in the "embarrassment the mothers felt" (DHS, 216) is gradually reversed until the unheard music of the "Dance of the Happy Shades" becomes a place from which we ourselves are judged. The hospitality of Miss Marsalles makes a space within which, however briefly, we may feel liberated from ourselves. That liberation, however, is profoundly ironic. We may feel a brief moment of moral superiority when we recognize the false and self-serving compassion of the neighbour who frets over Miss Marsalles. What we cannot escape, however, is our own misplaced pity for her. The narrator and her mother are dutifully kissed by Miss Marsalles, but the narrator comments: "It seemed to me that Miss Marsalles was looking beyond us as she kissed us; she was looking up the street for someone who had not yet arrived" (DHS, 217). The eyes of Miss Marsalles look on things that we do not see and it is this that teaches us the absurdity of our own self-importance.

When the special visitors do arrive, we experience a deepening shame as we have to admit, once again, to our own misplaced compassion. While the narrator plays her own "dogged and lumpy interpretation" of the "minuet from *Berenice*" (DHS, 220–221), the room is filled with the heavy bodies of the strange children. Their physical presence demands our attention and yet we are not able to join Miss Marsalles in her easy and innocent compassion. Situated between irony and compassion we experience the weight of the dilemma staged by Munro. We also see something of the view of art that will inform her subsequent stories. When Dolores Boyle plays, she "sits ungracefully" at the piano (DHS, 222), but her big body is the unwitting vehicle for a miracle. The fact that she is one of the "idiots," signals the importance that will be attached in Munro's fiction to the experience of the fool, to knowing the limits of our understanding. Like the name of the musical piece by Gluck, entitled "Dance of the Happy Shades," the story by Munro also entitled "Dance of the Happy Shades" will leave "nobody any the wiser" (DHS, 223) if we search for fixed meaning. There is an implicit story behind the music, namely Gluck's version of the story of Orpheus and Eurydice, but the descent and ascent pattern is now an allusion only, not something followed in the story as it was in "Images." Munro prefers to stay with the performance and with the surfaces of the world, aware of the flies that buzz over the food left too long in the kitchen.

These children, like the ones in Yeats's "Among School Children," remind us that both "nuns and mothers worship images" but that we must keep apart the bodies of real children from the images that "the candles light" for nuns (Yeats, 1963, 244). The awkward body of Dolores Boyle will not allow us to get to that place where we cannot "know the dancer from the dance" (Yeats, 1963, 245). Her "body is not bruised to pleasure soul" (244). Indeed, she seems untouched by her own music. Why, then, is it that her name makes one think not only of Mater Doloroso but also of dolour and of boils, of the kinds of protuberances denied by the mother in "Walker Brothers Cowboy"? There is only the slightest hint of comic effect in this story but that hint is a clue to the direction taken by Munro's subsequent fiction. Since the last lines of the story take away from us the inclination to say *"Poor Miss Marsalles"* (DHS, 224), we feel our own blindness. Miss Marsalles looks like "a character in a masquerade, like the feverish, fancied-up courtesan of an unpleasant Puritan imagination" (DHS, 217). The focus of the story is more on our misinterpretation of that masquerade than it is on exposing a truth that lies behind her disguise. If we look more closely we do notice that "the fever is only her rouge; her eyes, when we get close enough to see them, are the same as ever, red-rimmed and merry and without apprehension" (DHS, 217). With this clownish mock mother, Munro puts herself deliberately at an ironic distance from the real-life mothers. Doing so becomes a means of reappropriating, on another level, the compassion which is idealized in maternity.

Chapter 7

Lives of Girls and Women
Trying to understand the danger

CLOWNING AROUND THE DANGER SIGNS: "PRINCESS IDA"

Danger signs are everywhere in this book. Danger is the "quicksand hole" in the Grenoch Swamp (LGW, 2). Danger is the "treacherous crumbling" shoulder of the road taken by Princess Ida, who drives "all the time as if she would not be surprised to see the ground crack open ten feet in front of her wheels" (LGW, 65). Danger is the mother foxes killing their pups (LGW, 21). Danger is Madeleine beating her child or threatening to crack a stove-lifter down on Del's skull (LGW, 17). Danger is Addie being tied up and "*tortured*" by her big brother (LGW, 77). Danger is Bobby Sherriff saying: "'Said the spider to the fly, eh'" (LGW, 249). Above all, however, danger is getting pregnant. Del expects stories to go "round and round and down to death" (LGW, 79), but it comes as a shock to have that death associated with birth. This is the case with the story that Del's mother tells about her teacher. Miss Rush "had married, rather late, and died having a baby. The baby died too and lay in her arm like a wax doll, in a long dress, my mother had seen it" (LGW, 79).

This wax doll is one in a sizeable collection. Dolls multiply madly in the book – like a miniature army set up as an ineffective bulwark against the growing sense of danger. Bella Phippen, for example, gives a doll to every girl who gets married in Jubilee. "Deaf as a stone" and working "in a sort of nest she had made" in the library (LGW, 118), Bella is a grotesque Dickensian mother hen, generating Kewpie dolls. "They were all the same: a Kewpie doll on top dressed in this ribbon, which made a hoop skirt over the actual pincushion" (LGW, 118). Nile, in "Princess Ida," is like a doll: "Her skin was without a mark, like a pink teacup, her mouth could have been cut out of burgundy-coloured velvet and pasted on" (LGW, 84). Auntie Elspeth and Auntie Grace resemble mechanical dolls: "every flutter of the hands came to seem like something learned long ago, perfectly remembered, and each of their two selves was seen as something constructed with terrible care" (LGW, 59–60). The cumulative impact of these descriptions suggests a danger associated in some way with reproduction. *"Christ, have mercy upon us"* is a plea significantly juxtaposed with the reproductions done in Household Science, in the room where the girls "learned to knit and crochet and embroider and run a sewing machine" (LGW, 102). The room, with "its three ancient sewing machines and its cutting tables and battered dummies" (LGW, 102), looks to Del like an "arena of torture," and yet the scene being reproduced is simply the opening scene of "Walker Brothers Cowboy" – the image of a mother at her sewing. The woman who presides over this reproduction of mothering is "a fat little woman with the painted face of a celluloid doll" (LGW, 102).

My aim in this chapter will be (adapting the language of "Images" once again) to try to "understand the danger." The site of danger keeps shifting, but I have begun by watching "the shadows instead of the people" (DHS, 35), the dolls instead of the characters. These dolls (like the skirt of the Kewpie dolls) screen out what we find "disturbing and threatening" (Frye, 1980, 12). The clowning mock mothers will be, to adapt the words of Northrop Frye, Munro's way of returning this "screened-out" experience to us in a "bearable form" (Frye, 1980, 12). The carnival is now in full swing and a "fat naked lady with balloonbreasts" (LGW, 106) seems to be the main attraction. The language of the circus comes up with increasing frequency. Jerry Storey's mind, for example, is visualized by Del as a "circus tent full of dim apparatus" in which he performed "stunts which were spectacular and boring" (LGW, 197). It is not yet clear what stunts a female clown might perform as a means of resisting the role of the "lady in danger." Del's seal act, for example, a grotesquely seductive stunt performed for Art Chamberlain, appears to be ludicrously unhelpful. She admires her own "wonderful braying bark" – "copied from an old Mary Martin movie where Mary Martin sings a song beside a turquoise pool and the seals bark in a chorus" (LGW, 161).

Everything that Naomi and Del find out about sex makes it seem "more and more like a carnival for us to laugh or get sick at, or as we used to say, *laugh ourselves sick*" (LGW, 184). They have yet to find, however, a way to laugh themselves healthy. If the reader laughs while reading this book (and I do), that laughter itself initially becomes a screen blocking out what is threatening. As we confront that screen, however, the laughter changes. Naomi erects this screen when she announces: "'That Fern Dogherty was just a joke. . . . A joke, she was just a *joke*!'" (LGW, 183). Fern Dogherty's stomach pops out "in a pregnant curve" (LGW, 146) and (after being jilted by Art Chamberlain) she swells up "like a boiled pudding, her splotched skin . . . stretched and shiny" (LGW, 175). Naomi insists: "'That Fern Dogherty had a baby'" (LGW, 146), but although Del watches Fern for signs of "remorse, maternal longing" (LGW, 147), we do not know if the stretch marks are telltale signs of an earlier pregnancy or simply the result of obesity. Although this phantom pregnancy is a joke, we sense that Naomi and Del are in greater danger than Fern.

Sex with Garnet French may be like a "circus net spread underneath" (LGW, 214) everything else for Del, but the reader is made increasingly anxious when she tumbles into the net. When Del makes love with Garnet, she does "not fear pregnancy" (LGW, 231). Although Del's mother writes "to the Jubilee *Herald-Advance* that 'prophylactic devices should be distributed to all women on public relief'" (LGW, 176), these devices are conspicuous by their absence when Del needs them. The humour in the question "'Do you have a diaphragm?'" (LGW, 202) is loaded for Del with the possibility of a "shotgun wedding" (LGW, 206). Although French safes are "scattered like old snakeskins" in the pine woods behind the Gay-la Dance Hall, we register, with some alarm, the absence of either diaphragm or French safe when Del is with Garnet French. The reader is not able to abandon herself to the pleasure of the sex in the text; we are too afraid for Del, seeing the danger that she does not see.

The reality of biological reproduction is a lowest common denominator that threatens to reduce women to an animal level. Naomi pretends disgust when Bert Matthews (a poultry inspector who is a literary predecessor of Jarvis Poulter in "Meneseteung") keeps asking Molly if she is pregnant yet. He sneaks "around to get a look at her stomach in profile" (LGW, 185). Some readers may find this inspection amusing, since Molly is not actually pregnant as far as we know. Even those readers, however, will surely stop laughing when Naomi announces to Del: "I'm pregnant you know" (LGW, 234). Her own earlier words come back to haunt us: "'if a girl has to get married, she either dies having it, or she nearly dies, or else there is something the matter with it. Either a harelip or a clubfoot or it isn't right in the head'" (LGW, 119). The danger is not always so crudely envisioned, but that does not mean that it is not always there.

Trying to understand this danger must also involve trying to understand what the danger means in the life of the writer as a young girl. In the epilogue, the impregnated womb is a dead metaphor contained in the dead body of Caroline, who is herself a character in Del's stillborn novel. Caroline's womb is "swollen *like a hard yellow gourd in her belly*" (LGW, 79). The italics set the self-quotation apart, making the simile itself hard and opaque – like a gourd, a dead fragment of fake fertility from an abortive novel. Like the pink bowl in "The Peace of Utrecht," this fragment may pose as totality or it may break into smithereens. Here lies the double danger. One danger is embodied in the imagery of the dreams that Del has about her father. She dreams that he keeps "skinned and dismembered human bodies" in his shed (LGW, 113–114) and that he lines up the family to cut off their heads. "*It won't hurt*, he told us" (LGW, 114). These images of dismemberment are set against the other related "arena of torture" (LGW, 102). The opposite horror is the image of what is too "perfectly remembered," what is "constructed with terrible care" to follow a design dictated by a machine. Bella Phippen's perfect rememberings of the design of her Kewpie dolls are as frightening as the father's dismemberings.

These two terrors come to a point of intersection in "Age of Faith." Del wants to believe in a God whose design would eliminate the "strange, anxious pain that just seeing things could create" for her (LGW, 100). "It seemed plain to me," she writes, "that this was the only way the world could be borne, *the only way it could be borne* – if all those atoms, galaxies of atoms, were safe all the time, whirling away in God's mind" (LGW, 100). The italics emphasize the play on the word *borne*, and the contrast between an image of a world made by hand and a world born out of a womb. The Heavenly Maker is contrasted, significantly, with Del's "real-life" mother. The atomistic confusion, Del concludes, can be borne only by people who have faith in design. She adds: "How about my mother? Being my mother, she did not quite count" (LGW, 100). The "real-life" mother out of whose body Del is born, does not "quite count" in the design. What are the implications of this for a woman writer?

Munro's exploration of autobiographical form revolves around this question. The retrospective pattern characteristic of traditional autobiography is replaced by a kind of circus parade of stories. A clownish mother figure, "Princess Ida," is positioned in the middle of this parade. *Lives of Girls and Women* began, in a sense, with this story since Munro began with the intention of writing a conventional novel about Princess Ida (Tausky, 1986b, xiv; Struthers, 1983, 25). As an abortive novel, "Princess Ida" demonstrates that Munro's experiments with genre are directly related to her exploration of maternity. "Princess Ida" is both a character and a text. Other texts lurk behind the surface of this one and invade it – texts by Tennyson, Gilbert and Sullivan, Joyce, and Proust. *Lives of Girls and Women* is itself a reading; it reads the signs of its own invasion. The best example of the invasion of self as text is the name Ida – or is it Ada, or Addie? The multiplication mocks the daughter's efforts to reproduce the mother. ADA are the first three letters of the name Adam but Munro's parodic structure makes it impossible to begin at the beginning. There are many words, many lives, many selves, many stories. Adam, Ada, Addie, Ida: the slipping of the letters in the proper noun reflects the instability of language and of the self. The name Del forms part of the name Adelaide, reflecting the difficulty a woman has in saying I when her identity threatens to merge with that of her mother.

The allusion to the name *Isis* at the end of "Princess Ida" might seem like a defiant assertion of identity. The word *I* and the word *is*, however, are divided by crossing lines that intersect in a crossword puzzle. The story of Isis, furthermore, subordinates her identity to that of Osiris. She is responsible for putting him back together and making him a new penis.

Isis, in more ways than one, is the wrong answer to the puzzle (LGW, 91). Put the allusion together with Nile – the name of Uncle Bill's child bride – and the Egyptian echoes lead to Aida, a name conspicuous by its absence in the book. Take the I out of Aida and you are left with Ada. Kill the I off completely and you may be left with Addie, the dead mother in Faulkner's *As I Lay Dying*. Ada chooses, instead, to act out her reading of an old text by Tennyson. Better to clown than to be a corpse (like Faulkner's Addie) or to be buried alive (like Verdi's Aida).

Since *Lives of Girls and Women* was published two years after Nabokov's *Ada or Ardor: A Family Chronicle*, the multiplying allusions (related to the image of a molested little girl) might suggest to a contemporary reader that Alice Munro had read the story of "Ada in Wonderland" (Nabokov, 1969, 129). Munro's Ida, however, has not read *Ada*, nor has she read Gertrude Stein's *Ida*, both texts we cannot ignore if we read "Princess Ida" carefully. Ada's life is, in fact, an over-reading of Tennyson. In *The Princess: A Medley*, Tennyson's prince and his men manage to invade Ida's university because they are disguised as women. Parody gives way to romance when the princess, who was a frigid maiden, comes down from yonder mountain and wedding bells ring merrily. This happens because the men exploit, quite shamelessly, the woman's maternal feelings. The "lost child" is a powerful motif in Tennyson's poem because it keeps taking us back to the patriarchal view that a woman denies, at her peril, the madonna that is inside her. The final collapse of Ida's resolve is brought about because the maternal "instinct" is flushed out into the open when the prince becomes ill. Exit: Princess Ida as university professor. Enter: Princess Ida as nurse/mother.

Munro challenges not only Tennyson's ending but also that of Gilbert and Sullivan's "Princess Ida." The princess in that version is asked how "Posterity" is to be provided at all if all women are enlisted in the cause against "tyrannic Man." This is by now an anti-feminist cliché; as if a woman could ever forget that her body is a potential site of reproduction. With Gilbert and Sullivan as ventriloquists, however, the princess says: "I never thought of that!" and promptly reverses her mission, offering herself ("Take me, Hilarion") and presumably her body for the purpose of reproduction. The operetta ends: "with joy abiding, / Together gliding" (Gilbert and Sullivan, 1938, 340–341).

Lives of Girls and Women consists of a multiplication of such pairings-off which do not abide, partly because they are undermined (as the title indicates) by another kind of pair: mother and daughter. Miss Farris and Mr Boyce, Fern and Art Chamberlain, Del and Jerry Storey, Del and Garnet French – all these are abortive romances leading up to the mating of the pregnant dead body of Caroline with the sinister photographer in the epilogue. A fate worse than death, apparently, is to be left out of such a pairing, to be like Mother Goose, the old maid in the card game for children. Del's mother contrives, somehow, to be both the woman left over and a mother goose. She often mouths an acquiescence to the symmetries of the symbolic order, but her living arrangements stand as a resistance to that order since she and Del's father often do not live in the same house.

The changes envisioned by Ada are (in Munro's own words) "touchingly oversimplified" (in Hancock, 1987, 214). Princess Ida is like a Victorian joke that entertains us until it touches us, and it does so when we realize that she herself does not get the joke. She is appealing to the extent that her life as a reading varies from the books she reads; it is only the variation that makes us aware of her *as* a reader. Munro's "Princess Ida" is the uterus out of which is born not one perfect baby or one novel but multiple offspring. The reason it can form such a matrix is that it is not a perfect circle but a conscious blind spot. The parodic anti-structure of this book demands that we see the blind spot in the centre. The "abandoned novel," as Tausky describes, "in re-written form, became the middle section of the book, from 'Princess Ida' through to the story 'Lives of Girls and Women.' The two opening stories were written next, followed by 'Baptizing,' and, after much agonizing, the epilogue" (Tausky, 1986b, xiv). The heart of this "abandoned novel" becomes like the abandoned wing of the typical Gothic structure. The dark centre of this womb and of the house is the place that cannot be seen or represented, the place of origins that (like the cave-house in "Images") repeatedly shows us the surface of our own constructions – the kitchen linoleums with which we pave our deep caves (LGW, 210).

THE MADONNA AS "DAY-UD COW": "HEIRS OF THE LIVING BODY"

The figure of the madonna is nearly invisible in these stories because the powers invested in her are thoroughly domesticated. Since the ideal of the serene madonna is sustained by the work of real women, Del is misguided when she seeks in the House of God for some refuge from Household Science, from the "arena of torture" ruled over by a "celluloid doll." Del's prayer is quite simple: "please let me not have to thread the sewing machine on Thursday afternoon" (LGW, 105). Her mundane problem exposes as naive Ada's assumption that danger is most acute in the structures of religious belief, openly acknowledged. The symmetries of the symbolic order – the father/law as strong authority and the mother/madonna as gentle nurturer – are far more dangerous to a girl as they are invisibly imbedded in the daily routines of domestic life. The domestic house appears to be ruled over by the mother: "No sign of her father, or her brothers. . . . They did not linger around the house" (LGW, 75). The men are not around – or are they? Who made the ancient sewing machines? Who made the rules? And who, above all, made the madonna?

In her efforts to understand the danger around her, Del confronts the powers of the madonna as they appear in the body of a dead cow.

Cows frequently make their clumsy way through Munro's stories. The image appears fleetingly, for example, in "The Flats Road." As her husband advises Uncle Benny on his choice of a wife, Del's mother enters indulgently into the joke: "'Talk as if you're buying a cow'" (LGW, 10). In "Heirs of the Living Body," however, the joke has begun to stink. The shock is muted by the mediating presence of one of Munro's near-grotesque characters: Mary Agnes. She is the odd character who links up the two bifurcated parts of the story "Heirs of the Living Body," one dealing with the dead body of Uncle Craig, the other with the dead body of a cow. If we could accept the theory about death advanced by Ada, then it would be possible to wed these two corpses and become, as readers, heirs of one living body. Ada, coping with her brother's death, is as rhapsodic as any evangelical Christian: "'We would all be heirs of one another's bodies, we would all be donors too. Death as we know it now would be done away with!'" (LGW, 48–49). The sonnets of Shakespeare and Donne chime in to reinforce Ada's ringing conclusion and these oblique allusions are not, of course, without their consoling power.

E.D. Blodgett (1988) quotes Ada with approval: "'all these elements that made the person changing and going back into Nature again and reappearing over and over in birds and animals and flowers – Uncle Craig doesn't have to be Uncle Craig! Uncle Craig is flowers!'" This seems to Blodgett a "triumphant" demonstration of the "relation of human to nature as metaphor" (Blodgett, 1988, 40–41). If you hear an echo, however, of Faulkner's Vardamon saying "'My mother is a fish,'" then the metaphor no longer comes out smelling of roses. Blodgett fails to note that the mother speaks with "ominous cheerfulness" (LGW, 47) and that the speech initiates a coercive process which ends when Del bites Mary Agnes. The phrase "'Uncle Craig is flowers!'" is followed jarringly by Del's "'I'll get carsick. . . . I'll vomit'" (LGW, 48). Joined bizarrely in death, the dead bodies of Uncle Craig and of the cow refuse to be married.

The metaphor is there, yes, but it seems to have been dead for a while, just like the cow. Better to shift the focus (as Blodgett himself emphasizes throughout his book) to Del's efforts to understand. Del is a writer because she is a "*borderline case*" (LGW, 57), not because she shares her mother's vision of identity in metaphor. We gain distance from the metaphor if we pay attention to Mary Agnes who, in turn, draws our attention to the eye of the dead cow, which is likened to a jewel. Just before confronting the cow, Del notes that the cowpats are "dried like artifacts, like handmade lids of clay" (LGW, 43). When they come "upon a dead cow," however, the impression of artifice is sharply contrasted to the reality of what is born and dies. The cow's eye is "open, dark, a smooth sightless bulge" and flies nestle in one corner of it, "bunched together beautifully in an iridescent brooch" (LGW, 44). This iridescence is a fake iris. The decorative sightlessness of the cow makes us aware of Mary Agnes and Del as two readers engaged in the mutual act of looking.

Ironically it is Mary Agnes who makes this clear. She lays "*the palm of her hand*" over the cow's eye. She does this with a "tender composure that was not like her" but that allows us a fleeting glimpse of the maternity in *Mary* and the purity in *Agnes*. Where the landscape was eclipsed by the cow, the cow is now eclipsed by the hand. Mary Agnes stands up and holds her hand with the palm towards Del. The "fingers spread, so that it looked like a huge hand, bigger than her whole face, and dark" (LGW, 45). The image of a hand covering the eye, according to Cirlot "represents the clairvoyance at the moment of death" (Cirlot, 1962, 131). Here, however, it represents the opposite: the failure to understand. It is a human hand, however distorted, and it represents kinship between Del and Mary Agnes. Being human, neither Del nor Mary Agnes understand death. Inflated and fixed in this way, the hand is not something that works with clay. The hand itself is clay. The cowpats that look like "handmade lids of clay" are a gentle reminder of this scatalogical levelling. We may pretend to clairvoyance, to having triumphed with our theories over our mortality, but what we confront is ultimately the human hand, a screen blocking out what we do not see. On that screen we project our desires and fears. Unlike Mary Agnes, Del is conscious of herself as a reader responding to a text. Her words insist on this role: "'Day-ud cow,' I said, expanding the word lusciously. 'Day-ud cow, day-ud cow'" (LGW, 44).

I do not believe that the body of the dead cow becomes part of the living body mentioned in the title. It is rather something that is left out of the title, that shows up the title as a failure to encapsulate meaning. The funeral of Uncle Craig is the occasion to spell out the implications of this for a writer. Del's relation to the family and to other institutions and ceremonies is mediated by her second confrontation with Mary Agnes. The room in which the meeting takes place is like the abandoned room of a Gothic house. The aunts refuse to enter this room and say that it is "just like a tomb" but Del "loves the sound of that word" because she has it "mixed up with womb" (LGW, 54). She sees herself and Mary Agnes as being inside of "some sort of hollow marble egg, filled with blue light, that did not need to get in from outside." The windows are like the "never-quite-convincing windows in a doll's house" (LGW, 54). Del is entering the dangerously swollen body of a madonna who produces dolls. There is danger in thinking that this is a self-contained enclosure, in turning real windows into fake windows. Del is made vulnerable to the power of Mary Agnes because she gives in to that temptation. The outside world is present in a concrete form inside the baby carriage, where Del finds a "pile of old *Family Heralds*" (LGW, 54). If the egg-like room is a phantom pregnancy, then the mock baby is a text to be read, a text which heralds the power of the family.

The room is also, however, like a tomb. Del's pleasure in the hackneyed rhyme signals danger, tempting us to envision some kind of essence, some theological paradox that, like Ada's theory, would turn death into life. It won't work. All of this is a delaying tactic. The body of Uncle Craig is still there, whether Del decides to look at it or not. Del is like a mock baby in this room and she will be stillborn – or permanently infantilized like Mary Agnes – unless she can read the signs of invasion in this enclosure. She has to acknowledge that the light comes from outside and that the place of apparent essence is produced by machine – in this case, a printing press. While she looks at the contents of the baby carriage, Del hears her mother calling her name. The voice of her real mother calls her out of this mock womb. The naming is a summons to her to take her place in the family but it also marks, on a deeper level, her birth or emergence as a writer.

The hand of Mary Agnes, acting in conjunction with the disembodied voice of the mother, has a "shocking strength" (LGW, 55) as she attempts to coerce Del into viewing the dead body. When Del bites the arm of Mary Agnes and tastes "Mary Agnes Oliphant's blood" (LGW, 55), she thinks it is an act of "pure freedom" but although she bites herself free of Mary Agnes, "freedom is not so easily come by" (LGW, 55). The "demon power" of Mary Agnes is deflated by this act, but is then simply dispersed into the other mock mothers. Del now finds herself dangerously close to Aunt Moira, the mother of Mary Agnes, whose body hisses and trembles "like a monument about to explode" (LGW, 55–56). Aunt Moira's maternal rage is, in turn, defused and she is soothed by her sisters, who mock mother her as if "they were trying to keep the pieces of her together until the danger of explosion had passed" (LGW, 56). While Mary Agnes and Aunt Moira are mothered, Del too is "surrounded and taken care of . . . blanketed" and given cake and tea (LGW, 57).

No essence of maternal power, however, can protect Del from the "last look." Of all the staged reading scenes in Munro, the posing of a dead body to be viewed by a living body is the most unavoidable. In the later story "Privilege," Rose and her friends play at "the game of funerals" (WDY, 33). It is a game involving groups. As a writer, Del may be tempted to play dead, but ultimately she, like Munro herself, acknowledges her connection with the living. Being over-mothered and tucked in enables her to see, paradoxically, that she will never be able to escape but, by the same token, will never be without the comfort of the bodies around her. Her act of biting has marked her as a "*borderline case*" but it has not changed the reality that she is part of a family – the "badly brought up *member of the family*" (LGW, 57). The people in the house are "blunt old crayons" that are pressed together, with her "in the middle of them" in spite of being shut up by herself. This place – both middle and margin – is the place from which she writes – or crayons. What she writes will be coloured by the other crayons that surround and melt into her.

Being thus forgiven and mothered triggers the anti-epiphany of this story. Del experiences a "peculiar shame" and feels "held close, stifled." She has a vision of obscenity which is the "very opposite of the mystic's incommunicable vision of order and light" (LGW, 57). It is also contrary to her mother's view of mastery. "To be made of flesh was humiliation" (LGW, 57). Del feels a voluptuous helplessness, like the experience of being "tickled beyond endurance" (LGW, 57). After such a vision, the dead body of Uncle Craig is an anti-climax. His body is a thing prepared for viewing. The viewing itself is an ordered ceremony – a procession resembling the one in "Privilege," with the significant difference of actual death. This Uncle Craig cannot be said to *be* flowers, but the bottom half of him is covered with a lid which in turn is covered with flowers. We know that Del will be a writer because she is conscious of surfaces – the flowery surface of language itself, the surface of our conventions, our blankets, our enclosing houses, our masks, and our sacred cows.

ART CHAMBERLAIN'S WHORES

Sex, like death, may be hidden behind the skin of "ordinariness." Del thinks of the three prostitutes in Jubilee as "having gone right beyond human functioning into a condition of perfect depravity, at the opposite pole from sainthood but similarly isolated, unknowable" (LGW, 154). The "perfect depravity" of the Jubilee whores contrasts with the degradation suffered by Mary Agnes. Five boys take her for a walk to the fairgrounds and she is forced to make an exhibition of her body at the carnival. They "took off all her clothes and left her lying on the cold mud, and she caught bronchitis and nearly died" (LGW, 42). The fact that Mary Agnes has been prostituted has as little to do with Del as Fran's rape has to do with Rose in *Who Do You Think You Are?* The muddy body of Mary Agnes, like the "muddy toes" of Fran (WDY, 27), brings the image down to earth and shows it to us, at the same time, *as* an image.

Del poses naked in front of her mirror but clothes herself in images from the "reproduction of Cezanne's 'Bathers' in the Art Supplement of the encyclopedia" (LGW, 185). When she undresses for Jerry Storey, she feels "absurd and dazzling" but both of them reach instantly for language to clothe this confrontation. In a dialect "based roughly on the comic strip *Pogo*," Jerry comments: "'Yo' is shore a handsome figger of a woman'" (LGW, 204). Her absorption in the passive state of being looked at as a "figger" does not always end so benignly. Her way of looking at the "Art Supplement" is related to the fact that she does not see danger when it appears in the shape of Art Chamberlain, a man who seems to make a more benign appearance as Mr Florence in "The Progress of Love." In Del's fantasies it is Mr Chamberlain who views her when she is naked. "The moment of being seen naked" cannot be "solidified," however. Mr Chamberlain's "presence was essential but blurred; in the corner of my daydream he was featureless but powerful, humming away electrically like a blue fluorescent light" (LGW, 155).

When she is with Art Chamberlain, a woman is in the presence of danger, walking near an "abyss of irresponsibility, or worse" (LGW, 168). He is surely one of the most repulsive characters Munro has ever invented, and yet danger is so domesticated, so diffused into the hum of machinery, that it is hard to remain aware of it. Mr Chamberlain's character is a negation of violence. Nothing about him "predicted chance or intended violence" and yet "it was Mr. Chamberlain . . . who had been in the war" (LGW, 150). Neville Chamberlain's policy of appeasement comes to mind, but the war, for this Mr Chamberlain, is a "conglomeration of stories" and the stories are jokes.

Fern goes along with Art's defence, labelling his war as "one big idiotic good time" (LGW, 151). Del's mother blocks it out in a different way. Finding that Art was in Florence during the war, Ada brings out a book that has reproductions of a different kind of Art in Florence. "'There!'" she exclaims, "'There's your Florence. Michelangelo's statue of David'" (LGW, 151). The image seems harmless: "A naked man. His marble thing hanging on him for everybody to look at" (LGW, 151). Art Chamberlain's violence, unlike David's, comes fully clothed. The disturbing alignment of Art with Art repeats, in a different way, the questions that are raised in "The Office" when the landlord's dirty imaginings are placed alongside those of the writer. Mr Chamberlain's villainy is as invisible as his body, "his body that did not in any way disturb his clothes but seemed to be made of the same material as they were, so that he might have been shirt and tie and suit all the way through" (LGW, 150). Even his "light blue-green eyes" are "so pretty you would want to make a dress" out of the colour (LGW, 149–150). Here is a graphic demonstration of Kent's comment to Oswald in *King Lear*: "A tailor made thee."

It is significant that when Del enters the fantasy of being Art Chamberlain's whore (a "girl that a man could buy;" LGW, 153), she does not undress but rather dresses herself in her "mother's black flowered dressing gown" (LGW, 154). Of course she plans for the dressing gown to come off – perhaps "catch the material on the nail of a chair" – but what we see is the material and the fabrication of the gown itself. With Naomi, Del shares the adolescent obsessive desire to strip the body naked. In their drawings, the naked men and women have "startling gross genitals, the women's fat, bristling with needly hair, like a porcupine's back" (LGW, 145). The woman's pubic hair becomes the place where we confront the impossibility of discovering naked essence, and the adolescent Del anticipates this when she refers to the pubic area as a "vile bundle." Mr Chamberlain's molestings of Del are expressions of his fixation on the genitals. He does not bother with "a hug around the shoulders, fatherly or comradely" but goes "straight for the breasts, the buttocks, the upper thighs, brutal as lightening" (LGW,

162). Del, herself an adolescent, is not surprised. "And this was what I expected sexual communication to be" (LGW, 162).

The drive in the country is a mock-quest leading to a confrontation with his penis. Will she recognize the real thing, when compared to her own representations and to reproductions she has seen? The ordeal or shock is a reversal of expectations which is duplicated in the reader. Most readers, like Del, would surely expect the touches to escalate to more touch. What Del expects is contained in the single word *fuck*, and just before leaving with Art, she reflects on that word: "I had never been able to contemplate before its thrust of brutality" (LGW, 167). The shock of inversion begins when Mr Chamberlain does not use those words that give off "flashes of power." He speaks, not in his "dark chocolate" voice (LGW, 149), but in an "infantile voice": "'Birds are nice. Trees are nice. Nice you can come for a drive with me" (LGW, 167). At the very moment that Art is seeing her as his whore, he is simultaneously seeing her as a little "dirl" and as a mother. When Del does see his penis, she admits: "it did not seem to have anything to do with me" (LGW, 170). She claims to be "anxious to know what would be done to [her]," but in fact the word *fuck* captures her expectation.

Instead of being in the missionary position, however, Del is put in the position of the voyeur. The effect is histrionic. Mr Chamberlain "reached in to part some inner curtains, and 'Boo!' he said" (LGW, 169). This "Boo!" catches the whore in the act of looking. To be a watcher in this way *is* to be a keeper. The woman's role is to nurture the man's ego, and thereby to keep the man's phallus in place at the centre of the symbolic order. Mr Chamberlain withholds his power in a literal sense ("'Lucky for you? Eh?'") and this averts the danger of a literal pregnancy. His power is unleashed in more subtle ways that involve a negation. "Not at all like marble David's" is the negative phrase that describes his penis and the negation is a clue both to his perverted power and to her own means of empowering herself. "It did not seem frightening to me," says Del, comparing it to an animal "whose grotesque simple looks are some sort of guarantee of good will" (LGW, 169).

Del's comparisons, however ridiculous, are the exercise of her freedom as a resisting reader. The phallocentric position, so literally put, is a burlesque and the only possible response is laughter. Much later, she reproduces Art as a story to comfort Naomi when she is pregnant:

> I even told Naomi, all this time later, about Mr. Chamberlain, and how that was the first one I had ever seen, and what he did with it. I was rewarded with her pounding the bed with her fist, laughing and saying, "Jesus, I never yet saw anybody do that!"
>
> (LGW, 235)

The reproduction of the phallocentric position, done by one woman for another woman to the sound of hysterical laughter, offers both community and the resistance that comes from distance. It does not, however, provide safety. After Naomi has laughed "for some time," she grows "gloomy" again and raises herself to "look down at her stomach." "'You better be careful'" she says to Del (LGW, 235). The reproductions of Art are always mixed up with these other reproductions, and Art's seeds, splashing on Del's skirt, are too close for comfort. Like the man in "Wild Swans," this man does not actually rape the young girl. When she sees the landscape as "post-coital," Del is not being strictly accurate. Perhaps, however, it is accurate on some deeper level. Has Del been violated or invaded on some level that is much more destructive than a literal rape would have been?

If she has, then her strength is up to the task of fighting back. Her resistance will develop along with her abilities as a reader. Her reading of Art's exhibition augurs well, as does her ability to distinguish it from other kinds of art exhibitions. The mock affair with Art is initiated with Del as performer: she does herself being a seal. Art is the one who violates, with his molesting hand, the distance that would keep him in the role of audience. When he, in turn, does his performance, however, she is able to distance herself, to see herself as the audience. She sees his face as "blind and wobbling like a mask on a stick," his sounds as "theatrical, unlikely" and "the whole performance" as "fantastically and predictably exaggerated" (LGW, 170). The word "predictably" is a clue to the source of her strength. Like the "recognition" of the man with the axe in "Images," this one "does not surprise you" because it is "as if it was made, in the first place, from a wish of yours" (DHS, 38). During the scene in which Mr Chamberlain climaxes, Del is put in the position of a worshipper and the naked phallus is the mock religious icon. The journey, if this were to be taken seriously, would be a religious quest with a vision as the goal. After the exhibition, Mr Chamberlain makes only one comment: "'Quite a sight, eh?' was what he said" (LGW, 171). The sight Del sees and the one Art thinks she sees, however, are two very different propositions.

Del's confrontation with the thing hidden inside a man who is made by a tailor is an instructive one for her. Despite this experience, however, she remains vulnerable to danger. The scene is like a dress rehearsal for her affair with Garnet French. The sexual initiation leads her deeper and deeper into the illusion of the natural, the yearning for a place where the artifices of culture can be abandoned. Her passionate affair with Garnet French demonstrates that danger lies in the illusion that sexual pleasure happens outside the constructions of culture. Del wants to think it is all instinct. She thinks she loves "the dark side" of him, "not the regenerate Baptist." She sees the Baptist "as a mask he was playing with that he could easily discard" (LGW, 220). When his violence emerges, however, in the baptizing scene, she remembers the story of how he kicked the man at the beer parlour, and she realizes that she "never really wanted his secrets and his violence" (LGW, 239). What she sees, in retrospect, is something that looks like a kind of subtle prostitution. Fern and Art mock openly about the fact that they service each other. Garnet and Del clothe this in romantic ceremony but Del knows that they have used each other: "he rearranged me, took just what he needed, to suit himself. I did that with him" (LGW, 220). The phrase "to suit himself" evokes the image of dressmaking, an image that comes up again when Del confesses to the illusion that she could keep Garnet sewed up in his "golden lovers skin" (LGW, 197).

This broader application of the act of prostitution must be kept in mind when we confront the potent image of the molested child at just the point where Del may be most deeply hurt by Art's irresponsibility. When he gives her a sample of his handwriting, the text he writes is as follows: "*Del is a bad girl*" (LGW, 164). Del's worry is explicit: "Could he have hit upon my true self?" The issue is one of identity and of how the woman views herself. The way Del sees herself is at war with the way Art – in both senses – sees her. When we can see this, we are getting closer to an understanding of the danger.

CAROLINE AS ORPHAN ANNIE: THE DILEMMA OF AUTOBIOGRAPHICAL FORM

We have just visited, with Del, an Art exhibition which demonstrates that the power of the patriarchy (especially as it relates to art) is not in the penis but in the eyes. The inversion of Del's expectation underlines this point. A literal manifestation of the invading male gaze would have Del stripped naked with Chamberlain viewing her body – as Jerry Storey does. The greater power is exposed by the inversion: he controls her gaze – or thinks he does – by forcing her to see what he himself sees. The image of the eye multiplies in these tales like the beautiful "blind eyes" on a spreading peacock's tail (LGW, 159). Uncle Craig, for example, is blinded in one eye, which is described as "dark and clouded" and the eyelid has a "menacing droop" (LGW, 29). What fascinates Del most about the dead cow is the "smooth sightless bulge" of the eye (LGW, 44). When Ada expands on her theory about death, she comes to a focus on the eyes: "They are already able to transplant eyes, not whole eyes but the cornea, I think it is" (LGW, 48). The most significant, however, of all these eyes are those in the epilogue. The epilogue constitutes a powerful closure because it sums up this image and brings it into sharp focus. What is brought into focus, however, is the failure to focus and the limits of our seeing.

Like Art Chamberlain, "*The Photographer*" in the epilogue inverts our expectations of male strength. He has "a rather narrow chest and shoulders and a pasty, flaky skin" (LGW, 246). His victim, the suicidal Caroline, nevertheless seems by contrast a weak body: "She was the sacrifice . . . her frail body squashed into the mud and hen-dirt of barnyards, supporting the killing weight of men" (LGW, 246). Caroline's muddy body repeats the image of Mary Agnes, lying in the mud of the fairgrounds. The photographer, in turn, repeats in displaced and exaggerated form the power of Art Chamberlain. Like Art, he at first seems to be all material – all cloth. His body, like a pseudo-pregnancy, is "shrouded in his photographer's black cloth, a hump of grey-black, shabby cloth behind the tripod, the big eye" (LGW, 246). Although his body, when it emerges, contains a "wicked fluid energy," his power is contained in "the big eye."

The eye of the camera becomes, then, the circle we must enter in order to understand the danger posed by Munro in this book. The figure associated with this eye is the endangered little girl. Art Chamberlain refers to Del, in his mocking infantile language, as a "'little dirl'" (LGW, 168) at just the moment when he intends to control her eyes and coerce her into mothering his phallus. Naomi's father calls the story of the wise and foolish virgins a "'lesson for young girls.'" His "toothless mouth" is described as "sly and proper as a baby's" and when Naomi calls him a "'Stupid old bugger'" (LGW, 157) we are invited to see him as a dirty old man. The littleness of the female is everywhere exaggerated in this book, encapsulated even in the implied Proustian echo of the word *petit*, contained in the name *Madeleine*; Uncle Benny writes "Dear Lady" to her but Del's mother announces: "'She's a *child*'" (LGW, 16). Art Chamberlain miniaturizes the figure of the harlot and sees it as contained in the little girl: "'No older than Del here'" (LGW, 152). He thinks he has defined the real Del when he has her copy the words: "*Del is a bad girl.*" (LGW, 164). Like the photographer's pictures, his way of looking at her is intended as prophecy. In the photographs, "brides looked pregnant" (LGW, 247), but the question of pregnancy was, in fact, never established in the case of the woman, Marion Sherriff, on whose life Del bases the character of Caroline.

Del's story about Caroline is a kind of displaced autobiography. Del's question: "'Could he have hit upon my true self?'" is ultimately answered in the negative, but in Caroline she pictures the extreme opposite – the better to avoid it. Looking at the image of herself as pregnant, Caroline buys it and becomes it. Her "womb swollen" (LGW, 247) with this phantom, she then discovers what we knew all along, that the photographer is made up of cloth. His power is not his but is in the machinery of culture. When he vanishes, she walks into the Wawanash River. The power of the camera eye has destroyed any possibility, for Caroline, that a "true self" could exist outside the one constructed by the male gaze. Since her "real" name is Marion, however, her mad behaviour might lead us to picture the "unruly 'Marion' of carnival" whose name became "indissolubly linked to revolution" in France. In England she accompanied Robin Hood during the May games where she exchanged "lewd jokes with the Fool" (Stalleybrass, 1989, 54). The name "Marion," however, is simply another fiction and these layerings of propriety serve to white out the revolutionary potential of the carnivalesque. "[L]ooking at the picture the Photographer had taken" of Caroline's high school class, her brother sees that "*Caroline's eyes were white*" (LGW, 247).

We can begin to see why Munro has not written a traditional autobiographical novel. Del's eyes are the place of danger and also the place we watch as she develops resistance. The displacement of male autobiographical form is explicit when Del provides a sample of her writing for Uncle Benny and ends up mimicking a passage from James Joyce's *The Portrait of an Artist as a Young Man*. The quotation is distorted so that we see her as writing the name and location not of herself but of the man for whom she writes. As we read the words: "*Mr. Benjamin Thomas Poole, The Flats Road, Jubilee, Wawanash County . . . The Solar System, The Universe*" (LGW, 11) we see, like a layer in a palimpsest, the passage beginning: "Stephen Daedelus . . ." (Joyce, 1916, 15–16).

What appears to be a negation of identity, however, is the source of the growing resilience of Del's identity. The only protection against the menace of the drooping eyelid and the black cloth is in seeing a multitude of eyes. Each, individually, is as blind as the eyes on the peacock's spreading tail. Together they form "quite a sight." This multiplication is crucial to Munro's approach to autobiography. This book is not entitled *The Life of Del Jordan* and the epilogue shows why this cannot be. It is not just that there can be no single autonomous self and that the camera eye, framing the conventions of a technological society, brings this point home to us. "'Pregnant, naturally'" is not a natural fact but a creation of that technology. What is equally important to note, however, is that Del herself is already engaged in activity that parallels that of the photographer. He is not there as the objective correlative of wicked male power, but rather as a shocking reminder to her of her own power.

It is a repetition, in another form, of what took place at the end of "The Office." Del, as a writer, not only is aligned with the victim in the story but also holds in her hands the apparatus that could align her with the tyrant. The compassion of the keeper *must* be sustained in order to protect her from the corrosive impact of pure watching. As a camera eye taking in the town, she will be only a danger to them. The "unpitying smile" of the photographer, then (LGW, 246), is not duplicated in Del. She may reproduce the town so that it is full of "posters advertising circuses" (LGW, 247) but it is done with compassion and with humility. Her reproduction of Bobby Sherriff as a "plump ballerina" (LGW, 253) becomes a means of experiencing her limits as a writer. Bobby Sherriff is not simply her host in the final scene; she allows him to play the role of mock mother. "'Mother went to Toronto'" Bobby explains. His activities are described in painstaking detail, down to the last mint leaf, as if the specificity is there as a kind of bulwark, a protection. And so it is. The details are piled up to protect Bobby Sherriff from dissolving into her fiction. The epilogue constitutes a reversal of the book's approach to danger, a reversal which is similar to the one later documented in "Simon's Luck." Del describes how she planned to "annihilate Jubilee" and turn it into a "black fable," how "the people who really were the town" simply hooted their car horns, "never knowing what danger they were in" (LGW, 248).

In Caroline's suicide, Del pictures the annihilation of self – the opposite danger which forms an undertow in this book. Over and over again Del experiences the impossibility of posing herself as an autonomous identity. Parody and self-mockery are her "salvation" (LGW, 197). When Jerry calls her *Eggplant* in her "purply-wine" dress, we know that growth will come only from a carnivalesque pose recognized *as* a pose. An image of growth remains invested in both the word *egg* and the word *plant* and this is not in spite of but because of the absurdity which they represent when put together. The conjunction of playfulness and self-annihilation is most forceful in Miss Farris. Like Carmen, but more playfully, Miss Farris's performances represent her "surrender to the final importance of gesture, image, self-created self" (LGW, 184).

THE RESPONSE: MISS FARRIS AS PUPPET

Munro's response to the helpless figure of the objectified little girl is not to use her power as an artist to champion the cause of that girl as a victim. On the contrary, she abdicates, picturing the artist herself as a little girl – perhaps even a puppet or a doll. In this book that abdication and the paradoxical power that grows out of it is vividly pictured in the character of Miss Farris. The name itself is an encapsulation of the response since it absorbs, in condensed form, the danger coming from the hatred of boys who bear down on you with their bicycles. The image of a ferris wheel at first suggests entertainment, but like Catherine in "Lichen," whose voice goes up and down like a ferris wheel, Miss Farris is also seen as a sacrificial victim. The ferris wheel is a way of avoiding the Catherine wheel.

Miss Farris's re-productions of the operettas, going round like a ferris wheel, are a response to the dangers inherent in the reproduction of culture and of mothering. Miss Farris inspires devotion "to the manufacture of what was not true, not plainly necessary, but more important, once belief had been granted to it, than anything else we had" (LGW, 131). This kind of "manufacture" offers to the alert reader a means of resisting the sinister power contained in the kind of manufacture we associate with a technological society. Miss Farris is a mock mother birthing a mock world. This world – "with cardboard house fronts and a cardboard fountain" (LGW, 135–136) – is the place where the woman artist meets the visible world on its own terms. There is no safety in running for cover and hiding in essence, in archetypes about earth mothers and white goddesses.

Resistance to danger, Miss Farris teaches, will have to start out in the open, on the level of a production that is seen.

The manufactured thing – the operetta – is very like a phantom pregnancy. At first the operetta is contained in the two selves of Mr Boyce and Miss Farris, who are envisioned by the students as having a "hypothetical romance" (LGW, 122), but "when the time came they would let it loose, it would belly out like a circus balloon" (LGW, 123). Here the swelling belly is the place of child's play but also a site of invasion which offers hope for resistance and subversion. The balloon is huge; "growing and growing" it pushes down school rules and eliminates social barriers. The person who produces this spectacle, however, is slight – like the et in puppet or in operetta – and her ability to subvert the enormous powers of our technological society comes from her very slightness.

Unlike Et in "Something I've Been Meaning to Tell You," Miss Farris does not inspire fear and her power is not sinister. Hers is a labour of love in ways too complex for her adolescent students to grasp, which is why they displace that passion and reduce it to a romance between Mr Boyce and Miss Farris. In her intense but circumscribed way, Miss Farris offers Del an example of how the imagination may resist the forces that want to destroy the human spirit. We can see this in her response to war. She speaks "rather absently" about the fact that the boy – Pierce Murray – who played the part of "the captain in *The Gypsy Princess*" was "killed, in the air force." After doing the captain, "did it matter so much what else happened to him?" (LGW, 130). Miss Farris's own actions reinforce this emphasis. She picks up the cape he wore for the part and does Pierce Murray doing the captain. She makes a "swashbuckling swing" with the cape on – "'like this'" – and is caught in the act by Mr Boyce. His response: "'*Con brio*, Miss Farris!'" is always afterwards seen by the students as the "final touch to her; it wound her up" (LGW, 130–131).

If the image of Miss Farris as a mechanical wind-up doll is disturbing, the name "Pierce" might also make us wonder if Arthur's sword can be so easily sidestepped. Is this art, this dramatic performance by Miss Farris? Is it adequate as a resistance to the dangers associated with that other Art? As she twirls on the ice like a puppet, she seems like the town's possession – as did the mother in "The Peace of Utrecht" and Madeleine in "The Flats Road." We know, if we are not reading for the first time, that since Miss Farris is "impulsive and dramatic," her last act will also be seen by the town as a dramatic performance. Although Marion Sherriff is described by people as walking into the Wawanash River, "in the case of Miss Farris they said she *threw herself into* it" (LGW, 243). This narrative reproduction of her act is contrasted to the flat, abrupt one that comes near the end of "Changes and Ceremonies": "Miss Farris was drowned in the Wawanash River" (LGW, 140). Here the agency of death is not clear. It is simply something that "happened." In fact, the phrase "was drowned" has overtones of murder. It is what is done to kittens.

We watch with the children as Miss Farris throws herself into the production of an operetta. The children, however, disappear with her, "imprisoned in that time" (LGW, 141), as if by a pied piper, victims in some way of the "anarchy, the mysterious brutality" that we can never quite define, although we can see that women and children are the first victims. Munro's exploration of this danger is related quite specifically to the dilemma for the female pied piper who has no identity, who is a mechanical doll. During the performance of the operetta, Miss Farris wears a jacket with sequins – "in circus-military style" (LGW, 136). She is a woman warrior, but also, like a puppet, she is "dry and wooden and innocent" in her little girl clothes, living in "her own little house" (LGW, 122). She is an artist, in a sense, because she makes "all her own clothes" (LGW, 122). Although she may thus suit herself, so to speak, she is also a painful figure of isolation. Miss Farris's clothes are costumes, conscious disguisings and she herself is a kind of clown or fool. Her clowning is projected into the figure of the "Pied Piper." The pied beauty of his costume, the "cloak patched with various colours" and the "pointed cap, almost a fool's cap" (LGW, 135), could as easily suit Miss Farris herself. Like the Pied Piper who leads the children into an underground realm not accessible to adults bound by inertia and mechanized behaviour, Miss Farris herself leads the way for Del. The intensity she brings to her re-productions is a response to the "brutality" of the reproductions of culture within which she survives – for a while.

The death of Miss Farris and her obvious limitations cannot eliminate the redemptive energies released in her vision of theatre. There comes, however, a point when both Del and the reader protest the "unprotesting" death of Miss Farris. Miss Farris is a kind of literary mother; in the telling of her life, Del can briefly confront the horrifying possibility that the sacrifice of the mother is necessary for the life and writing of the daughter. The relation between Del and Miss Farris becomes so central that the sequence of abortive love affairs – Del and the Pied Piper, Mr Boyce and Miss Farris, Naomi and Dale – are diminished by comparison. The part that Del plays is, in literal terms, simply as one of the dancers. The part she plays on a deeper level is emblematized on the night of the performance. Here it is Del who plays the part of Miss Farris herself – the puppet inside the puppet show. Miss Farris herself is maternal in behaviour: "she glided, unlike herself, speaking softly, moving through all the turmoil with bountiful acceptance" (LGW, 136). Naomi is "apple-cheeked in her motherly kirtle" (LGW, 136). It is Del, by contrast, who now plays the part of the puppet inside the machine. Her headdress slides "disastrously to the side" of her head: "I had to tilt my head as if I had a wry neck, and go all through the dance like that, teeth clenched, glassily smiling" (LGW, 137). Her mother, with clumsy tact, later comments: "'It was lovely, did you have a crick in your neck?'" Naomi's response is more brutally honest: "'Everybody was killing themselves laughing, the way you held your head when you were dancing. You looked like a puppet with its neck broken. You couldn't help it though'" (LGW, 138).

The word "killing" and the image of the puppet with a broken neck confront us, on rereading, with the picture of a dead Miss Farris. The most frightening line is the one that seems the most innocuous: "'You couldn't help it though.'" The terror of being helpless, of being a puppet whose strings are pulled elsewhere, whose neck may be broken to the sound of people dying with laughter – all these images are disturbing only when unpacked in this way. At the time of the performance, Munro domesticates the brutality and entertains us at the same time. Del takes on the role of Miss Farris, the wind-up mechanical doll, but brings that puppet to life because she has her eyes open. After the performance, while the dancers are waiting to be photographed, Del tries to get her "headdress on properly." Dale offers his glasses as a looking glass and Del accepts, "though it was distracting seeing his lonely, crossed eye behind my reflection. He was making leering faces" (LGW, 138). The danger is that Del's image of self will dissolve into what is seen by the "lonely, crossed eye" of Dale. Safety, however, is in numbers, in refraction and doubled reflections. The person Del is concerned with at this point is not Dale but Frank Wales – the Pied Piper. He appears "suddenly between the curtains, after having his picture taken, alone, in his lordly, beggarly costume" (LGW, 137). When Dale suggests that Frank should walk Del home, he nods at Del and her head bobs in his glasses (LGW, 138). The broken neck and the severed head are images of danger that will be reduced to what is reflected back to her in Dale's eyes. The image anticipates and resists the death of Miss Farris: "My face swam in Dale's foolish eyes." Note that Del's face does not drown. It swims.

It is not an adequate response to danger to distract yourself by going round and round on the ferris wheel. Del also needs to make some progress. Failure to do this spells death for Miss Farris. What saves Del from that fate is her ability to put herself in the position of a reader. When Dale dares Frank Wales to walk her home, Del writes: "It was too much, too dangerous, to be flung like this into the very text of my dream" (LGW, 138). This text refers to the "often repeated" daydream in which he walks home with her "after the performance of the operetta" (LGW, 135). Dale's ability to spell out the dream, to put it in words, makes the dream itself a suspect and conscious cliché. What saves the Del who writes, as autobiographer, is the fact that she sees it as a "very text" – open to interpretation. If the symmetry of the fit – Dale's text and her daydream – is what is "too dangerous," then what will save Del is to multiply the texts and the readings of those texts.

DEL READS MOMMA'S COMPLETE TENNYSON AND OTHER STORIES

If there is any act that unifies *Lives of Girls and Women*, it is surely the act of reading, and if there is a single story told in this book, that is the story of how Del learns to be a resisting reader. The "lives" told in the book are unified by the fact that Del is reading them. Del, in turn, is constructed as a subject by virtue of the fact that she is the reader. If the lives of girls and women are readings, then it is important to define the special dilemmas confronting female readers. The problem is encapsulated when Del looks at a picture of a pioneering scene in Uncle Craig's office. What E.H. Gombrich (1960) has termed the "beholder's share" is defined differently by these two beholders. Del makes "the mistake of asking Uncle Craig if he [is] in the picture." He is indignant. "'I thought you knew how to read,'" he says, pointing to the date (LGW, 28–29). The comment seems to echo Uncle Benny's question: "'Can you write?'" (LGW, 10), but it is increasingly obvious that Del's way of reading and writing will go contrary to the expectations expressed by the two uncles. Del's way will not obscure her own presence in the picture. In the epilogue, the life of Del contrasts with the death of Caroline because Del is not written; she lives inside the story she is writing.

Munro's choice of autobiographical form allows her to try to understand the danger encountered by the woman who reads and writes. Caroline's empty eyes, in the epilogue, cannot read; she exists in the realm of what is read. Uncle Craig may be blind in one eye, but his eyes are in no danger of being whited out. A woman's way of reading, from his point of view, is beneath contempt. When the aunts suggest that Del should learn to "copy his way" (LGW, 62), they are counselling the death of Del as a reading subject. Del chooses to write as a reader, constantly open to new texts, constantly invaded by other worlds. This openness, paradoxically, is what will lead to the development of a resilient self.

There are dangers, however, in admitting to her presence in the picture. Del experiences this when she reads an article written by a "disciple of Freud's." "*For a woman, everything is personal . . . in works of art she always sees her own life, or her daydreams*" (LGW, 181). Reading such articles, Del responds with a heightened sense of danger: "I would turn the page quickly as if something was trying to bite me" (LGW, 181). Just picturing the danger in this way is already the beginning of resistance. Danger is in what is read and "understood" – assumed to be innate and natural, and for the woman the reality of this must be directed to the image in the mirror. Munro invokes, in mocking fashion, the old subjectivity for which women are notorious. Turning her back on her own reflection in the mirror is not a means to becoming a resisting reader. The woman must, instead, step out of the looking glass into her own body and write from inside that body.

The signs on either side of the door leading into the Town Hall give an example of how the world looks to a woman who does this. On one side, "were letters that read LAD ES REST RO M. On the other side they read PUBL C RE DING ROOM. The missing letters were never replaced. Everybody had learned to read the words without them" (LGW, 117–118). These ordinary labels would not arrest the attention of most men, and yet for many women they are an ominous way of spelling danger. The implications of this go beyond the theories about language advanced by Lacan in relation to the two doors "Ladies and Gentlemen" (Lacan, 1977, 151). Danger here is in what is understood – the lords that should join the ladies, for example, if the two sides were symmetrical. Danger is in this way of looking at the distinction between public and private worlds, relegating the ladies to the privy and the men to the public acts of reading.

For help in rendering the invisible letters visible, Del goes to the library. "Reading books" is considered a "habit to be abandoned" in Jubilee; "it persisted mostly in unmarried ladies, would have been shameful in a man" (LGW, 99). Since Bella Phippen is the librarian, she might logically be expected to give books as presents to the girls who get married in Jubilee. The fact that she makes dolls in the library and gives one to each bride is a graphic demonstration of the way the reader in the wife is eliminated. Del will not get her doll, but her consolation prize is almost incalculable. She loves to read. She describes the books in a way that emphasizes the tactile pleasure to be had. They are "shabby old friends," some with "slightly softened, slightly loosened, covers" and some known only "by their spines" (LGW, 118). The materiality of the books is a way of leading up to confrontation with the way they erase the body of the woman. Many of the books have "a frontispiece showing a pale watercoloured lady in some sort of Gainsborough costume, and underneath some such words as these:

> *Lady Dorothy sought seclusion in the rose garden, the better to ponder the import of this mysterious communication, (p. 112)."*

(LGW, 118)

Here there is a blank where the communication should be and we cannot "ponder the import" of this text within the text. The pleasure of reading is thus accompanied by an awareness of the flattened and devalued female body.

Del's library searches refuse to yield an image of the female body that corresponds to her own experience. Her description of *Kristin Lavransdatter*, for example, contrasts vividly with Munro's own representations of reproduction. The "place where Kristin has her first baby, hour after hour" is reproduced as "page after page, blood and agony, squatting in the straw"

(LGW, 119). Munro's method, by contrast, relates the belly of the woman to the book as material object. The "fat green *Kristin Lavransdatter*" read by Del implies that the text, like Kristin, is pregnant. This phantom pregnancy can come to represent the swollen female body as it is burdened with the invading expectations of the symbolic order. It is also associated with the size of books. The "boxes of Bibles" ordered by Ada's mother, the "volumes of the encyclopedias, their weight (of mystery, of beautiful information)" sold by Ada (LGW, 66), the Great Books read by Ada in her discussion group, Uncle Craig's exhaustive local history – all of these are mocking representations of texts that presume to be totality. When Del memorizes huge sections of the encylopedia and shows off her "freak memory" like a circus performer (LGW, 67), she mocks in herself this kind of phantom pregnancy. A similar self-mockery is contained in her account of how she read Uncle Benny's tabloids: "I read faster and faster, all I could hold, then reeled out into the sun . . . I was bloated and giddy with revelations of evil" (LGW, 5). The bloated body of the little girl is pregnant with texts that she cannot digest. If the object, the material thing that is the book, is related to the object as female body that is subjected to a male gaze, then where shall the woman go who wishes to be a subject? Over and over again Munro invokes the image of women reading to suggest an answer to this question. Del comments, for example, on having seen one of the prostitutes "reading the *Star Weekly* . . . I was surprised, in a way, that she would read a paper, that the words in it would mean the same things to her, presumably, as they did to the rest of us, that she ate and drank, was human still" (LGW, 153–154). Reading in this passage is imaged as a response to a basic human appetite.

When Naomi and Del are taken to a hotel with Clive and Bert, the shock sustained by Del is pictured as the elimination of the reader in her. Arriving at the Brunswick Hotel, Del cannot decipher simple signs. She registers as "utterly beautiful" the "bubble-shaped container of red liquid" (LGW, 190) at the end of a corridor but cannot make the next step of interpreting it as an exit sign. When Bert and Clive start to tell jokes, it is obvious that Naomi and Del have been crippled as readers. They are reduced to pretending to understand the jokes as the only alternative to being left "stupidly gaping" (LGW, 191). Clive's question "'You believe in equal rights for women?'" is designed as a trap. It sets Del up as a mock reader, follows up with an apparently serious question about capital punishment, then ends with the punchline: "'You believe women should be hung like men?'" (LGW, 190). The fact that the sentence is syntactically a statement (it does not begin: "Do you believe . . . ?") shows that Clive is standing on the same ground as Art Chamberlain. Like Art and like Freud, he appears to assume the male fiction of penis envy and it is this assumption that eliminates the possibility that Del might have an opinion about the particular issue raised. The fiction of penis envy reduces the women to the "fuckhole" (LGW, 117). Since the hole is always imperfect, the joke is always on the woman.

Since the denial of the reader in woman is related to the denial of the woman's own experience of her body (which has been reduced by these men to a lack, a hole), it is fitting that Del's escape should be occasioned by the fact that her body talks. "'I have to go to the bathroom,'" she announces, and that (like Clive's joke) is not a question but a statement. Bert, however, treats it as a question and responds like a mock authority figure: "'You have my permission'" he says. "'Go down the hall,'" he instructs, "'and go in the door where it says – '" He peers at Del closely, sticks his face into her chest, then concludes: "'ah, I can see *now* – *Ladies*'" (LGW, 192). Reduced to a hole, to what cannot be seen, the men add insult to injury and put a pretty label on this lack: *Ladies*.

The experience in the hotel room seems to shock Del back into life as a reader. When she returns from the bathroom, she sees the "bubble of red liquid" for what it is – the exit sign and makes her exit, down the fire escape. Returning to her own room, she feels "redeemed by childish things" (LGW, 193) – things like her copy of *The Life of Charlotte Brontë*, which she settles down to read. Del's sexual initiation, however, is by no means complete, nor will it be possible or desirable for her to recapitulate her mother's rejection of sex. Danger takes another form in her relationship with Garnet French. Unlike Clive and Bert, Garnet does not act aggressively to eliminate her as a reader. Unlike Art, Garnet is not simply looking for a place to exhibit. Unlike Jerry Storey, Garnet does not mock Del for reading fiction. Garnet, however, is sexy. He is simply, quite unexpectedly, there – as a body that she wants. During the "climax" of the book, however, Del is eliminated as a reader. "I could not have made sense of any book, put one word after another," she writes, "with Garnet in the room. It was all I could do to read the words on a billboard, when we were driving." She compares this world to "what I thought animals must see, the world without names" (LGW, 221), evoking an image of Alice in the forest of no names.

Del is assuming that her body's needs have nothing to do with the body of reading material that she is supposed to be covering for her examinations. This is not a surprising mistake, since the canonical texts to which she refers all erase the reality of female appetite, reducing the woman to an object or ignoring her existence. The quote from Browning's "Andrea del Sarto" (LGW, 217), for example, makes space for the voice of Browning who, in turn, has given voice to a male painter. The woman who poses for the painting, however, is voiceless. There is no trace of woman in the examination question about *"Englishmen in the eighteenth century"* who value "formal elegance and social stability" (LGW, 229).

Del's abdication as a reader may be understandable. It is also nearly fatal. An alert reader will see danger signs predicting trouble during Del's visit to Garnet's home, but Del herself seems oblivious to them. She notes that members of his family "never called me by name at all" (LGW, 222). Before she can be named by Garnet, she has to listen to him reading out the names of his previous girlfriends to his sisters and to his intended spouse – names carved "on the underside of one of the roof-beams of the porch . . . each one with an X after it" (LGW, 224). The catalogue of names, like a list of war dead, ought to be a warning to Del, as should Garnet's description of the X as a "military secret" (LGW, 225). But Del is proud to have Garnet carve her name "at the bottom of the list," putting a border of stars around it and drawing a line underneath it. When he announces "'I think I've come to the end'" and kisses her in front of his sisters, she does not "read" the incident as a mock wedding ceremony. The point of most intense danger has not yet been reached. Munro stages a near-death by drowning which allows us to observe Del in the act of repudiating the alternative represented by Miss Farris and Caroline.

The scene is existential and what is dramatized is the fact that Del's reading and writing will *be* a form of survival. In the case of Miss Farris and Caroline, no villain can be found but their death invites pity. In this case, power is distributed. Far from being a victim, Del here discovers her own power. Here it is impossible to define danger in a way that sets it apart from the act of love itself and this constitutes Del's loss of innocence. The mutual struggle, in the wrestling scene, is a relief from the mutual infantilization in the scenes with Clive, Bert, and Art. When Del fights back and holds her own, surfacing from the near-drowning with her self intact, she provides an example of how a woman may survive. Her "old devious, ironic, isolated self" begins to "breathe again and stretch and settle, though all around it" her body clings "cracked and bewildered, in the stupid pain of loss" (LGW, 240). This rebirth of the self is accompanied by the return of Del as a reader. After escaping from Garnet, she cuts through the Cemetery and tries to remember the text of a silly epitaph that she and Naomi once wrote on the Mundy mausoleum (LGW, 240). After her survival, moreover, the wrestling scene that might have looked like a circus stunt, is identified and labelled by the title of this story as a text – as a parodic version of an old religious ritual. Laughing in the face of danger, Del becomes a spectator both of her eventual death and of her survival in the present. The more important implications, however, have to do with how she will now talk to herself about herself. Having won the fight with Garnet, will she now assert her self as master? Will she affirm the isolated self as inviolable?

The answer, of course, is no. Like an orgasm, this kind of struggle is not an ending but something that will be repeated. The emergence that she describes will be duplicated in the ending of "Bardon Bus." *Who Do You Think You Are?* will demonstrate, what Del already sees, that a man and a woman may emerge together through that kind of struggle – "hate and fight and try to kill each other various ways, then love some more" (LGW, 240). Munro's rejection of the notion that Del is now master is reflected in the way in which Del herself looks at her own reflection after she leaves Garnet. The act of graphing connects the word *autobiography* and *photography* (not to mention *autograph*) and we may observe Del in this act when she looks in the mirror. As she reproduces for us as readers what she saw when she looked in the mirror, that reproduction embodies the image that we might see if a woman could in fact photograph her own self. The paralyzing "big eye" of the camera lens is not there, but we become gradually aware of the way in which the picture is invaded (see Bruss, 1980).

At the moments of most intense passion in the lives of these girls and women, Munro shows us her characters in the act of looking at themselves. Madeleine's violence, for example, is described as "theatrical" – "She was watching herself" (LGW, 17). There is danger in Madeleine's theatre; Del knows that she will crack the stove-lifter down on Del's skull if she feels the scene "demands" it (LGW, 17). The woman who reads the script with care (like Rose in *Who Do You Think You Are?*) has a different relation to the authors who do the demanding. The woman who writes her own script (as autobiographer) has still a different relation. To see herself in the picture she paints or photographs is to take responsibility for the end product. It would be wrong, however, to assume that her position is one of total freedom. Autobiography is a graphing of the place where a woman is watching herself and that place may offer a resistance to the Freudian view that women see only themselves in a work of art. I say this because Munro demonstrates that when the woman watches herself with such heightened awareness, she is also watching another. The mirror, in fact, becomes a window. Because autobiography is invaded by biography – the life invaded by lives – it also leads to parody.

Freud's image of the woman who views a picture as a mirror is inverted at the end when Del confronts a mirror and finds a picture. Waiting for Garnet to come, and yet knowing he will not come, Del looks "in the dim mirror" at her "twisted wet face. Without diminishment of pain," she notes,

> I observed myself; I was amazed to think that the person suffering was me, for it was not me at all; I was watching. I was watching, I was suffering. I said into the mirror a line from Tennyson, from my mother's *Complete Tennyson* that was a present from her old teacher, Miss Rush. I said it with absolute sincerity, absolute irony. / *He cometh not, she said.* / From "Mariana," one of the silliest poems I had ever read. It made my tears flow harder.
>
> (LGW, 241–242)

This scene is crucial to an understanding of Munro's response to the dangers she has explored. Del's ability to confront the mirror in this marvellously ambiguous way – herself and not herself, sincere and ironic, crying and laughing at herself – this is the ability that enables her to go on with her life.

Her pose recalls still another poem by Tennyson, "The Lady of Shalott."
In this case there will be no Lancelot coming to the rescue, no lord coming
to rescue his lady. We are not able, however, to celebrate absolute female
autonomy since the quotation from "Mariana" installs the presence within
the mirror of another lord: Lord Tennyson.

The old maxim goes: cry and you cry alone, but Del, by crying, gives
herself company. In "Tears, Idle Tears," the I in the phrase "I know not
what they mean" is the voice of Tennyson. In a later story – "The Spanish
Lady" – two women act "like high school girls" reciting "Tears, Idle Tears"
to each other as they laugh, on the "edge of hysteria" (SIB, 177). Controlled
hysteria is also what Del experiences here. You might say that she is beside
herself with pain. Del is still in that position ("watching myself still") when
she leaves the mirror and turns toward a different text: the want ads (LGW,
242), feeling a mild gratitude for these "printed words." Seeing the image
of the woman in the mirror as the image of a woman reading is a means
of survival. It is a way of ironizing and thus resisting the dismissal that
accompanies male response to the subjectivity of female reading. Beyond
irony, however, it also inverts that subjectivity, showing that the woman's
way of looking at the subject involves an embrace of the object – the other.
Del has come to a place where she no longer waits for Art or for Garnet or
for the bridegroom who cometh not. She can confront the picture – the *Bild*
– that is reflected in the mirror but this is no ordinary *Bildungsroman*. If
Del goes deeper and deeper into the depths of that mirror, seeking for her
origins, she will not arrive, as did her mother, at a feeling of hate directed
against her own mother. Neither will she find some mysterious *primum
mobile* or Great Mother. What we do glimpse in the murky depths of
the mirror is the image of the mother engrossed in a book: her *Complete
Tennyson*.

It is thus that Del discovers the other in mother and acknowledges the
impossibility of constructing herself as subject without pointing to that
figure. The mother herself may be in the blind spot, but unlike the
"day-ud cow" she is not blind. Miss Rush, the mother's teacher, did
after all leave behind something besides the dead baby doll (LGW, 79).
One way of reading this book is to imagine mother and daughter sitting
side by side reading "Mother's *Complete Tennyson* that was a present from
her old teacher, Miss Rush" (LGW, 241). As readers of this book, we form
a "strange diagonal" (to use a phrase from "The Princess"), as we read
over their shoulders. This image of reading as something that takes place
in dialogue, as part of a creation of community, contrasts vividly with Del's
lonely preparations for the final examinations. She shuts herself up in a
room which is like a "cell or chapel" (LGW, 207) and sets herself to the
mastering of facts. "Once I had mastered them," she writes, they "came
to seem lovely, chaste, and obedient" (LGW, 208). This mastery, serene
and controlled, stands in contrast to the image of the weeping woman in

the mirror, the image of the woman who lives inside her own experience of limitation, of being framed. The last scenes in the book capture that experience of limitation. Bobby Sherriff's mockingly maternal behaviour becomes like a screen on which Del sees a definition of her own desires. Bobby stands at the end of the book like a policeman blocking traffic, because this quest can have no end except in a repeated return to life itself, to the mysterious otherness of others – including the other in mother. It is the opposite of mastery. In the last act of this carnival, Bobby rises "on his toes like a dancer, a plump ballerina" (LGW, 253). It is a "joke" displayed for Del – a joke that cannot be understood. Del imagines it to have a "concise meaning," but it has no definable meaning for her or for us. We may associate him with pretty Bobby Shaftoe who went to sea, but once again the poetic structure of a performance makes it impossible to complete an old narrative. We cannot conclude: "he'll come back and marry me." The stunt is presented, instead, as "a letter, or a whole word, in an alphabet" we have not mastered.

Chapter 8

Something I've Been Meaning to Tell You
Coming to see the damage

"TELL ME YES OR NO": THE FIRST PERSON AS MOTHERLESS CHILD

Something I've Been Meaning to Tell You is a consciously experimental collection of stories. After the thoroughgoing challenges issued in *Lives of Girls and Women*, Munro seems to ask: what next? How can the female subject be constructed, after Del has confronted the white eyes of Marion as well as the "Mariana" in her looking glass? How should the issue of moral responsibility be dealt with, after Del has confronted the reality of her own power during her visit with Bobby Sherriff? How can the figure of the mother be represented, after Del has confronted her mother's disguises? The stories in this collection take new directions in response to these questions.

With the important exception of "The Ottawa Valley," they no longer foreground the mother–daughter relationship. The mother figure, instead, is displaced and distorted – even grotesque, like Robina in "Executioners." Munro moves to a method more dramatic than lyrical as she unpacks some of the "varied and powerful" implications that Del could not work out (LGW, 247) when she envisioned Caroline's white eyes.

In making this move, Munro is re-enacting an old struggle between the artist's need for subjective expression and a demand for objective representation (see M.H. Abrams, *The Mirror and the Lamp*, 1953). It is for this reason that I begin, not with the first story in this collection, but with a story in which Munro experiments with a new use of first-person point of view. I am reminded, as I observe how Munro transgresses generic boundaries, that Robert Browning developed the dramatic monologue in an effort to mediate between the subjective and the objective. In *Lives of Girls and Women*, Munro alludes to "Andrea del Sarto" (LGW, 216) and to "The Bishop Orders His Tomb" (LGW, 184–185). The aspect of Browning that is now increasingly foregrounded is his fascination with the relation between art and evil. Munro resurrects Browning's "Last Duchess" to play a bit part in the title story of this collection, but there is no easily identified villain and no clearly defined point of view. Indeed, point of view is a literary convention that is problematized increasingly in Munro's fiction. With his posturing male voices, Browning suggests that evil is somehow inherent in presuming that the self is autonomous – that nothing has invaded your framed point of view. Munro seems to share this view; the difference is that her narrating voices cannot even mime such singularity. As soon as she speaks, the female first person multiplies and changes shape like a chameleon.

There is often a vivid contrast in these stories between the women who are objectified characters in the stories and the woman who is the implied writer. The contrast is between Et and the et in the puppet Alicia. The character often has people at her mercy; the first person, in contrast, is at the mercy of her material. In the story called "Material," there is a male writer called Hugo, whose mastery and authority are contrasted with the first person, his former wife (the writer of the story) who feels herself to be "*at the mercy*" (SIB, 44). The contrast between how male and female writers look at their material is an explicit theme of that story. I have chosen to focus close attention, instead, on several lesser-known stories in which Munro's narrative technique alone tells this story. She gives us ironic distance from her grotesque maternal figures by clearing a space for the activities of the writing and reading "I." This space is not fixed but fluid, unstable, and alive precisely because it is a place of contingency and possible death.

In the story "Tell Me Yes or No," mothers and mock mothers are conspicuous by their absence. Munro here plays hide-and-seek with the words "I" and "You" and "She" in a way that challenges old ways of looking at first-person point of view. "Tell Me Yes or No" tells a very old story: the story of a broken love affair. He loves me; he loves me not. Yes. No . . . So the story goes round and round and round. As if to emphasize the bald and circular outline of the hackneyed tale, Munro strips the initial stages of the story of any other relationships that might distract from the one between the speaking "I" and her ex-lover: the "you" she addresses. Although the narrator describes the kind of life lived by mothers of young children, the relation between mother and child is not brought to the fore. The domestic details ring true, down to the "red corduroy dressing gown, wet across the stomach" (SIB, 106). Indeed, the love affair begins when the first person and the "you" go for a walk, pushing a stroller that "'had Jocelyn in it then'" (SIB, 108). The reader, however, does not meet Jocelyn. The naming of the child makes her stand out as Real, as other – in contrast to the nameless speaker and her nameless lover for whom the child is an obstacle.

In stark contrast to the opening domestic scenes, the first person asks us to envision scenes of death and murder. The speaker ostensibly tells her story as a passive fantasy of her lover's death: "Would you like to know how I am informed of your death?" (SIB, 109). In fact, she is trying to kill his memory. The reader may be a reluctant eavesdropper, at first, but as the first person goes on to imagine her visit to her lover's wife, the story changes quite dramatically and we are drawn deeper in and domesticated into the dialogue. The first person seems to forget about her lover. She forgets about her motive of revenge – forgets about one story and starts to tell a different story. This different story, although it takes up fewer pages than the details of the love story, is a ghost story that will change our response to the old love story.

The first person describes herself haunting a bookstore – "BARBARA'S BOOK MART" – and secretly observing the owner: the wife of her former lover. The bookstore is the setting for an eerie exchange. "I know her at once," writes the first person, "though she has changed. Her hair is grayer, grayer than mine, pulled into a bun" (SIB, 118). Even for readers who have never stepped inside a famous Canadian bookstore called *Munro's Books*, there is surely the suggestion that the speaker is looking into a distorting prophetic mirror. Although the story is not literally autobiographical, an uncanny sense of intimate recognition is repeated when the woman in the bookstore later says to the first person: "You look familiar to me. . . . You don't look much younger than I am . . ." (SIB, 123). If the only difference between the two women is in the shades of gray of their hair, that might simply be a trick of the lighting. The name *Barbara* derives from a Greek word meaning "strange" or "foreign" (Withycombe, 1977, 41), but this stranger looks familiar.

The image of the stranger you see when you look in the mirror provides an edge of magic realism to all the exchanges between "I" and "she," subject and object, in this story. Like Del, this speaker might say: "I talk to myself about myself, saying *she. She is in love*" (LGW, 231–232). If we know that Munro and her first husband ran a bookstore, we may glimpse an "I," for example, in sentences such as the following: "She has come from the back of the store carrying a couple of large art books" (SIB, 119). The first person who has just emerged from her love affair, however, does not feel as Del did after such a surfacing. She is not sure of her old "isolated self" (LGW, 240). She feels her identity, instead, as blurring into those of the other two women and more who are not named who all had the same man for a lover. Even with different men, the story is still repeated. When she is "low, very low, and gone" the first person reads, "for comfort," the stories of these other women: "Case histories . . . Martha T., mistress for five years to a man who deceived, mocked, and fascinated her . . . Emily R., whose lover was not married as he claimed" (SIB, 117). At such low points, when she is "gone," the first person brings herself back into existence by seeing her pain as shared, not a "particular agony, only some shopworn recognizable pain" (SIB, 117).

This story, then, is about sheer survival. The "Me" in the title both is and is not the same "me" as the first person and it is we, as readers, who help to bring both of them into being. Munro demonstrates this by interpolating the text of love letters by a woman called Patricia. The fact that Patricia is named keeps her in existence, just barely, apart from the first person. Her love letters are interpolated within a larger story that is itself a love/hate letter. The case history of Patricia, however, is different for the first person than those of Martha T. and Emily R. The first person dreads reading the love letters because she, like the woman in the bookstore, expects them to be a mirror. It is only when she sees that it is not her handwriting that she can "start to read" again (SIB, 121). Seeing her own life in the life of another woman, the first person can read it and gain some distance from it. Since the emotions expressed by the other woman are very nearly identical to those of the first person, the voice in the letter and the voice of the first person narrator are dangerously close to collapsing into each other. Brodzki and Schenck (1988, 9, 11) argue that such replacements of "singularity with alterity" are "dramatically female." Munro's strategy here is an example of what they term a "transgressive" practice. This story is not a dramatic monologue but neither is it autobiographical fiction. It is a strange hybrid of the two.

The first person in "Tell Me Yes or No" is in fact looking into a mirror when she reads the love letters. What she sees is a warning – an image of a woman in the act of erasing herself: *"Patricia. Pat. P."* (SIB, 121). The first name suggests nobility, the second a careless touch, the third echoes the "pee, pee" from an earlier story (DHS, 10). The last note is just a "large scribble" with no signature at all. This is what could happen to her if she is not careful. We sense, however, that it will not be enough to tell herself "to be careful" (SIB, 124). The ghostly voice of the first person is only saved from extinction if the reader cares enough to play the part of the "you" in a deliberate misreading of the title. This involves usurping the part of the man who is the intended reader of these letters. The "you" as lover is killed off and becomes, instead, the "you" as reader/mock mother. P's last words written to her lover (before she loses her name, before she is "gone") are: *"please, please, tell me yes or no"* (SIB, 122). As readers we can tell the "me" that yes, we do hear her, she does exist. What she is asking for, of course, is something quite different. If we stay on that literal level we have to conclude (with conscious cruelty) that she gets what she asks for when her signature dissolves into nothing. We must do, instead, as mothers are instructed to do with children: respond to the emotion behind the plea and not to the plea itself.

The women in the story cannot do either of these. The first person returns the letters to Barbara, saying: "'I didn't write these letters.'" The woman asks: "'You aren't her?'" and the first person replies: "'No. I don't know who she is. I don't know.'" She repeats this last line over and over: "'I don't know. . . . I don't know" (SIB, 122). The scene is a parody of Peter's denial of Christ: "I know not what thou sayest . . . I do not know the man . . . I know not the man" (Matthew 26:70–75). This is both self-betrayal and a betrayal of Patricia. The "me" in the title is casually killed off. "'I will just have to let her suffer,'" says Barbara (SIB, 123). No cock crows and nobody "wept bitterly" (Matthew 26:75). Nobody will tell Patricia yes or no in that other sense of affirming her as an other, a "you."

When the first person says: "'Eventually she will figure it out,'" the reader may be figuring out that this less-than-perfect lover is a parody of the bridegroom who comes (LGW, 156) – the one who is the "*Fairest of Ten Thousand*" (MJ, 111). Who is he, in actual fact, this parody of Jesus? "Who would this man be? He could be anybody. A soldier . . . or a farmer down the road" (MJ, 110). The men themselves are single but the paradigm is a collective configuration. The letters in question are private and yet the meaning is public. We experience this as a transgression, a violation of privacy, when the two women stand together, reluctantly admitting that they have read the same love letters. The betrayals are multiple. Oddly enough, we may experience the pain of these most vividly in the woman who is absent: Patricia. She is cut off from any community of readers who could confirm her very existence, because she is cut out of this story. When Barbara "makes a little bitter face, a swallowing face . . . that would dispose of you" (SIB, 123), she disposes of the other woman as if she were a bitter pill. Using the past participle of *eat*, as Faulkner does in *As I Lay Dying* and elsewhere, the other becomes something to be et, a disturbing echo of the Et who is the first person in the title: *Something I've Been Meaning to Tell You*. The first person sees Barbara as giving off a "shriveling light" (SIB, 123) that destroys any possibility of community or further dialogue.

The first person, too, has her ways of disposing of you. "I invented loving you and I invented your death," she says ominously. Reduced to this level, narration itself comes down to survival of the fittest. "I" is simply what is left when "you" is killed off. We are urged, unless we want to have our own death invented before our very eyes, to step into the part of "you" and make it come alive. This story is deeply disturbing partly because it is by no means clear how we can escape being implicated in the brutalities implied. The first person confesses that she does not understand the "workings" of her own "tricks" and "trap doors" (SIB, 124). Her tricks with the mirror threaten to make all these women into one woman. It is no answer to conclude that Alice Munro is really writing about herself, since she writes herself (and her readers) into this frightening cliché.

Confronting the bleakness of my own reading, I cast around for some comfort and found myself looking for maternal behaviour. Perhaps this is because the opening scenes of the story sketch a vivid picture of a community of mothers. Somebody should go comfort that woman, I said to myself, make her a cup of tea and say "Hang on" as Stella does to Catherine

(PL, 46). Mock mothers, however, are conspicuous by their absence in this story and the darkness is directly related to that absence, not to the breaking up of yet another affair. It's not that mothering characters are ever invoked by Munro as saviours: they cannot redeem either themselves or their men as they do in so much Victorian fiction. The clowning mock mother, however, not only offers comic relief but also makes possible, at a deeper level, laughter that breaks down barriers, making it possible to see things that are otherwise paralyzing. The reader may try to play the "you" as a mock mother, in this story, but the characters in the story remain beyond our help – like motherless children. The bleakness of this story shows, by negation, how necessary the body of the entertaining mock mother is to the evolution of Munro's splendid comic vision.

"HOW I MET MY HUSBAND" – THE FIRST PERSON MEETS ALICE KELLING

Once again the hackneyed tale of love betrayed is overwhelmed by a subtext when the "I" in the title threatens to conflate with the "she" – a woman called Alice Kelling. The meeting of bride and bridegroom is subordinate to the disturbing kinship felt between two women. When an author spells out her own name – especially an author who almost never plays such a trick – that name is immediately under a spotlight. The result, in this case, is that the first person – a maid called Edie – is dwarfed by the giant shadow of a nurse called Alice. "This Alice Kelling had on a pair of brown and white checked slacks and a yellow top" and Edie sees nothing "in the least pretty" about her (SIB, 55). There is nothing in the least like Alice Munro about this Alice Kelling. The sheer sound of the name, the act of comparing character and author, however, is a distraction that splits the reader's sympathy. We end up trying to see double – seeing with the first person and seeing from inside the other woman.

Edie, it turns out, is a reluctant mock mother, not self-less and filled with the milk of human kindness. When her employer asks her to fix a glass of iced tea for Loretta, she complains: "it galled me" (SIB, 56). When left in the house alone, she quickly does the housework, then abandons the mothering role to play at another part. Chris Watters sees her first while she is dressed in this disguise, wearing her employer's clothes: "You got dressed up and played queen," he says. The "hired girl" (SIB, 50) dressed up as a queen is a masquerade that captures an important reversal of power. Like Et, Edie acquires power from her ability to read – that is, to decode the visible world of signs, to "figure it out" (SIB, 123) and make it work for her. It is therefore significant that she faults Chris Watters's sign making: "The lettering wasn't all that handsome, I thought. I could have done a better one in half an hour" (SIB, 53). Edie is an uneducated farm girl, but she gains power because others do not see her as threatening. Because we enter the first-person point of view, we become increasingly conscious of her gradual, secret acquisition of power.

Like the lover who is called X in "Bardon Bus," Chris is associated with Jesus Christ. The addition of one letter would make up the name Christ. W.R. Martin refers to the "celestial significance of the airman" (SIB, 83) and describes his treatment of Edie as an "apparently refined and considerate tenderness" (SIB, 83). Alice – Alice Kelling, that is – does not view his behaviour with such equanimity. She is the intended bride of Chris, but (unlike the Intended in Conrad's *Heart of Darkness*) she is not content to wait at home while her man goes on his quest. Her challenge is all the more significant since this particular airman is a parody of a sky god: "SEE THE WORLD FROM THE SKY" (SIB, 53). His entry is dramatic and resembles a stunt at an air show. As the airplane descends, Mrs Peebles screams and the child predicts a "'crash landing.'" Although the father says calmly: "'It's okay . . . He knows what he's doing'" (SIB, 45), a reader tuned in to the mock-biblical echoes might well fear for the safety of the women and children. The father, with his easy act of faith, invites Alice Kelling to "sit and wait" for the bridegroom but she is an impatient bride – "wrinkling and straining at the sky" (SIB, 56).

Near the end of the story, Edie finishes her "reading" of this man whose letters never arrive to be read. Her reading goes directly contrary to Martin's "celestial significance," and she arrives at a simple conclusion: *"No letter was ever going to come"* (SIB, 65). Her reading is resistant because she refuses to do what W.R. Martin does. She refuses to read the last letter of the name as understood. She also refuses to wait. She knows that the letter t will never come to be added to the name Chris, making up the perfect lover: Christ or Logos. Like Del and like Tennyson's Mariana (and unlike the wise virgins), Edie knows that the bridegroom will not come. It is thus that the first person meets her husband, marrying the mailman instead of the man whose letter he was to have brought.

Edie gains power because she understands the simple symmetries of the symbolic order and makes them work to her advantage. Not so Alice Kelling. When she arrives on the scene, we start to see double. The fact that the women in question do not "recognize" each other contrasts with the reader's sense of their kinship. Despite her education – or rather, because of it – Alice Kelling is more vulnerable than Edie. Her training as a nurse constitutes an education in the reproduction of mothering. Like Naomi's mother in *Lives of Girls and Women*, Alice Kelling nurses the man she intends to marry (SIB, 56). Unlike Edie, Alice Kelling is not a reluctant mock mother. She is like Caroline, who runs after the photographer, tramping the hot roads looking for him. Caroline "waited and waylaid him and offered herself to him . . . with straining eagerness and hope and cries" (LGW, 247). Alice Kelling waits for Chris Watters and waylays him, willing to sacrifice her self, to nurse him.

Alice Kelling's name is invariably cited in full, as if the reader is invited to add an additional phrase: Alice Kelling – not Alice Munro and not Alice Laidlaw. With each repetition the name Alice Kelling becomes more opaque. The image of the woman is distorted, like Del's image when she looks at herself in the mirror through the blur of tears. The name *Kelling*, with the change of one letter, could be the world *killing* and is, in fact, the origin of that word according to Skeat. I think of the "killing weight" of men's bodies (LGW, 246) or of Del's discovery that lovers may "try to kill each other, various ways" (LGW, 240). The word *kell* refers to a shroud (*OED*), but in this case may also suggest *caul*. In view of the deformed babies referred to by Alice Kelling, readers might be reminded of another practical nurse – Naomi's mother – who insists that "babies born with cauls will turn out to be criminals" (LGW, 119).

The conflation of the term "caul" with the image of a criminal is significant because it points to the inescapable moral responsibility of the infantilized person. Giving in to the desire to be mothered is not an indication that the person has no power – only a possible indication that she fears her own power. Et, in the title story, describes Arthur as someone still in a caul. He sits "in the rocker with the quilt over his knees, foolish as something that hasn't grown its final, most necessary, skin. Yet in a way the people like Arthur were the most trouble-making of all" (SIB, 14).

The confrontation between Alice Kelling and Edie is the culmination of a process which shows us mock mother and infant as the two sides of a single character. When Edie confesses to having been "intimate" with Chris Watters, Alice Kelling undergoes a transformation. As Edie's mock mother pose was replaced by a queen, so Alice Kelling, the practical nurse, is replaced by a siren. Both Edie and Alice Kelling are characters in whom Alice Munro explores how and why women abuse their maternal power. It is tempting to see them as acting out the revenge of women for being excluded from the quest. On another level, however, they both behave like little girls. Tears are running down Alice Kelling's face and she is sobbing while she talks. In response to her rantings, Loretta Bird takes over the part of mock mother, saying "'Don't get yourself upset'" (SIB, 63). Alice Kelling describes "little country tramps" having diseased babies, and Loretta Bird remembers a "'bad woman here in town had a baby that pus was running out of its eyes'" (SIB, 63). When Mrs Peebles follows up with "'You don't want to have a baby, do you?'" Edie herself is infantilized by the thought of having an infant. She starts howling "just like a six-year-old" and protests: "'You don't get a baby from just doing that!'" (SIB, 63). It is Mrs Peebles who now takes over the mock mother role, saying "'Calm down. Don't get hysterical. Calm down. Stop crying'" (SIB, 63), just as Loretta Bird tried to calm Alice Kelling.

There's not a man in sight during this scene – just four women in various stages of hysteria. It doesn't take too much imagination to see

Alice Kelling's rage at Edie as a displaced anger which ought by rights to be directed at the men she describes. "'Men despise girls like you,'" she says to Edie, "'He just made use of you and went off, you know that, don't you? Girls like you are just nothing, they're just public conveniences, just filthy little rags!'" (SIB, 63). The word *filthy* is repeated three times, and although we know that Edie uses rags to clean up other people's filth, we are still not sure who to blame for spreading filth. We do get, however, a clarification of the issue of power as it relates to identity. Edie becomes a kind of looking glass for Alice Kelling. It is easier for Alice Kelling to confront the idea of being used in the person of another than for her to concede that she herself is being used.

The blurring of individual identity is crucial to the empowering of women and this is suggested by the fact that Edie seduces or is seduced while she is masquerading in Mrs Peebles's clothes. Alice's efforts to catch up in a car with a man who flies is as absurd as it would be for Loretta Bird to fly. Edie's actions, however ironic, suggest an alternative avenue to female empowerment. She visits Chris in a tent in an abandoned fairground, and the context of this scene makes clear to us that she could be any woman. The true lovers' meeting is a kind of staged circus accident – a failed stunt. The tent is a place where the performance on "one of these fold-up cots" (SIB, 59) will briefly hold the old narratives still inside this makeshift structure – just long enough for us to gain ironic distance from them. This is not a corrosive irony: both Edie and Chris are briefly nourished. She brings him cake and he gives her tender kisses. This abandoned fairground, like the one in which Mary Agnes is raped (LGW, 42) is, however, a bleak setting. It takes courage for Edie to look back at "the fairgrounds with the full-blown milkweed and dark teasels" and to confront something that is "plain and true": "*No letter was ever going to come*" (SIB, 65). The positive consequences of this vision of milkweed are not realized in this story but they are implied as part of Edie's present perspective, which she articulates when she tells about how she lied to Alice Kelling for Chris: "Women should stick together and not do things like that. I see that now, but didn't then. I never thought of myself as being in any way like her, or coming to the same troubles, ever" (SIB, 61). Seeing herself as a conscious cliché makes it possible for Edie to come to a different end than the one prescribed in the old formula. That is how she comes to marry the mailman.

The question of how the female "I" meets her husband is a dilemma repeated again and again in Munro's fiction. The metaphor that lies behind the deceptively ordinary surface of the story is that of the bride of Christ preparing to meet her bridegroom (see LGW, 156). That metaphor not only militates against the construction of the woman as an I but also sets woman against woman. The meeting of the first person and Alice Kelling – like the meeting of the first person and Barbara in "Tell Me Yes or No" – tells a sad story of sisterhood betrayed – a story that threatens to overwhelm the predictable story of sexual love betrayed. For female readers the word "I" in the title sets up a mirror mockingly tempting us to read in the way that the Freudian disciple predicts we will – seeing our own lives in the work of art (LGW, 181). To do so is to become another Freudian "Case history" (SIB, 117). Better to acknowledge in advance that the female "I" is not an autonomous identity so much as it is a place of invasion. Then the dialogue may begin – a conversation between the overlapping faces in the mirror. By naming herself, then pushing herself away from that name, Alice Munro enables us to join her in distancing ourselves from the structures within which we all live.

"SOMETHING I'VE BEEN MEANING TO TELL YOU": SAY HEART AND LET IT GO

This story takes place amongst wreckage of the kind envisioned by Adrienne Rich in "Diving Into the Wreck" (Rich, 1975, 65–68). Watching Blaikie as he narrows his gaze on women, Et pictures him as a "deep-sea diver diving down, down through all the emptiness and cold and wreckage to discover the one thing he had set his heart on, something small and precious, hard to locate, as a ruby maybe on the ocean floor" (SIB, 3). "BLAIKIE NOBLE, DRIVER, GUIDE" (SIB, 1) does not, however, guide pilgrims into an underworld. He takes female tourists to see "the sights" (SIB, 2). This story, in fact, stays relentlessly with a visual world. The "sun dazzling on the water" (SIB, 6) seems like a defence weapon, preventing us from making entry or descent, and Et complains of so "much white it hurt your eyes, the ladies' dresses and parasols and the men's summer suits and Panama hats" (SIB, 6). The reader, like the speaker in Rich's poem, has to "explore the wreck". If we take with us the "book of myths," then we may at least come to see the "evidence of damage." The first myth to question is the quest myth itself.

The surface of the story is mannered and the characters brittle. It is not possible, as it was in "Images," to trace in the narrative a descending and ascending quest pattern, nor is the recurring departure/return pattern enacted. Instead, the story is like a crazy quilt, shifting among time levels in a way that disorients a reader. The experience of reading is roughly analogous to the feeling of being at the mercy of temporality itself – felt not as narrative sequence but as unpredictability, as contingency. Blaikie is imaged as being on a treasure hunt and Arthur is certainly on a quest for the Holy Grail. The narrative discontinuity, however, derives from the fact that the goal is not so clear for the female characters. Like Penelope, Et stays at home. We might be tempted to think that if she could tell the story that is "on the tip of her tongue" (SIB, 23), a sequential order would be restored. If we depend on Et for meaning, however, then we, like the characters in the story, will be at her mercy.

In this story Arthur's sword is not "snatched out of the stone" (LGW, 117). As long as Et – in a characteristic maternal gesture – can keep the quilt over the bottom half of Arthur's body (SIB, 14), she herself can wield her "sharp tongue" and her needle as invisible swords. In another maternal gesture, Et feeds Arthur and watches him drink "with an eager noise, like a child" (SIB, 13). As long as Et can see herself as protecting Arthur from the danger of Char's "slow poison" (SIB, 13), so long will she be blind to the danger she herself presents. Imagining Char murdering Arthur does give Et a little pause.

> She did think maybe she was going a little strange, as old maids did; this fear of hers was like the absurd and harmless fears young girls sometimes have, that they will jump out a window, or strangle a baby, sitting in its buggy. Though it was not her own acts she was frightened of.
>
> (SIB, 14)

Et sees danger everywhere except in herself. Indeed, it is by taking care of Arthur, and of everything that goes with his name, that Et takes care of herself. It is by taking care of others, by mothering them, that she harms them. "She's a terror, they said about her, Et's a terror" (SIB, 18). She may not be frightened of her own actions, but clearly others are. The phrase captures a major shift in Munro's fiction. The mock mother is now a figure less likely to invite pity. We do not say of her what Naomi says of Fern: "'A joke, she was just a *joke!*'" (LGW, 183). This mock mother stirs up both pity and fear. In exploring her power, Munro returns to the sinister connotations first evoked by Mary McQuade in "Images."

Et's power should not be taken to imply that Arthur has no power – as Et herself notes when she comments that people like Arthur are "the most trouble-making of all" (SIB, 14). Arthur's name, after all, contains the distilled essence of the ancient paradigm that Et invokes destructively in this story. His acquiescence to the old patterns is frightening. He is the passive mock-female against Et's mock-male aggression. Et's needle is not so much mightier than Arthur's sword, as it is a miniaturized version of that weapon. It is absolutely imperative, then, that we find a place to stand from which we may offer resistance to Et's manipulations. If Et cannot see herself as dangerous, then we must see her from some other place if we are to understand the danger she represents. Alicia, I will argue, makes this other place.

If we think of the "I" as hiding behind the puppet called Alicia, then we experience, in a very immediate and radical way, the abdication of the author who, by this gesture, makes a space for us. There will be no authorized version of the "something" that Munro means to tell us. The puppet Alicia is controlled by a "lady ventriloquist" (SIB, 9) and she dances in step with another puppet called Alphonse. The name *Alphonse* echoes the sound of *Alpha* but it may also allude to the figure of Mother

Alphonsa, the daughter of Nathaniel Hawthorne (see Burton, 1956). A gender-blurring dance of Alphonse and Alicia is at least the beginning of resistance to a fixed notion of a male deity who is Alpha and Omega, beginning and end. The reader is invited to join the dance, but on terms which make it clear that it is not an act of absolute freedom.

The dancing puppets are images – representations of visible earthly bodies. They challenge the Pauline notion, developed in a famous chapter on the resurrection, of the first Adam's "living soul" contrasted to the "quickening spirit" of the last Adam (I Corinthians 15). Char misquotes a portion of that chapter when she says: "'O Life, where is thy sting'" (SIB, 12), a significant inversion that turns Paul's hierarchy upside down. The image of the dance is often used in this way by Munro. It is associated, in her fiction, with a spiritual world, but with the recognition that the spirit expresses itself only in a body, however awkwardly, otherwise there is no dance at all. In "Dance of the Happy Shades," for example, the unearthly music does not come in spite of but out of the earthly body of the retarded child. When Miss Farris gives her "dancing directions," she rails, by implication, against the separation of soul and body, telling the children that they dance "like fifty-year-old arthritics." *Con brio* – the phrase that winds up Miss Farris (LGW, 130–131) – means "with spirit" in Italian. She is, in a sense, a "quickening spirit."

If we keep this biblical allusion in mind, the puppet Alicia begins to look more and more like a skeleton doing a dance of death. Although the "lady ventriloquist" speaks to Alicia and Alphonse "as if they were real people" (SIB, 9), they sit in her bed, "one on each side of her" as images of the brittle characters that people this story. The ventriloquist is a mock mother and the puppets are her mock babies: "'She sits up in bed,'" Blaikie tells Char, "trying to feed them bits of bacon and talking to them and doing them answering back" (SIB, 10). They are visible replicas of what will remain of Char – skeletal remains – if she swallows enough blueing. Only the reader can quicken them with life. The puppets are not free to answer back. They take dictation in a sense, and the "lady ventriloquist" could be seen as playing the part of the "bad or false mother" described by Derrida as a "functionary of the State" (Derrida, 1985, 35–36). Unlike them, however, we can talk back. The reader, in short, stands in the only place in the story that is alive and the reader thus bears the burden of freedom.

From this position, then, we may protest the sacrifice of Char. No resistance to that sacrifice is offered within the story. It can come only from the reader – outside the narrative structure – who looks at Et's looking. Et's watching is itself a dangerous way of keeping. The words of the story's opening paragraph focus on Et in the act of watching: "'Anyway he knows how to fascinate the women,' said Et to Char. She could not tell if Char went paler, hearing this, because Char was pale in the first place as anybody could get. She was like a ghost now, with her hair gone white" (SIB, 1). It is as if Et's very act of looking robs Char of life. A similar act takes place in Timothy Findley's *The Telling of Lies*: "Based on the notion that mothers – even surrogate mothers – have a right to keep an eternal eye on their children, Arabella took her role as watcher far too seriously. This woman could watch a person to death" (1986, 149). Et's descriptions of Blaikie and Char imply that she is watching them to death. Blaikie has a "bleached" quality (SIB, 5) and when she compares him to a "vanilla ice-cream cone," we know that he is in danger of being et. This is the world of the dead and the voice of the devourer is a ghostly voice, bloodless and heartless. Munro's ironic method urges us to find a different way of balancing the competing claims of the "watcher" and the "keeper."

Arthur, too, is a watcher who tries to keep or possess the object of his gaze. For him "Char was above, outside, all ordinary considerations – a marvel, a mystery. No one could hope to solve her, they were lucky just being allowed to contemplate her" (SIB, 17). She is his Holy Grail. Despite her sarcasm on the subject (SIB, 3), Char is not able to resist Arthurian designs on her body. Her body is sacrificed to make the legend come true once again. Her womb may not be in shreds like Dotty's (SIB, 32), but Char does suffer a miscarriage (SIB, 16). Char is dead at the time of the story's narration; in her name we hear the sound of ashes. She is remembered for the part she plays as a statue "draped in white crepe" (SIB, 15). She cannot be still enough, white enough, dead enough for those who want to fix her in the role of Beauty. Personal hygiene was the subject of hysterical laughter in *Lives of Girls and Women*. Here, the hysteria is carried to bizarre lengths when Char swallows laundry blueing. All the blueing in the world cannot make her womb clean enough to be Arthur's Holy Grail. She has failed to keep the vessel clean and her act of adultery is the sign of that failure. Blueing is "not in the book" consulted by Et and not in the "book of myths" referred to by Rich (1975, 68). Suicide, as so often happens in real life and in Munro's stories, is one way for the woman to take up the place assigned to her in the myths. The comic effect offers the only clue to a possible means of escape. The clowning of Alice as Alicia make a tiny space of hope.

All that is left of Char, to be watched by Arthur and Et, is a framed photograph – "the one taken of her in her costume for that play, where she played the statue-girl" (SIB, 23). The image may allude obliquely to the ending of Shakespeare's *Winter's Tale*, especially since Et suspects that Arthur thinks of Char as a "heroine out of Shakespeare" (SIB, 17). It is closer, however, to the inversion of the Pygmalion/Galatea story seen in Browning's "My Last Duchess." Like the Duke, Arthur thinks he possesses his wife more surely in death than he ever possessed her in life, but we sense that Char, like the duchess, escapes his clutches. Et is a negation of everything that Char stands for and thus, by inversion, we do intuit a sense of Char's life. The contrast of good and evil is subsumed, as it is in Browning, by the contrast of life and death. What is evil is life-denying. We experience evil as Et's denial of the presence of a heart in the bodies of the women that she treats as dressmaker dummies. We end up enlarging exactly the things that Et wishes to diminish. The inversion is similar to the one enacted by the reader of Browning's poem who responds to the "spot of colour." The duke wishes us to hold the duchess in contempt and we never get outside his point of view; how is it then, that when he is done, many readers see her as innocent?

When Char dies, "the old doctor said heart and let it go" (SIB, 23). Et chooses to interpret this one-word post-mortem in a literal way. Her gloss refers back to Char's bulimia: "Perhaps it really was the heart. All that purging would have weakened anybody's heart" (SIB, 23). Whatever else the "something" would achieve, if Et ever told it, it would confirm that there was a subject inside the object – the statue; it would colour a red heart on the battered dummy. Et "let it go, day to day" and thus keeps Char in her state as serene, remote object. Both the doctor and Et are described by the comment that they "let it go," but I feel the betrayal of the sister more deeply. The reader, however, need not let it go at that. W.R. Martin sees Char as "disdainful, statuesque" (Martin, 1987, 81). He approves of the fact that Et "makes do with Char's" husband, and he sees Et as someone who "achieves her own happiness" in "this Cinderella story" (Martin, 1987, 80–81). This drastic misreading of the story results from a failure to notice the ironic distance that Munro so carefully makes available to us. Even if Char were a beautiful statue containing a nice clean Holy Grail and even if Et were a kind, nurturing motherly figure – the Cinderella story would still not fit. Like Et, Munro knows "a good fit from a bad" (SIB, 18) and Et does not fit into Cinderella's glass slipper. It is Char whose name would be associated with the Cinderella story and even she does not fit. There are not two stepsisters conspiring against the one pure-blooded daughter, nor is sheer beauty a ticket to a happy ending.

The fact that the Cinderella story is a pattern that does not fit is a useful clue for readers of this story. It will not be enough to take a red crayon and sketch a bleeding heart on the battered dressmaker's dummy and "let it go." That would simply be to substitute Juliet for Cinderella. It is never enough (SIB, 44) and never time to "let it go." The various stories alluded to in this story should be seen as clashing against each other and acting as a catalyst for thought. We are left with remnants of old stories, not with a completed costume. In order to achieve the goal of dialogue and growth we must eschew Et's desire for a neat fit and for a closed ending. We must choose, instead, to dance with the puppet Alicia. From that vantage point we may observe that Et's readings of events are conditioned by her own needs. The performance she directs might be called *Lovers* and the two people she watches most intensely throughout the story are Blaikie and

Char. "*Lovers*" to her is not a "soft word, as people thought, but cruel and tearing" (SIB, 14). She sees it this way not only because she feels protective of Arthur, but also because she denies her own sexuality. Blaikie and Char are acting out the story that she has repressed; she is living her life through them because she lacks the courage to live it through herself.

Comparative reading is what Et cannot do and what we are asked to do. When she suspects, for example, that Char is poisoning Arthur, Et recognizes her suspicion as unoriginal. "What awful nonsense. Like something you read about, Agatha Christie" (SIB, 13). She is not able to resist the nonsense, however, because she wants to believe in her reading of events. She needs to see Char as being cruel to Arthur and she needs to see Blaikie as being cruel to Char. She is so determined to prove that her reading of events is the correct one, the one that fits, that she ends up making it happen. Her fatal weapon is a story based on her reading of events so far, a one-sentence story: "'I hear he's taken up with a well-to-do woman down at the hotel'" (SIB, 21). The fact that she describes the story about Blaikie as hear-say is neither here nor there since she did not actually hear anybody say it. She manipulates Char not by what she says, but by what she carefully refrains from saying. She proceeds to tell Arthur (speaking, in fact, to Char indirectly) about Blaikie and the "lady ventriloquist" (SIB, 21). She remembers "even the names of the dolls, though of course she left out all about Char" (SIB, 21). Et's storytelling technique is a trap – a kind of practical joke. Char is invited to fill in the blank – "all about Char." That phrase encapsulates the heart that has been excluded from the picture of the statue. What Char is also trapped into doing is to fill in all about Blaikie – his treachery and cruelty.

The story is not in fact recapitulated in detail at this point and this leaves a space for the reader to rewrite it – making alterations. We may treat the story the way Char treats Arthur's "black scholar's gown" and rip it up (SIB, 16). What we can hope for is something like the multicoloured patchwork of the Pied Piper's costume, but only if we include the "bright blue" of Char's dress (the colour that "did not show" on the photograph; SIB, 6), the bright red implied in "heart," and the "green stuff" clogging Sandy's nostrils (SIB, 11). The ironic method of this story, then confronts us with our own subjectivity. Even as I write, indeed, I am conscious of my own subjectivity and of the fact that I may be judging Et too harshly. There is no escape, however, from subjectivity, only a choice between a subjectivity that is acknowledged and one that is not. The world of this story will remain a black and white negative, unless the reader adds the colour. The heart of any story we reconstruct from the pieces will be determined by what it is that we have set our hearts on – by desire. Et has set her heart on Arthur as surely as Blaikie has "set his heart on" the ruby at the bottom of the ocean (SIB, 3). We are conscious of Et's repressed hunger for Arthur. Had she herself been conscious of the heart, the feeling in her own body, she would have been able to make allowances for it when cutting and altering the story to fit her needs. As any good scholar knows, the only way to ensure that your reading takes into account the inevitability of subjective bias is to know your own bias and to keep checking the facts. Et does not do either.

There is something frighteningly predatory in this story. Et, Blaikie and Arthur are all intent on narrowing their gaze to that "something small and precious" that they wish to possess. At the moment when Blaikie and Char appear to have made the acquisition, Et perceives Char as having "lost her powers, abdicated. Sandy drowned, with green stuff clogging his nostrils, couldn't look more lost than that" (SIB, 11). The deep-sea diving scene becomes an analogy for the act of storytelling. The heart of the story is something that cannot be told. It can only be lived. We may examine the wreckage and come to see what damage is done, but we cannot pinpoint blame or make it all better again. Perhaps we do have to say "heart" and "let it go" in the end. What we gain, however, in the midst of such a bleak setting, is a potential increase in compassion that accompanies our ability to see the irony. This compassion, for example, may give us enough distance to realize that there is something besides the sexual object that is "small and precious" under the water, namely the "little brother who was drowned" (SIB, 7). Like the later story "Accident" (MJ, 77–109), this one introduces the fleeting image of a dead child in a way that makes us uncomfortable about our fictions. That death makes the quest myth itself seem "slightly beside the point" (SIB, 190). We are left, instead, with questions.

"THE OTTAWA VALLEY" – GIVING UP

If the majority of the stories in *Something I've Been Meaning to Tell You* are a "*conscious* effort to get away from personal material" (Munro, in Struthers, 1983, 22), then "The Ottawa Valley" certainly looks like a conspicuous collapse of that resolve. This is one of Munro's most moving stories and her most profound and subtle tribute to her mother. It is the last story in the collection and also came last in the order of composition (Struthers, 1983, 27). Munro describes this story and "Winter Wind" as a "going back to earlier material" (in Struthers, 1983, 27). She goes back, however, in order to construct and confront a crisis that has been apparent, in one form or another, in all the stories in this collection. Her reservations about using "life" to make "art" are made explicit in "Winter Wind":

> I have used these people, not all of them, but some of them, before. I have tricked them out and altered them and shaped them any way at all, to suit my purposes. I am not doing that now, I am being as careful as I can, but I stop and wonder, I feel compunction.
>
> (SIB, 201)

Munro, in fact, almost stopped for good. Tausky reports that after writing "The Ottawa Valley" Munro "seriously contemplated giving up the writing of fiction altogether" (1986b, xviii). In conversation with Tim Struthers, Munro turns the crisis into a joke and compares herself to "all these people that are always making final concert tours and saying good-bye [laughter]. Then they're back with the next [laughter]." She adds, however, that she often does "quite *genuinely* feel . . . *tormented* by the inadequacy and impossibility" of writing fiction. She describes herself as looking – in "The Ottawa Valley" – at "real lives," confronting the "inadequacy" of the way she represents them, and questioning her "right to represent them at all" (in Struthers, 1983, 28). Central to her compunctions is the representation of the mother and this fact is crucial to an understanding of Munro's evolving attitude to the act of fabrication. This story is more explicitly autobiographical than any other story by Munro, but it controls and objectifies subjective expression in a way that moves beyond "The Peace of Utrecht" and that could not have been possible without the experimenting Munro did in the preceding stories. Those stories now make it possible for Munro to confront subjectivity more boldly and daringly than she did in earlier stories.

Curiously enough, given the wrenching subject matter, it is in this story that Munro returns to her exploration of comedy. An important feature of this story is the clear split between the "real-life" mother and a mock mother figure who is more obviously a fiction. This division is central to our experience of other divisions in this story – in particular the division between laughter and crying. The division is a return to the split initiated in her earliest stories. It's almost as if the circus cannot go on without these maternal clowns. Munro here grieves after the death of her "real-life" mother. Although I weep each time I read this story, what is heard *in* the story is the sound of laughter. It comes primarily from Aunt Dodie, a mock mother who enjoys practical jokes (as does Mary MacQuade in "Images") and who laughs "at the end of every sentence" (SIB, 228). In this story the mock mother is sentenced to be an old maid and the "real-life" mother is sentenced to death.

No such clear demarcation between real-life mother and mock mother occurs in "Winter Wind," where the daughter herself gains "the upper hand" over her mother by taking on the mothering chores:

> After all, it was I who heated tubs of water on the stove and hauled the washing machine from the porch and did the washing, once a week; I who scrubbed the floor, and with an ill grace made her endless cups of tea.
> (SIB, 202)

Commenting on this role, the daughter notes: "I did not get tired of it so easily, in fact I did not get tired of it at all" (SIB, 202). This is in stark contrast to the fear expressed by the daughter in "The Ottawa Valley":

"I was very much relieved that she had decided against strokes, and that I would not have to be the mother, and wash and wipe and feed her lying in bed, as Aunt Dodie had had to do with her mother" (SIB, 244). The daughter's enjoyment of her power in "Winter Wind" is replaced, in "The Ottawa Valley," with an experience of powerlessness. The difference is marked by the fact that the object of hygiene changes: the act of washing and scrubbing the floors is replaced by the act of washing and wiping the body of the mother. The mother's body, the site of our birth, is also the place of anxiety in the face of death.

In this story, as in "Images," the powers associated with birth and death are projected into a mock maternal figure whose relation to the family is ambiguous. In "Images," the mock mother acts as a powerful midwife. Here she is a screen on which the narrating daughter witnesses the collapse of her own powers. The image of powerlessness is contained in the warning that Aunt Dodie issues when she predicts that "someday" the mother will have a big stroke: "'You'll have to learn to be the mother, then,'" she predicts: "'Like me.'" Like the mother in "Images," Aunt Dodie's mother is swollen up "like a big balloon" (DHS, 33) but there is a difference: "'She was all swollen up; what she had was dropsy'" (SIB, 243). It ought to be a joke, Aunt Dodie seems to say when she describes how they "'took it out of her by the pailful.'" When the narrator asks "'Took what out?'" and Aunt Dodie answers "'Fluid'" we could see this as another hysterical pregnancy. Aunt Dodie describes how her mother, like a big baby, begged to be turned on her left side: "I got hold of her and turned her – she was a weight! I turned her on her heart side, and the minute I did, she died" (SIB, 243). The narrator does not write "I cried," but we know that she cries from Aunt Dodie's maternal response. Aunt Dodie laughs at her to cheer her up and protests: "'What are you crying about? I never meant to make you cry! Well, you are a big baby, if you can't stand to hear about Life'" (SIB, 243).

As the narrator weeps for her own mother by weeping for Aunt Dodie's mother, so I too weep for my own mother by weeping for Alice Munro's mother. It is a displacement which is crucial to the special power of this story. A community of readers is formed by this process and the mutual vulnerability, the risk of exposing subjectivity is crucial to that experience. When we set up this kind of analogy as readers, we enter into the heart of the dilemma that Munro is exploring. There is both a comfort and a kind of reproach in this action. It is comforting to say "like her, so also I" or "like her mother, so also my mother" but the likeness breaks down when daughter attempts to pay tribute to mother. At that point my mother and Munro's mother become like each other only in the sense that they are both silenced by death. To push the likeness any further is to conspire with the forces that deny their lives, their difference. By the admission of failure, however, Munro clears a space where the mother is allowed to be Real in a way that is not contained in the fiction.

In contrast to the daughter in "The Peace of Utrecht," this daughter is not given a consciously fictitious name, nor does Munro play cleverly with the word "I" as she does in other stories in this collection. Referentiality is no longer one thread only, as it was in the earlier story. This story, in fact, could be said to be *about* referentiality. "I think of my mother" – this is the opening phrase of the story and the rest of the paragraph leaves us in no doubt that the "I" is Alice Munro and the "mother" is her own mother, who died slowly of Parkinson's Disease. The story opens with the mother and her daughters in Union Station, Toronto, about to leave for the mother's "old home in the Ottawa Valley" and the time is "one summer during the War" (SIB, 227). These specific details ought to be reassuring. Coming along with the invocation of the old quest pattern – departure and return home – the prologue ought to unite myth, history, and geography in a satisfying wholeness. Precisely the opposite happens as the quest for identity is replaced by a confrontation with separation and difference. The fact that the mother is already dead is the most important historical detail. It lends a specious quality to the whole story, as though the story admits, from the beginning, to being "slightly beside the point" (SIB, 190). The blind spot here threatens to engulf the entire narrative – like the blackness of the Ottawa Valley: "My mother waved at the blackness on either side of us. 'Children! Children, this is the Ottawa Valley!'" (SIB, 229). The word "valley" – like the inside of the mother's body out of which we were born and like the "valley of the shadow of death" into which we vanish – does not refer to what can be seen. The dislocation is central to the impact of this story and to our sense that words and appearances cannot be trusted. "It was no valley," writes Munro, "I looked for mountains, or at least hills, but in the morning all it was was fields and bush, and Aunt Dodie outside the window holding a milk pail for a calf" (SIB, 229).

Hovering over this, the most "realistic" of Munro's stories, is the sense of unreality that accompanies all our confrontations with death. The result is an experience of radical fragmentation. Loss of wholeness is experienced almost viscerally in this story and is directly related to the loss of contact with the mother's body. The mother/child split is evoked in the image of the "moderately famous" pianist named Mary Renwick, whose parents "said that they would give up all their daughter's fame for a pair of baby hands. *A pair of baby hands?*" (SIB, 228). Hands are associated with power, but since no baby is born, the image – like the hands – is severed and becomes a dead metaphor that lies as an obstruction between Mary Renwick and her parents. These and other fragments in the story contribute to an experience of powerlessness in the face of death. There is a sense of dislocation, as if the sound and the sight are not synchronized. Union Station in Toronto looks "like a street with its lighted shops and like a church with its high curved roof" but the sounds do not correlate with the sights. The "thunder of trains hidden" is as ominous as the mention of the distant War. The trains tempt us to hope for unions and meetings even as they enforce alienation and threaten chaos. We sense this in the "amplified voice, luxuriant, powerful, reciting place names that could not quite be understood" (SIB, 228).

The mother waits here for a "cousin she was planning to meet, for a between-trains visit" but the cousin does not show up (SIB, 227). The word "Union" is ironic in the circumstances. Aunt Dodie refers to the "cousin" as "Her Majesty" but we are informed that she "was referring to the legal secretary, who was in fact her sister. Aunt Dodie was not really our aunt at all but our mother's cousin. She and her sister did not speak" (SIB, 229). Aunt Dodie herself is an isolated fragment of the family. She lives "off her cows" but she is not full of the milk of human kindness. In our first sight of her she is "laughing and scolding and hitting" the calf and calling it a "'greedy little bugger'" (SIB, 229). Her "milking outfit" is "many-layered and -colored and ragged and flopping like the clothes a beggarwoman might wear in a school play" (SIB, 229). Like the Pied Piper in *Lives of Girls and Women*, whose cloak is "patched with various colours," Aunt Dodie could be seen as wearing "almost a fool's cap" (LGW, 135). "A man's hat without a crown was shoved – for what purpose? – on her head" (SIB, 229). The absent crown is an anti-symbol, and if we make the interpolated question more than rhetorical we note that Aunt Dodie survives because she is willing to play the fool's part. The hat without a crown contrasts with the "large black hat" (SIB, 227) worn by "Her Majesty" – Aunt Dodie's sister (SIB, 228–229) and with the "hat like a buggy wheel" worn by Durrand's wife (SIB, 242). Aunt Dodie's ability to laugh at this upside down world goes along with the material of her dress: slub rayon. A slub is a twist in the thread which prepares it for spinning, but *slub* can also refer to "thick sludgy mud; mire, ooze" (*OED*), a relevant association if we remember Aunt Dodie's insistence on the "chicken dirt" scraped off the boots of "Her Majesty" (SIB, 229).

The denial imaged in "Material" in the character of Dotty, is here repeated in the very material of Aunt Dodie's dress. The similarity of the women's names invites us to connect the aspects that are separated in them: the sexual and the maternal. In Aunt Dodie Munro challenges, as she does elsewhere, the unsexing of the mother figure. The old maid who never marries is the one who mothers her own parents and it is she who bears (like Maddy in "The Peace of Utrecht") the burden of the old ideology. Aunt Dodie's disarming entertainments enable us to venture close to the brutalities inherent in the system. Sexuality, for Aunt Dodie, seems to be a juvenile joke. Aunt Dodie's adolescent stance, however, is a pose – a form of mimicry. It is, in fact, the first of a sequence of three jokes that structure this story. The miniature autobiography, a joke told by Aunt Dodie, becomes a place from which to think about genre. At first we are invited to see her life story as a tragedy: "The tragedy in her life was that she had been jilted" (SIB, 230). This genre, however, is immediately undercut by the very next sentence: "'Did you know,' she said, 'that I was jilted?'" By the simple act of telling her own story, Aunt Dodie makes it impossible for the listener or reader to see her life as tragedy. She says the word "'jilted' proudly," as one might name a "bad important disease" (SIB, 230). In this she resembles Miss Havisham, in *Great Expectations*, who spoke of her broken heart "with a weird smile that had a kind of boast in it" (Dickens, 1965, 57). She also anticipates Marietta in "The Progress of Love," whose tragedy is encapsulated in the consciously important statement: "Her heart was broken" (PL, 13). Turning her "tragedy" into a joke, Aunt Dodie offers resistance to the tyrannical powers that decree either tragedy or divine comedy as a choice of endings.

That kind of comedy can clearly not be the right genre either, for Aunt Dodie is the bride whose bridegroom never comes. Like Aunt Dodie, Miss Havisham is left in the lurch on her wedding day. Unlike Aunt Dodie, she does not take off her wedding dress or her "long white veil" (Dickens, 1967, 55). In the act of taking off her wedding dress, Aunt Dodie also divests herself of the old structures and gains a kind of freedom, however circumscribed. Aunt Dodie's wedding dress is not, in any case, the traditional white satin but a "nice dark red merino wool, because of it being a late fall wedding." While waiting in vain for the bridegroom, Aunt Dodie remembers not only the time of year ("late fall") but also the time of day: "'It got dark, and I said, time to go out and do the milking! I pulled off my dress and I never put it back on. I gave it away" (SIB, 230). The "wedding dress" is replaced by the "milking outfit" and this masquerade is a clue to the way women like Aunt Dodie are seen to survive in Munro's stories. The "milking outfit" fits as the costumes of tragedy and comedy do not. By *telling* her life as a joke, Aunt Dodie makes herself at home in her "milking outfit" and resists *being* a joke. If this is comedy, it is not the old kind of comedy that leads to great expectations of weddings as closure. It is more like the "carnivalesque" of Bakhtin that challenges old patterns – including that version of comedy. "Lots of girls would've cried, but me, I laughed" (SIB, 230).

All this is not to say, of course, that Aunt Dodie's life is necessarily a happy one. The mother does not remember the laughter; she remembers that she "used to wake up and hear [Aunt Dodie] crying in the night. Night after night" (SIB, 230). This story, however, draws us into Aunt Dodie's defended territory. Watching her performance, we allow her to be, in this sense, our comforting mock mother. In the second of this story's three practical jokes, we see Aunt Dodie going a step further than self protection. The victim of the first practical joke becomes the victimizer of the second one. In terms of chronology, of course, this cannot be seen as simple revenge since the joke was played on Allen Durrand when Aunt

Dodie was an adolescent. The telling and the timing of the joke raise important questions about power. Miss Havisham takes her revenge by training Estella to break hearts. Presumably, each time a heart is broken, she could say: "Like me." Aunt Dodie's revenge is less melodramatic but it is a more conspicuous failure.

Allen Durrand, the victim of the joke, is not like the man who left Aunt Dodie in the lurch (about whom we know nothing at all). As the hired man, he is not in a position of power and this is part of what makes it a bad joke. The power in this little anecdote – "'Oh, the cruelty of it!'" – is not in either the victim or the victimizers of the story. It is in nature: in the hot weather and in the needs of the flesh. The body of Allen Durrand resembles what used to be called a Wettums doll – pour in liquid at one end and it comes out at the other end. This is precisely what the girls do. Because they also sew shut the fly of his overalls, Allen Durrand is forced to take them off when he urinates. Aunt Dodie insists that they "'had the full view'" from their knothole and that there "'wasn't a thing we couldn't see'" (SIB, 236).

In their actions the girls reappropriate the powers taken away by the male vision of the female as a lack, a "fuckhole" (LGW, 117). We might even see this exposure as a revenge for the kind of exhibition ("Quite a sight, eh?"; LGW, 171) that Art performs in *Lives of Girls and Women*, but Munro gives us ironic distance from the juvenile humour. It is true that the young females objectify the male as they themselves are objectified and manipulated by the symbolic order. The barnyard setting does hint that Aunt Dodie may be a domesticated version of Circe; for the moment of urination she has Allen Durrand in her power in a condition no different from the animals. This fact, however, must be taken in conjunction with the reality of the present and with the information that triggers the memory in the first place. Aunt Dodie reads in the "daily paper" about Allen Durrand, "'a big Holstein man now,'" and speculates that he "'wants to get nominated'" by the "'Conservative Association'" (SIB, 233). Durrand's very name suggests the conservative structures that endure. Doubtless, he will win. The cows will lose.

As the story of the crude practical joke nears its conclusion, we instinctively prepare for a reversal in the role of victim. While Aunt Dodie remembers how both girls kept their eyes to the knothole, the daughter's gaze is fixed on the mother's face: "My mother looked from me to Aunt Dodie and back with an unusual expression on her face: helplessness. I won't say she laughed. She just looked as if there was a point at which she might give up" (SIB, 236). This "point" signals the most painful reversal in the story, a turn away from Aunt Dodie's stoicism. The point of almost giving up is mimed in the crisis triggered for Munro as writer: that she considered "giving up the writing of fiction altogether" (Tausky, 1986b, xviii).

In a short section immediately following, Munro interpolates (with uncharacteristic abruptness) a passage from Fishbein's *Medical Encyclopedia* which outlines the inexorable stages of Parkinson's Disease and, by implication, reduces the mother to a case study. As the objective words roll on, we are left with a mental picture of the mother's face. "Helplessness." That single word is the best that the daughter can do. The inadequacy of her own effort at mimesis *is* a mimesis of the mother's inarticulate condition. Both of these stand in stark contrast to the illusion of control contained in Aunt Dodie's practical joke. The controlling factor there was the involuntary urge to urinate after drinking. In what is surely one of Munro's most breathtaking risks as a storyteller, she now introduces an intensely subjective image: the mother's face and body, subject to involuntary spasms and paralyzings.

This face, like that of a helpless puppet, is inserted between two practical jokes that might both be described by the phrase *"no pants"* (SIB, 240). One takes place in a barnyard, the other in a graveyard. We see the disintegration of the mother's face and body, but our desire to resist her destruction is thwarted by the intrusive interpolation from an objective, scientific textbook. This is how we define authority, by virtue of a style of writing which denies the personal and renders the impersonal. The interpolation is itself like a joke. It resembles the word game called "dictionary" in which contestants compete in writing mock dictionary entries in an effort to capture the illusion of objectivity.

> *The onset is very slow and often years may pass before the patient and his family observes that he is becoming disabled.*
>
> (SIB, 236)

In the narration that follows, we switch gender easily: "Just her left forearm trembled . . . she could hold the arm still by stiffening it against her body" (SIB, 237). With the ease of reading experience, we conflate the body of the man in the medical case study with the body of the mother. What makes this poignant is our awareness that the final levelling of death will make the distinction irrelevant.

Do we dare to look at the face of the mother that lies behind the narrative outlines of this story? Do we dare to represence the body of the mother when it involves such a radical confrontation with the knowledge of our own death? The face of this mother reflects back to us our own helplessness. It is subject to *"various tics, twitches, muscle spasms, and other involuntary movements"* (SIB, 236). The image is that of a facial grotesque but in this case it cannot be redeemed by seeing the mother as a clown. A clown is a performer. This face cannot mimic or express her *"passing moods"* (SIB, 237). Confronted with this face that is not the face of her mother, Munro here goes beyond the mimicry of the daughter in "The Peace of Utrecht." In that story Helen carries in her mind a "picture of her [mother's] face" which seems "too terrible, unreal" (DHS, 201). The strongest feeling in the earlier story is of waste: "All wasted, our pride; our purging its rage in wild caricatures we did for each other (no, not caricatures, for she was one herself; imitations)" (DHS, 195). In "The Ottawa Valley," the daughter's imitation of the caricature is displaced into the act of writing itself. The muscles on the mother's face, like the limbs of the puppet Alicia, perform a dance of death. The face of the mother who is a victim of Parkinson's Disease, when confronted this way, becomes a way of defining the way mimicry itself offers an *illusion* of control. Disease is not so much a metaphor as a means of experiencing the limits of metaphor. The controlled gestures of dance or mime are unavailable to the mother. She tries, instead, to hide the parts of her body that are moving: "The thumb knocked ceaselessly against the palm. She could, however, hide her fingers, and she could hold the arm still by stiffening it against her body" (SIB, 237).

Not all the fragments in the story are as horrific as the one from the medical encyclopedia. So visceral, however, is the experience of the mother's denied body and of her silence, that I become conscious of myself in the act of looking for comfort. In the section that immediately follows the interpolation about Parkinson's Disease, we are reminded of the fact that when we feel ourselves losing control we often reach, ironically, for a drink. The drinking song that Uncle James sings in the car when they are "coming home" has to do with still another journey: "*As I was a-goen over Kil-i-kenny Mountain*" (SIB, 238). What comforts is the up and down lulling rhythm of the "voice rolling out the black windows." The "perfectly black night" is filled with the sound of the voice: "*But I take delight in THE WATER OF THE BARLEY*" (SIB, 238). Like many drinking songs, this one evokes an image of fertility associated with John Barleycorn, but the strength of the comfort comes not so much from the image of seasonal renewal as it does from the singer's "delight" in the sheer sound of his own voice and from the spell cast by that voice.

Northrop Frye has noted that charms are made to keep away those who threaten the "cleared and protected place" of community. He cites, as example, a drinking song which condemns those who refuse the toast to lying down, down, down "among the dead men" (Frye, 1976, 128–129). As she rides along inside the car, the narrator is inside a blind spot, carried forward (like a child after a pied piper) by forces beyond her control. The voice is that of the male driver, reminding us that the "compulsion inherent in charm means that authority and subordination are integral to it" (Frye, 1976, 129). The narrator's experience in the car is a good analogy for the reader's experience of this story. She cannot remember the whole song and we cannot construct a total, meaningful design using the "bits of the words" (SIB, 238) that we have. If we do achieve some comfort in the end, it will define our protected place in a community.

The narrator needs all the help she can get as she sets herself up for the last practical joke. It takes place in a community of sorts: a graveyard. The first thing the visitors do in the graveyard is to stop at "two stones, on which were written the words *Mother* and *Father*" (SIB, 238). The post-Saussurean emphasis on language as arbitrary is here taken to an extreme that can only be borne if we comfort ourselves with the sheer materiality of our bodies. We laugh and sing and drink because we do not yet lie down, down among the dead men and women. We may laugh at the fact that one of the "two wooden toilets" behind St John's Church is "the Ladies" (SIB, 240) but the laughter itself is a comfort. Like the clichés on the gravestones – "*Until the Day Break . . . In Pacem*"(SIB, 239) – the word is not comforting because of its content but because language, like clothing, is a way of deferring our knowledge of death and dissolution.

Nobody is ultimately safe from death, the last practical jokester. The three jokes develop a changing relation between the seen and the unseen: Aunt Dodie's unseen crying in the night, the sight of Allen Durrand urinating, the mother's face and body gradually erased, unseen. Now, with the church setting, we might think of a biblical context: "Now faith is the substance of things hoped for, the evidence of things not seen" (Hebrews 11:1). In actual fact, of course, we are firmly in a visible world that includes Durrand himself as member of the audience. The church is a middle-class world of appearances in which people act in accordance with the way they want to be seen. Like the mother in "Walker Brothers Cowboy," this mother wants to walk into the church "serenely like a lady . . . like a *lady*" (DHS, 5). What prevents her from doing this is the fact that she has walked into "the Ladies" and sacrificed the safety pin from her slip strap to her daughter. The result is that her slip slides down "half an inch" and shows "in a slovenly way at one side" (SIB, 241).

Who is the victim of this practical joke? Who holds the power? In contrast to the first *no pants* joke, this one is not the result of a trick. It is sheer coincidence that the elastic of the daughter's underpants snaps in the graveyard just before the service. The daughter cannot imagine "walking into church in a blue taffeta dress and no pants. Rising to sing the hymns, sitting down, *no pants*. The smooth cool boards of the pew and *no pants*" (SIB, 240). There is a sense of a shared danger from which no safety pin can preserve us all. Having just visited the graveyard, what we imagine, by inversion, is not the body without pants but the pants without the body, the wedding dress without the bride.

The description of what takes place after the service takes, to an absurdly exaggerated level, the bourgeois emphasis on appearances. It seems to parody the biblical comfort that assures believers that although we now see through a glass darkly, then we will know as we are known. The figure of Allen Durrand, victim of the earlier practical joke, now regains power by the simple refusal to participate in the illusion: "'Didn't you see him?'" "'I didn't see him.'" "'Maybe he didn't know me. Or didn't see me.'" Munro aligns her own "realist" method with the mother's concern with appearances. The western tradition of mimesis, like the mother's gray and rose outfit, is a way of fending off the knowledge of death. The subtext of the story suggests that acquiescence to this tradition and to the accompanying mythology may also involve a denial of the mother's body and of her life. As a response to this dilemma, Munro repeats the image of the mother's retreating back. As they walk through a cow pasture, the daughter demands something more than a safety pin. "'Is your arm going to stop shaking?' . . . I demanded of her now, that she turn and promise what I needed" (SIB, 244). The "familiar bulk" on the path ahead of her turns "strange, indifferent" and the mother withdraws, darkening in front of the daughter. As she darkens, the mother enters into the blind spot. This scene may look like a final abandonment if we imagine it as something to which the mother gives "her consent." In fact, of course, we are seeing a final powerful gesture of the daughter's craft. It is the daughter who allows the mother to walk out of the frame of her story. By visualizing the mother's exit, the daughter allows the other in mother to remain alive.

It is appropriate, then, that Munro ends the story with a staged community of readers in which the mother is a reader of the old Ontario readers. "One night" during the visit to the Ottawa Valley, the mother, Aunt Dodie, and Uncle James play the old parlour game of capping quotations. In this group recitation there is a response to the meaningless recitation of place names in Union Station (SIB, 228) with which the story began. Sight and sound will never come together perfectly and we will never know as we are known. At the end of this story, however, we do emerge into a social world which acknowledges and accepts different perspectives even as it enacts a unity of sorts. The canonized texts from which the group recite are not given in full. The result is that we still experience dislocation but in a new way.

The passages quoted by Aunt Dodie and by the mother are from poems about war, with the female voices taking the male part. The poems chosen assume the irrelevance of gender with an abandon that we now question. Death is universal but women do not tend to die in wars except as victims. The female voice cannot seek to appropriate, without embarrassment, the powers inherent in the stories of male heroism. "'*How can a man die better* . . .'" Aunt Dodie cries "cheerfully" – quoting from Macaulay's "Lays of Ancient Rome." The dying mother might well counter with "How can a woman die worse." The mother, instead, recites – with an "embarrassing tremor" in her voice – two passages from Tennyson's "Morte d'Arthur" that are oddly cut apart by a passage from Charles Wolfe's "The Burial of Sir John Moore at Corunna." Once again, it seems, the joke is on Momma and she does not see it. Like the involuntary movements of hand and face, the tremor in the voice is not necessarily an expression of deep emotion.

It represents, more radically, the being taken over by a power beyond her control.

The dismembered fragments of poetry here are excerpts from the sad stuff "'they put in the old readers'" (SIB, 245), but when human voices give substance to the words, we are instantly aware of the power structures that produced the readers. Uncle James claims not to "remember a bit of it," but then recites "without a break" from a poem about the coming of winter. This pretty poem will be recognized immediately by many Canadian readers as Wilfrid Campbell's "Indian Summer." Munro, however, does not identify any of these quotations. The parlour game thus involves all readers as we align ourselves with a variety of different communities. British readers will presumably be more likely to recognize the passages from Macauley and Tennyson. There is, in addition, a generational split and the gender split already mentioned.

What this multiplication of contexts achieves is an awareness that the point here is not to affirm a specific poetic vision. The point is rather, quite simply, to affirm the mother's perspective, however limited, as one among many to be respected. These quotations become opaque as we question our understanding of the structures within which we live. The story cannot end with an answer; instead, the mutiplying charms lead to the ultimate riddle of death itself. Any answer, as Frye notes in another context, will be "wrong because it is an answer. . . . The answer is another way of trying to get control over things, the conceptual way, and renouncing it means, again, being set free to create" (Frye, 1976, 147). It is thus, then, that this story – far from putting a stop to Munro's writing – can be seen as a courageous confrontation with failure – a giving up or renouncing that set Munro free to do increasingly creative clowning.

Chapter 9

Who Do You Think You Are?
Blaming the king of the royal beatings

FLO: THE STEPMOTHER CLOWNS IN THE DUMP

If a failure to "get rid" of the mother is like a failure of hygiene (Jacobus, 1986, 193), then it should be no surprise that the book following "The Ottawa Valley" is full of scatalogical imagery. We are in the upside-down world of a winter carnival, where the warm body and what goes in and out of it are exaggerated in opposition to a frozen world. Topos here is often "the toilet locale," and the ice sculptures are "turds copious and lonesome . . . preserved as if under glass" in the "heaped snow under a glaze of ice" (WDY, 23). "To be made of flesh was humiliation" – this was Del's discovery (LGW, 57–58). In her vision "helplessness . . . was revealed as the most obscene thing there was" (LGW, 58). In *Who Do You Think You Are?* Munro returns to this vision with a difference, after confrontation with the "helplessness" of the mother's face in "The Ottawa Valley." After a beating, Rose is humiliated by her own appetite. The description of what she eats in "helpless corruption" is detailed down to the "rich streaks of Vita-Malt" (WDY, 19) in her chocolate milk. Later, envisioning her appetite for sex, she imagines herself "ashamed of, burdened by, the whole physical fact of herself, the whole outspread naked digesting putrefying fact" (WDY, 169).

The word "outspread" here hints at the centrefold pages of a girlie magazine, anticipating the decomposing photograph of the naked Dina in "Lichen." The reproductions of culture loom like a massive background to these stories. Munro is now close to Baudrillard's notion that "obscenity begins when there is no more spectacle, no more stage, no more theatre, no more illusion, when everything becomes immediately transparent, visible, exposed in the raw and inexorable light of information and communication" (Baudrillard, 1987, 21–22). The helpless body of Mary Agnes, exposed in the cold mud of the fairgrounds (LGW, 42), is restaged with a difference in Franny. This time everybody gathers to look at "relations performing" (WDY, 25).

Signs and words are similarly staged in this book, like the "parade" of words (WDY, 185) in "Spelling." The materiality of the sign is here not only an impropriety but also something produced involuntarily – helplessly. As the diapered old crone strains to produce a word, Rose thinks "she might be going to have a bowel movement" (WDY, 183). Rose imagines Flo in a different involuntary process, "her death moving in her like a child, getting ready to tear her" (WDY, 185). Adapting Bakhtin, then, we might say that Munro hurls her objects "down to the reproductive lower stratum, the zone in which conception and new birth take place. Grotesque realism knows no other level; it is the fruitful earth and the womb" (Bakhtin, 1968, 21).

But Munro's carnival is also a radical challenge to old ways of looking at our origins in an Earth Mother. That old fruitful womb sticks in the woman writer's throat like the hard-boiled egg Rose's mother imagines herself having swallowed:

> Her mother had died. She said to Rose's father during the afternoon, "I have a feeling that is so hard to describe. It's like a boiled egg in my chest, with the shell left on." She died before night, she had a blood clot on her lung. Rose was a baby in a basket at the time, so of course could not remember any of this. She heard it from Flo, who must have heard it from her father.
>
> (WDY, 2)

The absurdity of the image is designed to shock us out of our complacent assumptions about what is natural, especially as those assumptions relate to maternity. This opening image condenses the stages examined so thoroughly in *Lives of Girls and Women*. Here the pregnancy is hysterical from the beginning and here the seeing eye, from the beginning, is a hidden camera eye.

The time period covered by this book begins prior to the fact of television. The first stories take place during a time when, in the words of the radio interviewer, the people "made [their] own entertainment" (WDY, 21). Munro's way of making this book, however, is profoundly influenced by television. The name Flo may remind us that "the central television experience [is] the fact of flow" (Williams, 1974, 95). When Rose (a television actor) concludes, in the very last words of the book, that Ralph Gillespie's life is "one slot over from her own" (WDY, 206), we may remember that television flow consists of slots (Williams, in Heath and Skirrow, 1986, 15). Television changes the old quest pattern in which the hero departs from home and returns. Rose, with one breast bared, returns to Hanratty in a television production of *The Trojan Women*, making of the television set a Trojan horse "pregnant with social disaster" (Durling, 1981, 74). The passivity once associated with the woman who waits at home for the hero to return is now an emblem for television viewing. Perhaps this is why woman is frequently identified with the "monster mass culture" (Modleski, 1986, 163). Studies of television have tended to focus on reception rather than on production, perhaps due to the difficulty of identifying the source of production control. The industrial complex is an invisible power; what we can see is the passive spectator and passivity is traditionally female. If the male spectator is offered distance and mastery "though projecting the experience of submission and defenselessness onto the female body" (Modleski, 1986, 163), what is the female viewer to do?

Munro seems to me to call the television spectator to a kind of battle. We are enlisted in a fight against loss of consciousness, as the images from the screen threaten to batter us into insensibility so that we are like Franny, "stunned, bewildered, by continual assault" (WDY, 26). Consciousness alone, however, is not enough; it proves nothing more than that we are still awake enough to push the remote control button. "Consciousness, by itself," as Northrop Frye notes with relation to Wallace Stevens,

> is simple awareness of the external world. It sees; it may even select what it sees, but it does not fight back. The consciousness fighting back, with a subjective violence corresponding to the objective violence of external pressure . . . is the consciousness rising to imagination.
>
> (Frye, 1976, 277)

"Imagine!" – this is Flo's often repeated imperative and it rings like a call to arms while, at the same time, it oddly echoes John Lennon's famous peace anthem. Munro does "imagine all the people" but she does not posit an "essence of the people" in the past that may be nostalgically reconstituted in the present (Williams, in Heath and Skirrow, 1986, 7). Flo is the clown who helps us resist such nostalgia. In contrast to the old image of an alma mater, Flo is an entertaining "aspera matera" (a phrase coined by Eleanor Cook in another connection: 1988, 34). Her tartness counterbalances the overpowering sweetness of mass culture – amply represented in Munro's fiction with mountains of candy.

What is important is not only the sheer particularity of Flo's world but also the fact that she is constantly and exuberantly in the act of constructing. Flo's irony is itself ironic, since she (like Isis remaking the penis of Osiris) reinstates and reaffirms the patriarchy even as she appears to challenge it. She threatens to force Rose (who refuses to eat tongue) to live on a diet of "boiled baloney" and when a boy exhibits himself to her, she claims to mistake his penis for a "baloney sausage" (WDY, 11). Flo makes us aware that popular culture is not raw but cooked, not transparent as a sheet of ice but opaque as the preserved turds or the "pickled arseholes" (WDY, 12). Once you can see stories as in the process of production, then you can move towards finding your own tongue and empowering yourself (as Rose does) to participate in that production. The preparation of food becomes a forceful image for the production of meaning and Flo is the most important housekeeper. From inside the house that she keeps, she watches the world around her. The writing on her wall reads "THIS IS MY KITCHEN AND I WILL DO AS I DARNED PLEASE" (WDY, 68). Such freedom is illusory, of course, and that sign is given by Rose as an example of what poverty "meant" (WDY, 67). But meaning is not so easily reduced in this book. The sign is a cliché but Flo's clowning makes it possible for her to reclaim some of the power expressed so defiantly.

The images of enclosure in this book reflect the development of Munro's aesthetic which has now more fully absorbed the reality of an electronic culture and the relation of this to class divisions. Electronic culture blurs many old distinctions and sets up new ones. It is significant, for example, that Flo's place is a combination of store and house that blurs the categories of public and private life. The walls of electronic culture are like the beaverboard partition between bathroom and kitchen in Flo's house and the result is a challenge to the very nature of identity: *Who Do You Think You Are?* Del, retreating to a store room to avoid the last look at Uncle Craig, found old magazines in the baby carriage. Imagine the additional blurring of her isolation if the room had contained a television on which was projected the reproduced image of Uncle Craig's body. Such a fluidity confronts the characters in this book as they seek to define their separate identities. The person who occupies one space (the toilet) must not be acknowledged as the same person who occupies the other space (the kitchen) (see WDY, 4). The person who spoke nonsense in his workshop and the person "who spoke to [Rose] as her father were not the same" (WDY, 4).

These pre-television images communicate a post-television reality. Joshua Meyrowitz argues that the sharing of information systems undermines class division (1985, 5). Munro's stories are a strong qualification of this assumption. Despite the invading images of an electronic culture, her characters continue to have a "sense of place" – both geographic and economic. Munro never turns a blind eye to the realities of power and money; class division is a simple fact in this book. Members of the working class are not depicted, moreover, with contempt. They accept fakes or technological reproduction, for example, in a way that makes them less vulnerable to some illusions than the middle and upper classes. If you assume from the beginning, as Flo does, that maybe somewhere in the world there could be a green plastic swan, then you will be less likely to dream (as Patrick does) of living your life in a "rose garden" (WDY, 83). It will also be more difficult to create out of your origins some nostalgic and genteel essence.

Where Rose comes from is a kind of horror for Patrick but it is, after all, only a house, a construct. "'You would think the place I lived in was a dump,'" (WDY, 75) Rose says to Patrick later, and he does. "'You were right,' said Patrick as they left Hanratty on the bus. 'It is a dump. You must be glad to get away'" (WDY, 87). As Rose is busily getting away, however, her image still flickers on television screens in Hanratty. Every dump, after all, has a television set. Rose's flowery name is like the dew on the dump full of images in Wallace Stevens's "the Man on the Dump": "heads / Of the floweriest flowers dewed with the dewiest dew. / One grows to hate these things except on the dump" (Stevens, 1967, 163). The rose as dead metaphor will be deadheaded in this book so that we will be able to glimpse the rose *as* the rose "(All its images are in the dump)" (Stevens, 1967, 164).

The reproduction of mothering should be seen, I believe, in this startling new context. Flo is only the most highly visible of many mock mothers in this book. Jocelyn, for example, is described as "nurturing" Clifford like a long-suffering mother (WDY, 103). Clifford's seduction of Rose, in turn, looks suspiciously maternal. He "put his arms around her and rocked her . . . 'Oh Rose, Rose baby. Never mind, Rose'" (WDY, 109). Simon is described as speaking "almost maternally" (WDY, 155) and Rose is later cast in the part of a "pseudo-mother" in a television series that concerns "a family, or pseudo-family, of eccentrics and drifters" (WDY, 171). This pseudo-family is a good image for what used to be called the family of man as it has adapted to the electronic culture. The investigation of the mother within that culture must begin by repudiating the notion of some essence of maternity that is sacred and set apart from this world of cultural constructs.

Munro's narrative technique helps us do this. The story of the death of Rose's "real" mother, for example, is a copy of a copy of a copy: "She heard it from Flo, who must have heard it from her father" (WDY, 2). It comes to a stop, deceptively, in the figure of the father, but it is impossible to invest this sad paternal figure with ultimate authority or to blame him for being the "king of the royal beatings" (WDY, 1). The father's writings, on "scraps of paper and torn envelopes," defy all efforts to construct a master pattern. His speech is similarly fragmented. The words hang "clear and nonsensical on the air" but the list is like a shopping list that doesn't work: "'Macaroni, pepperoni, Botticelli, beans – '" (WDY, 4). Baloney or boiled eggs could be added to this list without solving the mystery. Referentiality is challenged by the absurd association of the egg with a blood clot, but the image is also not a metaphor pregnant with meaning. The main focus, rather, is on the act of telling itself. "Her mother had died" – this sentence appears to be written from a third person omniscient point of view. That point of view, however, has already been made profoundly ambiguous by the very first words of the story.

Flo's complicated role in this book is signalled by the fact that the first words of the first story are spoken by her and yet not spoken by her. There are no quotation marks around the phrase that is also lifted up into the title: "*Royal Beating*. That was Flo's promise. You are going to get one Royal Beating" (WDY, l). The absence of quotation marks combines with the odd third-person voice to question Aristotle's famous distinction between history and fiction. History would be one beating that happened and fiction the one kind of beating that happens. In this case, however, the phrase is colloquial and the word *one* is there for emphasis. We will not be given the narration of one, specific beating nor will the beatings combine to represent one mythological story. Neither history nor fiction offer an escape from our own sense of involvement in the story. The more the sly narrator indulges her mock-improvisational imaging of one beating ("Suppose a Saturday, in spring": WDY, 10), the more we feel our own involvement. We are drawn in to play the part of the understood *you*: "[You] suppose a Saturday." This influences our response to what appear to be straightforward items of information: "They lived behind a store in Hanratty, Ontario. There were four of them: Rose, her father, Flo, Rose's young half brother Brian" (WDY, 1).

As the story moves through the telling of the death of the mother, the narrative voice loses its transparency and becomes increasingly opaque. Our eyes follow the voice as if we are following the movement of a blind spot, instead of a movement of increasing vision. The undermining of the fake omniscience and this sense of growing darkness materializes in the image of the hard exterior of an egg – a parody of the egg of infinite potential laid by the Great Goddess (Graves, 1960, 248). Having discarded the symbol of womb as Holy Grail, Munro seems to seek for an alternative image of enclosure and artifice. If you look to Flo for milk or eggs you will find only gall and gallstones. Although one of her fifteen gallstones is "'as big as a pullet's egg'" (WDY, 188), there is no room in it for the old symbolism. Munro reaches back, instead, to restage a revised version of the ancient fool festivals. Willeford cites an East Lancashire Easter custom in which "boys dressed as girls and girls dressed as boys went around accompanied by the 'fool' or 'tosspot' and asked for presents of eggs" (Willeford, 1969, 86). This book can be seen as such a "tosspot" and it is full of fools and eggs. "'Oh Simon, you idiot,'" says Rose, and I think of Simple Simon. The old costumes still seem to fit: Becky Tyde as dwarf-fool; Milton Homer as festival-fool; Ralph Gillespie as court-fool; Flo as Mother Folly.

The figure of the fool challenges old symbols of maternity. Flo implies that Rose's mother is a fool: "when she said that Rose's mother mentioned a hard-boiled egg in her chest she made the comparison sound slightly foolish" (WDY, 2). Rose seeks to represent her mother as a non-fool, but she has "nothing to go on but some egg cups her mother had bought" (WDY, 2) and these empty egg cups are as mocking as the "egg whole." The egg cups, like the pink bowls in "The Peace of Utrecht," cannot bear the burden of too much meaning. Flo's "mobile, monkeyish face" (WYD, 9) will let you know when you have gone too far.

Since the "helplessness" of a mother's face was such a strong image in

"The Ottawa Valley," it is interesting to note that Flo cannot resist "making faces, at herself and others" (WDY, 9). Flo and Rose are like the non-fool looking at the fool in the mirror in Holbein's illustration to Erasmus's *Praise of Folly*. The fool has the expression of a man "attempting to learn something about who or what he is; as he does so, his image seems to stick out its tongue at him" (Willeford, 1969, 35, Plate 8). A similar shock is felt by Rose at the end of "The Beggar Maid," when Patrick, coming upon Rose unawares, makes a face at her, as you might do at the "sudden, hallucinatory appearance of your true enemy" (WDY, 96). Patrick's face is both "infantile" and "savagely warning." Face to face with her television guests, Rose imagines these *"personalities"* wanting, like Patrick, "to make a face. . . . They were longing to sabotage themselves, to make a face or say a dirty word" (WDY, 96–97).

The dialogue of stories that move back and forth between Flo and Rose is a structural acting out of this strange face to face experience of fool and nonfool, infant and mother. Flo and Rose, however, contrast with the clown mother and child act often included in the circus parade. The traditional clown mother is "usually a transvestite man, with babies in a buggy, often twins or triplets, identical with one another and (despite their difference in size) with her" (Willeford, 1969, 177–178). Something of this clownishness invests the figures of Hattie and Mattie Milton, who are mock mothers to the most important fool in this book: Milton Homer. Flo and Rose, however, are different. Theirs is a world of variety and protean disguise, not of identity. What unites them is a shared pleasure in their mutual foolishness as they make faces at each other.

I do hear the fool in Flo, but she is a revised version of the figure of Mother Folly, who (in Willeford's words) "reigned supreme" over the medieval fool festivals.

> The momentary abrogation of the Pope's authority in the joke of the fool festival, allows the representation of the feminine within the cult, the Virgin and the Bride of Christ, to be opened to kinds of femininity that are excluded from that representation. Within the cult, selfless maternal compassion is represented, but jealous rage is not; chastity is represented, but whorishness is not. . . . During the fool festival the walls of the pure feminine vessel admit for a moment the coarse and seemingly chaotic vitality of the Mother Nature to whom the fool belongs.
>
> (Willeford, 1969, 177)

In Munro's carnival, mother and daughter keep each other from collapsing into these old symbols. The mother–daughter dialogue forms the main line of resistance to the old Virgin/Whore binary.

Although Flo enjoys seeing people "brought down to earth" (WDY, 23), she is a parody of an Earth Mother. At an awards ceremony for Rose, Flo's hair is "covered by a thick gray-blue wig, pulled low on her forehead like a woollen cap" and she wears beads that look like "strings of white and yellow popcorn" (WDY, 186). Flo's popcorn that isn't really popcorn and her hair that isn't really hair poses her as a parodic pop-culture version of Ceres, the corn goddess. At the end of the story, Rose brings that same wig to Flo in the County Home and Flo compares it to a "dead gray squirrel" (WDY, 187). When Rose sticks the wig on her own head, "to continue the comedy," Flo laughs so that she rocks "back and forth in her crib" (WDY, 187). Like the image of being tucked in, the image of being rocked is a potent feature of maternal behaviour. Here, however, the old mother–daughter paradigms (including the story of Demeter and Persephone) are undermined by the mutuality of the laughter:

> Mothers and daughters often the same way. It was always in them. Waves of craziness, always rising, irresistible as giggles, from some place deep inside, gradually getting the better of them.
>
> (WDY, 174)

This book is a new kind of comedy that comes "from some place deep inside," not a divine comedy that comes down from above like the pattern of Dante's celestial rose. As we join in the laughter, however, we do well to be wary. There is a fine balance in this book between what is "helpless, involuntary" and what is "boldly calculated" (WDY, 194). That balance is not handed to us by Munro; the reader has to work to perform this part of the circus. We cannot perform at all, however, unless we see Flo – the mother – *as* a performance. To celebrate the end of one beating, and to distract her family from the fact that she has "never heard of the planet Venus," she performs a trick with her body, keeping it "stiff as a board" and turning herself around in the air between two kitchen chairs. Like the imaginary American airship sent up to "rival the heavenly bodies," Flo's artifice competes with Nature.

It is possible to see Flo's stunt as a parody of the Egyptian goddess Nūt (mother of Isis and Osiris) and Barbara Ibronyi's painting (see cover) encourages me to do so. In Egyptian paintings, Nūt is usually represented as a naked woman with an "elongated body arched over the earth" (Ions, 1965, 46–48). Unlike Nūt, Flo is not naked; she has somehow "managed to tuck her dress modestly between her legs" during her stunt (WDY, 20). As a mock-heavenly object, Flo's body is a visible challenge to the symbol of both sky goddess and Earth Mother. "Just as Flo turned herself Rose got a picture in her mind of that airship, an elongated transparent bubble, with its string of diamond lights, floating in the miraculous American sky" (WDY, 20). Her father gets the picture too. "'The planet Venus!' her father said, applauding Flo. 'Ten thousand electric lights!'" (WDY, 20). A string of carnival lights cuts across the mythological allusion and as it does so we experience a domestication of outer space. It becomes the setting for a family circus.

Munro intercepts her mythological allusions while she is in the act of making them. *Flo*, for example, is a cutting from *Flora*. Here, as elsewhere, Munro indicates her suspicion not so much of fiction itself as of the place where fiction hardens into symbol. The birth of Venus and the origin of roses cannot be brought together here, despite the earlier allusion to Botticelli. The egg from the mother's throat cannot be put into the egg cups and the nettles cannot be taken out of Hat Nettleton's name and added to the roses in Patrick's family rose garden. If you follow the bee that buzzes among the cigarette trees in Flo's song (WDY, 10), you may get to the title of the song: "The Big Rock Candy Mountain." You will not, however, gain the strength of Samson or arrive at the perfect commonwealth of bees envisioned by Theocritus. You may end up, instead, with the honey dumper or else with the bee that "buzzed itself to death" (WDY, 174) in the hair of a crazy old woman in "Spelling."

Munro makes an unusually clear distinction here between the two kinds of imitation that have traditionally been confused: the imitation or copy of an object (say a rose) and the imitation or miming of an action (see Sparshott, 1982, 540). Since the mimesis of the object is what tends to harden into symbol, she emphasizes the action. That action, however, is a performance, not a narrative. Patricia Mellencamp has described how performance may undermine and question the enclosing power of narrative (1986, 80–98). Where the symbol of maternity might be in traditional fiction, we here have Flo's physical performance. Flo absorbs and condenses the old myths into her rigid turning body, then reflects them mockingly back to us, daring us to disown them. As readers we are in the uneasy position of the family of the hysteric, whose histrionic behaviour is designed to immobilize the family and turn it into a passive audience.

Flo's entertainment is a diversion that now enables us to enter the dump and examine the entertainment industry that reproduces these images. The best slot to tune in to, if we wish to clarify the moral issues, is Flo's telling of the story of the death of Becky Tyde's father. How does the mock earth mother respond to the image of the male body as surrogate king, sacrificed in so many fertility myths in order to keep the world and the seasons going round? Nature, in these stories, is like a dismembered human body whose shape we cannot quite remember, but is it a male body or a female body? Rose and her friends looked "at the part of Mr. Burns that sagged through the hole" in the outhouse. "For years Rose thought she had seen testicles but on reflection she believed it was only bum. Something like a cow's udder, which looked to have a prickly surface, like the piece of tongue before Flo boiled it" (WDY, 25). Testicles, bum, udder, tongue – this image of a dismembered body is like the "anatomic enumeration of the parts of the body" in medieval carnival (Bakhtin, 1968, 196), but the parts do not form a whole. Burns is the name of a major meat-packing company in Canada. If we process scraps like the name *Burns*, we are more likely to end up with baloney than with a fertility ritual. The image of a dismembered or beaten human body recurs in this book. It does not easily align itself, however, with "the carnival dummy of winter or of the dying year" who is "mocked, beaten, torn to pieces, burned, or drowned" (Bakhtin, 1968, 197). Mr Burns does sing, while defecating, about a green hill on which *"the dear Lord was crucified / Who died to save us all"* (WDY, 24). But the numerous beatings in this book cannot be captured in the cauldron of myth. Although Rose claims, for example, that her own father is "king of the royal beatings" (WDY, 1), he is himself a beaten man who beats her because he sees in her a surfacing of all the "things he had beaten down" in himself (WDY, 45). Rose later remembers how Patrick "beat her" (WDY, 95), but she also imagines wanting to "beat and beat him" (WDY, 92).

Who, then, is the "king of the royal beatings"? Who can we blame for all this violence? Becky Tyde's father is the villain/victim figure whose body – stood up in the snow and beaten bloody – becomes a disturbing focus of our desire to find a villain. "The story being that the father beat them, had beaten all his children and beaten his wife as well, beat Becky more now because of her deformity, which some people believed he had caused (they did not understand about polio)" (WDY, 7). We hear this melodramatic story from the mouth of the clowning mother. Flo reports local speculation that Tyde impregnated his own daughter and then sold the result in his shop: "'They used to say go and get your lamb chops at Tyde's, get them nice and tender!'" (WDY, 7). Flo domesticates this grotesque parody of the slain lamb of God. The making of meaning is again like the preparation of food. The image of cannibalism, however, is just that – a conscious image. We know this from Flo's reluctant admission that these are "'all lies.'"

As always in Munro's fiction, however, we are also aware of the reality that is left out of these lies. Flo's exaggerated telling assumes the immunity of a carnival victim who cannot feel since he is a dummy. The horsewhippers "began to beat him and kept beating him until he fell. They yelled at him, *Butcher's Meat!* and continued beating him while his nightgown and the snow he was lying in turned red" (WDY, 8). Rabelais describes a similar scene, in which a character is "beaten to a pulp . . . pounded into mincemeat," and although "blood spurted from his mouth, nose, ears, and eyes," Bakhtin describes the carnival thrashing as having a "gay character; it is introduced and concluded with laughter" (1968, 201–202).

The laughter in Munro's story is more ironic. This is partly because the beatings multiply to suggest a mechanical, pornographic reproduction of the image that changes the very nature of an action which was once a ritual repetition. Raymond Williams contrasts the time when "drama was important at a festival, in a season" with our own culture, where drama is "habitual experience" (Williams, 1989, 4). Watching is especially problematic when drama is no longer occasional (1989, 3). This fact is a clue to Munro's continued reflections on the conflicts between watching and keeping. Becky Tyde watches "all the way through" as her father is beaten. She watches as one watches television. The role of the clowning stepmother is to give us a grotesquely exaggerated picture of the child-victim. The ironic method asks us to question the image of "the butcher's prisoner, the cripple daughter, a white streak at the window: mute, beaten, impregnated" (WDY, 8). Becky, with her position as ironic watcher, rejects the Dickensian role that would make the child into her father's keeper. Her new role, however, is no more satisfactory.

The multiplied beatings are so consciously put to us as an "entertainment" entitled "Royal Beatings," that we are left with a troubling moral ambiguity. "But the authorities got wind, Flo said. The case came to trial. . . . A farce, said Flo" (WDY, 9). The figure of authority breaking wind is consistent with carnival convention. Where the figure of the father should be in this book we find that collapse of authority which is the precondition of any carnival. Although our sense of the collapse is intensified if we are aware of the impact of electronic culture, the image itself is consistent with classical and biblical mythology. What is unique is Munro's way of positioning the maternal voice and body in relation to that mythology. Female gossip here acts as a domestication of a central dilemma. *Schadenfreude* (pleasure in another's pain) is here spelled out as the very heart of the entertainment industry, an electronic version of the old scapegoat story. A sensational tale is best for a boring winter day. This irony was raised in the story "Postcard" and is now explored in depth.

The place of the collapse of paternal authority in this book is occupied by the usurping stepmother who watches the beating of Rose. In this way Munro's version differs from other rewritings of carnival convention in which the mother is kept on a moral high ground, apart from the degradation. In Robertson Davies's *Fifth Business*, for example, Dunstan Ramsay rescues Mary Dempster by turning her into a fool saint barely distinguishable from the Passchendaele Madonna. She has a snowball's chance in hell of remaining human once Davies brings his Jungian categories down on her. Munro's challenge to the old essentializing mythology is much more radical. Her women are spectators and participants, watchers and keepers. It is Flo who has the power to "put the lid down on the story" (WDY, 9) of Tyde's death. The image is significantly domestic, evoking the kitchen territory of pots and pans.

That's not to say, of course, that the lid could not come off again. It does come off, in a sense, at the end of "Royal Beatings." Rose is in her "apartment kitchen" (WDY, 21) when she hears, on the radio, an interview with Hat Nettleton, one of the men involved in the beating of Tyde. The radio voice makes it impossible for her to remain *apart* in her apartment. She is involved, as we are, and we have to respond without

Flo's authoritative presence. Flo, by this time, has "stopped talking" and sits in a "corner of her crib" at the "Home" (WDY, 22). The disembodied radio voice usurps her authority. Munro's narrative technique, however, has anticipated and acted out that collapse. As the stepmother clowns in the dump our comforting old notions of authority are hurled down to a scatalogical level that cannot be easily seen as a "fruitful earth" (Bakhtin, 1968, 21). "Flo said further that Cora had no father, you might wonder what her mother worked at, and who was her grandfather? The honey-dumper!" (WDY, 36). A direct narration could have read this way: "Flo said, 'Cora has no father.'" The indirect narration mimes the collapse of authority. If we search for a paternal origin of narrative, we will find "no father." All we have to go on is the filtered and repeated act of storytelling.

CORA AS MADONNA: ROSE PLAYS DEAD

Had Rose been able or willing to play the part of Patrick's madonna – either as beggar maid or white goddess – then this book could have been a domestic comedy miming a divine comedy, ending with the ringing of wedding bells and the integration of society. Her rebellion spells the collapse of that kind of comedy. Patrick and Rose, instead, are seen as playing out a power struggle that replicates a mother–child relationship. While Rose suffers herself to be nearly stifled by an absurd mother hen – Dr Henshawe – Patrick, in turn, seeks mothering in Rose. Dorothy Dinnerstein's account of infantilism is apt. Patrick pays "heavily hostile, costly, magic homage to the original magic protector; not to woman herself but an abstraction of woman as captive goddess of an archaic realm" (Dinnerstein, 1976, 205). Patrick, in fact, admits that Rose reminds him of *The White Goddess* and of "The Beggar Maid." Like the Duke in Browning's "My Last Duchess," Patrick points out to visitors his sculpture of Neptune – with the difference of a fig-leaf (WDY, 116). But this beggar maid, like the last duchess, resists framing and possession. When Rose looks it up in the Library, she cannot fit herself into the picture of "milky surrender." She imagines Patrick bringing her a "huge egg, maybe, of solid silver" and "begging her to take some of the weight of it off him" (WDY, 77). Rose's refusal to carry the crushing burden of that egg is a matter of survival. The only way to survive death as a madonna is to play dead.

Since the madonna is revealed in these stories as a dead metaphor, it is appropriate that we should find her posing in a coffin. Here is a fertility rite with a difference: "When things were flowering – lilacs, apple trees, hawthorns along the road – they had the game of funerals" (WDY, 33). Donna, Cora, and Bernice play the part of triple goddess. Each has a name that suggests the mother–daughter relation in some way: Donna is a fragment of Madonna; Cora is the daughter of Demeter; Bernice is a martyr often confused with Veronica, a name associated with icons and with the woman who captured the face of Christ on a cloth (Withycombe, 1977, 288). Each of the three girls gets her "chance to be dead" (WDY, 33), which is a chance to escape from the burden of being herself. Flo's insistence that Cora has a mustache is like graffiti scrawled on the face of the Mona Lisa, mocking our rigid gender distinctions. The madonna, thus defaced, is a challenge to the very *being* of the woman. Rose "wanted to be Cora, now. . . . Trying to *be* her" (WDY, 32). Cora, in a brief moment of reciprocation, mirrors this feeling back to her: "'That's a pretty name, Rose. I like it. I like it better than Cora. I hate Cora'" (WDY, 32). Self-disgust is the basis of this love; Rose sees her hand, held in Cora's hands, as a "small, disgusting object" (WDY, 32).

Like a mockery of elegiac form, Rose mourns over the body of Cora. "She lay heaped with flowers, lilac, and wore her rose crepe dress" (WDY, 33). In her rose dress, Cora plays back to Rose a death contained in Rose's name. The game is a parody of ancient stories like *Snow White* and *Sleeping Beauty*, in which a woman appears to be dead but is in fact alive. Munro poses a situation in which the old subject–object split (with the body of the woman as object) is replaced by shared subjectivity. Rose wanting to *be* Cora and Cora wanting to *be* a Rose is an "indelible folly" (WDY, 33) by means of which Munro resists the bleakness of Rose just being. "By being," Brownstein notes, the rose

> inspires ennobling, enabling love. Her whole business is to be. The story of the *Roman de la Rose* is the Lover's story; the Rose is his objective. It is her nature to guard herself; by being what she is she tests his mettle; her glory is that she is unattainable, his glory that he desires to attain her.
>
> (Brownstein, 1982, 35)

In her mock-death Cora, too, is a parody of the love-object as unattainable ideal. The fact that only girls play the game of funerals becomes a means of questioning a gender-based subject–object split. These girls insist on a mortality and a subjectivity that Robert Graves denies to his white goddess. "Man is a demi-god," Graves argues, "he always has either one foot or the other in the grave; woman is divine because she can keep both her feet always in the same place, whether in the sky, in the underworld, or on this earth" (Graves, 1960, 110). Referring to *Snow White* and *Sleeping Beauty*, Graves concludes that the "deaths are therefore mock-deaths only – for the Goddess is plainly immortal – and are staged" (Graves, 1960, 421).

Munro's staging, however, is effective because we are aware that woman too has one foot in the grave. This dethroning of the old Muse has important implications for Munro's generic innovations. It is impossible to reconstitute the original folktales with the bits we are given. There is a wicked stepmother, a witch who threatens poisoning, a dwarf, and several sleeping beauties. The body of the text cannot be made whole, however, because the bodies of these woman are mortal. They will decompose, making both gender and genre as unstable and fragile as the words *Mother* and *Father* on the tombstones in "The Ottawa Valley." In the meantime, however, the circus must go on, but the performance keeps undermining the narrative. Rose makes up "stories of danger and rescue, accidents and gratitude. Sometimes she rescued Cora, sometimes Cora rescued Rose" (WDY, 32). Taking turns at playing prince and princess in this way is crucial to Munro's parody. Rose, with the candy for Cora "tucked into the elastic top of her underpants," presses her arms "tightly against her waist to hold everything in place" (WDY, 34). This phantom pregnancy is transparently ridiculous and Rose knows very well that what she is doing is "clownish, unlucky." Cora, similarly, turns into what Flo terms a "monster of fat" – another kind of mock pregnancy.

However absurd these games are, they are liberating in the sense that they render clownishly visible the icons and symbols which threaten, when invisible, to fix and destroy women's lives. Munro's clothing imagery works in a similar way. When Cora later joins the air force and her body ends up "bunched into their dreadful uniform," Rose is "not much bothered by this loss, this transformation" (WDY, 36). She simply speculates that Cora's personality "could not survive the loss of her elegant dresses." The dresses, in any case, were not Cora's. Cora's name, like her clothing, is a castoff. Munro makes it impossible for us to equate Cora's mother with Demeter. Cora's mother may inhabit another world, but the clothing she sends into the story from that realm is historically encoded.

> Perhaps she worked as a maid, and she was able to send castoffs. Cora had plenty of clothes. She came to school in fawn-colored satin, rippling over the hips; in royal-blue velvet with a rose of the same material flopping from one shoulder; in dull rose crepe loaded with fringe.
>
> (WDY, 30)

As the blue rose and the rose crepe suggest, Rose's own name forms a part of this costuming. Cora's mother is simply in our blind spot, living in a historical context which we may deduce from these clothes.

Munro's use of these names is an example of what Kaja Silverman refers to as "thrift-shop dressing." The name Rose is a "visible way of acknowledging that its wearer's identity has been shaped by decades of representational activity, and that no cultural project can ever 'start from zero'" (Silverman, 1986, 151). Munro's thriftiness is not simply condensation but also resistance. The problem cannot be resolved by simply introducing the boys to the girls' game and thus turning phantom pregnancy into real pregnancy. The body of Franny negates that solution. The "sartorial strategy" as defined by Silverman remains on a decorative level; Munro, however, gives it a structural application with her deliberately failed rewriting of a romance of the Rose. "A beautiful virgin walled off from an imperfect real world is the central figure in romance" – this is Rachel Brownstein's encapsulation of the story (1982, 35). Munro alludes obliquely to that story when Patrick's mother shows Rose the rose garden, which has "many low stone walls," walls built by Patrick: "'He built all these walls'" (WDY, 83). The life of Rose in the traditional romance must be "passed in staring at the bare insides of garden walls" (Brownstein, 1982, 36). Munro rereads the ancient romance by changing the point of view. Brownstein's words are so apt that they seem to refer to this book:

> Love or life, from the Rose's point of view, can hardly seem a perilous quest to be validated and ended by the capture of a reward. What is it, then? A confinement terminated by release? an ordeal of solitary waiting? a spectator sport? a pain or a luxury?
>
> (Brownstein, 1982, 35)

We are aware of these implied questions as Patrick mobilizes the structure by reaching out for Rose. The moment of Rose's acquiescence to the strangling pattern is one of the bleakest in Munro's fiction.

But "The Beggar Maid," like "Princess Ida," is an abortive novel. Munro has rewritten the old romance of the rose, scripting a new and active role for the woman to play. Adapting the Pygmalion myth, we might imagine this as the coming to life of the madonna. This humanizing process cannot happen within the old generic boundaries. The rose traditionally symbolizes completion and perfection but here Rose challenges the very notion of a centre. "'I'm Rose,'" says Rose to Flo when Flo does not recognize her and the failure of mother–daughter recognition overwhelms the old romance structure. These stories cannot be construed as making up concentric circles like Dante's celestial rose. They form something more like an encircling spider web from which the woman must extricate herself in order to be, to construct herself as a subject rather than as the object of somebody else's desire or worship. Barbara Clarke Mossberg (writing about Stein's "The Autobiography of a Rose") sees Stein's famous saying as a picture of entrapment in what she calls the "daughter-construct." Each repetition

> constitutes a possible moment of freedom in which this rose can be or become something else. . . . But there is a letdown as the rose reappears: rose again, always rose, rose forever. The case is hopeless if one values growth or change.
>
> (Mossberg, 1985, 200)

Munro's Rose, by contrast, does repeatedly – as an actor – "become something else." Her growth is not the end result of an old quest pattern, but of her performances at this winter carnival.

The madonna may look like an ice sculpture but when Patrick kisses the "snowy face" (WDY, 79), he finds a "corner of her mouth" that is flesh and blood. There is a rare moment of tenderness as Patrick and Rose wrestle in the snow, like winter sculptures come to life. It cannot last, however, and we know this because he is bewildered by her irony when she addresses him as her "White God" (WDY, 78). Patrick has not, after all, read *The White Goddess*. He is more at the mercy of its contents than he would have been had he read it. It's only a book that he owns and he thinks of owning Rose when he looks at the title (WDY, 78). The competent reader, however, is encouraged to make better use of the library. If we do, we may observe Patrick in the act of reassembling his madonna, each time Rose shatters it. The wintry setting of this book beguilingly helps us to resist the temptation to walk into his hothouse of roses. Munro makes no specific reference to roses in Dante, Yeats, Shakespeare, Joyce, or the Bible. She doesn't need to. Thrift is the name of this game. Teresa de Lauretis comments (with reference to Eco's *The Name of the Rose*), that

> the very term *rose* . . . is so dense with literary allusions, references, and connotations that it no longer has any, and thus appears to refer to what Baudrillard has called the implosion of meaning: a rose is a rose is a rose is a black hole, as it were.
>
> (de Lauretis, 1987, 58)

Munro does not, however, allow her stories to vanish into this black hole. When the madonna plays dead, the old roses are deadheaded. The act of playing or clowning makes a space for real growth and change. Munro's winter carnival does not simply re-enact the old story that Robert Graves said was the one and only story of the waxing and waning year. She constructs, instead, performances that go against the grain of the old narratives, piling up mountains of Canadian snow to act as a mock obstruction. The very sound of "*snows*, a poetic-sounding word" (WDY, 59) is ominous when used by the mock father in "Wild Swans," all the more so when it echoes an image sung by Flo (who is mimicking an undertaker/seducer): "*Her brow is like the snowdrift / Her throat is like the swan*" (WDY, 57). These hackneyed images are re-invested with an uncanny power. Against that power Munro sets the conscious cliché of a harsh Canadian climate. The most explicit inversion of the *Romance of the Rose* pattern occurs in "Providence." Here the snowstorm replaces the medieval labyrinth surrounding and protecting the rose. The quest pattern is inverted: it is Rose who hunts her man, whose name is Tom Shepherd, recalling both the "big striped Tom" (LGW, 227) and Flo's wall motto: "THE LORD IS MY SHEPHERD" (WDY, 68). When the blizzard blocks the path to Shepherd, Rose is relieved of the burden of making the pattern happen. The resulting moment of tenderness with her daughter allows us a glimpse of alternative ways of making a "progress of love." We begin to understand, perhaps, that the progress of love will be made possible only if we think of the old patterns, like the madonna herself, as made out of snow.

FRANNY AS HARLOT: RELATIONS PERFORMING

As we unpeal the onion-like layers of Munro's structural quotations, we are led into the very heart of that labyrinthian structure which was, traditionally, emblematized by the petals of a rose. I have deliberately mixed the metaphor to suggest that Munro questions the very concept of "heart." In *Heart of Darkness* the Intended waits in the margins for the return of the male quester. When the figure of the woman is, like the rose, at the centre it is even more problematic. Is she a goddess or is she a victim prostituted for our pleasure? Is she the object of worship or of torture? Like an actor refusing to play a stellar Hollywood role when it is offered, Rose (after refusing the part of the madonna) is left playing many varying parts. We become acutely conscious of her own power and responsibility with relation to those in the story who play other parts. We can see this most clearly if we imagine Rose saying "I am Franny" instead of "I am Cora" or "I am Rose." The whore is an image for a moral dilemma that is inseparable from Munro's radical disruption of traditional narrative patterns. Over and over again her narrators confront the need to avoid prostituting their subjects as Hugo prostitutes Dotty in "Material." At the deepest level of Munro's writing is her constant awareness that a writer, in the act of writing, is *using* people. Munro positions the act of prostitution in such a way as to diffuse but not defuse the moral issues that we normally like to package into the figure of the whore – the better to condemn and dismiss them.

W.J. Keith is particularly offended by the closing scene of "Mischief," in which Rose and Clifford have intercourse with "Jocelyn looking on, almost cheering from the side-lines" (Keith, 1989, 158). He faults Munro for "covertly defending (or at the very least refusing openly to condemn) an action that seems irresponsible and even repellant" (Keith, 1989, 159) and insists that the reader must make a "firm moral judgement" (158), one that puts us at a moral distance from Munro. But Munro herself (although she never fixes a moral judgement) is at a considerable distance from Rose here. Clifford and Rose using each other is explicitly and ironically placed in the context of Jocelyn's triumphant conclusion: "'We're Consumers! And it's Okay!'" (WDY, 131). Rose is "too sluggish to reach for" that level where she feels "appalled and sad," but surely the reader is urged not to be so sluggish a consumer. Our position as voyeurs of the voyeuristic Jocelyn is extremely uncomfortable. Shortie makes use of Franny while Rose watches, as Clifford makes use of Rose while Jocelyn watches. What is the difference? One difference is that Rose also uses Clifford. Another difference is in the size of the audience. Franny is prostituted in both a literal and a literary sense. She is used not only by Shortie for sexual release but also by the group for purposes of entertainment and distraction.

It is tempting to see the body of Franny, the object of repeated assault, as some kind of symbol for an aesthetic rejected by Munro:

> The use Shortie was making of her, that others made, would continue. She would get pregnant, be taken away, come back and get pregnant again, be taken away, come back, get pregnant, be taken away again. There would be talk of shutting her up, when she died suddenly of pneumonia, solving the problem.

(WDY, 26)

As we watch Rose watching this performance we are put into a dilemma that is not unlike the one we experience as voyeurs of the scene in "Mischief." Here, however, the challenge is more explicit. The challenge is to avoid turning Franny into a symbol, a figure, a metaphor. In order to meet that challenge, we must find a connection between Franny and Rose that does not dissolve them into metaphor. We cannot say that Rose *is* Franny. Rose does not even love Franny. Rose herself sees no connection: "An act performed on Franny had no general significance, no bearing on what could happen to anyone else. It was only further abuse" (WDY, 27).

Rose's *refusal* to identify with Franny is the first step in the process of humanizing the sister-whore. Franny is *not* a symbol for the victimization that happens to Rose and other women within the symbolic order. Munro leads us into the heart of a labyrinthian structure which has prostituted women, but we have no hope of developing resistance to that structure if we indulge in a glib homogenizing process that makes victims of all women. Rose cannot *be* Franny any more than she can *be* Cora. Rose thinks of Franny when she "comes across the figure of an idiotic, saintly whore, in a book or a movie," but she thinks of Franny not because Franny fits the picture but because the picture *leaves Franny out*. Franny is relentlessly real. She is not a metaphor for anything. *Who* she thinks she is outside this figure we do not know but we know *that* she is and we know it because of what we do not see, because she is raped in Rose's blind spot. Munro refuses to represent Franny as a "figure" during the assault. She allows Franny a voice: she "let out howls, made ripply, phlegmy, by her breathing problems" (WDY, 26). During the performance, Franny keeps "jerking one leg. Either the shoe had come off, or she had not been wearing shoes to start with. There was her white leg and bare foot, with muddy toes – looking too normal, too vigorous and self-respecting, to belong to Franny McGill" (WDY, 27). Franny is allowed to exist by Munro's refusal to represent her as a totality. "That was all of her Rose could see." Franny cannot stop her rape, but her jerking leg refuses and is, for that reason, "self-respecting." Munro's affirmations of moral integrity do not come in grand statements but in such small self-repecting refusals to yield.

Ruby Carruthers is another example. She sits on the veranda steps, "with the dirt from underneath all over her clothes and in her hair" and refuses the offer of a cigarette or cupcakes. She draws a "self-respecting" limit by insisting: "'I think I got a right to know who I'm doing it with'" (WDY, 42). She is the victim of a practical joke within the story that Rose tells Flo about "'those jokers'" (WDY, 14). We may join Flo in seeing the joke as entertainment, thus prostituting Ruby, or we may give her our respect, thus allowing her to escape the imprisoning fiction. We are not enouraged to sentimentalize Ruby – she is a "slutty sort of girl" who seems (unlike Franny) to welcome the boys who use her. While Del looks for Ruby in the house, Horse is getting her "to do it" under the veranda. When he is finished with Ruby, Horse goes in search of Del "not to enlighten him but to see how the joke was working, this being the most important part of the proceedings, as far as Horse was concerned" (WDY, 41). With this casual comment, Ruby is eliminated. In the male telling she is not even allowed to exist as the primary victim of the practical joke. Rose's telling reinstates her as victim but it does more than that for the reader. Ruby's first protest (when she hears footsteps above her) is reported by Rose: "Said Ruby, who is that? And Runt said, oh, that's only Horse Nicholson. *Then who the hell are you?* said Ruby" (WDY, 41). Her protest recapitulates the question of identity posed in the title of this collection. It does so, however, with an irony that escapes both Flo and Rose. Flo's exclamation, twice repeated, is to say: "'*Jesus Murphy!*'" (WDY, 41). But Ruby is neither Bride of Christ nor Whore of Babylon. We know this from the part of the story that Rose does not tell Flo. "Rose did not bother with the rest of the story" (WDY, 42). The "rest of the story" is given to the reader by the narrator behind Rose's back. Ruby's refusal to smoke or eat with the jokers is information we may use as we take up our positions with relation to this "entertainment." In simply having listened to the story – even if we did not crack a smile – we have been compromised. The implied moral questions are painfully ambiguous by comparison with the judgements made by the storytellers: "'She'll get what she deserves,' said Flo philosophically" (WDY, 42).

In all her representations of whores, Munro's method leads us to a confrontation with our own participation. The issue always revolves around the questions of use. It is a hackneyed story. "'Hackneyed,'" says a character in the later "Hard-Luck Stories": "'That's a word you don't often hear'" (MJ, 195). The word is taken from the Old French meaning "an ambling horse or mare, especially for ladies to ride on." It may also refer to a "woman that hires her person, a prostitute" (*OED*). This etymology traces the connection made by Munro between the characters of women who are used and the responsibility of the writer who uses words. The word Rose, for example, is hackneyed – "worn out, like a hired horse, by indiscriminate or vulgar use" (*OED*). Flo and Rose project their own fear of helplessness onto the body of Ruby Carruthers. Franny's "self-respecting" leg and Ruby's self-respecting words are there to make us aware of the otherness of these women, of the reality that is not included in the representation. That reality, however, is not sentimentalized. There is no question that these women are severely constricted in their freedom, if not utterly helpless. Ruby has a "bad squint." Under the veranda, the shadows are so deep that she cannot see at all. This image of partial vision indicates that we have not yet come to see the full extent of our dilemma.

ROSE AS ORPHAN: INVASION, AND WELCOME

We begin to understand the full force of the dilemma if we observe how the figure of the prostitute often blurs into that of the child. Becky Tyde is a kind of mock-child – a "town oddity and public pet" (WDY, 8). She is a "big-headed loud-voiced dwarf, with a mascot's sexless swagger, a red velvet tam, a twisted neck that forced her to hold her head on one side, always looking up and sideways" (WDY, 6). This kind of prostitution may be sexless but it does require human bodies. The description of the wry neck not only recalls Del's performance in "Changes and Ceremonies" (LGW, 139) but also is repeated when we are told that Flo, while telling "lurid" stories about Becky's father, "would incline her head" (WDY, 7). Becky behaves as if it is her "duty to be always on display" (WDY, 5) and the need for such a public display is by no means unique to Hanratty. Enid Welsford describes the custom of keeping dwarf-fools (Welsford, 1935, 58). Ivan the Terrible and Peter the Great, for example, "surrounded themselves with dwarfs and fools and grotesques of every description" (Welsford, 1935, 186).

Since Rose eventually puts herself on public display as a television actor, it is useful to read with particular care those parts of the book that deal with her initiation into that role. The story called "Wild Swans" ends with an expression of Rose's yearning to be a movie star. By means of an odd analogy, Munro sets up a scenario that enables us to examine the inner workings of our popular culture as they might look from the point of view of the prostituted orphan-fool. In its original published form, the story was subtitled "The Dirty Old Man of the Imagination" (*Toronto Life*, April 1978). It's not hard to see why Munro abandoned the subtitle; the sensational surface details of the story could be easily misread. This story is a kind of mock allegory. The domes and towers seen by Rose when she "comes" to Toronto may be briefly seen as merging with the radiant domes in Yeats's Byzantium poems – but only briefly. The illusion lasts only for as long as a good orgasm. The story is basically anti-apocalyptic. The site is that of the Canadian National Exhibition and the apotheosis is as suspect as the exhibition of Art to Del in the earlier book. The literary echoes are loud in this story but in the end Munro's version of Yeats's "Leda and the Swan" is powerfully parodic.

In the story, Rose travels alone (for the first time) on a train to Toronto. A strange man who claims to be a United Church minister sits down beside her. Under cover of his newspaper, his hand invades her and brings her to orgasm. Rose takes her pleasure and we have to think twice before judging her for that. Tania Modleski, thinking about women and mass culture, argues that women have been "denied access to pleasure while simultaneously being scapegoated for seeming to represent it. . . . At the very least, we might like to experience more of it before deciding to denounce it" (Modleski, 1986, 164). Rose's orgasm is a place in this book where Munro presents this dilemma. Rose's pleasure is represented to the reader in such a way that we become implicated in her compromise. The first words of the story alert us to danger:

> Flo said to watch out for White Slavers. She said this was how they operated: an old woman, a motherly or grandmotherly sort, made friends while riding beside you on a bus or train. She offered you candy, which was drugged. Pretty soon you began to droop and mumble, were in no condition to speak for yourself. Oh, Help, the woman said, my daughter (granddaughter) is sick, please somebody help me get her off so that she can recover in the fresh air. Up stepped a polite gentleman, pretending to be a stranger, offering assistance. Together, at the next stop, they hustled you off the train.

> (WDY, 55)

To become a white slave – to be thus sold into prostitution – first involves destruction of the mother–daughter relationship. Flo's almost casual threat also conjures up an image of the destruction of self: "You wouldn't want to go home, then, maybe couldn't remember home, or find your way if you did" (WDY, 55). The image is similar to Jeanette's experience in "Marrakesh": "Another thing likely to happen was that Rose would get her purse stolen."

In Flo's story, the villains are identified: "watch out for White Slavers" she says. The clear identification of moral turpitude, however, is immediately blurred by the disguisings within disguisings. A trickster mock-mother lures the mock-daughter into white slavery and this seduction recalls the song sung by Flo in "Royal Beatings." According to "Haywire Mac" McClintock (the busker who claimed to have written the song), the *"soda-water fountains"* and *"cigarette trees"* of the "Big Rock Candy Mountain" (WDY, 10) were used as a sales-pitch by tramps "to snare a kid to do their begging and pander to their perversions" (McClintock, quoted by Leisy, 1966, 27). The "hobo pied piper" (Leisy, 1966, 27) in Flo's scenario, however, is not a dirty old tramp but a mock mother who offers drugged candy to her victim. Candy is a recurring image in

Munro's fiction and when it is offered as a gift it is especially problematic. If this were a traditional winter carnival, wine would flow freely and if this were a traditional temptation scene, we would have an apple. What we have, instead, is women secretly indulging in sweets. Rose gorges herself on chocolate to comfort herself in "the Beggar Maid" and steals candy for Cora in "Privilege." In this story she is caught in the act of stealing pleasure: "But what harm in that, we say to ourselves at such moments, what harm in any thing, the worse the better, as we ride the cold wave of greed, of greedy assent" (WDY, 63). Unlike wine (which may symbolize blood), candy does not mean anything. Rose's orgasm, she wants to insist, just *is*.

What, then, is the significance of Rose's pleasure and how does the woman compromise herself? "Pleasure (or 'comfort' or 'solace') remains the enemy for the postmodernist thinker," Modleski points out, "because it is judged to be the means by which the consumer is reconciled to the prevailing cultural policy, or the 'dominant ideology'" (Modleski, 1986, 158). What is compromised, in a sense, is the very idea of an autonomous identity, and this compromise is most evident from Flo's part in the seduction. Rose cannot stop getting "Flo's messages" even when she gets to Union Station, but Flo's messages assume a fluid identity. The story about Flo's friend Mavis leads to a confusing proliferation of names. Here the act of disguising is repeated in a way that illuminates the significance of the earlier disguises. Frances Farmer, Florence Farmer, Flo, Mavis – all are disguises that are as false as the "black and mother-of-pearl" cigarette holder used by Mavis. Rose likes to imagine herself indulging in such transformations of identity, "preposterous adventures" undertaken in her own but "newly named skin" (WDY, 64). This desire translates, in vulgar terms, into her desire to be a movie star. On a more subtle level, however, it suggests that Rose's experience on the train has, in some way, involved a similar dissolving of identity. Rose's coming dramatizes a question put by Derrida in "Coming Into One's Own." We must think of autobiography, he argues, in an "entirely new way" when every autobiography "is the going out and the coming back of a fort; da, e.g. this fort; da. But which one?" (Derrida, 1978, 136).

Which one indeed, I wonder, as Rose comes into Toronto. The identity of the molester is as fluid as that of the victim: "Watch out, Flo said as well, for people dressed up as ministers. They were the worst" (WDY, 55). Flo's warning is prophetic but her very accuracy is ironic. The people dressed up as mothers and the people dressed up as ministers are obviously equally dangerous.

The question becomes absurdly epistemological as Rose wonders whether or not it is a hand. In between the lines Kant and Locke engage in a playful wrangle as she speculates: "What if it is a hand? . . . But what if it was a hand? What if it really was a hand?" (WDY, 61). She concludes: "It was. It was a hand. It was a hand's pressure" (WDY, 61). With the epistemological question settled, we confront the ethical question. His imagined reality is at war with hers: "She could not insist that it was there, when he seemed to be insisting that it was not. How could she declare him responsible, when he lay there so harmless" (WDY, 61). His outward appearance of harmlessness recalls that of Art Chamberlain in *Lives of Girls and Women*. Where we might expect an assault, we now have a man who is like a ridiculous male inversion of a sleeping beauty. His eyes are closed as his hand performs. Her eyes are open, looking out of the window. When he stands up afterwards, he is seen to be lacking in "ordinary grown-up masculinity," his face is "pink and shiny" and his manner "crude and pushy and childish" (WDY, 64). His babyishness puts the moral question of responsibility back to us at just the point where we want to condemn the villain. And yet (it *was* a hand, after all) we cannot conclude that Rose has done it to herself.

This spiritual father, then, is another absurd candidate for the king of the royal beatings. It is her desire for pleasure that makes Rose complicitous with his aims but it is also a desire for a loss of the burdensome need to construct herself as a subject: "She had a considerable longing to be somebody's object. Pounded, pleasured, reduced, exhausted" (WDY, 61). In the act of submitting Rose escapes the need to write autobiography, to construct herself as a subject. The child that is beaten in "Royal Beatings" here becomes the wandering orphan but her eyes, like those of the narrator in "Images," are burned out Orphan Annie eyes that reflect a world made up of her own desires: "Her imagination seemed to have created this reality, a reality she was not prepared for at all" (WDY, 61).

The imagination has not, however, totally eliminated the real world. Rose goes into this with her eyes open. The minister "would not lift his eyelids" but Rose is in an inbetween world, a threshold where the actual and the imaginary may meet (to borrow words from Hawthorne's famous definition of romance). As long as her legs are crossed, Rose can "lay claim to innocence" and may even be associated with the medieval iconography that associates crossed legs with virginity. As Rose's legs open, however, we also note that her eyes are open: "Her legs were never going to open. / But they were. They were. As the train crossed the Niagara Escarpment above Dundas, as they looked down at the preglacial valley . . . she would make this slow, and silent, and definite, declaration" (WDY, 63). Inside this snaky train, Rose is also travelling inside the very structure of a phallocratic society. But she is not blind and what she sees is a kind of map of Ontario. This may account for the fact that Joseph Gold concludes "Rose's orgasm blows up Ontario" (1984, 8).

Ontario, alas, comes back. Munro's strong sense of place here becomes a means of resisting the "popular visions" which threaten to turn the "painted domes and pillars" of the "Exhibition Grounds" into a vision of a new Jerusalem. The proper nouns act as barriers, making it impossible to dissolve the constructed world into the natural pleasure of sex. "Victim and accomplice she was borne past Glassco's Jams and Marmalades, past the big pulsating pipes of oil refineries" (WDY, 63). The painted domes float "marvelously against her eyelids rosy sky," suggesting that her eyes are closed. This sleeping beauty, however, is just pretending – like the man who ministers to her.

Let's not deny the pleasure. It is like being asleep and yet being awake enough to enjoy being asleep; like having your eyes closed and yet being able to see through the "eyelids' rosy sky." The word *rosy* here and the suggestion of rose-coloured glasses, hint at the danger in this to the identity of Rose which is now powerfully invaded by the dirty old man of the imagination. "Invasion, and welcome, and sunlight flashing far and wide on the lake water; miles of bare orchards stirring around Burlington" (WDY, 63). The stirring of the orchards reminds us that we are "traveling south, out of the snow belt, into an earlier spring, a tenderer sort of landscape" which is "as different from home as the coast of the Mediterranean would be" (WDY, 63).

The images of renewal associated with spring, however dubious, are also almost impossible to resist – particularly in the context of a book so often snowed in. At the same time, however, we suspect the freshness of spring; it is aligned with the false mother who asks for "fresh air" for her daughter and with the minister's feeling "refreshed" after ministering to Rose. Spring may be just another trick, we suspect. And yet something does stir, however guiltily, and his hand is able "after all, to get the ferns to rustle and the streams to flow, to waken a sly luxuriance" (WDY, 62). This image of an awakening, moreover, is repeated when the conductor (after the orgasm) passes through the train "to stir the travelers, warn them back to life" (WDY, 63). There is a sense of betrayal at the heart of this spring but we feel it, at an intensely intimate level, as a self-betrayal. Just here, I think, is where we experience the limited affirmation of the carnival, with its promise of seasonal renewal. Here too we may glimpse some of the reasons why Munro seems to opt, instead, for the physical performances that characterize circuses.

Like the child-victims of the hobo pied piper, Rose is implicitly urged to read the signs of danger by decoding the hidden messages. At this stage, however, she is a paralyzed reader. The newspaper that is draped over her lap hides her pleasure but is no text for her. It provides no guide to the reality outside the window, just as the spiritual father offers no authority. Flo and the minister, in fact, are a mocking parody of mother and father. The minister's earlier description of the wild swans invades and fathers Rose's vision at the moment when she would appear to be abandoning herself to simple pleasure. The ironic title is a sign that the orgasm is not a place in this book where the reader can relax in a place called nature. If that were the case, the birds should at least be Canada geese. The wild swan image is like a conscious literary trick; the mock mother conspires with the mock father to make a fool of Rose. With Flo's opening warnings in mind, we cannot reduce this story to an Oedipal scenario. When there was still time for more resistance, the "solution, so obvious and foolproof, did not occur to her." Rose did not think of acting, of whispering *"Excuse me"* and setting his hand "firmly on his knee" (WDY, 61). What Rose discovers, in fact, is that there is no "foolproof" solution. When Flo put her on the train, she cracked jokes which had Rose as the butt of humour. Those jokes made no impression on the conductor. At this deeper level, however, mock mother and mock father have made a fool of Rose. With her knowledge of the trick, Rose is cut free, orphaned.

MILTON HOMER AS PUPPET: FOOLING AROUND WITH THE AUTHOR

I have suggested in earlier chapters that Munro's response to her vividly conceived dilemma is to abdicate and that the figure of the puppet may be seen as a kind of autograph at the site of abdication. Miss Farris in *Lives of Girls and Women* (a puppet wound up by *con brio*) and the puppet Alicia in "Something I've Been Meaning To Tell You" are earlier examples of this visible abdication. In this book there are several characters who take on a version of the puppet role. Each of their performances sketches out a poetic space which challenges the cyclical narratives of carnival. One is the old woman in the story, "Spelling." The Crafts Center at the Wawanash County Home is a mocking version of an artist's studio. It is located on the first floor of the Home, where the old people who are still "bright and tidy" are busy painting pictures, making rag-dolls, constructing snowmen out of Styrofoam balls – "with sequins for eyes" (WDY, 182). The old woman is not found on this level. There are inmates "whose tongues lolled, whose limbs shook uncontrollably." Although this recalls the image of the victim of Parkinson's Disease, the old woman is not on this level either. It is on the third level that Rose confronts the old woman. She is a grotesquely exaggerated version of the dying mother in "The Ottawa Valley." She has lost full control of her muscles. She has "lost much of the power to shape sounds. What she said seemed not to come from her mouth or her throat, but from deep in her lungs and belly" (WDY, 183).

Deep inside the belly of an old woman: this seems to be a good image for the place of origin in *Who Do You Think You Are?* The oblique but powerful references to Parkinson's Disease link the new emphasis on circus performance to Munro's repeated exploration of maternal figures. It is this slight but tough connection to referentiality that prevents Munro from taking the image of the maternal belly in a primitivist direction. It may be possible to challenge old chronologies with what Mary Daly has termed a "crone-ology" (Daly, 1978, 16; quoted by Godard, 1984, 46), but such a method will inevitably take us back to a rereading of the old histories. The quest for our origins keeps leading back to the act of constructing and the old woman is engaged in such an act. However minimal her activity, it is a reduced and condensed image of the artist at work. The old crone is a performer and she has an audience. Her reproductions are less intricate than those in the Crafts Center and this enables us to observe as the activity is performed in slow motion. She bends "all her energies to master" each word (WDY, 184) as Munro bends her energies, in these stories, to master the reality that comes out to meet her. The nurse invites her performance as if it were a freak show at the circus. I am reminded of Lucky's speech in Beckett's *Waiting for Godot*. "'Hello Aunty. . . . You're spelling today.'" When the woman reproduces the word *weather*, she strains "forward, grunting to get the word" and Rose thinks "she might be going to have a bowel movement. 'W-E-A-T-H-E-R'" (WDY, 183). Although Munro appears to use the words *carnival* and *circus* almost interchangeably, this performance in fact helps to understand how a circus stunt makes a poetic space within which to question the narrative patterns of carnival.

Although Rose finds this old crone on the top level of the County Home, the associations of her art, thus drastically minimalized, are with the lower part of the body. What is normally relegated to the lower levels of art is here given, by carnival license, a priority. By using the word "Spelling" as her title, Munro aligns the old woman's activity with her own activity – the spelling out of the details of this story. Because the woman's humanity is so concentrated in this single activity and because we sense that she would be dehumanized except *for* that activity, we see the activity itself *as* an expression of her humanity. Her mastery is severely limited and yet she is not, despite appearances, a slave to her dictator. She is not a crone of immense power (like those described by Barbara Walker in *The Crone*). She is certainly no mother goddess or oracle, and yet, as Barbara Godard notes, her act may be seen as "a vestige of the sacred art of spelling, the casting of spells being a sign of power. Each letter uttered thus becomes both less and more than ordinary language" (Godard, 1984, 46). The scene resembles a burlesque episode in the Italian *commedia dell'arte* in which a stutterer has trouble producing a word. The man "makes a great effort, loses his breath, keeping the word down in his throat, sweats and gapes, trembles, chokes" until Harlequin hits the man in the stomach with his head. "The difficult word is 'born' at last" (Bakhtin, 1968, 304).

The women break the conversational ice by talking about "weather." Munro respects each word, set apart, just as she respects the woman who spells them. She also indicates, however, that all our spellings and conversations take place within a set of conventions that are collectively determined. Although Rose, offered the role of dictator, can at first think only of suggesting "obscene and despairing" words, the old woman initiates a word "without prompting" – the word *forest*. When Rose suggests the next word: *celebrate*, an antiphonal process is condensed as a dialogue which, although pared down nearly to vanishing point, is no less than humanity itself. The woman mirrors back to Rose an image of what Rose does as an actor, recreating words that have been assigned to her. At the same time, however, her tiny gesture of liberty is an indication that although she spells words like a puppet, this puppet threatens to take on a life of its own, rebelling against the nurse who plays the part of lady ventriloquist.

"Spelling" is the penultimate story in this collection, coming before the title story "Who Do You Think You Are?" As a mocking image of a primal mother who gives birth to words, the old woman in "Spelling" goes in advance of Milton Homer, not heralding his appearance as a John the Baptist before a Christ, but as an image coming before, coming first – an image that questions and challenges the one coming later. Barbara Godard notes that the "paternal lineage is revised" (1984, 50) but that this is not achieved by denying the "spirit of the fathers": "Creation by inclusion, not by elimination" (Godard, 1984, 51). The old crone is part of a chronological sequence of figures that can be extrapolated from the last two stories:

1 Homer (blind)
2 Milton (blind)
3 Chapman's translation of Homer
4 Keats looking into Chapman's Homer
5 The old crone (blind)
6 Flo mimicking the crone (in Rose's dream)
7 Milton Homer doing the authorities
8 Ralph Gillespie doing Milton Homer
9 Rose doing Ralph doing Milton Homer
10 Munro doing them all.

Thus spelled out, however, this sequence of figures is suspiciously linear, whereas Munro suggests a "pattern that is circular, not linear" (Godard, 1984, 46). Godard notes that Harold Bloom foresees a challenge to this line in a feminist poetics: "Homer will cease to be the inevitable precursor, and the rhetoric and forms of our literature then may break at last from tradition" (Bloom, 1975, 31; quoted by Godard, 1984, 50). Although it is true, however, that Munro "creates distortions and loops in *literary* tradition" by going "back to the primal scene of language" (Godard, 1984, 45), Munro does not allow women writers to escape the anxiety of influence by affirming a primal essence. The old crone in "Spelling" does not really fit into the sequence I have laid out but the reason is not that she necessitates a quest to some cave of primitive authority. The reason, rather, is that she is simply doing a performance. What is constructed is not a line of narrative but a poetic space – or rather, a series of spaces that are like the tableaus set up by a float parade (see Sparshott, 1988, 326).

The old crone, diapered in her crib, performs a masquerade on the site of our belief in primal essence and Flo's mimicry of the crone re-enforces the challenge. Milton Homer absorbs this masquerade and enlarges it for all to see. In so doing, he helps us to see the powers of the earlier figures. His distracting and inflated body balloons out to take up all the visual space. In Milton Homer, Munro displaces and burlesques the figure of the mother. On one level he is simply a particularly explicit example of the "grotesque body" of carnival. This accounts for the fact that he is eating almost constantly: "All he did was stuff himself at an unbelievable rate. It seemed as if he downed date squares, hermits, Nanaimo bars and fruit drops, butter tarts and brownies, whole, the way a snake will swallow frogs. Milton was similarly distended" (WDY, 197). Milton ought, if this were a traditional carnival, to be a jovial and appealing figure of excess. Bakhtin describes the "act of eating" as the most full revelation of how

> the body transgresses here its own limits: it swallows, devours, rends the world apart, is enriched and grows at the world's expense. The encounter of man with the world, which takes place inside the open, biting, rending, chewing mouth, is one of the most ancient, and most important objects of human thought and imagery.
>
> (Bakhtin, 1968, 281)

Milton Homer's role becomes more complicated because he usurps the roles of both mother and father and it is for this reason that his performance has the power to arrest the old cyclical carnival patterns. When he does his incantation after the birth of a baby, he performs a ceremony which usurps the role of a spiritual father, but his ritual chanting and his rocking of the baby are the actions characteristic of a mother. Milton Homer is "overcome by a stammer" with the result that we are intensely aware of the process of production and of the materiality of the sign. Usually we see what goes into his mouth. In this case we see what comes out. He "opened his mouth wide and rocked back and forth, taking up each phrase with a deep grunt. 'And *if* the Baby – *if* the Baby – *if* the Baby – *lives* – '" (WDY, 191). The intensity of the focus is on the word *if* and this directs us to think of contingency, of possible accident, of our own inability to control even the death or life of a baby. That image of a failure of control taps the anxieties of the mother who seeks to protect her infant from harm. As Milton Homer rocks and chants, the repeated explosions of the word *if*, however, lead up to "the major explosion of *lives*" (WDY, 191).

Contained within this burlesque is an account of the powers and the limits of the artist as puppet. Milton Homer, like Garnet French in "Baptizing," presumes to perform a religious ritual "on his own authority" and the resulting questions about responsibility lead us to historicize the grotesque body of Milton Homer, situating it in the sequence I have listed above. The float parade puts increasing emphasis on mediation and on the responsibilities attached to the act of translation and of reading. Milton Homer is not a good translator because he is blind to his own image. When he draws whiskers on himself, he does it "without the help of a mirror," with the result that the whiskers curl up towards his "bloodshot foreboding eyes." His mouth, the place of the origin of voice, is similarly blocked. "He had put the pen in his mouth, too, so that ink had blotched his lips" (WDY, 198). Although he is a "mimic of ferocious gifts and terrible energy", he cannot "do" himself as does the father in "Walker Brother Cowboy." Hattie Milton's question "'Who do you think you are?'" – if directed at Milton Homer – would have no answer. The question, however, is directed at Rose. Her identity becomes, in fact, of particular importance in the sequence of creators that I have listed. The last in the parade, she is a woman who bears the name of the most hackneyed of objects exploited by our literary forefathers. Unlike Milton Homer, who is blind to the allusions in his own name, Rose must become a reader of her own name.

THE READER AS FOOL: LARGE PINK WOMAN LOOKING INTO MILTON HOMER

Munro reaches back to the ancient fool festivals as a means of invoking one aspect of tradition against another, more tyrannical aspect, of the same tradition. By this means she achieves the definition of Rose as a reading subject. Rachel Brownstein notes, at the end of her discussion of romances based on the rose/woman as object, that the "persistence" of the old plots shows "how hard it is to alter formative fictions" (Brownstein, 1982, 295). The fool is one means of resisting the old designs. Munro's fools, up to a point, correspond to Geoffrey Bush's description of Shakespeare's fool: "The fool is not in progress towards himself, the fool is always himself, and he preserves what he is by ignoring a world rushing headlong toward weddings" (Bush, 1956, 31; quoted by Willeford, 1969, 174).

Unlike traditional fools, however, Munro's fools do not become repositories for wisdom and this difference is directly related to Munro's rewriting of the role of Mother Folly. Milton Homer seems, on the face of it, to be an example of what Willeford terms the traditional "mother-boundness of the fool" which, according to Willeford, is the "most abiding form of his relationship to the feminine" (1969, 175). But mother, in Munro's fiction, is no final authority and Milton Homer is in fact motherless. The maiden aunts who serve as his mock mothers are like conspicuously failed versions of the lady ventriloquist: they cannot control what comes out of his mouth.

Milton Homer's imitation of a priest is reminiscent of the medieval "fool figures" who "played the priests and nobles of the normal world, but behind these burlesque figures of conventional – and masculine – authority Mother Folly reigned supreme" (Willeford, 1969, 175). Munro resists such an essentializing of maternity. In her stories we confront maternal figures as cultural constructs. Munro does not reach back to the ancient carnivals in order to affirm nature over culture. She reaches, rather, for a useful repertoire of conventions and stages them to achieve an ironic effect that could be called Socratic.

The conspicuous antics of Milton Homer issue a challenge like the one described by Willeford:

> when we see a fool we do so in ignorance of the fool within ourselves. This ignorance is more specifically the blind spot that keeps us from knowing in advance the point of the fool's trick or joke; it also keeps us from being aware of the larger fool show into which the trick or joke will dissolve, eluding our understanding.
>
> (Willeford, 1969, 51)

Munro's fiction acts as this kind of practical joke. The question in her title – *Who Do You Think You Are?* – is addressed, also, to the reader and can be seen in the context of medieval carnival tricks: "The question thus stated – Who is the fool? – was the basic rhetorical trick of the late medieval fool literature and is at least implicit in virtually every presentation of fools" (Willeford, 1969, 46).

This repeated return to the irony inherent in Socratic dialogue is all very well, but how does a reader deal with the moral issues so vigorously stirred up by this book? There is a danger that has always been part of carnival: after such a release of energy, the people may fall into even sounder sleep. The sanctioned safety valve of the carnival performance may result in a strengthening of the status quo. Enid Welsford notes that clownage might act, paradoxically, as a "social preservative" (Welsford, 1935, 321). Willeford, similarly, notes that

> since the disorder of which [the fool] is the spirit is largely contained in his show, he serves the boundary of which he is the enemy; and in doing this, he sometimes even demonstrates an authority proper to the central figure of the established order (such as the king . . .).
>
> (Willeford, 1969, 133)

This paradox is defined by Linda Hutcheon as a central feature of parody which, in her terms, both subverts and reinstates conventions (Hutcheon, 1985, 76).

Munro's response to this risk is easiest to clarify if we notice her aversion for the singular. *Lives of Girls and Women* is a title that signals the multiplication that is generally true of Munro's fiction. That book, like

Who Do You Think You Are?, is a float parade of stories that resists absorption by the old narrative cycles. There is not only one fool, not only one author, and not only one reader. All of these participate in a collective process. As soon as Mother Folly participates – like the old woman in "Spelling" – in a dialogue with others, she is only one of many. This multiplication is inherent in the crucial fact that Rose is an actor. An actor *is* a reader and the image therefore serves as a very useful paradigm for the place where Munro seeks to define the nature of female subjectivity. If a woman follows King Lear in asking those around her if anybody can tell her who she is, then we must not neglect to address this question in its new context. The question, in short, is not the same question when it is asked by a woman and when it is asked by someone from the working class.

The best example of all this, as so often happens in Munro's fiction, is a practical joke which acts as a text within the text. This particular joke offers us two readers, one sitting behind the other, one male and one female. The boy who sits behind Rose in school taps her on the shoulder and shows her his alteration of a canonized text: "He had stroked out *Chapman's* in the title of a poem and inked in the word *Milton* so that the title now read: *On First Looking into Milton Homer*" (WDY, 194). Like the Monty Python famous first drafts, this one is reductive and crude. We may unlock the condensed meaning of the joke by asking, as I have asked of other practical jokes in Munro's stories, who is the victim of the joke? In this case, significantly, it is almost impossible to tell because power is so evenly distributed among all the characters.

The most obvious victim, of course, is Milton Homer. "Any mention of Milton Homer was a joke, but this changed title was also a joke because it referred, rather weakly" to Milton Homer's habit of exposing himself to the people behind him in a line-up. The teacher, Miss Hattie Milton, must be added to the list of victims: "the alteration in the poem was the more daring and satisfying because it occurred under her nose" (WDY, 195). The list of victims grows rapidly if we imagine the line-up as related to the line-up of literary names suggested by Milton Homer's name. Milton Homer's performance in a line-up, indeed, seems to be a replaying of his performance at parades. In the line-up of literary fathers, leading back to Homer, Milton Homer thus stands exposing his penis to those behind him. What are we to make of this crude clowning? The joke is on Milton Homer, on his aunt, on the town, on the school, on Milton, on Homer – and so on. But the joke is controlled – so we might be tempted to say – by Ralph and Rose. Not so. Ralph and Rose are conspiratorial not only as figures of the power that comes from mutual understanding, but also as figures mutually aware of their own foolishness. Munro here exploits what William Empson has described as the "contradictions that appear in the doctrine" of the folly of the wise. These, as Empson notes, were "felt to be a gain, not an obstruction, because they brought out this feeling of mutuality: 'I call you a fool of one sort speaking as myself a fool of another sort'" (Empson, 1951, 107–108; quoted by Willeford, 1969, 45).

As readers of this practical joke we are positioned, in a line-up, behind Ralph who sits behind Rose. Looking over their shoulders at the text of a poem by Keats we find this experience of mutual foolishness made available to us. Although Keats waxes rhapsodic about a particular text, the content of that text is a deliberate ellipsis in the sonnet. "When I heard Chapman speak out loud and clear" is a phrase followed by a very conspicuous colon. The content of Chapman's speech is, of course, a translation and is thus in fact Homer's speech. By implication, then, Keats anticipates a contemporary attitude opposed to the autonomous voice of the individual speaker. The signs in "On First Looking Into Chapman's Homer" do not point inwards into a coherence that has transcendental significance. They point, instead, out of the poem itself and to the local library where the text in question may be located on the shelf.

Munro's practical joke offers a reading of the poem by Keats which redefines the very idea of reading and of art. She joins Keats in challenging the idea that the work of art is a well-wrought urn – or even a well-wrought book. The alteration of one word slyly and thriftily displaces the object of Keats's attention, replacing a book with a penis. Milton Homer's self-exposure, like almost every detail of his behaviour, may be seen in the context of the traditional fool, who often carried a rod, in mockery of a king's scepter. The symbol of authority is mocked by rendering it literally phallic. The traditional jester's bauble, in addition, frequently incorporated the idea of a self-image, since what was at the end of the stick might be a mirror or a "human image reduced to the fool's head and the exaggerated phallus" (see Willeford, 1969, 37, Plate 10). Milton Homer's self-exposure and his ceremony with babies could be seen as two different and mocking versions of that authority. Willeford shows how the "ventriloquist with his dummy" and the "behavior of children with dolls and other toys" can be deduced from the "uses of the bauble" by medieval clowns (Willeford, 1969, 33). If the bauble becomes a baby, then the fool begins to play a mock maternal role. Such a hermaphroditic conjunction of male and female roles is consistent with carnival tradition; what is distinctive, however, is Munro's insistence on the real thing – as distinct from the symbolism of carnival. Both the thing exposed by Milton Homer and the babies subjected to his ceremonies are relentlessly *real* and they cannot dissolve into each other as aspects of the same symbol. Willeford sees the "lump" on a traditional fool's rod as maternal, presumably suggesting pregnancy. Munro's phantom pregnancies, however, are invariably ironic because they are so clearly constructions. Milton Homer's swelling belly is full of items of real food. These items are listed for us, down to the last brownie. By the same token, furthermore, we know that the babies he rocked were not impersonal lumps, symbols of some essence of maternity. We know this because Rose herself was one of those babies, as was her brother Brian. Both have an aversion for imagining themselves in the humiliating form of a baby helpless to prevent the actions of a fool.

A modest affirmation emerges as we look at Ralph and Rose together as they look at the text of the poem about looking into Homer. In the doubling of the two readers – a man and a woman – Munro insists on difference and community simultaneously. Ralph and Rose, in their mutual and conspiratorial foolishness, share not a mutual sense of being victimized and marginalized, but a mutual experience of their power as readers. Rose considers and rejects the possibility that what she felt for him was simply "sexual warmth" (WDY, 205). Had Munro reduced the relation between this man and this woman to sexual desire, then the epilogue could have made a last minute dash to join the "world rushing headlong toward weddings" (Bush, 1956, 31). By seeing her activity mirrored in Ralph's mimicry (who, in turn, sees his mirrored in Milton Homer), Rose rejects the carnival cycle and opts for the float parade. She also escapes a danger pictured vividly for us in Milton Homer – the danger of working "without the help of a mirror." The fact that no powerful autonomous subject can be constructed does not negate the importance of knowing who you think you are, of knowing the limits of yourself, the place where the boundaries of self dissolve and flow into the self of some other. Munro pictures the pain of isolation and offers as comfort a sense of community – however small.

Ralph, according to Flo, has to be put together "from scratch" after his war injury, but Rose refuses to play Isis to his Osiris. The death of Ralph, however arbitrary and "literary," is brutally real. Even as his "fatal head injuries" lure a reader into symbolic associations, the reader is made to feel the fool. In the phrase "Rose didn't tell this to anyone," the word *this* has no clear antecedent. The life of Ralph cannot, it appears, be told. What can be told, however, is the affection that existed between Rose and Ralph. The very last lines of this book place his life "one slot over from" Rose's own life. The use of the word "slot" and the fact that Rose and Ralph are both performers encourages us to relate this conclusion to the challenge of electronic culture.

Spinoza's "*All things are alive*" is a phrase slipped into the text early enough (WDY, 3) to be useful to the reader in search of affirmation. Life is in the making and remaking of conventions presumed dead. Destruction of the old precedes this as surely as the deadheading of old roses, but the new that is created is never created "from scratch." Munro attacks the paralyzing powers of nostalgia with the same strategies that shatter the old icons of maternity. When Hat Nettleton, interviewed on the radio, speaks proudly of a time when people made their own entertainment, we have been prevented (before we even hear that interview) from experiencing simple nostalgia. "*Didn't have no T.V. Didn't have no radio. No picture show*" (WDY, 21) – his words make a deceptive contrast between the time before and after the technology of the reproduced image. What Munro does is to expose the constant – the fact that we are responsible for our makings and remakings of entertainment.

Milton Homer is a performer whose actions make visible a huge blind spot. His behaviour is made up of historically coded liturgical patterns. As he performs his travesty of religious ceremony, his maternal rocking leads us to see, hovering massively behind him, the figure of maternity as essence. When Rose does Ralph Gillespie doing Milton Homer, she performs a new way of looking into Milton Homer, a new way of understanding our literary tradition. She is an active reader, but one who consciously reads within communities. Rose opens herself up ("invasion, and welcome") to the texts that demand to be looked into in new ways. As we are made conscious of the rose coloured glasses with which we read, our identities flow into the space made by the dialogue between Flo and Rose. The space is like the "dress of cobwebby cotton, shading from pink to rose" worn by Catherine in "Lichen" (PL, 33). Caught in the webs of popular culture, we can do more than sit back and enjoy the show. We can join the parade. This large pink woman not only reads with a man behind her, but also *does* Milton Homer with an audience in front of her. And Munro, herself a "mimic of ferocious gifts" (WDY, 192), is everywhere at the same time, like a good hostess. She walks courageously in her own parade of mothers and other clowns, walks against the grain of centuries of narrative convention.

Chapter 10

The Moons of Jupiter
Picking up the pieces

UNFRAMING THE FATHER

By selecting "The Moons of Jupiter" as her title story and giving it added weight as the last story in the collection, Munro invites us to associate this book as a whole with her response to the death of her father. Death triggers a testing of the values which we take for granted and briefly renders visible our usually invisible means of support. The codes that gird up our lives suddenly loom large, exposed, and open to question. Like Ted in "Accident," we may see ourselves as overcome by a "flood of nonsense" and by "superstition." The "powerful nonsense" may nevertheless be "impossible to stop, impossible to disregard" (MJ, 88). Are the principles of order that surface after a death equal to the task of comforting the bereaved or do they offer as much punishment as comfort? These questions are directed in this book so that we take a new look at the figure of the father. Munro has given steadily increasing power to surrogate mothers in her preceding collections. A phrase from "Accident" could be used to apply to *Who Do You Think You Are?*: "'Those women are capable of anything. The father's just a shadow. The women are terrors'" (MJ, 101).

Although the groups of women in the opening two stories in *The Moons of Jupiter* continue this pattern, the death of the father now requires that he step out of the shadows so that we may look at his relation to these women and to the symbolic order. When he does emerge we recognize him as the gentle clown from "Walker Brothers Cowboy" who will now direct us to see a new kind of elegiac comedy. The return in "The Moons of Jupiter" to a comfort anticipated in "Walker Brothers Cowboy" is striking because of the horrors we have glimpsed in the intervening fiction. No fatherly comfort is present, for example, in *Lives of Girls and Women* when Del scares herself by trying to imagine "all those atoms, galaxies of atoms." Del concludes that they must be "whirling away in God's mind" because that is "the only way the world could be borne, *the only way it could be borne*" (LGW, 100). The father in that book is usually absent, appearing in a nightmare as a tyrant acting calmly to dismember human bodies and to behead the members of his own family. In *Who Do You Think You Are?*, this collapse of fatherly comfort is made visible by a restaging of ancient carnival rituals. A mock-king is beaten to death in the first story and Rose's own father speaks incoherent nonsense.

In startling contrast, we now have the homely figure of the father sitting in his hospital chair on "his last night" and telling his daughter "the moons of Jupiter." He did not, she observes, look "out of place. He looked thoughtful but good-humoured, an affable host" (MJ, 232). Although the father's good humour is partly the product of "happy pills" or tranquilizers, he also shares the deeper "tranquillity" (DHS, 3) of the father in "Walker Brothers Cowboy." I am not saying that fatherly support was not actually there for Munro during the intervening years. I am simply suggesting that when a support is removed by death, a constructive grieving process acts to define and consolidate what was taken for granted.

The Moons of Jupiter deals with the impact of various kinds of loss on narrative structure and there is no easy elegiac reversal. In "Accident," for example, the bereaved mother is almost obscured. We glimpse her behind the melodramatic spectacle of the grandmother who rocks and wails. These maternal figures issue a powerful challenge to the consciously glib surface of the story which tempts the reader to accept the neat closure represented by the marriage of Frances and Ted. The bereavement is trivialized by the image of a punitive Father God and by the master-narrative that goes along with that image. Adelaide, "stocky and maternal," spells it out for Frances when she speculates gleefully that the death of Bobby may be God "paying back" Ted for his adultery (MJ, 94). A near accident in "Labor Day Dinner" similarly reinforces Munro's challenge to the idea that "'things happen so symmetrically'" (MJ, 149). Roberta notes: "'I don't think you get your punishment in such a simple way. Isn't it funny how you're attracted – I am – to the idea of a pattern like that?'" (MJ, 149).

The attraction of any pattern, of course, lies in the illusion of control and in the denial of chaos. There is an emphasis in these stories on severed words, objects, and letters, but also on severed family relations. The challenge to find a relation and make a "connection" is urgent. The severed head of Sir Walter Raleigh is left lying around in "Bardon Bus." There is also a lover called X, and – in other stories – a package of seaweed, a stone, a pie, and a gibbous moon. The narrator of "Connection" notes that Richard wished her to be amputated from her past (MJ, 13) and Kay, in "Bardon Bus" has a lover who pictures her with "an ominous blue fire around her neck, a yoke or a ring." He leaves behind a "book on anatomy which showed real sliced cadavers" (MJ, 115–116). *The Moons of Jupiter* is not, however, a static anatomy of grief. It puts the reader on the spot. The reader is like Isis who has to decide how to put Osiris back together again.

The woman's dilemma is dramatized urgently in this, however, because as she puts him together, she may be eliminating herself. This danger is posed by Dennis in "Bardon Bus" when he compares the buried soldiers whose "legs and torsos and heads have to be matched up" to X's women (MJ, 120). It is tempting to go along with the narrator's insistence that the analogy is false and that the women come and go of their own free will. The crisis of dismemberment, however, is not so easily averted.

With this collection Munro returns to the piecemeal method of narration that she initiated in *Something I've Been Meaning to Tell You*. The result is a foregrounding of the activity of a reader in the text who is confronted with a crisis. Often this reader is a woman struggling to come to terms with the competing roles of "watcher" and "keeper." Prue, in the story "Prue," is an image of the reader as kleptomaniac; she cannot give meaning to the cuff-link that she steals from the man who betrays her. Betrayal itself has no meaning if there are no vows to be broken and in this abbreviated story the ideological structures are conspicuous by their absence. If the reader refuses to be kept by Prue, refuses to be one of that group of "people who always feel cheered up after listening to" Prue (MJ, 129), then the reader outside "Prue" is at an ironic distance from the reader inside the text. Our own compassion is made possible by that ironic distance. This distance is also evidence of our horror at the possibility that the world – like Prue's collection of stolen objects – might be a random collection of things that have no meaning.

In "Mrs. Cross and Mrs. Kidd," the readers in the text are senior citizens living in a "home." Their efforts to construct meaning *are* an effort to construct a home, but they are crippled by the fact that they are amputated from their past, severed from their families. We observe the two women engaged in mock-maternal activity. Mrs Cross "takes over" a newcomer to the home who has been severed (by a stroke) from his age group and his family. His vulnerability awakens in Mrs Cross an "old managing watching power." After they quarrel during a scrabble game, Jack's violently petulant gesture leaves the "letters scattered all over the floor" and Mrs Kidd notes: "We can't do much about picking them up," and adds: "If either one of us bends over we black out" (MJ, 178). The challenge issued to us as readers is explicit: can we pick up the pieces and make something meaningful of them before we black out? In so doing, will we use the mythological patterns associated with words like *cross*? Will we think of sacrificing a kid or will we kid ourselves that we can do without these? Mrs Kidd's children love to hear her say that "the Lord and his disciples" appear to be eating hamburgers on the picture with the halo that lights up. The reader of the story, however, is distanced from such a facetious response and made uneasily aware of the power that remains in the picture.

The old paradigms (like the picture on the wall) are there even when the reader *in* the text is unaware of them. The Holy Family, for example, hovers invisibly behind the story "The Turkey Season" and the scene in the turkey barn becomes a grotesque parody of the nativity scene. The bloody interior of the barn stays in our memories as three women walk, at the end of the story, through a snowy "Christmas card" scene, singing "We Three Kings." The gender confusion undermines the rigidity of the old story. Herb may be used to season the Christmas turkey but the character Herb, a homosexual, is marginalized and left out of the picture. In this story it is Herb who is the "keeper"; he is the only one who might qualify to play the part of the mother. The scene cannot be restaged, however, and this "Christmas card" is a picture with bleeding edges.

In one form or another, many of these stories invoke some version of a family system. When you take away the father, the head of the traditional family, the whole system is brought into question. Kinship structures are so central to our way of ordering social life that it is astonishing to see them looking so eerily unfamiliar in a Munro story. We find ourselves staring uncomprehendingly at the labels "Mother" and "Father" on the tombstones in "The Ottawa Valley." The inscriptions on the "splendid white stones" in the Australian cemetery in "Bardon Bus" are similarly arbitrary: "Our Wonderful Mum" and "A Fine Fellow." Even the name Poppy Cullender, in "The Stone in the Field," seems to act as a mocking echo of the word Papa, a possibility that is heightened by the narrator's observation that her father "could imitate him very well" (MJ, 20). Poppy's homosexuality and his friendship with the narrator's mother make of the name "Cullender" an absurdly perforated vessel, somewhere between Holy Grail and witch's cauldron.

Poppy is a kind of fool, like Milton Homer and Bobby Sherriff. When people said "he was queer, they just meant queer; odd, freakish, disturbing" (MJ, 21). There is an edge to Poppy, however, that is missing from those other fools, for Poppy is not a freak at the circus: Poppy is, in fact, "queer" in the sense of being a homosexual. Poppies are associated with the macho image of war, but although Poppy's elimination is less spectacular than that of a soldier, it is no less brutal. "'Poor Poppy,'" says the mother, "'. . . Some people can't survive in a place like this. It's not permitted. No'" (MJ, 21). Thinking of Poppy's fate and of his "greasy black clothes," we might adapt a conversation from "Labor Day Dinner" and conclude: "'It's just something black that rises. . . . 'Oh, there's always something black'" (MJ, 149).

If there is something black in this book, however, there is also a corresponding depth of comfort that is found in the courage to laugh in the face of blackness. As the moons of Jupiter make their appearance in the last story, we conclude that there is "No perpetual darkness after all" (MJ, 231). Munro does not offer, however, any easy comforts. Her stories insist on a process whereby we are forced to confront false comforts and recognize them as such. After the loss of a lover in "Bardon Bus," the narrator searches obsessively for the perfect ear-rings. Prue in "Prue" grabs a cuff-link. The daughter in "The Moons of Jupiter" has a similar experience prior to her father's death:

A preoccupation with fashion and my own appearance had descended on me like a raging headache. . . . I recognized this obsession for what it was but had trouble shaking it. I've had people tell me that waiting for life-or-death news they've stood in front of an open refrigerator eating anything in sight – cold boiled potatoes, chili sauce. . . . Or have been unable to stop doing crossword puzzles. Attention narrows in on something – some distraction – grabs on, becomes fanatically serious.

(MJ, 229)

The absurdly inadequate substitutions here show that the clowning impulse is always just below the surface as Munro, like the father in the title story, mocks her own search for comfort. In "The Stone in the Field," for example, the father offers his daughter a story about some "lace curtains" that were used as a shroud to bury her great-great-grandmother. He does it as if shyly offering her a present, then adds "brusquely, 'Well, that's the kind of a detail I thought might be interesting to you'" (MJ, 32). Munro subsequently recycles this detail in later stories. In "Bardon Bus" the narrator remembers dressing up "as a bride in old curtains" and then having no place to go (MJ, 126). In "Labor Day Dinner" Munro picks up the curtains again. Eva wears "several fragile, yellowed lace curtains draped and bunched up. . . . One of the curtains is pinned across her forehead and flows behind her, like a nineteen-twenties bridal veil." Under the veil her face is "lewdly painted" with "violent colors" (MJ, 135). Like the woman in "Bardon Bus" who has to learn to say "'I know what a spectacle I am'" (MJ, 126), and like Alice Munro herself, Eva is "an acrobat, a parodist, an optimist, a disturber" and this helps us to gain distance from the cultural forms she mocks, from the generic laws that dictate a headlong rush towards weddings. The painted face of the clown leers from behind the bridal veil. Since the father's example has made it possible for the daughter to do this kind of parody, it is fitting that the curtains should be a gift from the father, part of the daughter's legacy.

Like the pretty pattern of the lace curtains/bridal veil/shroud, the patterns in this book are self-mocking and unstable. The curtains may, in fact, be glimpsed in the image in "Hard-Luck Stories" of buried bodies like "layers of rotting fabric" (MJ, 196). If we are tempted, for example, to see the "gibbous moon" in "Labor Day Dinner" as related to the moons in the title story, we find ourselves being returned to the act of gibing or mocking or perhaps even to speaking gibberish. The hope for a resilient source of unity is not in any shape – gibbous or otherwise – but in the process of mutually discovered meaning, a process encapsulated in the conversation during which father and daughter join in naming the moons of Jupiter. This father knows very well that his writing daughter will not turn the lace curtains into some symbol with transcendental significance. His gift comes with no strings attached. She can use the curtains for a clown costume or for a wedding dress. The father's gift is not an icon or a thing but rather a gesture that affirms not only the process of storytelling but also the possibility of comic performances that might undermine the old stories. His gesture implicitly blesses the daughter's future tellings without prescribing what form they should take.

The father's gesture, moreover, is now married to gestures made by the mother as if they are joining to make up a circus family. The mother in "Walker Brothers Cowboy" was left out of the father's joke. Now she does her own stunt and the performance of a maternal clown arrests, for one brief moment, all the narrative sequences. "My mother, most amazingly, put on a pair of my father's trousers and stood on her head" (MJ, 4). In her brilliant analysis of this scene, Smaro Kamboureli reads Mrs Fleming's act as an assertion of her "subjectivity as woman, subjectivity in the sense of a speaker's or a performer's capacity to posit herself as subject" (Kamboureli, 1986, 34). Her disappearance inside her husband's clothes, argues Kamboureli, is a "radical absence that marks, from within, the deconstruction of the codes of absence that have silenced her. It calls into question the subject's non-presence since it is the subject herself that initiates her disappearance" (34). Kamboureli argues persuasively that the "figure of authority, the logos, the phallus, is not simply displaced as the host of his house by his wife and her visiting cousins. The phallus becomes the figure of the fool" (Kamboureli, 1986, 34).

This father, however, who is identified with the law and who is the displaced host cannot be equated with the "affable host" in the hospital (MJ, 232). It is hard to conceive of that father making any objection to having his trousers used for the purpose of parody. That father is a self-confessed fool and is himself engaged in self-parody. Family history refuses to dissolve into myth and the rejection of such symmetry is crucial to Munro's way of marrying her maternal and paternal tributes in these stories, of making hers the hosting parents at a family circus. This circus, however, is located in a specific place and it is the father who provides the deepest connection with the history of that place.

Munro's first book was dedicated to her father, Robert E. Laidlaw, and the first story in that collection features a father who directs his daughter to think about her place in relation to time. "The tiny share we have of time appalls me," confesses the narrator of "Walker Brothers Cowboy," but she adds: "my father seems to regard it with tranquillity" (DHS, 3). It is a contrast frequently invoked by Canadian writers: the stark contrast between our short human history and an ancient geological time span. The daughter shrinks from consideration of this vastness and confesses that she is not "even able to imagine the shore of the Lake when the Indians were there" (DHS, 3). At the end of that story her father's past is compared to a familiar landscape, "darkening and turning strange" (DHS, 18). In "The Ottawa Valley," similarly, the mother's "familiar bulk" turns "strange, indifferent. She withdrew, she darkened in front of me" (SIB, 244). The father's life, like the mother's life, turns into "something you will never know, with all kinds of weathers, and distances you cannot imagine" (DHS, 18). In the context of *The Moons of Jupiter*, this imagery now suggests the turbulent conditions in the Jovian atmosphere. The father in the title story speaks of the unimaginable distances of outer space but the father in "The Stone in the Field" is concerned with the details of local history. With these father figures, Munro points implicitly in the direction of her own father's writing.

Just before he died, Robert Laidlaw wrote a book entitled *The MacGregors: A Novel of an Ontario Pioneer Family*. It was published after his death, during the same year (1979) that saw the publication of Munro's "Chaddeleys and Flemings." In his preface, he gives as his aim a desire to record a "partial history of this part of South Bruce and North Huron counties." The preface concludes: "Thanks are due to my wife Mary Etta, who corrected my spelling, and to my daughter, Alice Munro, without whose encouragement this book would not have been written" (Laidlaw, 1979, vii). The formulaic phrase is unusually moving in this instance. The fact that Munro's father was writing, so to speak, side by side with her just before his death adds a poignancy to the father–daughter dialogues in this collection.

The differences between his fiction and hers are instructive, however. Where Laidlaw chooses to write a continuous chronicle, an "imaginary account of a man's life from the 1850s to the 1920s" (Laidlaw, 1979, vii), Munro rejects, as always, the extended narrative line. There is subtle irony in Laidlaw's writing, but the linear novelistic structure he chose blocked the development of that irony. Munro's now large and flexible repertoire of narrative tricks, by contrast, enables her to give full expression to a comedy that is only a potentiality in her father's novel. The gently clowning father figure in "The Moons of Jupiter", then, is a shorthand representation of his much larger oral influence. That father offers a way of mediating between two extremes of atomism – the atomism of local detail and the atomism of cosmic detail. The "galaxies of atoms" in "Age of Faith" are associated with the "strange, anxious pain that just seeing things could create" (LGW, 100) and this pain is related to the inevitable failure to capture "every last thing . . . every smell, pothole, crack, delusion, held still and held together – radiant, everlasting" (LGW, 253). At the other extreme of this centripetal pull is the centrifugal pull outwards to a vast distance from which our galaxy is reduced to a kind of atom: "one of millions, perhaps billions, of galaxies. Innumerable repetitions, innumerable variations" (MJ, 231).

In this book, then, the father is a mocking master of ceremonies at a family circus that restages the Copernican Revolution. "The death blow to the Aristotelian/Ptolemaic theory," writes Stephen Hawking,

> came in 1609. In that year, Galileo started observing the night sky with a telescope, which had just been invented. When he looked at the planet Jupiter, Galileo found that it was accompanied by several small satellites or moons that orbited around it. This implied that everything did *not* have to orbit directly around the earth.
>
> (Hawking, 1988, 4)

Munro's book is not so much about the Copernican revolution as it is about our inability to take it in. By the act of naming them according to our own mythologies, Simon Marius reappropriated the moons for all of us; we can pretend that they still do orbit around the earth, that we have mastered them with our classical narratives. By recapitulating that act of naming in the title story, father and daughter participate in this construction of an illusory comfort; they unite in a refusal to be paralyzed by the meaningless vastness of space. Alice Munro in turn, by her choice of title, acknowledges her participation in this mutual human foolishness. The understood imperative in the title [Tell me] *The Moons of Jupiter* involves the reader in the same process.

There is a dark side, of course, to the comfort of naming. The moons are either female (a few of Jupiter's many paramours) or, like Ganymede (Jupiter's homosexual lover), mock-female. Either way the names lead us to imagine them revolving around a powerful male body. The challenge to the woman who writes and who feels the pain of "just seeing things" is to minimize the gesture of imperialism that comes with the very act of telling the names. Once again, comedy offers a response. The mother's body, standing upside down in the father's trousers in "Connection," is a crucial exhibition at this circus. It is a way of holding things still so that we can question the old narrative flow. If we allow for narrative relativity, the father may be seen to offer (in one story) the use of his trousers for this purpose (in another story): "He was bare-legged, wearing a hospital gown" (MJ, 232). The parental stunt offers a place of laughter where the daughter may be at home, may resist being torn to pieces by the competing atomistic forces – centripetal and centrifugal. The father gains power in the very abdication of power; an imitation of this abdication is the heart of Munro's fictional strength. Unlike the Father of carnival narrative, this father does not have to be killed or beaten. The daughter, instead, mimes his abdication of his own power.

Since the father's abdication takes place in the opening and closing stories, we may observe how the loss of paternal power works to change old narrative orderings. "The Stone in the Field" and "The Moons of Jupiter" make up a frame that breaks up or dissolves. These two stories deal explicitly with visits between father and daughter in the hospital just prior to his death. The names Janet and Richard are used in both stories and the hospital setting is identical. The title of the collection isolates the hospital visit and puts the daughter in position as a mediator for her father's last bedtime stories. The frame comes apart in her hands, however. If you put one visit on top of the other like a double exposure, you have the figure of the bereaved daughter, left behind to discover the meaning, to pick up the pieces of the broken frame and to respond to the father's abdication. This figure – the reader in the text as bereaved daughter – is what gives three-dimensional depth to the picture.

It is not possible for the daughter to construct a master-narrative from the broken pieces after the father is unframed. This collection exists, rather, to destroy its own frame from within. The collection as a whole exemplifies the contradictory desires described at the end of "Bardon Bus" – the desire for closure and the desire for what thwarts closure, the pleasure in "seeing how the design wouldn't fit and the structure wouldn't stand" that coexists with "whatever there is that wants permanent vistas and a lot of fine talk" (MJ, 127–128). *The Moons of Jupiter* is a structure that won't stand because the Father and the father, the Host and the host, cannot be aligned. The father's dialogue with his daughter leaves the structures of patriarchy as exposed and naked as his legs. The element of referentiality distances the father in the autobiographical "frame" from the more sinister paternal deity who appears in stories like "Bardon Bus" and "Accident." When the father, with wry humour, makes conversation about Jupiter – that other Father – he (like the upside-down mother) helps the daughter to crack the old frames. He does this almost in spite of himself, a fact reflected in his irritating suggestion that she should have stayed on as Richard's satellite. The "real" father, sitting in his hospital chair, is not by any means devoid of power, but he is not identified with the father/lover who rules over this sorry mess that we call the symbolic order. This distance from a repugnant metaphor puts him in a unique position to suggest alternative sources of comfort.

"BARDON BUS": MASQUERADE IN BLACK VELVET

Having established a healthy distance between real-life father and symbolic father, Munro is freed to explore the "dreary sort of sex" (MJ, 78) that goes on between father and daughter in the old myth. The place where symbolic father and perfect lover come together with greatest intensity is in the story "Bardon Bus," where the absent lover is designated by the letter X. That this X is related to the man who died on a cross is made explicit by the "stubborn virgin's belief" in "perfect mastery" and by the hymn she sings: "*He's the Lily of the Valley*" (MJ, 111). In no other story by Munro is there so overt a reference to the metaphoric goal that underlies the generic rush to weddings. The five wise and foolish virgins are alluded to in *Lives of Girls and Women* and the woman waiting for the bridegroom who never comes is parodied in numerous stories. Seldom, however, does Munro move so boldly right into the very heart of this identification. "Bardon Bus" reads like a parody of the Song of Solomon, rewritten as it might look to an abandoned woman walking on Queen Street in Toronto. Munro's usual method is to reject overtly meta-symbolic fictions, but here the lover is explicitly connected to the one in the Bible who is worth waiting for and who becomes, in the book of Revelation, a bridegroom wedded to the Church as Bride of Christ.

The connection, of course, is made by the reader. X, like a sign in an equation, could stand for anything. The dramatization of a reader's dilemma, however, is powerful because it operates against this vividly evoked backdrop. What we witness here is a woman who, like Patricia in "Tell Me Yes or No," is in danger of being wiped out, dispossessed. The task of learning to be a resisting reader is, for her, a matter of sheer survival. She sees herself as an old maid who keeps, for comfort, "the one letter, hidden under maidenly garments, never needing to be opened or read because every word is known by heart, and a touch communicates the whole" (MJ, 110). The inadequacy of this way of reading is exposed by another letter that appears in her dream after X has left her. The transparency of what is known "by heart" is here replaced by opacity. "I dreamed that X wrote me a letter," she writes. This letter is "all done in clumsy block printing and I thought, that's to disguise his handwriting, that's clever. But I had great trouble reading it" (MJ, 114).

The great trouble experienced by the woman reader is pictured vividly in this story as the pain of a betrayed love. We feel this because the affair itself is an experience of mutual reading. This woman is not like Del, whose sexual pleasure with Garnet French is an entering of a world with no names. The shared pleasure of reading is here inseparable from the pleasure of sex. While in Australia, they read as separate individuals, he going "downtown to the research library" while she looks at "old newspapers on the microfilm reader" (MJ, 113). They also read together, however. She brings home texts from the stones in the cemetery as well as the remembered text of the tattoos on the body of the sexton. The woman savours the "pleasure of going home and telling X" and he, in turn, brings her "conversations on the bus; word derivations" (MJ, 113). The emotion is intensified by the shared geographical dislocation: "I wondered what this meant, about Australians, and then I thought how we are always wondering what things mean, in another country, and how I would talk this over with X" (MJ, 113). With love betrayed, all the shared texts are robbed of meaning, like the abandoned cuff-link in Prue's collection. Unlike Prue, however, this nameless narrator does retain a commitment to the idea of a vow and it is for this reason that she suffers.

There is great danger in this story but we are not allowed to point the finger of blame simply at X. The danger is also in the woman herself, in her longing for "the moment when you give yourself up, give yourself over, to the assault which is guaranteed to finish off everything you've been before" (MJ, 111). She cannot resist this lust for her own elimination. In the "scene" she imagines, she is simply "a woman": "The woman, who has almost lost consciousness, whose legs are open, arms flung out, head twisted to the side as if she has been struck down in the course of some natural disaster" (MJ, 123). The "head twisted" here recalls the "twisted neck" of Becky Tyde (WDY, 6) and the "wry neck" of Del (LGW, 137). The image of sacrifice is vivid, superimposing the centrefold of pornography on an image of the crucifix. The threat is made explicit in X's post-coital comment: "'We almost finished each other off'" (MJ, 124). It is easy to see that the survival of the woman depends on distance, on being a resisting reader, but sexual pleasure collapses that distance. Here, as in "Wild Swans," however, Munro refuses to give sex a hygienic place that is in pure nature, apart from cultural constructions. If it is related to reading, then it is also related to the reading of pornographic texts that are mechanically reproduced. While the woman allows herself to be read in this way, she herself loses the power to be a reader and is like a doll with a broken neck.

This woman tries "vigilance and reading serious books" but cannot stop herself from sliding into her tormenting memory of such scenes. It is a blessed relief when she emerges to congratulate herself on how lucky she is "to be sitting in Rooneem's drinking coffee" and listening to people "speaking Spanish, Portuguese, Chinese, and other languages that you can try to identify" (MJ, 128). The woman is led to this place by a comic performance which dramatizes the idea of love as it is defined by Kay: "'It's nothing but the desire to see yourself reflected'" (MJ, 117). Multiplied in the three-way mirror of a dress shop, a "beautiful young lady who is not a young lady at all but a pretty boy dressed up as a lady" performs this as a masquerade (MJ, 125). The frame of the mirror allows the woman who looks at him looking at himself to hold something still long enough for her to remember the time when, as a child, she dressed up as "a bride in old curtains" (MJ, 126). When the boyish voice of the lady says "'How do I look, Momma?'" the watching woman confronts the reality of infantilization underneath all the poses. The blurring of gender distinction makes it possible to unfix the ideology that envisions the father as a brutal lover. Munro reclaims the mirror image that is often used to condemn women to narcissism. Once again the poetic structure of a physical performance stops the narrative rush to weddings.

The reader in "Bardon Bus" is a woman estranged from her lover, a woman for whom the world therefore threatens to be totally bereft of meaning. The fact that she has no name lets us know how close she comes to oblivion. She comes into existence for us, however, as she reads her own story. Comfort and identity come from having enough distance to be able to read at all. She will doubtless go on to love again, as do Kay and

X, but comfort is not in the old generic structure. It awaits her, rather, in self-parody, in saying: "'I know what a spectacle I am" (MJ, 126). Her acts of mutual reading with X were also an acceptance of difference and her view of love, in fact, is not as cynical as that of her friend Kay. This, as I read it, is why Kay, in her "dark-green schoolgirl's tunic" becomes fixed as the eternal pupil, cast in the role of Holy Mother of God in the sublimated Pieta scene with which the story ends. It is tempting to say that Kay and X deserve each other. The narrator, by contrast, escapes being framed in that scene and she does so by being a wary but compassionate watcher who dares to look at the blackness of self-love. The boy-lady is dressed in "a black velvet dress with long sleeves and a black lace yoke; black pumps and gloves; a little black hat with a dotted veil" (MJ, 126–127). The velvet blackness of this masquerade is a place where the woman can view her own oblivion and step back from it.

"CONNECTION": IRIS IN–IRIS OUT

Turning to the first two stories in the broken frame of this collection after confronting the blackness at the mock-centre, we find ourselves watching a parade of clowning mothers who are followed by a cluster of women who reject the parade. The two stories are paired under the umbrella title of "Chaddeleys and Flemings." The propriety of these proper nouns make it a consciously inadequate title. The book's first lines are a catalogue of proper nouns: "Cousin Iris from Philadelphia. She was a nurse. Cousin Isabel from Des Moines. She owned a florist shop. Cousin Flora from Winnipeg, a teacher; Cousin Winifred from Edmonton, a lady accountant" (MJ, 1). This catalogue, in contrast to epic catalogues in which lists of men killed convey the magnitude of a battle, comes with a gloss that confirms the mock-maternal roles of these women. Whether they take care of patients, flowers, children, or people's accounts, they are all keepers. The sheer size of their mammary glands, however, challenges our assumptions about the maternal role: "Their bosoms were heavy and intimidating – a single, armored bundle" (MJ, 1). As a group – they arrive "en masse" – they make up a kind of alternative community, a collective grotesque maternal body pregnant with mischief. They look after themselves by looking after others. Their bodies "swell and ripen" like circus balloons, but the size and shape of these bodies "had nothing to do with sex, everything to do with rights and powers" (MJ, 1). Power comes clothed in patriarchal language; as soon as we are made conscious of that language, power is denuded and made visible: "Maiden ladies, they were called. Old maids was too thin a term, it would not cover them" (MJ, 1).

These bodies, thus foregrounded, mock the body of family history, imaged as an organic wholeness in the metaphor of the family tree. The family tree is a kind of text for the cousins. The more they fail to read it, to derive any useful meaning from it, the more we are aware of the awkwardness and unwieldiness of the metaphor. The "overseas branches" may or may not be connected, but the reader is definitely out on a limb. What we are left with is the sheer sound of proper nouns and as Munro repeats them we feel the numbing effect of such a list. The family estates were near Canterbury, says the mother, and the narrator parenthesizes: "(Canterbury pilgrims, Canterbury bells)" (MJ, 7). The names ring bells but they end up as signs that have significance, for the narrator, in a system that is not quite her own, place names in a country that is not her country. As she writes about the "Chaddeley family, my mother's family," the word Chaddeley, by repetition, becomes increasingly opaque. "Isabel and Iris were not Chaddeleys by name, but their mother had been a Chaddeley; my mother had been a Chaddeley, though she was now a Fleming; Flora and Winifred were Chaddeley's still" (MJ, 7). A woman's tenuous relation to surnames makes them sound absurd even as they threaten her elimination from recorded history. Pretensions to aristocratic connection are no help: "Lord Cholmondeley" is a branch that cannot hold the weight of these stories.

"Connection" is a story in which it would be easy to miss the forest for the family trees. The bewildering geneological complexities are in fact organized around two family visits in which female impropriety challenges the structures made up of proper nouns. Janet's memory of the time when her cousins visited her mother in Ontario is followed by her memory of the time when Cousin Iris visits her in Vancouver. The two visits are divided by the death of the mother. (In "The Stone in the Field," two visits will similarly divide time into before and after the death of the father.) The image of organic unity is undermined by the fact that two separate family trees (one English, one Scottish) have to be awkwardly brought together by the sheer fact of marriage. If she wishes to pay tribute to both her maternal and her paternal heritage, then the narrative point of view itself will split the family tree in half. Janet's acceptance of this is reflected in the bifurcation of the stories. This contrasts with the cousins in this story and the aunts in the next story. Both groups of women define themselves with relation to a powerful paternal figure who subsumes the matrilineal progression. For the cousins, the "sum total" of all the names is embodied in an old "gentleman": Joseph Ellington Chaddeley. The narrator, in contrast, searches for some way of making this her mother's story, of discovering a maternal line.

The central feature of Munro's narrative strategy here, as Smaro Kamboureli has indicated (1986), is the idea of performance. With their clownings, the cousins subvert the very order to which they pay homage when they talk. "Audience and performers, the cousins were for each other, every waking moment. . . . Drama enough already" (MJ, 4–5). Performance allows for expressions that are forbidden in the narrative itself. This is most apparent when the cousins "put on a concert" (MJ, 4). "They dressed up in old clothes, in old straw hats and my father's overalls, and took pictures of each other" (MJ, 4). The mother's headstand, as I have already indicated, is the most significant stunt performed. The upside-down mother is like a parody of the family tree and her stunt exposes family history as something arbitrary and open to question.

The image registers and stays in our minds as we move on to the second visit in this story. The "visit of Cousin Iris" is given as a reason why Janet no longer cares about family trees. A letter comes from "an elderly lady" in England who is "working on a family tree" and the letter contains information about the Chaddeley ancestry. "By the time the revelation came," writes Janet, "I did not care, one way or the other. . . . I had already had my eyes opened to some other things by the visit of Cousin Iris" (MJ, 10). The visit mimes the "iris in–iris out" movement of the camera eye in silent films. It is offered as a revised approach to family history. In her "peacock-blue dress" (MJ, 14) which is described as "iridescent" (MJ, 16), Cousin Iris, like Iris in *The Iliad*, is a messenger of hope. She offers hope for escape from the white eyes of Caroline in *Lives* and from the eyes of Orphan Annie – eyes without pupil or iris. This is not, however, because she has oracular power or herself possesses any special insight. She is a colourful character, yes, but what we learn is that we see the vivid colour of the iris only if we first acknowledge the reality of the blackness at the centre of the pupil – the blind spot.

It is because he does not see this – he does not see what he cannot see – that Richard ends up with pie in his face. His verdict after the visit is simple: "'What a pathetic old tart'" (MJ, 17). The word *tart* is an ironic totality, contrasting with the piece of pie. He thinks he sees it all but Cousin Iris exists in his blind spot. Richard, after all, is in the next room during the visit. Janet throws "the Pyrex plate at his head" and hits him with a piece of lemon meringue pie, a "moment of amazement" that is compared to an episode in an *I Love Lucy* show. Patricia Mellencamp, as we saw earlier (p. 23), has explored the ways in which the *I Love Lucy* show was able to resist the containment of woman, only to be subject, at the end, to the "resolute closure" of television comedy (Mellencamp, 1986, 94). Munro's burlesque scene is not thus defused and contained. Her strategy is to upstage narrative itself with a clowning performance and in this she does mimic Lucy. Mellencamp notes that "if Lucy's plots for ambition and fame *narratively* failed, with the result that she was held, often gratefully, to domesticity, *performatively* they succeeded" (Mellencamp, 1986, 88).

What is it, then, that Janet succeeds in doing for us when she hits Richard (whose name echoes that of Ricky Riccardo) with a pie in the face? What is it that she sees when she has her eyes opened? It is a practical joke that we witness, and a trite one at that. The point is not simply to find a male scapegoat for the old jokes. With distance from the conscious cliché, however, we also gain a distance from the nostalgic yearning for unity and connection that permeates the story. The reader with eyes opened by this visit must double back in the story to read the family tree from a new perspective. "There was his name on the family tree: Joseph Ellington Chaddeley. The marriage register gave his occupation as butcher's apprentice. He had married Helena Rose Armour, a servant, in 1859" (MJ, 10). The "iris in–iris out" mimicry helps us to focus the camera eye so that we can spy, just before it vanishes, something that is pink: Helena Rose Armour. Her life, however, disappears almost immediately into the blind spot: "His wife, whether she was seduced servant or not, bore him eight children, then died" (MJ, 8). This mother (whose life story is thus brutally condensed) is hidden behind the group of mock mothers whose presence dominates this story. The "single, armored bundle" (MJ, 1) of their massive mammary glands acts as an obstruction, however, that may paradoxically reveal the existence of this other Armour. The name Helena Rose Armour is recorded but her life vanishes even as the letters of her name take shape. Such are the nearly invisible silent butcheries of recorded history.

After the pie in the face there is no return to some "natural" narrative of past events. There is, rather, a sense that "real life" is in the *now* of listening to a sequence of performances. At the very end of this story, Munro switches to the present tense, as the narrator goes back to the memory of that first visit: "My parents, all of us, are on holiday" (MJ, 18). The pace, with the change in tense, becomes breathtakingly slow; Munro uses print to act like a slow motion camera working on the sound of voices. The "pattern of rounds" – "*Row, row, row*" (MJ, 4) – ends with "two voices striving" like a final powerful image of marriage.

> Then the one voice alone, one of them singing on, gamely, to the finish. One voice in which there is an unexpected note of entreaty, of warning, as it hangs the five separate words on the air. *Life is*. Wait. *But a*. Now, wait. *Dream*.
>
> (MJ, 18)

The word *dream* hangs in the air, just one of many fragments in this book. The anatomizing of this song is a distillation of the process that unites this book, but the silencing of the voices, one by one, is the kind of silence that follows a good concert. This performance is what we are given as a replacement for the final union of man and woman that is prescribed by the symbolic order. The series of concerts, like the parade of clowns, becomes a means of resisting the erasure of the mother's life. We experience this most vividly when mother and daughter remember the same concert. When the daughter visits the mother – "near the end of her life" – the mother remembers the earlier visit: "'Oh, Lord, do you know what I was thinking of? The water-pistol. Remember that concert? Winifred with the water pistol! Everybody did their stunt. What did I do?'" (MJ, 13).

The daughter, acting as one part of a shared memory, reminds the mother of her act: "'You stood on your head.'" We experience the full power of shared memory in the mother's exclamation: "'Ah yes I did'" (MJ, 13). The absence of commas allows for an uninterrupted release of tension now like an escaping breath.

"THE STONE IN THE FIELD": THE MOTHERING OF MR BLACK

The mother who stood on her head in the first story is seen, in this story, as engaged in other kinds of unorthodox behaviour. Her friendship with the "freakish" and "queer" Poppy Cullender (MJ, 21) is isolated as a cause of disruption of the old orders. The drive to the aunts' house is made in Poppy's car, with the result that the father does not drive. "This," the daughter notes, "made the whole expedition feel uncertain, the weight wrongly distributed" (MJ, 23). Her discomfort with the distribution of power is crucial to her growth in this story. The family circus balancing act will fail if father is not given more weight than mother and if it is not clear whether Poppy is masculine or feminine. Once again, the father's parody offers a way of responding. The visit to the aunts puts the father right in the middle of a patriarchal setting and he responds by joking and teasing, turning romance itself into a farce. "He said they were a bad lot, they wouldn't get married because they'd rather flirt; why, he couldn't hold up his head for the shame of them" (MJ, 27). Jokes of this sort may reinforce existing kinship structures but they may also do the opposite. Like the father who jokes with Mary in "Images," this father mocks the romance structure that dictates a rush towards weddings. He invites his sisters, in effect, to join the parade of mothering clowns. Although giggles break from them (MJ, 27), they refuse. These sisters are brides on a symbolic level – perpetual virgin brides to their own father. They pay homage to the Father daily in their actions, acting as mock mothers to the symbolic order, working fiercely to maintain "propriety and self-control".

The single challenge to the brittle order sustained by these women comes in the form of a man called Mr Black – the man whose tombstone is referred to in the title. The old newspaper report (entitled "HERMIT DIES NEAR DALGLEISH") makes reference to "the nursing care being provided by the young Misses Fleming, who reside at home" (MJ, 33). Mr Black is a consciously arbitrary name, typical of the kind of change made by many Canadian immigrants who choose to dissolve the oddity of their linguistic past. His name could really be *Schwarz*. "'He was an Austrian or some such thing. Black was just what he was called, or maybe he called himself'" (MJ, 32). The act of naming is related to existence itself: Mr Black does not exist unless we call him something and the same is true of the aunts. Telling their names is as hard as telling the moons of Jupiter. This may be because their lives, like the moons, revolve around a powerful male name. The narrator rehearses the names with her parents' help:

> I started saying the aunts' names.
> "Susan. Clara. Lizzie. Maggie. Jennet was the one who died."
> "Annie," said my father. "Don't forget Annie."
> "Annie, Lizzie. I said her. Who else?"
> "Dorothy," said my mother, shifting gears with an angry little spurt.
>
> (MJ, 24)

Both parents try to help in the process of remembering each specific woman. In this case, however, the effort is sadly futile: "'Lizzie. Dorothy. Clara.' / It was no use, I could never get them straight. They looked too much alike" (MJ, 25).

"The battle of proper names," notes Derrida, "follows the arrival of the foreigner" (Derrida, 1974, 113). The Fleming women's world is like the "virginal space" described by Derrida with reference to the study of the Nambikwara made by Levi Strauss. This space, Derrida notes, is "connoted by the scene of a game and a game played by little girls" (1974, 113). The aunts, in their doll-making and shy scurryings, are like perpetual little girls, their "hair cut short in a plain childish style" (MJ, 25). This is supposed to be a family visit, and yet the guests are like intruders, like the eye of the foreigner that "calls out the proper names, spells them out, and removes the prohibition that covered them" (Derrida, 1974, 113). The virginal space is violated by the voice of the narrator.

The threat of extinction here is felt acutely. Janet has to reassure herself that the aunts had a voice ("'Could they scream?'"). The aunt who tells a story about the clothespin dolls she makes does briefly find a voice: "'Here's a lady. She went to church with her wig on, see? She was proud. What if a wind comes up? It would blow her wig right off. See? You blow'" (MJ, 23). The aunt, however, is not aware of her stories *as* stories. To her this is simply a lesson on pride. By reconstructing the doll and the story for us, Munro turns it into a text for us to read, but the aunt herself is not a reader. "No radio; no newspapers or magazines; certainly no books. There must have been a Bible in the house, and there must have been a calendar, but these were not seen" (MJ, 26). The aunts live by orders and ideologies that are taken for granted. That the texts are hidden shows how very far these women are removed from learning to be "resisting readers" of the stories that constrict their lives. The ideology that prescribes the rejection of vanity threatens to eliminate their very selves: no masquerade in a mirror here. The story that the doll-making aunt tells about the wounded soldier is childishly transparent and impersonal. It inscribes historical detail – even a proper noun from history – but it is unaware of itself as a text. By imagining these stories and recapitulating them ("I am certain she talked") the narrator briefly gives substance to the transparency, but the story remains eerily threatened with its own extinction. The aunts cannot construct themselves as subjects and would not exist if the narrator did not label them. They would vanish into the "block of shade" where they sit in their "straight-backed chairs." The result is a radical imbalance in the distribution of power. The weight is "wrongly distributed" (MJ, 23) and the narrator is clearly uncomfortable with her own power.

The space inhabited by Mr Black is very black because it is a condensation of this state of dispossession and the father's story in the hospital offers a way of responding to that blackness. When Janet speculates that the "gravestone" might have been a joke, he responds: "No joke. That would be it. Mr. Black was buried underneath there" (MJ, 32). The joke is no joke at the point where we stop to respect the "truth of the lives laid down" – a truth that makes the narrator in a different story aware of the "silly sound of [her] own voice" (MJ, 196). Mr Black is a blind spot. He challenges all our fixings of historical truth. The newspaper reports that "he gave the name Black and did not reveal his history" (MJ, 33). Since he "at some point in his life had parted company with one of his legs," we may be tempted to correlate him with the one-legged soldier doll made by one of the aunts. Such orderings, however, are suspect. Because the father is dead, the narrator can no longer compare memories with him. This is the pain of her grief. But her memory of his storytelling in the hospital becomes a crucial way of focussing on the limits of memory. The stone in the field is overtly anti-teleological. There may be a faint ironic echo here of the stone that is rolled away in the Bible, but there are no women left behind to weep the loss of their divine Father/Lover and there is no ascension with transcendental significance. By its very absence, the stone is a challenge to the pillar which lists the names of the Fleming women, daughters of a tyrannical patriarch. Mr Black, who is several times referred to as a hermit and whose burial place is marked by a stone, is a parody of a herm.

> Hermes's phallic spirit protected crossroads throughout the Greco-Roman world, in the form of *herms*, which were either stone phalli or short pillars with Hermes's head at the top and an erect penis on the front. During the Christian era, the herms were replaced by roadside crosses.
>
> (Walker, 1983, 396)

Since this herm cannot be located, however, we are returned to the word hermit, which comes from Latin words meaning "desert" and "uninhabited." In Mr Black we confront such a desert – a life hermetically sealed and resistant to historical investigation. In their love affair with that blackness, the Fleming sisters conspire in their own erasure.

If this confrontation with blackness does not lead to despair, it is because of the father. Although she abandons the search for the stone, the daughter does not therefore abandon storytelling. It is because telling is so highly valued that we feel the intensity of the narrator's frustration at her failure to involve her aunts in that process. The infrequent contacts with them are like the lowest common denominator of the speech act. The cards that Janet receives from them at Christmas are formulaic and yet the gesture itself is not totally devoid of meaning. It is "an act of faith for them to write and send those sentences to any place as unimaginable as Vancouver" (MJ, 31). This story is itself an act of faith made possible for the daughter by the memory of her father's faith in the storytelling process. The visit of daughter to father in the hospital is a crucial staging of a mutual expression of this faith. In the stories of his own life, the father pays compassionate tribute to the courage of his pioneering ancestors, even as he acknowledges that the "courage got burnt out of them" (MJ, 30). By exaggerating and performing a single phrase about looking "up the arseholes of cows" (MJ, 30), he turns his own father from a tyrannical patriarch into a human being. His comic stance acts as a filter as the daughter goes back to the farm. The place revisited has changed because she brings with her the memory of her father's story about Mr Black. That story, with its conspicuously placed blind spot, offers new ways of distributing the weight and new ways of telling the old quest story about a heart of darkness.

The lives of the father's sisters, acting as mock mothers and mock lovers to Mr Black, revolve around a blackness that is like the hermetically sealed centre of the symbolic order. The blackness, however, is finally seen not as a horror at the heart of darkness, but simply as the limit of what can be known. Experiencing that limit in the company of her father, the daughter can take up with him a position of mutual foolishness. This protects them both from slipping into the kind of humour that is simply a form of contempt. Munro's jokes are not there to objectify the victim but rather to make us aware of ourselves as readers of the joke. "'There used to be a joke about Mr. Black,'" comments the father, "'They used to say he built his shack there because he was sweet on Susan. I don't think so'" (MJ, 31). Janet asks: "'So you don't think she had a romance?'" and her father replies: "'I wouldn't think so. It was just a joke'" (MJ, 32). Romance with an Intended is a family joke, a text to be read warily, and the most easily available stimulus to such wariness is the fact of death. The stone, unlike the romance, is "'no joke'" (MJ, 31).

"THE MOONS OF JUPITER" AND THE COMFORTS OF THE FAMILY CIRCUS

"I found my father in the heart wing, on the eighth floor of Toronto General Hospital" (MJ, 216). The first sentence of the title story appears to nail down the framing hospital visit that is given such prominence in this collection. On the face of it, the sentence is straightforward and the language referential: Toronto; the Toronto General Hospital; the eighth floor; the heart wing. These exist. That is where she found her father. This narrowing-down process is ironic, however, as we can feel from the tense: "I found my father . . ." The phrase can be inverted to say: "Now I cannot find my father." The phrase: "The other bed was empty" may likewise make us think of graves that are newly filled.

The words "I" and "father" are severed by the past tense of "found" and this makes a mockery of the possessive "my." This hospital in Toronto is no heavenly mansion where I and the Father will be one. When the father later speaks of going "under the knife," the very words are sharp at the edges with our awareness of severed relations. The specific details ("on the eighth floor") are in themselves irrelevant. What is important is that we are plunged into the process: "Attention narrows in on something – some distraction – grabs on, becomes fanatically serious" (MJ, 229). In the story that follows, the father will help his daughter to avoid being trapped in such fanatically serious patterns, but humour is already there in the ironic undercurrent in the opening sentence. She found her father "in the heart wing." Here the father is in the heart instead of the heart being in the father, an inversion that resembles the image of the mother who dies with an imaginary egg stuck in her throat in "Royal Beatings." The identification of heart with wing is equally absurd. Are we to think of the father taking the "flight that concerns everybody" (DHS, 208)?

Munro's stories are increasingly dense and ironic. They demand such close readings. The anatomizing may be frightening but it would be self-deception (for a literary critic, at least) to pretend that it is not also exhilarating. When the foolish reader has acknowledged this much, then she is on the way to seeing how our lives feed on other people's deaths. At the same time, however, the process makes us feel our own mortality in a visceral way. We experience an uncanny sense of our own absence and Munro brings this emotion into focus by framing it on the "small screen" which displays the "behaviour" of her father's heart. "On the screen a bright jagged line was continually being written. The writing was accompanied by a nervous electronic beeping" (MJ, 217). The idea of writing itself seems, thus inadequately framed, to be inseparable from the knowledge of death. The line on the screen, like the line of narrative, and like the "story of our days" (MJ, 122) is not endless. It is like a parody of a television screen for this line tells no story; it is the ultimate paralyzing soap opera. We will never get to the heart of this story, but the line is nevertheless "dramatizing what ought to be a most secret activity" (MJ, 217).

The image of the writing on the screen is a way of saying that the death of this father will be explored in terms of its implications for the daughter's writing. The behaviour of the heart will be crucial to this investigation, but Munro does not sentimentalize. The potential for abuse of power is always there. When, for example, the father expresses disapproval of Janet for having left Richard, Janet has to "look out the window and down at the traffic to control" her anger (MJ, 228). When she turns back, she finds herself "looking at the line his heart was writing." The potential for blackmail is there and redemption comes only with the father's abdication and with mutual awareness of the reality of power. "He saw where I was looking. 'Unfair advantage,' he said" (MJ, 228). The power of histrionics is explicitly repudiated and she accepts this by issuing a mock threat: "'I'm going to have to get hooked up, too'" (MJ, 228). The laughter and the formal kiss between father and daughter are suffused with affection and with a special contained intensity that I (as a westerner) associate with the reticence of Ontario's Anglo-Saxon people.

The reader, too, is involved in this act of looking. We look at the daughter looking at the screen and then we look at the father looking at the daughter looking at the screen. What is exposed on the screen is surely of negligible importance by contrast with the comforts available to us as a community of readers. The emphasis on oblique vision is encapsulated in the title, since moons are an image of reflected light. The daughter does have to turn away from the world outside the window, from the notion of language as such a window looking out transparently on the traffic below. That "reality" is as illusory as Plato's ideals. The daughter turns inwards into the cave of the hospital room, to watch the reflections. Like the much younger daughter in "Images," she watches the shadows instead of the people. Unlike the inhabitants of Plato's cave, she is not left only with such inadequate consolation, not with just the screen and not with just the reflecting moons. What she has is more existential; it is the shared act of naming. The game of telling the moons is a way of killing time while they wait for him to go "under the knife." In an odd rereading of "The Lady of Shalott," however, this act of naming insists on the reality of the space out there.

Much of this book is about false comforts – cuff-links, dulse, ear-rings, etc. – and here father and daughter join in a rejection of false comforts. The father, it turns out, is an exemplary wary reader. He is conscious of being tempted to play tricks on himself to deny death and the temptation takes the form of reading material. In the hospital he finds one of "'those tabloid sort of things. . . . I started reading them. I'll read anything handy'" (MJ, 226). They are stories about near-death experiences. He resists the temptation of them because he is a comparative reader. "'And if you're going to believe it, take it seriously, I figure you've got to take everything else seriously that they print in those papers'" (MJ, 226). The conquest of death (so triumphantly celebrated by the mother in "Heirs of the Living Body") is here put ruthlessly on a level with "rubbish" about "baldness cures."

Munro uses a contrasting text to show the power of reading from yet another angle. Like the mother in "The Ottawa Valley," this father is educated to quote poetry. Such recitations contrast with the kind of reading that happens to be "handy" in the hospital. This reading is handy because it is stored in the memory, waiting there to be a possible comfort like the memorized psalms were to St Augustine. The lines that go through his head, however, offer no such encapsulated tranquilizing power. "'Behind him lay the gray Azores, / Behind the Gates of Hercules; / Before him not the ghost of shores, / Before him only shoreless seas'" (MJ, 225). The word that escapes his memory briefly is *shoreless*, which is thus isolated for our special attention. The brief failure of the father's memory anticipates death. The word *shoreless* evokes a seascape without horizon or limit, something beyond comprehension like the "horrible immensities" she glimpses in the planetarium. As readers we are privileged to share in the warmth created as father and daughter join in a confrontation with this blackness. An "appalling rush of love and recognition" is felt by the daughter (MJ, 226) partly because she shares her father's readings of the articles in question. Reader response here will presumably vary depending on whether or not we recognize and share that reading. The consequence of a mutual resistance, however, a shared rejection of false comforts, is a mutual experience of being exposed to the full impact of the loss.

If we are not to dissolve, along with the father, into those shoreless seas, then we must look for another frame and we must face towards the future as well as towards the past. An unusual reversal takes place in this story to make it possible for life to go on. The picture on the screen turns itself inside out so that background becomes foreground. All through the conversations in the hospital, the reader is never allowed to forget the background: Janet's anxiety *as* a mother, her obsession with her daughter Nichola's absence. The telling of the names of the moons of Jupiter is in part a distraction to prevent her father from naming Nichola and asking after her. The voice of the woman mourning her father's death is simultaneously the voice of the absent mother, the one who exists in her daughter's blind spot. "'Does Nichola not want to see me?'" says Janet to her other daughter Judith. Our consciousness of the narrator as an anxious and protective mother is a factor that mutes the pain of the father's loss.

It is hackneyed, that experience of discovering when you yourself are a parent, that you did this to your own parents. "How thoroughly we dealt with our fathers and mothers," writes the woman who has just written stories dealing with her parents, ". . . how competently we filed them away, defined them beyond any possibility of change. What presumption" (MJ, 222). The narrator's response to Judith and Don is petulant: "'I decided that his beard and hairstyle were affected'" (MJ, 222). The petulance is conscious and self-mocking and in this we see that the father's way of dying is a means of helping his daughter in her role as a mother. We observe this as a result of Munro's dislocation of the last stage of the story. The chronology is disrupted in a studied sort of way. The phrase "When I left the planetarium that afternoon" does not fit into a neat linear pattern beginning with "I found my father." The temporal dislocation answers to that eerie spatial dislocation that we felt in the first sentence. The story ends with the narrator going "back to the hospital" when we already know that her father must have died in the white space that separates the penultimate from the last section of the story. The refusal to narrate the actual death is like a refusal to look directly at the jagged line of writing on the screen or directly at the sun or directly at the moons of Jupiter. We look at a reflection of a reflection, but this is not cause for despair. As the daughter emerges from the planetarium show into slanted "late-afternoon sunlight," she enters a "Chinese garden" that is not in China. The sense of human limits is strong, embodied in the high grilled iron fence that separates the garden from Bloor Street.

She watches the people on Bloor Street and what she sees is a "girl who reminded me of Nichola." The moment she writes it down, she contradicts the recognition. The girl was "not really much like her at all – but I thought that I might see Nichola." The eye plays tricks on her, a product of maternal longing and intense protectiveness. She tries desperately to let go – to relinquish the role of keeper: "If I did see her, I might just sit and watch" (MJ, 233). This mental picture of herself seeing Nichola is a releasing one only if we put it beside the picture of her father dying and the screened picture of the sky in the planetarium. The narrator explicitly compares her experience, indeed, with the near-death stories read by her father: "I felt like one of those people who have floated up to the ceiling, enjoying a brief death. A relief, while it lasts" (MJ, 233). Which is not very long, to be sure, and the moment of epiphany is hypothetical and ironic, oddly reminiscent of the mother's body that threatens, in "Images," to "bob up to the ceiling" (DHS, 33). Nichola resolutely refuses to walk into the frame of this story – or rather, her mother refuses to put her inside the frame. That very refusal becomes a way of showing respect for Nichola – a way of acknowledging that she needs no patron Saint Nicholas and no fussing mother to take care of her. Janet's self-dramatization of herself dying is trite, like threats of suicide used as emotional blackmail. It is precisely what the father repudiates when he speaks of his "'unfair advantage.'"

"My father had chosen and Nichola had chosen" (MJ, 233). Chosen what? Did the father choose to die? Did Nichola choose to eliminate her mother? What stops us from resorting to facile answers or from wallowing in self-dramatizing despair is our sense that the choices are much more minimal, much less ultimate. We choose, for one thing, what to see and what not to see. "I meant to get up and go over to the tomb," Janet writes, "to look at the relief carvings, the stone pictures, that go all the way around it. I always meant to look at them and I never do. Not this time, either" (MJ, 233). We can choose not to see a particular picture, not to read a particular text. We can also, however, choose to let others be or choose to let them go – into death or into life. Janet's father moves into death. Her daughter moves into life. With this movement, Janet herself escapes being trapped in the role of keeper. The end of this section is not really the end and going backwards *is* going forwards. Not seeing Nichola is not the end. When Janet goes "back to the hospital," she plays the game of naming that is implicitly acted out in all these stories. Iris, Isabel, Flora, Winifred, Susan, Clara, Lizzie, Maggie, Jennet, Annie, Dorothy, Io, Europa, Ganymede, Callisto, Nichola. The act of naming is an act of faith. These are names that record the lives of women threatened with extinction.

If we view this hospital visit, however, as overlapping with the one in "The Stone in the Field," then we can make a crucial addition to the list: Mr Black. Mr Black's inclusion is a sign that the respect for difference is not restricted by gender, although women may be more sensitive to it because of a history of dispossession. The story of Mr Black, as told by the father is an example of the father's tolerance and skepticism. It shows us a way to be both wary watchers and compassionate keepers. As the father joins his daughter in this act of faith that is storytelling and, as we continue the process, we begin to experience something of Munro's revised version of elegiac reversal. In the tradition of elegy, a loss turns into gain if only we can find the appropriate paradigm. If we can see Milton's Lycidas as Jesus Christ, then Lycidas too will be "sunk low, but mounted high" and Lycidas will no longer be dead. No such reversal is available in Munro's fiction, for each tested paradigm crumbles as it is being tested. The very idea of reversal, in fact, is challenged by the restaged Copernican revolution that now seems to direct us to make some effort to accept the theory of relativity. In the last words of this collection, the daughter speculates on some future time when she may "go over to the tomb" in the Chinese garden. She tells that she went inside to have something to eat before going "back to the hospital." In this reversal the past and the future become relative and we begin to experience the comfort of this family circus that is restaged in a new space that is both inner and outer. This is the only elegiac reversal we will have, this refreshed experience of the *now* of reading, the now of discovering shared meanings only so as to question them all over again.

Although orphaned, this daughter is not left with Orphan Annie eyes. The pink bowl that shattered after the mother's death in "The Peace of Utrecht" is briefly reconstructed as the upside-down "bowl of the ceiling, which soon turned dark blue" (MJ, 230) but which later turns into a "blooming pink sky" (MJ, 231). The inside of the bowl is no longer a trap but is rather a text which the daughter reads with her father. Like the stains on the ceiling in "The Progress of Love," these signs are meant to be read. The "show" that takes place on this "sky-screen" (MJ, 230) replays what Northrop Frye would call a recovery of projected gods, but the daughter in this story cannot read this projected text without simultaneously reading that other "small screen" on which the behaviour of her father's heart is being written (MJ, 217). In this sense she becomes like one of the children who make up the audience in the planetarium: she too has a "natural immunity" to the "echo-chamber effects" (MJ, 231) because the life of her father – his heart – protects her from being stunned by these "horrible immensities" (MJ, 231). The "faint rim of light all around the edge" of this "sky-screen" (MJ, 230) is like a one-ring circus. When she is alone, the daughter sees this circus as a "slightly phony temple" (MJ, 232), but the father's restaging of that show transforms it for her. He is "thoughtful but good-humored, an affable host" at this more comforting family circus.

Chapter 11

The Progress of Love
Making a spectacle of yourself

"THE PROGRESS OF LOVE": A CIRCUS ACT GOES WRONG

The father steps back into the shadows as Munro returns, in this collection, to her foregrounding of maternal behaviour. Mother figures multiply, especially in the title story, where a careful ambiguity makes it hard to tell whether the story is happening to the mother or to the mother's mother. In "The Progress of Love" the narrator's mother is a child called Marietta who makes up an audience of one as *her* mother performs a mock-suicide. Standing high on her chair, with the rope dangling near her neck, the mother's mother makes a spectacle of herself. Whereas Flo's stunt with kitchen chairs was a relatively benign performance, this one is a maternal practical joke that is profoundly ambiguous if not malignant. This mother, pretending to hang by her neck like a puppet, asks us to rethink our response to the mother who stood on her head in "Connection." It will not be enough to take the poetic structure of the performance as a place of some liberation from the old generic laws. Having done that, we are still left with the responsibilities that accompany liberty – however modified.

The increasing density of Munro's fiction is in part a consequence of her effort to locate a maternal lineage. In its first publication in *The New Yorker* (7 October 1985), this story was written in the third person. In *The Progress of Love*, however, the story is written in the first person, from Phemie's point of view. The revision seems to me to reflect Munro's struggle to find room, within the old conventions of narrative, to suggest the maternal line. By settling on the first person, she once more puts the focus of this exploration on the issue of the construction of the female subject. The question is more clear this way: how does the writing female "I" position itself with relation to the lives of her foremothers? The generational span here is that of a novel but although the density results in confusion, this is a necessary part of Munro's staging of the dilemma.

The middle stories in *Who Do You Think You Are?* demonstrated how the old narrative structures eliminate the lives of our mothers in the very gesture of putting Mother or White Goddess up as an object of worship. In the title story of that collection, Munro makes her alternative explicit in the image of the parade. The title of this collection implicitly poses a question arising from that choice. When Swift used the title ("Phillis, Or, The Progress of Love"), his ending was an ironically "exact Poetick Justice: / For John is Landlord, Phillis Hostess; / They keep at Stains the old blue Boar, / Are Cat and Dog, and Rogue and Whore" (Swift, 1967, 172). Once they have repudiated the trap of being hostess in "the old blue Boar," however, what is there left for Munro's women? Having rejected the progress of romance narrative in favour of a parade of clowns, we have to address an important question: do we make any progress in this parade? What is our responsibility to those that come behind us, mimicking our mimicries? The fact that the narrator of "The Progress of Love" calls herself Fame may be a self-parodic touch. Munro's own fame, by now established, leads her not into complacency but into deeper levels of self-interrogation. Acts of irresponsibility are often viewed with a kind of horror in her stories and here she reflects again on the storyteller's own responsibilities.

Responsibility, in "The Progress of Love", is hard to define because child and adult keep blurring into each other. The child mother here is not the single Dickensian grotesque but is, rather, separated into different layers in time. Munro's new approach to temporality suggests that if we could disentangle these layers and achieve an idea of history that includes the mother, then we might also be able to begin defining this responsibility. The story of Marietta's mother's hanging is a little historical text. Like a miniaturized parody of Mary, Mother of God, the mother of Marietta (who, in turn, is the mother of Fame) may be examined like a marionette, or like a high-wire circus act gone wrong. If we telescope time in this way, however, we must be careful to ensure that we ourselves do not become victims of this practical joke. Marietta's mother only pretends that she is a puppet whose strings are manipulated by an absent father. It is not easy to see who holds the strings or how the marionette is operated.

Fame confesses to having had a "childish notion" that the word Mother suited her mother "better than it did other mothers. Mother, not Mama" (PL, 9). She sees Marietta, the little girl, as "separate, not swallowed up in my mother's grownup body" (PL, 9). Fame's Aunt Beryl protests: "'I'm not used to being anybody's aunt, honey. I'm not even anybody's momma. I'm just me. Call me Beryl" (PL, 14). As readers we can no more disobey this imperative than we can say no to Melville's "Call me Ishmael." We agree to call one woman Marietta and the other woman Beryl simply because the story would otherwise dissolve into confusion. Marietta and Beryl play out a conflict within Fame. As they do so, however, we observe the kinship structure emerging in a new way. If Marietta could make her peace with the body she inhabits – the "grownup body" of Fame's mother – then perhaps she would not be so silent at the dinner party. If Beryl could accept her responsibilities as Fame's aunt, then she might be less subject to the tryannical expectation that she be a barrel of fun.

Munro's exploration of maternal ancestry is intimately related to language and to the process of storytelling. The self-conscious naming of the mother and the aunt reflects the fact that they construct themselves as subjects while they tell their stories and play their jokes. For Fame, however, the two versions of the story about the mock-suicide are not just any two versions. One version takes up a privileged position because it is her mother's story about *her* mother. The matrilineal story is open to the challenge issued by Aunt Beryl's story, but that does not eliminate its unique power.

Since Sophie (or "Old Norse") in "White Dump" regularly rereads *The Poetic Edda*, I venture to suggest that the mother figures in both the opening and closing stories of this collection are of particular interest with relation to a succession of maternal storytellers. Munro here turns back to the idea of inheritance that was explored in "Heirs of the Living Body" (see Godard, 1984, 50–58). The most visible image of this is her repetition of the theme of the rejected money; in "Princess Ida" it is used to buy Bibles; here it is burned. The inheritance from the father is thus repudiated, but that still leaves the problem (already opened up in "Connection") of how to recover a maternal heritage. Sophie directs us to approach this problem by thinking about stories. She is not telling her own family stories, but the stories compiled in *The Poetic Edda* are stories about families that were constructed by an oral process.

Jacob Grimm defined the word *edda* according to the way it is used in "one of the poems, the *Rigsthula*, where, rather conjecturally, it means 'great-grandmother.'" Henry Bellows notes that the word "exists in this sense nowhere else in Norse literature, and [that] Grimm's suggestion of 'Tales of a Grandmother,' though at one time it found wide acceptance, was grotesquely inappropriate to either the prose or the verse work" (Bellows, 1923, xvi). Maybe so. The etymology may be false, as is, no doubt, the association of *edda* with the earth in Mother Earth (Walker, 1988, 339). The associations, indeed, threaten to become nonsensical if we hear the word *Nurse* in the word *Norse*. These days, however, we are not so quick to assume that an association with grandmothers diminishes the power of a tale. Munro traces her own ancestry back not to James Hogg himself but to the mother of James Hogg, to the woman who helped Sir Walter Scott compile *Minstrelsy of the Scottish Border*. It is Hogg's brother who is Munro's direct ancestor.

Like James Hogg, Munro develops her craft by revising techniques that go back to an oral tradition of storytelling and the mother – whether Scandinavian or Scottish – is often the repository of that tradition. The naming of Old Norse shows that this is not a sentimental primitivism, but rather a sophisticated adaptation of methods that unite popular cultures throughout the world. Like James Hogg's stories, those of Alice Munro are often most sophisticated when they are most popular. Like Hogg, also, Munro rejects traditional novelistic structures and is concerned with alternative ways of framing stories. Indeed, she maintains brevity by focussing not so much on the story itself as on the telling, on the process of framing.

Like Hogg (who quarrelled with Sir Walter Scott on this issue) Munro challenges the idea of history implied in romance structure and opts for a more open-ended, almost improvisational approach. Barbara Godard refers to the efforts of women writers to reclaim "literary foremothers" (1984, 52) and this takes on a special significance in Munro's case. Hogg's mother recited to Scott many of the ballads in *Minstrelsy of the Scottish Border* but they did not give her fame. Alice Munro makes a claim to fame by adapting the methods of Hogg, not of his mother. Her literary "forefather," indeed, resembles the self-parodic father figure in "Walker Brothers Cowboy," "The Stone in the Field," and "The Moons of Jupiter." Like that father, Hogg delighted in *doing* himself. Like Hogg, Munro works with layers of oral stories. Unlike Hogg, she uses these layers to make us aware of the potential erasure of the maternal line.

The image of overlapping wallpaper in the title story is apt for Munro's way of seeing the process of storytelling. The whole collection is like what Michel De Certeau terms a "palimpsestic site" (1985, 144), like a meeting place for variations of the same stories. When De Certeau refers to a "promenade-like unfolding of the stories silted up on a site" (144), he seems to describe the parade of Alice Munro's stories. Local legends "create exits, ways of leaving and re-entering, and thus habitable spaces" (142). It matters not which of the stories a reader begins with – which is exit and which is entry. The site is a place of insight. It is also a piece of real estate and Fame is a real-estate agent (PL, 3). As the site is bought and sold, changing hands, the stories come and go and demonstrate the social and economic context of all fictions.

The most flexible image for our observation of human behaviour on that site remains the family circus. The mother who pretends to hang herself in "The Progress of Love" and the grandmother who appears naked before her family in "White Dump" – these mother figures are making a spectacle of themselves. Their very exhibitionism challenges our notions of innate motherhood and this, at the same time, results in a transgression of the boundaries between stories. Both stunts are necessary to survival. The mock-hanging makes visible the body of a mother that would be eliminated in traditional narrative and the body of "Old Norse," floating alive on the lake, is a quietly defiant answer to the drowned bodies of the women in earlier Munro stories. The mock mothers in different stories now declare themselves alive and well. Indeed, they seem to reach out to each other, like acrobatic sisters touching each other in violation of the walls separating stories.

I am not suggesting that each of these stories cannot stand alone. The more firmly Munro opts, however, for the short story form, the more we begin to sense that the walls between the stories are permeable. The emphasis on the response to this performance, moreover, puts reader and writer on the same site. Unlike the audience of a traditional circus, we are never allowed to sit back passively. Like the boundaries demarcating the various rings of a multiple-ring circus, the sights and sounds from various stories overlap and intermingle. As they do so, we too feel ourselves to be contained within the rings. "'Conversations tend to be widespread around here,' says David to Catherine. 'Notice how none of the partitions go up to the ceiling? Except the bathroom, thank God. It makes for a lot of family life'" ("Lichen," PL, 37). At the same time, however, as the "family life" of the circus emphasizes togetherness, it makes us conscious of the vast distances that separate individual performers.

The distance between Beryl and Marietta recapitulates the "desert" that lies between Helen and Maddy in "The Peace of Utrecht" (DHS, 190). Like those sisters, these "do not really share" a past at all; rather, each thinks "privately that the other has turned alien, and forfeited her claim" (DHS, 190). There is a difference, however, in the place of the mother. The absent mother in "The Peace of Utrecht" is now represented as a mother in the act of staging a performance. How we interpret that performance is less important than the fact that she is there, doing it herself, clowning to make herself visible. Since the daughter is herself now a mother, she knows from experience that this act of picturing and composing herself will conflict with the demands of mothering. That struggle, however, is miles away from erasure of the mother – as we see in "Miles City, Montana." "Watcher" and "keeper" are at war with each other in that story, but both mother and daughter do survive. Both, moreover, know how to swim.

These various stagings of survival scenes, however, do undermine our assumption that there will be a safety net of maternal care waiting if we fall. The mother may not get our "signal" (PL, 105); she may be busy composing herself or she may be reading Old Norse. The need of the child who is "a spectacle" howling "'Mama!'" (PL, 12) runs counter to the need of the mother who, in a competing spectacle, yearns for freedom, for being itself. How do we negotiate our lives between these conflicting needs and desires? Munro's stories urge us to begin by accepting the reality of spectacle itself instead of turning a blind eye to it in our hunger for maternal essence. If all the world is a stage, then we must take full responsibility for our part in the performance. The mock-hanging scene in the title story is a staged event that leads us to catch ourselves in the act of looking. Because the daughter's way of looking at the mother conflicts with the mother's way of looking at herself, this staged circus accident leads to the breaking of a heart. "Marietta's mother laughed, and Marietta blacked out. . . . Her heart was broken" (PL, 13). Whose heart is broken? The question directed to Mrs Sutcliffe's comment "'She was silly'" could be directed at the whole story: "Did she mean Marietta's mother or Marietta herself?" (PL, 13). "Her heart was broken" – the phrase is repeated and given the power of ending the story as told by Marietta: "That was the end of it. Those words lifted up the story and sealed it shut" (PL, 13). The image recalls how "Flo put the lid down on the story as if she was sick of it" (WDY, 9).

It is only the beginning, of course, for the process documented in this story. The unsealing of the story is achieved by the simple device of allowing the little Mary to grow up. The child Marietta (now the narrator's mother) is present in the story as a person with a reading of events, with a story to tell. At a dinner party during a family visit, Aunt Beryl tells the same story but from a different angle and as one in a series of jokes. As she does so, we see that what is constructed or performed is not just the story but the self of the teller. The object of the story, in fact, is the subject in the act of constructing herself and this is true for each of the storytellers. In Aunt Beryl's story she constructs a flattering image of herself as a little girl. "'I was just a little squirt,'" she says proudly, "'but I was the one noticed that rope. My eyes followed that rope up and up and I saw it was just hanging over the beam'" (PL, 22). When Beryl *does* the German lady, we should view this as a performance *of* a performance in order to see the irony in the finger of blame. In Beryl's story the "'German lady starts wailing, "Oh, Missus, come down Missus, think of your little *kindren*" – "*kindren*" is the German for "children" – "think of your *kindren*," and so on'" (PL, 22). Since Beryl was one of those "*kindren*," she is both inside and outside the story she tells.

How then can the reader sort out the pieces of the broken heart? Fame's father sets an example. At the restaurant he picks up "a table napkin the size of a diaper" and asks the daughter "in a loud whisper, 'Can you tell me what to do with this thing?'" (PL, 20). When the father clowns, then the napkin, the rope, the "rooster" in the pot, the butter that looks like "Shirley Temple's curls" – all these become, like items at a circus, susceptible to transformation. The main focus of this change, however, is the subject caught in the act of looking at herself. The stories told act as layers that reveal the different stages of that transformation. Beryl has bright red fingernails and toenails, a "big red mouth" and a "loud laugh." Her hair is "of an unnatural color and a high gloss, like cherry wood" and Fame sees her as "noisy and shiny" (PL, 16). She resembles a kind of ceramic clown and we watch as she scrubs her face clean after the performance: "there was such a change that I almost expected to see makeup lying in strips in the washbowl, like the old wallpaper we had soaked and peeled" (PL, 17). In Beryl the glossy clown comes alive because her story clashes with her sister's story. We can avoid being sealed up in our own compositions, when we encounter their contradictions in the stories told by others. As we trace these stories to their origins, moreover, we do not end up in a place of primal essence. All we have, at every turning point, at every entry and exit, are the makings of local legends. All we can do to achieve momentary focus and to survive is to make choices in the *now* of narration.

As Fame and her companion Bob Marks approach her old home, we experience a graphic visual illustration of this focus on makings. What he identifies as "'that hippie place'" she describes as "'where I was born'" (PL, 25). The place of her origin has been displaced by hippies going back to nature. We see, however, the continuing ironic relation between nature and art in the decorations on the old homestead. The hippies have "painted a rainbow across the side of the barn that faced the road." There were "some letters that looked Egyptian painted on the wall of the house" and pictures of giant sunflowers, an enormous dove, and an equally gigantic butterfly on walls inside the house. All these images are signs with a history but the exaggeration of scale conveys anxiety about a loss of history. Since butterflies are associated with Psyche or the Soul, we might even call it a fear of loss of soul, certainly of loss of identity. The flaunting of instant group identity seems absurd, given the communal stories that lie behind the images. Inside this place of unacknowledged historical resonance Munro positions a man and a woman as readers. The conflict of their readings is set against the materiality of the signs in the present. The process – *now* – of investing them with meaning necessarily interacts with meanings constructed in the past.

Bob and Fame stand side by side, as beholders and readers. They confront "two human figures painted on the wall. A man and a woman holding hands and facing straight ahead. They were naked, and larger than life size" (PL, 26). The two figures could represent Adam and Eve or they could represent John Lennon and Yoko Ono (PL, 26). What is more important is the fact that they confront Fame and Bob, like a mockingly distorted mirror image. This undressing is, in fact, a dressing up. Full frontal nudity is here a confrontation with the impossibility of being naked and the scene illustrates Gombrich's challenge to Ruskin's notion of the "innocent eye." We are aware of the "beholder's share" (Gombrich, 1960, 14, 30). Gombrich's *Art and Illusion*, indeed, may actually have been on Munro's mind. One of my students, Brock Pennington, without knowing of the connection I had already made, found an echo from that book in this story. A famous passage by Leonardo da Vinci is quoted by Gombrich; in it Leonardo suggests that the "spirit of invention" can be quickened by looking at "certain walls stained with damp" (quoted by Gombrich, 1960, 188). Mr Pennington drew my attention to the following passage. Fame remembers looking at "chimney stains, old or fresh" and her husband tells their children: "'See, your mom's folks were so poor, they couldn't afford

TV, so they got these stains on the ceiling – your mom had to watch the stains on the ceiling!'" (PL, 5).

The fact that my student and I arrived, independently, at echoes from Gombrich's book confirms my sense that these issues are an important feature of this story. The story reaffirms what has been recurrent in Munro's fiction, namely that there is no place of innocent vision, no place of natural origin that can be discovered. These found images on the ceiling, like the projected ones on the ceiling of the planetarium in "The Moons of Jupiter," dislodge the fixed values of high art that we associate, for example, with the ceiling of the Sistine Chapel. The abandoned "hippie" dream stands as only one version of an ancient illusion. What is exposed is not nakedness but layers of this illusion of nakedness. The style of the painting, the "little pigs' tails of yellow hair . . . decorating their not so private parts" draws attention to the surface and to decorative detail. What we see is not what they represent but the fact of signing as it confronts the clothed man and the woman who look at the ostensibly naked man and woman. When Fame peels away the layers of old paper, she discovers a fragment of "the cornflowers on a white ground" – paper she remembers putting on with her mother. The desire to "see more of the cornflowers" results in a "little shower of dried plaster" (PL, 27).

So much for the search for a white ground or a pure blue virginal origin. The only way to avoid being fixed by those "staring blue" eyes is to enter into the process itself. That is what Fame does when she tells her version of an important story. The money-burning episode isolates the response of Fame's mother to her paternal inheritance. In the telling of that story, we glimpse a maternal storyline. Fame's grandmother's mock-suicide was an act of anger and hatred at her husband. Marietta – Fame's mother – recapitulates that legacy of hatred in another way when she burns the money inherited from her father, thus going against her own view that one "drop of hatred in your soul will spread and discolor everything like a drop of black ink in white milk" (PL, 6). In the concluding scene of "The Progress of Love," Fame chooses to make the progress of love by "remembering" the way her own father allowed her mother to burn the money. Bob Marks notices "'a lot of hate'" in the money-burning scene – hatred of the mother's father. Fame, on the other hand, says: "'That isn't the point. . . . My father letting her do it is the point. To me it is . . . I consider that love'" (PL, 26). Since we have just learned that the father was not actually present, we know that Fame's "memory" is in fact a fiction. This does not eliminate the comfort but rather directs it away from the facts and into the act of telling itself. Irony remains in the gesture that Fame enacts to protect Bob Marks from her own awareness and thus from her discovery of strength. Even if we say that he excludes himself by his way of looking at the past, we are still left with a muting of the affirmation. "Moments of kindness and reconciliation" seem not as important in themselves as is our desire to *believe* in those moments, to work towards them and thus affirm the "progress of love."

"LICHEN": DOMESTICATING THE CAT ACT

The title of this story points to one kind of pussy but there is another less conspicuous pussy in the story – "a large ginger tom with ears mutilated in battle, and one grayed-over eye. His name is Hercules" (PL, 35). An image used in "The Progress of Love" anticipates this displaced "cat act." Marietta is pictured as walking past men laughing: "Armed by God, she walked through their midst . . . safe as Daniel" (PL, 12). In circus language, "*lion's den* stands for *circus cage*." Paul Bouissac notes: "This biblical expression is sometimes used in presenting a lion act (a 'cat' act in circus talk)" (Bouissac, 1976, 91). Marietta's immunity to male aggression, however, is precarious since her armour is borrowed from a patriarchal ideology. A more effective method is for the woman to find her own way of performing at the circus. Munro achieves this in "Lichen" by dwarfing Hercules, the tom, and enlarging the other pussy – Dina's pubic hair. The result could be described as a thoroughly domesticated performance of a cat act. The renowned feats of Herculean strength achieved by the mythical male are mocked in this house cat. "'Lazy beast,' says Stella. 'He's getting about as bad as Daddy'" (PL, 35). David's inability to tame Dina's pussy, furthermore, parodies the male handler of a wild animal at the circus. Traditional male power appears to shrink, then, but the presence of the camera eye (focussed on the female genitals) will bring it back and make it visible in its new, more diffuse form.

The apparent collapse of both male and female power is alarming in this story. There is no Herculean strength that will hold the crushing weight of the world as it is felt here and Stella's father is totally blind in more ways than one. The mutilated ear and the single blind eye of Hercules are images often repeated. Stella thinks there is something wrong with Catherine's eyes (PL, 39–40). Catherine "makes Stella think of an amputee. Not much cut off, just the tips of her fingers and maybe her toes" (PL, 44). Dina's pubic hair on the photograph is "like the dark pelt of an animal, with the head and tail and feet chopped off" (PL, 42). Dina's very name is an amputee: "'Her name is Dina. Dina without an "h." She's twenty-two years old'"(PL, 42). Since David calls her a "'little witch'" (PL, 42), we may remember that a cat is often a witch's familiar. We may also hear an oddly distorted echo of that other Alice's chattering: "'Dinah'll miss me very much tonight, I should think!' (Dinah was the cat)" (Carroll, 1960, 19).

The characters in this story cannot read these allusions as signs of danger. They fail to recognize the patterns within which they act and Munro's narrative method mimes this danger. Her allusions are subtle, deeply embedded in the domestic details of a particular visit. Lulled by

Stella's charm, we begin reading this story with only a vague premonition of danger. Stella tells stories about "wrecks on the Great Lakes. Catherine knows something about wrecks. She has a boyfriend – a former boyfriend – who is a diver" (PL, 43). We may be reminded of Blaikie's "diving down, down through all the emptiness and cold and wreckage" (SIB, 3), but the full awareness that Catherine is a wreck comes to us only after the dinner party is over. The stories about wrecks remain just that – stories told at a dinner party. When the cat acts, we hardly notice it. As Catherine "spreads out her long legs in a tomboyish way" in an unconscious imitation of Dina's pose, the tom "takes a determined leap and lands on what there is of her lap" (PL, 45). The woman's lap is conventionally the place that receives those in need – the head of Christ or an infant – but the *tom* in *tomboyish* (like the *Cat* in *Catherine*) reminds us that it is also the site of sexual welcome. We know that Dina failed to get a part in a movie "because of some squeamishness about holding a tame rat between her legs" (PL, 49). On Catherine's lap, Hercules performs a mocking version of such a balancing act. When Catherine snores lightly, he "doesn't take fright, but tries to settle himself more permanently, getting his claws into her dress" (PL, 46).

In a story about deceit and betrayal, Munro's narrative is itself a conscious deceit. Our eyes are lulled into after-dinner sleepiness as we watch Catherine and Hercules, both of them asleep. The words in the story dissolve into each other in a dreamlike challenging of boundaries. Are ginger and rosemary the names of a cat and a woman or are they what Stella uses to prepare her feast? It is possible to excavate ancient stories from subtle allusions, but much harder to know what to do with them once you have unearthed them. We can feel that some Catherine wheel is in operation, but we cannot easily determine how it works. As Munro unleashes, in increasing amounts, an implied female anger, she also makes it increasingly clear that the anger has no easy target. David, of course, is a cad. His shoulders, however, are too weak to bear the magnitude of suffering that is glimpsed in this story. Although David claims that Catherine believes in horoscopes (PL, 41), no zodiac or stellar sign is here offered as an easy way of decoding the intersecting stories and allusions that point to this suffering. Since we are in the presence of real danger, this is no small problem.

While Catherine and Hercules sleep together, then, it remains for us to set up the antagonisms that are denied in the story. While Stella and David avoid all expressions of hostility, it remains for us to define the opposition denied by their amicable separation. The circus act is made nearly invisible because the camera draws us so close to the object: woman. This circus lady is endangered by the male gaze but the male in question is simply enacting an old pattern. David reproduces, on one level, that other David, the one who sees "a woman washing herself; and the woman was very beautiful to look upon" (II Samuel 11:2). By our awareness of the allusion and by our sense of David's *un*awareness of it, we are able to work towards a definition of our share as beholders. The woman who is the object beheld by the king's eyes is not simply given a voice by Munro. Instead, one detail is blown up to the point where you can't see the woman for the pussy. This is true, however, only if we allow Dina to live in David's pocket. When the secret is hidden out in the open – flaunted in the title itself – then the cat becomes the reader's familiar.

The eight sections of this story are woven into a web that exposes the process of its own production and reproduction and we become conscious of participating in that reproduction. The Greek word for web, *erion*, is also the word for pubic hair. In his essay on "Femininity," Freud sees weaving as woman's way of concealing her "genital deficiency." Nancy Miller sums up Freud's argument: "In weaving . . . women re-enact nature's art of concealment by which pubic hair comes to hide what is said to be missing" (Miller, 1986a, 289). Lichen, of course, is not artificial but tenaciously natural, clinging to rocks and growing where little else will grow. I assume that Munro chooses it instead of the word *moss* because *lichen* sounds like *liken*. "Lichen" is to lichen like the "art that doth mend nature" in Shakespeare's *Winter's Tale*. The question implied is: who controls this art? Who does the mending? Catherine's dress is "of cobwebby cotton, shading from pink to rose, with scores of tiny, irregular pleats that look like wrinkles" (PL, 33). Despite the cobwebs, however, Catherine is not the Spider Woman who weaves the web entitled "Lichen"; although Stella has the power of naming *lichen*, she also is not the weaver; although Dina, in a sense, *is* lichen, she has no power to weave it. This story does not allow for an easy identification of the source of power. The story is an interweaving of a triple exposure of images: Dina, Catherine, and Stella. Behind this trio lies the woman Rosemary, David's first affair; her name echoes delicately like the name of a chosen chinaware pattern. Who makes the patterns, whether for the dishes or for the fabric? Do the women in question have any control?

These questions are bound up, at every turn, with Munro's own awareness of herself in the act of patterning and arranging. The limits of her power are pictured, however, in the ironic figure of an absent weaver. Stella tells the story: "'This woman has her own sheep. . . . The weaver woman. She has her own spinning wheel. She spins the wool and then she weaves it into cloth'" (PL, 36). David responds to Stella's description with an exclamation: "'Holy shit.'" Unlike the Lady of Shalott, Penelope, and Arachne, this weaver woman appears totally self-sufficient, controlling the entire creative process from start to finish. Her power, however, is made consciously illusory because she is a character in a story told by a character. The weaver woman may be seen as the place where Munro pictures the limits of her power. The weaving author, like the weaver woman, does not have total control over the garments worn by the characters in the story. The fashionable cobwebby cotton of Catherine's dress is manufactured in a factory. When Stella emerges from the shower after the conversation about the weaver woman, she is wrapped in a towel: "the bottom corners are flapping dangerously free" (PL, 36). Like mock stage curtains, the towel (woven by machine) is all that protects Stella from the blackout suffered by Dina, whose identity is eliminated by the web of pubic hair. When Stella gets dressed, furthermore, we see that her clothing is clearly not made by the weaver woman. It is not fashionably natural but is, rather, the sort of stuff you might order from a Sears catalogue. "'I have two new summer outfits. One is flamingo and one is turqouise. I can mix and match. Either way, I look stupendous" (PL, 36). Mixing and matching with already reproduced patterns, Munro fabricates something like the "many-layered and -colored" milking costume worn by Aunt Dodie (SIB, 229). The cloth called "Lichen," woven in imitation of lichen, will be consciously synthetic – not natural.

The first figure we look for in this fabric is the figure of Dina. The opacity of the title is a sign that we will not find her and her absence is, indeed, made conspicuous in the story. The telephone defines her exclusion from the story itself. "David, in the phone booth, begins to dial Dina's number" (PL, 46), but Dina never answers the phone. David pictures Dina's place: her "windup toys" – frogs and bears and "space monsters" are "all the same size" (PL, 47). He imagines her as she "squeals, and even screams with excitement," but the operator's voice destroys the illusion: "'There doesn't seem to be any answer, sir'" (PL, 47). Dina's silenced voice is central to the power of this story and, ironically, to her power over David. Unlike Miss Farris, who is like a toy wound up by the phrase *con brio* (LGW, 131), Dina is totally absent from this story. She might as well be a "windup toy" in outer space. The title shows that we begin by confronting her place. The toys and the childish glee cannot disguise the fact that Dina's place is no place. It is the blackness that is Kore or the perpetual little girl. The name Dinah is Hebrew for "law suit" and the brothers of the biblical Dinah slay the man that loves her because, they argue, he dealt with their sister "as with an harlot" (Genesis 34:31). Dina, however, with the h chopped off, does not operate within the law of this or any other narrative. She does not exist as a character within this story and the result is that we are ironically compelled to "read" her through David's eyes. Since there can here be no vengeance under a law, our reading is itself the only possible place of resistance.

Dina is hidden behind the name of the man who is her "last, and perhaps not quite finished with, boyfriend" – Michael Read. The telephone operator tries to help: "'Yes, there is an M. Read, living on Simcoe Street. And another M. Read, R-E-A-D, living on Harbord'. . . . 'All right. Try Reade, R-E-A-D-E'" (PL, 47). The name *Read* is repeated over and over again as the male reading obliterates the voice of the woman. She is pure object. Since her presence is excluded from the story she cannot exist as a subject, as a reader. This is the objectification that we see enacted in the "hand holding the picture" (PL, 42). Stella eventually announces obediently "'Well, I can see now'" (PL, 42) and her act of seeing becomes the central act in this story. Like Stella, however, we will not be able to read or "see" the blind spot that is "Lichen" until we study the superimposed picture of the second woman in the triad: Catherine.

Dina's "flattened-out breast far away on the horizon" resembles the distant flattened image of Catherine as she sits "looking out at the water. . . . She could be posed for a picture" (PL, 39). Dina's "legs are spread wide" and between them her pubic hair resembles the "dark pelt of an animal" (PL, 42). Catherine "spreads out her long legs" and between them sleeps the cat Hercules. The pictures, however, cannot be merged into a single image. We can see this if we pick up the echo in Catherine's name. Munro herself has called *Wuthering Heights* the "BIG influence" on her writing and commented that she still knows "parts of that book by heart" (in Horwood, 1984, 124). The choice of the name Catherine, then, is bound to open up a rereading of that text. In *Wuthering Heights* Catherine says "I am Heathcliff" and her abandonment of self is related to the mother–daughter identity of the two Catherines. Munro's Catherine does not say "I am David," and we feel her isolation partly because there is no mother around for her to identify with. The paired women in this story are more like mock daughter and mock mother, a relation similar to that between Lily and Mrs Ramsay in Woolf's *To the Lighthouse*. Stella stands at the window looking at the lighthouse in an oblique allusion to that novel (one of many pointed out to me by my student Clare McMartin). Catherine, in an inversion of Lily's beholding of Mrs Ramsay, becomes the one beheld.

As we intercept these overlapping lines of vision we become conscious of the island setting and of the way the allusions, like invading waves, threaten to erode the shores of the story. Catherine refers to an "Ingmar Bergman movie where there is a family living in a summer house" and notes: "The girl was going crazy" (PL, 36–37). The girl that goes crazy in that film (*Through a Glass Darkly*) is called Karin and her father is an author called David. As we are alerted to the displaced family relations exposed by this allusion, we are also increasingly aware of the urgent need for Catherine to read the "signs of invasion" before she, like Karin, is dispossessed. David's comment, in "Lichen," about widespread conversations going through partitions is apt since the walls of "Lichen" are invaded by Bergman's imagery. Karin's brother complains that "the walls in the house are so thin, and I can't help hearing when you and Martin are making love" (Bergman, 1967, 21). Stella's good humour counters Bergman's intensity. Over "the bedroom wall" she pronounces Bergman movies "sort of bleak and neurotic" (PL, 37). No spider-god will materialize here as he does in the Bergman film and the overheard bedroom conversation is about cars, not sex.

Despite – or because of – these absurd diminishments, we experience a heightened sense of danger as we unpack the allusions in the name Catherine. Catherine was a martyr who was tortured by "the wheel which bears her name (a diabolical engine consisting of four wheels armed with knives and teeth turning different ways." A Catherine wheel also names "a kind of firework which rotates while burning; or a lateral somersault" (Harvey, 1967, 150). Catherine's voice "goes up and down like a Ferris wheel; it dips and sparkles" (PL, 44) but, like Miss Farris in *Lives and Girls and Women*, her pleasure is not far from pain. Like the boys in that book, who act as if they "wished there were knives on the wheels" of their bicycles (LGW, 117), David takes pleasure in wielding his power: "'Sometimes I think the best thing would be to give her the big chop. Coup de grace. Coup de grace, Catherine. Here you are. Big chop" (PL, 43). If the place of greatest danger is the elimination of the reader in the woman, however, then David fails to give Catherine the final chop. The name M. Read blacks out Dina, but David cannot black out Catherine. While Catherine sits looking out at the water, David tells Stella that Catherine cannot read: "'I don't think she's ever read a newspaper," he claims. "'I don't think she can read a map." The idea of her as a reader is a joke: "'Do you know what she did? She went to Ireland to see the Book of Kells. She'd heard the Book of Kells was in Ireland. So she just. . . . And you know what, she found it!'" (PL, 41).

Stella's subsequent interrogation of Catherine corrects this misreading. "'You read the newspapers?'" asks Stella, and Catherine responds: "'I read parts. I get one delivered. I don't read it all'" (PL, 45). This deceptively casual exchange points back to the biblical passage echoed in the title of the Bergman film. Catherine sees through a glass darkly; she knows in part and does not claim to know as she is known. An example of Catherine's reading ability is offered in her shrewd reading of David: "'If you feel dependent on somebody, then you can be mean to them. I understand that in David'" (PL, 44). This particular reading is shared with Stella, who understands the same thing about David. Catherine's reading, however, also defines her as apart from Stella. While Stella and David were observing her, while Stella was seeing her as someone who could be posing for an advertisement, Catherine was, in fact, reading the message sent to her by the waves: "'He loves me, he love me not'" (PL, 44–45).

Catherine reads the waves. For the reader who has read *The Waves*, this opens up further levels of irony. In that novel Virginia Woolf issues a challenge to old illusions about the autonomous self: "It is not one life that I look back upon; I am not one person; I am many people; I do not altogether know who I am – Jinny, Susan, Neville, Rhoda, or Louis; or how to distinguish my life from theirs" (Woolf, 1931, 237). Such a fluid sense of identity, however, is a crisis for the parade of David's women. Catherine, as she reads the waves, is fighting for autonomy, fighting to resist the drowning that overtook both Miss Farris and Virginia Woolf. We fight with Stella, in turn, to resist her identification with Dina and with the reproduced women who pose for advertisements.

Contradicting David's claim that she is a vegetarian, Catherine compliments Stella on the meal: "'It was fantastic, that roast. Did you put garlic on it?'" and Stella replies: "'Garlic and sage and rosemary'" (PL, 45). Engorging the pattern Rosemary and digesting it is the only hope of survival for women like Stella and Catherine (see Auerbach, 1985). As I turn now to the cook – the third and last image in the triple palimpsest – it is with an awareness of coming home without coming home. We are in "Stella's domain" (PL, 33) and this is certainly preferable to being at Dina's place. Stella's home, however, is a site of invasion and her house is one that we have seen before. "It was and is a high, bare wooden house, painted gray – a copy of the old farmhouses nearby" (PL, 32). It is also a copy of other houses constructed by Munro which, in turn, are copies of houses in earlier literature. Like that "barest, darkest, tallest of all old frame houses" in *Lives of Girls and Women* it has "something terrible about it" (LGW, 75). It's very familiarity is uncanny. It is the house, in fact, that reminds Catherine of the Bergman film (PL, 36–37).

Stella is the cook, but we can never be sure what she put into her meal. Like a good hostess, she makes us feel pleasurably at her mercy. The story makes us feel her power, however, in order to confront us finally with the limits of her power. The nature of her power is intimated with David's "fuming" comment that "'She's turned into a troll'" (PL, 32). *Troll* is a Swedish word meaning to charm or bewitch and Stella does have a bewitching power. The word also means "to go round and round" (*OED*) and is thus associated, like the Catherine wheel, with circularity. As a verb, the word is used for the act of moving or passing a vessel around the company: "to circulate; be passed around" (*OED*). Like the host at a eucharist, Stella does circulate among her guests. Her main power, however, inverts that image. She has the ability to *troll*: "to turn over in one's mind; to revolve, ponder, contemplate" (*OED*).

Stella is the main reader within this text. It is she who trolls or revolves the picture of Dina around in her mind like a still photograph turned into a moving picture. She is a character of tremendous vitality. In a particularly endearing gesture, she hides the last glass of home-made mead behind the blender and takes occasional sips as she cleans up. "'I have a fine life. Yes'" (PL, 44) she says to Catherine, and we want so much to believe her that we do. Yes, we say, yes. She offers, I think, a particular temptation to feminist readers because she nourishes herself while she feeds her mock-children: David and Catherine. If the picture of Dina is eclipsed by the blind spot and Catherine seems to have something "the matter with her eyes" (PL,

39), Stella is associated with vision. The word "stellar" points to the stars but it is not really her way of looking that endears Stella to us. She is an entertainer. Her bright clothes are compared to balloons and in her performance at the "Balm of Gilead Home" she acts as a balm to the inmates: "She called out various names in answer, detoured to press hands and drop kisses. Vibrating here and there like a fat hummingbird" (PL, 50). She nourishes the inmates as she nourishes her guests, singing about herself as a "*little sunbeam*" (PL, 50).

Stella finally says: "'Well, I can see now'" (PL, 42), when David confronts her with the picture of Dina. What is it, then, that she comes to see or that we see by her stellar light? Stella makes us comfortable in a kind of post-prandial way. Even as we make ourselves at home, however, we start worrying about the drugged Catherine. In the cold light of Stella's final revelations, we have to confront the questions with her. Can the daughter who performs as a little sunbeam compensate for the total blindness of the father? The biblical allusion to the Balm of Gilead demands that we pay attention, also, to the health of the daughters:

> For the hurt of the daughter of my people am I hurt; I am black; astonishment hath taken hold of me. / Is there no balm in Gilead; is there no physician there? why then is not the health of the daughter of my people recovered?
>
> (Jeremiah 8:21–22)

It is hard not to read this lamentation now as an ironic comment on post-feminism, especially since Atwood has invented the Republic of Gilead in *The Handmaid's Tale* (1985). "For they have healed the hurt of the daughter of my people slightly, saying, Peace, peace: when there is no peace" (Jeremiah 8:11). Despite visible advances by women in the public world, there has been no decrease in the number of women who are battered and raped.

Stella's own hurt becomes visible only when we see that the daughter in her is eliminated when she mothers her Daddy. As King and Author, the father ought to be the villain, but like the old woman in "Spelling," the father in this story communicates at the lowest common denominator of speech: "It was the core of each syllable that was presented, a damp vowel barely held in shape by surrounding consonants" (PL, 51). Stella's father is not given a name; he is, in fact, more often referred to as David's "father-in-law." This deflection of the law of the father puts the awareness of power repeatedly back on each individual character. The "wet cave deep inside" the father-in-law (PL, 50) is no more a place of origin than was the old woman in "Spelling." Jeremiah's question may be rephrased. "Is there no physician there?" becomes "Is there no father there?" and "Is there no mother there?" Who will worry about the health of the daughters in this story while the men talk about cars?

As we feel these questions pressing on the story, we become increasingly aware of the limits of Stella's power. Our mental picture of her has acted as an unconscious bulwark protecting us from confronting the bleakness of Dina's place. It is David, ironically, who finally holds our picture of Stella up so that we have to confront what we have helped to make:

> David had a picture of her as she had been twelve or fifteen years before. He saw her coming across the lawn at a suburban party, carrying a casserole . . . . Why did this picture please him so much? Stella coming across the lawn . . . Of course the food she brought would be wonderful, and she brought not only food but the whole longed-for spirit of the neighborhood party. With her overwhelming sociability, she gathered everybody in.
>
> (PL, 53)

Why does this picture please *us* so much, we might ask? It is easy enough to reject David's picture of Dina, but what if the composition of that picture depends on the composition of this picture of Stella? This picture, unlike the one of Dina, is one that easily gathers us in along with David. If we look at it closely we may confront our own participation in the reproduction of the web called "Lichen." Like the others in the company who conclude that she is a "wonderful person at a party," we easily add our voices to the chorus: "Sometimes she was a riot. *Your wife's a riot*" (PL, 53).

"Riot" is a word suggesting chaos. Like David, we have felt such "benevolence" towards Stella (PL, 53) that we may be shocked to find that our notion of her role is not "a notion Stella shared at all" (PL, 53). We cannot count on Stella to be the authoritative reader in the text. When David addresses her as "Madam Stella, the celebrated mind reader" (PL, 54) she places this in the category of "bitter and wounding things" that have now become "stale, useless and formal" (PL, 54). Earlier in the story David has compared the smell of a woman, when he is finished with her, to stale meat. Like the Gray-Dort (a car briefly made in Ontario) and like filmy pink dresses, a woman may be used up, obsolete. The older woman, Stella, who is discarded for a younger woman, Catherine (nearing 40), who is discarded for a still younger woman, Dina, leads mockingly not only back into infancy but also forwards into the final obsolescence of death. That Stella's hair is white and David dyes his hair is a mark of David's terror of his own mortality. Contingency, the fact that "what's to come is still unsure" (PL, 46) is what we feel with an intensity rare even in Munro, when Stella looks at the Polaroid snapshot of Dina for the second time.

The double-take comes with a difference. In between is not only our growing sense that a Catherine wheel is in operation, but also a lapse of time, the action of the sun. It is no longer a snapshot of Dina. The black pelt is now "bluish or greenish gray" (PL, 55). The figure of the naked woman is blotted out by time but now she becomes visible by being hidden. The only escape from total obliteration is to turn the title into a verb: to liken. It is Stella who has done the likening, who is conscious of herself in the act of comparing and reading.

> She remembers what she said when she first saw it. She said it was lichen. No, she said it looked like lichen. But she knew what it was at once. It seems to her now that she knew what it was even when David put his hand to his pocket. She felt the old cavity opening up in her. But she held on. She said, "Lichen." And now, look, her words have come true.

(PL, 55)

"She held on" is a phrase that echoes Stella's words to Catherine: "'Hang on'" (PL, 46). A woman may hang on, may resist the decomposition of her self but the "old cavity," like the "older woman" is older than the house, older than Lake Huron, and older than the cat (PL, 33). The "old cavity," in fact, is imaged in the horror of the "wet cave" that is the father's "post-human" mouth (PL, 50–51).

Who is responsible for the "hurt" of the daughters in this story? On the one hand, Stella wants to blame David: "This is David's doing. He left it there, in the sun" (PL, 55). On the other hand she is disturbed by the power inherent in the very act of beholding. In no other story by Munro does the battle between the "watcher" and the "keeper" reach such intensity. Watching the changes in the picture, Stella gains ironic knowledge. To what extent is she, by the same token, her sister's keeper? Having seen the pattern of the Catherine wheel and watched it "come true," was it enough to offer Catherine a glass of water? Like Jonathan Swift's Stella, Munro's Stella is a woman who "freely entertains / With Breeding, Humour, Wit, and Sense." Like Swift, we may conclude that she "So little gets for what she gives / We really wonder how she lives" (Swift, 1967, 213). Our increasing awareness of Stella's power has set up an undertow, however, that gradually exposes the collapse of her power. Stella is afraid of her own visionary power – unhappy that her "words have come true." We, in turn, have to recover the power we projected into her and this is not easily done. To look at the web we have woven in "Lichen" is, in the end, to cut the umbilical cord tying us to our mock mother. As we come face to face with our own power, the sheer fact of mortality comes to be a consolation. It is oddly comforting to be reminded that the power of the sunlight on the Polaroid shot is greater than that of the "*little sunbeam*" who acts as a mock mother at the "Balm of Gilead Home."

"THE MOON IN THE ORANGE STREET SKATING RINK": MOTHER AS TRICKSTER

"'She was dead but she was still bleeding,'" says Miss Kernaghan. The body in question in this bloody story within a story is the dead body of Callie's mother, lying on a hotel floor. In Miss Kernaghan's version she is a nameless thing, "howling and yelling" and "puffed up to a terrible size." That size is the place of Callie's beginning, and Miss Kernaghan – her adoptive mother – describes the birthing: "'The baby popped right out of her on the floor'" (PL, 150). The French-Canadian driver bites the umbilical cord and tries to stop the blood with snow. In a moment of terrifying violence he kicks the dog across the room while a strange woman screams. The dog lives but the mother dies: "'Blood was coming out of her as dark as fly poison – it was spreading across the floor'" (PL, 150).

This spreading maternal blood is lurid, melodramatic – as artifical as the moon itself. It is a contrived sign that draws attention to itself. I begin with it because it is a danger sign in the story, warning of a "kind of trouble whose extent you couldn't know and punishments you couldn't fathom." Edgar can feel "something being prepared – a paralyzing swipe" and Sam senses "larger implications" but neither of them know what or whom to fear. The question is inseparable from the issue of what is "real" and what is "artifice." The death of the "real" mother seems to leave a space, as it did in "Royal Beatings," for the storytelling of the mock mother. Like Sam, however, we may suspect that her stories are "probably a lie." "Callie, supposedly a foundling, was said by some to be Miss Kernaghan's daughter" (PL, 134). To adapt words used to describe the mock father in "Wild Swans," Miss Kernaghan could be a real mother dressed as if she were not, or, stranger still, a woman who is not a real mother pretending to be real but dressed as if she is not (WDY, 64).

It seems impossible and yet urgently necessary to extricate ourselves from this web of illusions. It helps to avert our eyes for the moment from the maternal blood and think about the storytelling process itself as it relates to the mother–daughter relationship. The daughter in question here appears as a "sickly looking thing" in the birthing. While the story is told, however, Callie performs as Slavey. She is a marginalized member of the audience, listening to the story of her own origins. She it is who comes out of the terrible puffed up blackness of the pregnant woman and she is thus the centre of the story within the story, the hole in the story without which we could not see. But she, in a manner different from Dina, is blacked out. Callie is polishing the black part of the stove during this telling. She is "smudged from head to foot. Even her eyelids were black." But she is not silent. Like an unheard descant over the telling, she sings "Oh, my darling Nellie Grey." As we tune in to her performance, we gain a kind of release, but one that can be achieved only if we read the signs of her invasion. Munro's method puts us at a distance from the child-mother who is the pupil at the heart of this story. The framing visit pictures Callie as "quite painted up herself, under a pinkish-blond wig" (PL, 133). This story poses some of the questions that wrinkle the "deep, blue-painted nests around her eyes" (PL, 161).

The scene of biological procreation polluting the public space is ironic because the main focus is in fact on cultural reproduction and on artifice; the nests are painted. Callie is herself an artifice, a conscious literary reproduction. Like Rose she plays out a distorted version of the Cinderella role. We may think of the black slaves of the American South, or of Blake's little black thing in the snow. The foundling theme touches on Dickensian echoes. We may think of Charley, the maid in *Bleak House* or, more likely, of Jenny Wren, the doll's dressmaker in *Our Mutual Friend*. Like many of the surrogate child-mothers in Dickens, Callie is miniaturized. Jenny speaks of her father as a "bad, bad child" and Callie, too, treats grown men like babies. Unlike Jenny, however, Callie does not weep behind a bower of bright hair. She laughs, rather, under her "pinkish-blond wig" (PL, 132). Where Dickens pictures child-mothers as victims, Munro shows Callie acting out the revenge of a trickster mother who was once the dispossessed child. The blackness out of which Callie comes is accentuated because she is the victim of a kind of double rape.

The story told by Sam includes an image that fits all too neatly into the story told by Miss Kernaghan about Callie's birth. "Something very important is missing from Sam's memory of that morning – blood" (PL, 145). If it is a phantom rape, then will the subsequent pregnancy also be phantom? Sam assumes that the sign of the real means that there has to be blood. In this tallying of stories – one with too much blood, the other with no blood – there is a grotesque symmetry which makes of Callie a bloodless doll. In Irigaray's phrase, there is a blind spot in this old dream of symmetry and Munro explores that blind spot in depth by means of the bizarre setting of the skating rink. Like the underground house in "Images," the rink is a place to explore issues concerning reflection and representation of images. The arena makes a good place for circus acts if only you can penetrate it. Like Callie's womb, it is at first impenetrable but it is Callie, ironically, who enables Sam and Edgar to invade the rink.

Unlike Callie's birthing, her "rape" is no melodramatic scene, no violent dispossession and this is primarily because of her mock acquiescence. Her pubic hair, unlike Dina's lichen, is a "tuft of dead looking hair." "It was as if they had used a doll or a compliant puppy" (PL, 146). The power inside Callie is projected and displaced into the arena where it can be unpacked and examined. There we may watch "the shadows instead of the people" (DHS, 35), shadows created in this pseudo-Platonic cave by the action of a fake moon. There we may observe the shenanigans of two acrobats and the mimicking actions of Callie, the "pretend-boy" (PL, 155) called Cal.

Here, surely, is the mocking heart – or rather, uterus – at the centre of *The Progress of Love*. The gender conflict is played out like a choreographed dance or circus act. Sam and Edgar want to become acrobats, but Sam

> could not picture Edgar and himself in a circus. They were not dark enough, for one thing. (He had an idea that the people who worked in circuses were all Gypsies.) He thought there must be acrobats going around on their own, doing stunts at fairs and in church halls.
>
> (PL, 135)

Paul Bouissac observes that "acrobatic acts are very often followed by, or even carried out simultaneously with, clown acts, which constitute a part of the act. The role of the clown is to provide laughter through parodic or absurd acrobatic behaviour" (Bouissac, 1976, 44). Munro's adaptation is startlingly close to a conventional sequence described by Bouissac:

> A group of acrobats begin their exercises, and as soon as the first introductory movements have been completed, a grotesque figure comes forward and makes known his desire to join the acrobats. His first attempts are failures. He gives the impression of copying their gestures, but in vain. He falls or gets caught up in the accessories, and shows through mime that he overestimated his physical strength or courage.
>
> (Bouissac, 1976, 44)

Sam and Edgar begin their exercises by performing in a vacant lot. Callie, the clown, is not present. "If Callie watched, it was from behind windows. She always had her work" (PL, 136). Callie is too busy performing the maternal function to join the performance yet. Their success as acrobats depends, in fact, on her absence. "They shaped their bodies into signs – into hieroglyphs – eliminating to an astonishing degree their separateness and making the bumps of heads and shoulders incidental" (PL, 135). These hieroglyphs, however, are signs without significance until they collapse into failure (see Bouissac, 1990a, 409–443). When the "creations toppled, everything came apart, arms and legs flew free, and grappling bodies reappeared – just two boys' bodies" (PL, 135).

Enter Callie, the clown. The clowns described by Bouissac are male, but here the role is accentuated because the clown is female. "The function of the clown," as Bouissac observes, is to represent

> a biologically inferior being, one who would not survive in many animal species because of his peers or his predators, a being toward whom aggression is expressed. And laughter seems to be one of the expressions of aggression in the human species.
>
> (Bouissac, 1976, 46)

At first Callie's clowning role seems consistent with her inferior position as a female. When the boys first meet her she is the very image of the working-class mother whose work is never done. "It is a hard life," writes Hoggart, "in which it is assumed that the mother will be 'at it' from getting up to going to bed: she will cook, mend, scrub, wash" (Hoggart, 1958, 42). Like a perfect super mother, Callie even finds time to do needlework and has a scrapbook of newspaper clippings as evidence of the competitions she has won. Like Arachne who competes with Athena in a "contest of representation" (Miller, 1986a, 272), Callie competes with the implied icons of the maternal role. She is also the very embodiment of a Protestant work ethic: "In her own estimation, she was no slavey but a prodigy pitying the slothful lives of others" (PL, 142). Her pride in her work is exposed as an overestimation of her strength. She cannot refuse a dare: "Jokes and dares were what finally disarmed her" (PL, 142). The rape of Callie, in this sense, is a kind of practical joke, but it is Callie who has the last laugh. Clownishly lying flat on her back for the boys, she would appear to be at their mercy, disarmed and biologically inferior.

Callie's staged weakness, however, is her means of achieving strength. The card she later sends, pretending to be Chrissie, is like the mimicry of the white-faced clown by the "clown proper" who "'wrongly' repeats words, which, out of this context, would not have any meaning" (Bouissac, 1976, 45). As the circus progresses, however, Callie's role is revealed as more complex. The clown who performs alongside acrobats often sheds his "grotesque costume and performs the most difficult exercises of the group" (Bouissac, 1976, 45). Callie's performance fits this description. Her aerial act in the skating rink is like a daring competition with Sam and Edgar. When she climbs through the roof of the rink, "risking a fall to the ice below and broken bones or even death" she does no more than what is done by many another boy: "But boys risked that all the time" (PL, 141). So why did others, boys especially, "not manage the same trick. . . . And why was Callie not noticed?" (PL, 141). Her balancing act is not like the "magic balance" achieved by Sam and Edgar as acrobats (PL, 136). It is a staged survival scene.

Bouissac notes that in some cases the clown who copies acrobats may ostensibly diminish the stunt. The clown, for example, may walk on a sidewalk while pretending to do the same trick there that the acrobats did on a trapeze. Initially Munro's story seems to reverse this situation, with the acrobats performing on solid ground and Callie doing an aerial act. As we observe the larger pattern of Callie's manipulations, however, we can see Callie playing out her power on a nearly invisible mundane level. When she traps Edgar into a romance pattern (with herself in the role of the bride) she outmanoeuvers the men. Her calm serene happiness on the train when she prevents their escape resembles that "smile of ease with which [an acrobat] ends his exercises" (Bouissac, 1976, 45). These are not merely exercises; they are stunts necessary to survival. Whether the clowns and acrobats are on the sidewalk or on a trapeze, the performance can be "defined as a series of compensations for loss of balance. From a biological point of view, both sequences are acts of survival" (Bouissac, 1976, 45).

Callie, then, is a mothering clown with tremendous power. She knows how to exploit her own marginality, to turn her weakness into power. Her stunts (in the skating rink and within the conventions of romance narrative) are based on an instinctive but profound understanding of the rules of this pseudo-Platonic game. First masquerading as a child-mother, then appearing as a "pretend boy," Callie withdraws deeper and deeper into disguise, seeming to be just another boy's body, only to emerge with startling effect as the stereotyped image of an over-nurturing mother. I am reminded of Olive Schreiner's rhetorical question: "Has the pen or pencil dipped so deep in the blood of the human race as the needle?" (quoted by Parker, 1984, 15). If Huck Finn, in disguise as a girl, gives himself away by his clumsiness with a needle, then Callie, the "pretend boy" gives herself away by her skill with a needle. The patterns she uses, however, are not her own creation. When the boys ask if she makes up her pictures, she is "incensed" and informs them that she sends away to Cincinnati for them.

In whatever factory they are reproduced, the patterns enacted by Callie are distressingly familiar. When Sam returns to Gallagher after many years, he finds Callie reading: "*My Love Where the High Winds Blow*, by Veronica Gray" (PL, 132). The title is a clue to the nature of Callie's special power as a reader within this text. Like a steel structure imbedded within the chiaroscuro shapes of this story is the pattern of a formula romance. Far from sneering at Callie's reading material, Munro shows how the formula is acted out in the day-to-day lives of ordinary people. Callie's strategy of disguise, being so bound up with story patterns, invites comparison with Munro's own narrative strategies. We are enabled to maintain ironic distance from Callie's way of reading. As Arthur is contained within Et's story in "Something I've Been Meaning to Tell You," so Edgar falls victim to Callie's designs. We gain distance from this because we enter the story with Sam, who is foregrounded as a reader in the text. The failure of the acrobatic stunt makes it possible for Sam to be a spectator of Edgar's collapse.

Edgar is described by Callie, in the end, as having "had a little turn" (PL, 158). The symptoms of his illness, however, appear much earlier in the story. Callie pictures his malady in the "get-well card" that she sends him during his first illness.

> It showed a green dragon in striped pajamas propped up in bed. On the front of the card were the words, "Sorry to Hear your Tail is Draggon," and inside "Hope that Soon, You'll have it Waggon." Down at the bottom, in pencil, was written the name Chrissie.
>
> (PL, 147)

Callie succeeds with her clumsy piece of subterfuge because it is an imitation of Edgar's own "seduction" of Callie. He proposes to show her "what I do to my girlfriend. Here's what I do to Chrissie" (PL, 145). In all this there is an implied image of rape followed by castration. The dragon's tail drags instead of becoming part of a circus parade. Like the cat in "Lichen," it is a sadly diminished mythic beast. In medieval embroidery patterns, St Margaret, the patron saint of childbirth, is shown as victoriously spearing the dragon. St Margaret triumphed over the dragon that swallowed her up just as she was making the sign of the cross; the cross took shape within the dragon, it split open and Margaret escaped unharmed (Parker, 1984, 36). In Victorian versions, according to Parker, Margaret loses her spear and gains power from the glorification of her suffering as she meekly raises her eyes to heaven in supplication.

Callie's help, by contrast, does not come in either of these ways. She helps herself by wielding her needle like a sword and her power comes from her reading ability, from her understanding of the embroidery patterns of narrative. Callie's tale is a devouring dragon. She might be said, using Nina Auerbach's phrase, to have engorged the patriarchy even as it threatens to engorge her. In a parody of Christian sacrifice, she acts *as* Chrissie voluntarily after having been coerced into being Chrissie during the rape. Like the name Chris in "How I Met My Husband," the name Chrissie acts almost as a kind of anti-allusion; it asks us to think not so much about the transcendental significance of a signifier as about the power of the person manipulating the sign. With her performance as Chrissie, Callie turns the narrative pattern to her own advantage. The echo of Little Bo Peep in the "get-well card" reflects the radical diminishment of the dragon. Callie's sheep will come, wagging their tails behind them and Edgar is like a lamb led to the slaughter.

Simply an ordinary woman reading a formula romance in her store, Callie represents a person who can get inside the story that has been imposed on her and, by performing it, suit it to her own needs. The get-well wishes and the hopes for Edgar's future are deeply ironic and the zany, juvenile humour cannot disguise the "paralyzing swipe" that immobilizes the acrobats. This wagon of the eternal child in us that longs for mothering will not make the progress of love. St Margaret's imitation of Christ kills her dragon. Callie's imitation of Chrissie defines the dragon as a patient. The woman gains her power simply by *being* the nurse and the man's striped garb indicates that he is a prisoner of his own design.

It is significant that Callie does not, biologically, become a mother. Although she lies obligingly under them both as they take turns "jabbing and prodding," the results are "bafflement" (PL, 146). There was no need for Sam and Edgar to run away from Callie or for Edgar to marry Callie. "There was no necessity – none that Sam could see. Callie was not pregnant and, in fact, as far as Sam knows she never became pregnant. Perhaps she really was too small, or not developed in the usual way" (PL, 160). The shadows cast by the fake moon as the rinkie dinks pull the wires construct a scene in which all the roles are confused and a man has the hysterical pregnancy. Callie gains her power by repudiating the biological essentialism of traditional views of maternity and embracing, instead, the fiction that embraces her. She understands that the moon is a bulb in a syrup tin, that mother may be a little boy and that boys may be mothers to each other. Callie is our guide to an underworld which is not a primeval cave but a world of mirrors and artifice. The strategy she uses to gain entrance into the skating rink is a shadowy reflection of the strategy she uses to draw Edgar into her world. This is a kind of inverted birth, a hideous infantilization of Edgar that returns him to the womb and destroys his life.

Since Callie is described as a slave with a "spitting, mocking, fierce look" (PL, 143), she might be seen as a distorted literary echo of Caliban. No Miranda and Ferdinand are seen to be pairing off in a brave new world, however. No Prospero acts with magical creative power. Who, then, is it that manipulates and deceives the eye with sleight of hand; who controls this illusory world? Munro herself, by the unusual self-consciousness of her strategy, seems to clownishly act out this role. "Magic" is a word that was used with regard to Sam and Edgar's acrobatics. It is also used in connection with Callie's power, but as Munro unpacks the word we gain further insight into her response to her own creative power. On the train, Sam and Edgar see Callie as "exercising powers that didn't fall far short of being miraculous" (PL, 155). Their tendency to label her as a magician is itself a function of their own weakness as readers, a weakness that derives from their desire to essentialize power. In Callie's actions there was "lucky timing and lucky guessing every step of the way – but that was all. It was not magic, not quite" (PL, 155).

Callie's achievement, after all, is nothing more complicated than the fact that she makes the boys see her as a woman. At first, as a "pretend boy," she sits on the train, just outside their line of vision. The men find, however, that they cannot travel any longer "without really looking" at her (PL, 155). The sexual connotations of the phrase "to know a woman" are ironic here:

> Sam would never know exactly when he first knew it was Callie, or how the knowledge came to him, and whether he looked at Edgar or simply knew that Edgar knew the same thing he did and at the same time.
>
> (PL, 155)

In their earlier collapses, Sam and Edgar became "just two boys' bodies" (PL, 135): this collapse leaves us with the bodies of two men and the body of one woman. When Callie first joins them she has "her boy's look on" and is a "good-humored boy, more or less, with reasonable expectations" (PL, 156). Her real desires, however, are based on the fact that she is a woman and this is what makes for the collapse of the circus act. As they collapse in a heap, the three experience the euphoria of a brief carnivalesque moment. Sam

> saw power – Callie's power, when she wouldn't be left behind – gener-ously distributed to all of them. The moment was flooded with power, it seemed, and with possibility. But this was just happiness. It was really just happiness.
>
> (PL, 156–157)

This happiness might have lasted if the three – two male acrobats and one female clown – could have joined the right kind of circus. We know, however, that "Callie's presence was bound to bring them all sorts of trouble once they descended into the real world" (PL, 156). Callie's presence is predictably problematic because that "real world" operates on the assumption of the absence of her body.

It would be easy to read the story by simply condemning Callie. She is certainly a wicked trickster whose revenge on Edgar seems out of proportion to his crime. If I am right, however, then we are being asked (here, even more than in the case of Et) to look at the story pattern itself, more than at the person manipulating the story. The action resembles that in Dante's *Purgatorio* as described by Durling: "The trickster cooks up his scheme, the victim swallows his story, and once the victim has swallowed the story, he is caught in it. The deceiver seeks to make the victim swallow what will then swallow the victim" (Durling, 1981, 80). Callie is swallowed by the story but then swallows it and deceives Edgar into swallowing his own story.

These convolutions become impossible to negotiate unless we pay atten-tion to Munro's way of framing this story. The story is framed by Sam's visit to Callie and Edgar's home. One result of this frame is that we define ourselves as readers with relation to Sam's response. As Sam visits, looking at the wedding picture and looking at the marriage of Callie and Edgar, we stand at a further remove. The biblical echo in Sam's name ironically suggests vision but this Samuel does not have designs revealed to him in a dream by God (I Samuel 3). This Sam is just another reader, like us. His inadequacies are so painfully apparent and so clearly work alongside Edgar's paralysis that we are urged into activity as readers. The shadowy memory of the actions in the skating rink are contrasted to the colours of Callie in the present tense. Sam sees in her store "hand-lettered signs in red and blue crayon" warning against "alcohol, fighting, loitering, and swearing" (PL, 132). These signs correspond with the image of Callie as the perpetual virgin, even puritanical. Callie will always live, in a sense, on Orange Street, with values reflecting the fiercely protestant world of rural Ontario. "Callie's place upstairs is stunning" and Sam sees himself there "crisscrossed by veins of black and silver" in the "dull-gold mirror" (PL, 158). The betrayal of that moment of happiness and recognition on the train is now total. It is impossible to tell image from reality. Edgar is himself a "polished ornament." Like a doll, he sits watching, on television, a young woman interviewing an older woman who makes dolls: "The dolls are made of dough" (PL, 158).

This image recalls the doughnuts that Edgar cannot eat when his panic about Callie's possible pregnancy makes him "half sick" (PL, 148). Who is eating and who is being eaten? The question continues to reverberate in Munro's fiction. The frames are no less constricting for being brittle. A picture of wedded bliss stands on the "false mantel over the electric fireplace" (PL, 159) and Sam remembers that the picture was staged long after the wedding itself. The temporal dislocation takes us beyond this particular story. "Callie looks a good deal older than on her real wedding day, her face broader, heavier, more authoritative. In fact, she slightly resembles Miss Kernaghan" (PL, 159). As mock mother, Callie achieves her power almost invisibly because she is such a good mimic. Edgar is helpless. When Sam notes that he does not "'want to go out after all,'" Callie simply says: "'No. He's happy'" (PL 161).

Most readers, however, will surely be very unhappy by now. We leave Callie's stifling world behind with relief. There is no possibility of making the progress of love on Orange Street. Since the paralysis is at least partly associated with a particular kind of theology (colour it orange), it may not be farfetched to see Callie and Cal as names associated with Calvin. In "Caliban upon Setebos," Robert Browning offers a useful reading of Calvinism and of *The Tempest*, useful because it teaches us that we do wrong to project horrifying power into figures external to us. Browning's Setebos lives in "the cold of the Moon," but Caliban has in fact created Setebos in his own image. Caliban's cave, in which he projects images of his tyrannical god, is not totally unlike Munro's skating rink. We are always, with Munro, in a world of images constructed and projected by people. Even Hattie and Mattie Milton, in "Who Do You Think You Are?," control their own projector. Edgar, however, denies his own acrobatic powers when he projects them into the woman who nurses him.

The horrors in this story are imaged in flashes of melodrama. A touch of orange here. A splash of blood there. The fact that we need so little with which to scare ourselves exposes our fear of our own freedom. The real danger lies not in some villain who is preparing a "paralyzing swipe" for us but in our willingness to project power into villains outside ourselves. Callie is a victim who makes a spectacle of herself and thus risks becoming a villain. She makes it possible for us to question our own powers and the limits of those powers. We catch ourselves skating in circles, our vision controlled by the rinkie dinks, our actions subject to maternal powers. As happens almost invariably in Munro's story, we are left with a staged dilemma that asks questions and offers no answers. We are made conscious of our desire to abdicate our freedom and crawl back under the covers.

Simultaneously, however, we can also see that this is no way to make the progress of love.

"WHITE DUMP": THE SURVIVAL OF DESIRE

"White Dump" concludes this collection and points forward to the detailed unravellings of marital infidelities that take place in Munro's most recent stories. The infidelity in this story is dramatic because it pulls against the grain of our expectations of mothers. Beginning with "Walker Brothers Cowboy," the father has always been allowed his infidelities. In "Progress of Love," for example, the father is easily forgiven by his daughter Beryl for a possible sexual indiscretion: "'He was supposed to be interested in some girl that kept coming around to the works. Well, he was a big good-looking man" (PL, 21). In "Walker Brothers Cowboy," the echoing phrase "'Just don't tell your mother'" is directed in large part to the daughter's shared knowledge of her father's secret life of desire. In "White Dump," by contrast, we are reminded that there is sex after mothering. Isabel's affair with a pilot recapitulates aspects of Edie's desire for a pilot in "How I Met My Husband" with the important difference that Isabel, unlike Edie, is a mother.

We can track the progress made by Munro's women if we observe their changing relation to the telling of jokes. When Sophie becomes the brunt of jokes in the family, she is not, as was the mother in earlier stories, the object of our pity. "Denise's mother and father had a name for Sophie that was a joke between them, and a secret. Old Norse" (PL, 280). Laurence announces: "'My mother isn't quite your average mom. She can read Old Norse. In fact, she *is* sort of an Old Norse" (PL, 280). This identification of Sophie with what she studies and "reads" as a scholar becomes central to Munro's oblique way of salvaging Sophie's very existence. The power of the secret nickname is dwarfed by the power of Sophie's "secret" knowledge of Old Norse stories, a knowledge that makes her more than an old nurse. Denise is the one who seems to sense this. When Laurence says "'Never tell Grandma about this game, Denise,'" Denise asks: "'Wouldn't Grandma think it was funny, too?'" (PL, 281).

These questions are clarified when Sophie becomes the victim of a practical joke. Floating naked on her back in the lake, looking at the "high bank of pine and cedar, poplar and soft maple" – the poplar leaves flashing "like coins in the sun," Sophie could be seen as at one with mother earth. By the simple act, however, of swimming in the heart of Ontario's familiar cottage territory, she performs a stunt that protests the fate of Miss Farris and other drowned women in Munro's earlier stories. When an audience comes to view her performance, however, Sophie's power is tested. The nameless figures steal her clothes and (in a parody of the Prometheus story) her cigarette lighter. Sophie eventually returns to the house and stands naked before her family. This second stunt is much more daring than the swimming stunt but also much more crucial to the survival of her own fiery spirit. The mother who did the headstand in "Connection" was clothed in the father's overalls. This one, as Isabel seems to know, is clothed too: "Crafty innocence. The stagy old show-off. Showing off her purity, her high-mindedness, her simplicity. Perverse old fraud" (PL, 301). Her aim, as Isabel sees it, is to "make her own son look foolish. To make him look a fool in front of his wife and children" (PL, 301).

Isabel – Denise's mother – blames her affair with the pilot on this image of the naked body of "Old Norse." "It was the idea of herself, not Sophie, walking naked out of the water toward those capering boys" (PL, 305). Here, as in "The Progress of Love," the generations blur into each other. A maternal line is there – Sophie to Isabel to Denise – but it is disrupted. Sophie, in fact, is Isabel's mother-in-law and this dislocation is accentuated by the fact that Denise is talking to Magda, her father's new wife. As we observe this palimpsest of maternal figures, the disruption of linearity helps us to question our assumptions about what they ought, naturally, to be doing.

Isabel herself, on that fateful day, is busy organizing Laurence's birthday party, seeing "her day as hurdles got through. . . . Not much to her credit to go through life thinking, Well, good, now that's over, *that's* over" (PL, 303). What Isabel does for Laurence was foreseen by Sophie, who knew that Laurence would have to be "propped up, kept going, by constant and clever exertions on her part, by reassurance and good management; he depended on her to make him a man" (PL, 304). The nurturing or mothering wife props up the phallocentric system. As Isabel yearns for release, then, it is not so much release from Laurence as from this ideology. Sophie's body becomes an embodiment of an image of liberty as she swims vigorously, floats serenely, walks towards the male gaze, and as she performs for the family circus. In all these ways Sophie's attention to herself goes contrary to the behaviour of Isabel who pays attention to her family. Isabel is oppressed by her caretaking role and longs for liberty:

> Freedom – or not even freedom. Emptiness, a lapse of attention. It seemed all the time that she was having to provide a little more – in the way of attention, enthusiasm, watchfulness – than she was sure she had. She was straining, hoping not to be found out. Found to be as cold at heart as that Old Norse, Sophie.
>
> (PL, 303)

Freedom, however, is not so easily achieved as the pilot's short flights might suggest. The affair itself, like those flights, may be only a cheap thrill. Although it does serve to free Isabel from her life with this family, we discover that she is already contained within another pattern. Isabel ends up living on a farm in British Columbia with a "commercial fisherman who used to be a TV cameraman" (PL, 277–278). They rent out the farm to "a man who raises goats" and this fact is used by Laurence in an effort to make Isabel the victim of a practical joke. He locks up his image of her in "some sort of ghastly outdated idealism" that is encapsulated in the image of goat milk. He whites her out, in a sense, with this mock maternal metaphor. Although the image of milk might suggest that Isabel remains a captive of ideological assumptions about maternal self-sacrifice, the complexity of this joke allows for a possible escape. Like Sophie, indeed, Isabel may be released by her very victimization since Laurence, given the comfort of this mock power, leaves her alone. His daughter Denise, however, remains disturbed by his distortions as he jokes: "'Enough counterculture left out there to buy goat milk'" (PL, 278). His new wife Magda is similarly braced to see herself as a possible victim: "'Is this the new in-joke?' says Magda. 'What am I missing? Goat milk?'" (PL, 278).

Who is the victim of this joke – Denise's mother Isabel, her stepmother Magda, or Denise herself? "Don't tell Momma" is an imperative that cannot be easily obeyed when we are no longer sure which woman is Momma. Laurence's relations with his new wife Magda, his mother Sophie, his ex-wife Isabel, and his daughter Denise are disturbingly similar. Each of them is required to prop him up. The conflict is focussed in Denise, who fights against the fragmentation of her family, but it is experienced with greatest intensity by Sophie. When Sophie goes up in a small plane for the first time, she feels herself shrinking. The date is 1969, the "year of the moon shot" (PL, 278) and the image used to convey Sophie's fear mimes the images she would be seeing on television, an image of a shrinking earth. She imagines the whole family "whisked off and cancelled, curled up into dots, turned to atoms" (PL, 296). Atomistic detail frightens here, as it did in *Lives of Girls and Women* and in "The Moons of Jupiter." Isabel's brief intimacy with the pilot is a response to this danger. The mother who has to try to keep the family circus act together by getting through "hurdles" (PL, 303) falls into the safety net of sex.

The affair with the pilot takes place on the ground but (like the scene in "How I Met My Husband") it is like a circus accident, a fall from the combined family high-wire act. The "small white house that had obviously been hauled here from somewhere else" (PL, 308) is a deliberately makeshift structure, like the tent in "How I Met My Husband." Adultery, unlike a marriage, arrests the forward movement of narrative flow. It is a staged performance that does not fit into the family circus at all and for that very reason it serves to make visible the body of the mother. Before her affair, Isabel is an "understood" element of the circus, the one behind the scenes who keeps the group performance going. After the affair, she is in some way liberated but that liberation is by no means absolute. The geographical distance between Ontario and British Columbia intimates the vaster distances of outer space that become an image for the distances that separate the members of the family. Like the "negative experience" staged at a circus, the near accidents, the collapses of relationship, the missed communications – all of these appear to be performed by "the core members of a family." Adapting Paul Bouissac, I note that "the situation is such that their respective position in space makes it impossible for them to rescue one another in case of difficulty" (Bouissac, 1990a, 440).

Although the details in "White Dump" evoke the counterculture of the 1960s, the emotional core of the experience is not new. Sophie recognizes it as something that she had "as a child. A genuine shrinking feeling, one of the repertoire of frightening, marvellous feelings, or states, that are available to you when you're very young" (PL, 296). The comparison (in a story about children eating candy) leads implicitly to an image of Lewis Carroll's Alice, shrinking almost out of existence because of what she eats. Although Denise sees herself in a kind of caretaker role in this family, it is impossible for her to play the part of child-mother. Her mother and her grandmother are in no need of rescue. The fact that they do not need her mothering leaves Denise with a dilemma. She blames her mother for not keeping the family circus together: "Her fault, Denise thinks. Isabel's" (PL, 288).

Blame, however, doesn't stick easily if we keep in mind the mountain of candy that represents our insatiable desires. In "The Big Rock Candy Mountain" (WDY, 10), the betrayal can be identified in the vague figure of the "hobo pied piper" who recruits poor children with a fantasy of "children in wonderland" (Leisy, 1966, 27). An implicit political question becomes increasingly insistent in Munro's stories as the very depth of her compassion makes it impossible to point a finger of blame. The "kid's dream" (PL, 306) comes out of an anonymous "biscuit factory" but Denise's anger needs a target if it is not to turn into despair. Her dilemma is pictured as she watches herself in the "darkening glass" of the window, carefully setting the table (PL, 288). The darkness behind her own image is picked up in the stories read by her grandmother and the image of cannibalism disrupts the dinner party here as it did in "Lichen."

> "In those old poems she reads," said Isabel, "you know those old Icelandic poems, there is the most terrible gore and hacking people up – women particularly, one slitting her own kids' throats and mixing the blood in her husband's wine. I read that."
>
> (PL, 281)

The muffled cries of these children in the distant background mingle disturbingly with the implied cries of the women who come to the "Women's Centre in Toronto" – where Denise works at getting "beaten women into shelters" (PL, 276). The ancient cries have become part of the entertainment we call Literature but Laurence collapses past and present when he taunts his daughter by suggesting that the women she helps are "enjoying all the attention they are getting, claiming to be battered and raped, and so on" (PL, 276).

In the face of such familiar dispossession, a woman reader might well feel like Sophie, "heated by a somber, useless rage." Like Sophie, then, the reader must take time "to compose herself" (PL, 292). Like Jeanette in "Marrakesh," Sophie has everything stolen and takes the composition of herself as her own responsibility. By the time she appears at the house she is ready to make a spectacle of herself. When she surfaces from the near-dissolution of her identity, she is no longer naked but clothed in nakedness.

> She didn't hurry past the family. She stood in the sunlight, one foot on the bottom step of the veranda – slightly increasing the intimate view they could all get of her – and said calmly, "Down there, I was dispossessed of my bathrobe."
>
> (PL, 300)

Sophie's daughter-in-law, Isabel, assumes that Sophie is enjoying the attention she gets from having claimed a kind of rape. We, however, are at an ironic distance from the various spectators. Sophie, after all, claims dispossession only of her bathrobe – not of her very self. Although she drapes herself in the tablecloth that her son throws at her, Sophie will not be eaten. She refuses the role of family hostess. The family does not consume her attention; she always has time left over for Old Norse.

A matrilineal tradition of anger is hidden in this story but Denise is blocked from contact with it, partly because she cannot read Old Norse. Isabel refers to "those old poems she reads" and adds: "'I read that'" (PL, 281). Denise, however, has no access to this shared text. While Laurence (her father) is content and Isabel (her mother) "has no regrets" (PL, 288), Denise continues, however, to feel a rage that makes a potential connection with her grandmother. The three women who fail to come together in actual communication seem to come together, ominously, in the story's final allusion. At the end of the day that is seen by Denise as marking the end of the family, Sophie reads *The Poetic Edda* while the rest of the family plays charades. She leaves the book behind when she goes to bed and Isabel picks it up and reads this verse:

> "*Seinat er at segia;*
> *sva er nu radit.*

(It is too late to talk of this now; it has been decided.)" (PL, 309). By this simple device, Munro prevents the erasure of Sophie. She remains before us as the body of a woman in the act of reading. Although the disturbing contents of what she reads serve to block a euphoric celebration of women's reading power, there is no question that the act of reading or beholding is crucial to the woman's survival. As we observe the mother (Isabel) reading what the grandmother (Sophie) read, however, we are also made conscious of the fact that the daughter (Denise) is left out of this line. Were Denise to join in that process and investigate the text in question, she might find a way of expressing or directing her anger. The story seems to acknowledge that efforts to open up a space for a maternal line in history cannot get around anger.

The exaggerated fatalism of the quotation, however, is ironically hopeful. "It is too late" is a phrase that invites repudiation. The reader can protest and contradict the finality, then get down to work and construct an alternative vision. The details of that story make clear the enormity of this task and the responsibilities of this potential power. The quotation that ends the book comes from Stanza 26 of *Atlamol*, a story about a woman who takes revenge on her husband by killing her own children and feeding them to their father. Such gruesome tales seem very far from the amicable separations here pictured. If we think, however, of the revenge of the trickster mother as seen in Et and Callie, we may interpret this as an oblique distillation of a complex danger envisioned by Munro in any exercise of power. We envision the ultimate horror of infanticide in order to repudiate it and that repudiation returns us to the act of reading itself. The challenge is for the woman to forge a matrilineal tradition that does not lead from "somber, useless rage" into the violence of such vengeance.

While it is by no means clear just how these women will be able to make the progress of love, we sense that they must learn to balance the acts of watching and keeping. Sophie's watching, like Stella's in "Lichen," is associated with a dangerous, almost prophetic vision. The very title of this story, however, belies her futuristic vision just as it challenges an ironically fatalistic conclusion. The shape of things to come has not been decided and it is not too late to talk about our desires. The two words "White Dump" refer specifically to a mountain of white candy remembered by Isabel:

> "You know we used to have the White Dump? At the school I went to – it was behind a biscuit factory, the playground backed on to the factory property. Every now and then, they'd sweep up these quantities of vanilla icing and nuts and hardened marshmallow globs and they'd bring it in barrels and dump it back there and it would shine. It would shine like a pure white mountain. Over at the school, somebody would see it and yell, 'White Dump!'"

> (PL, 306)

This "kid's dream" gleams like a parody of Shelley's "Mont Blanc." Unlike Shelley's mountain, it is not the seat of a power that "dwells apart in its tranquillity, / Remote, serene, and inaccessible" (Shelley, 1905, 534). The association with Shelley's image of a "still, snowy, and serene" mountain (533) is more immediately apparent in the image that triggers Isabel's memory. Laurence tells Isabel about seeing the silica quarry from the plane. "'It was like a snowfield'" he comments. "'White marble,' said Sophie, quoting. 'Pretentious stuff. They've put it on all the park paths in Aubreyville, spoiled the park. Glaring'" (PL, 306). The word *quoting* draws a parallel between this phrase and the one that forms the title. That, too, is a quotation. "'White Dump!' said Laurence – who, at another time, to such a story might have said something like 'Simple pleasures of the poor!' 'White Dump,' he said, with a mixture of pleasure and irony, a natural appreciation that seemed to be exactly what Isabel wanted" (PL, 307). This ephemeral moment of understanding when husband quotes wife is elevated in importance when Munro selects it as a title.

"Exactly what Isabel wanted," of course, we can intuit from her affair with the pilot. Isabel's desires for secret sexual pleasure undermine this surface level of words and quotations. Laurence's name, Vogelsang, means bird song in German and picks up one of many anti-romantic echoes. Unlike Shelley's Mont Blanc, this dump is accessible; Isabel remembers the children "scrabbling away at that enormous pile of white candy" (PL, 306). Munro, however, does not allow us to stay in the relatively stable position that is assumed by "The Man on the Dump" in the poem by Wallace Stevens. This dump is not so much a dump full of stale images as it is an image of vanity and excessive desire, reminding us of "poor children" in a consumer society. The whiteness that is observed by Sophie from the plane, like an alien moonscape, captures a little of what we might feel if we could take in the Copernican revolution. Sophie "felt as if it was she, not the things on earth, that had shrunk" and she continues to shrink until she reaches an "awareness of exquisite smallness. Her stomach shrivelled up: her lungs were as much use as empty seed sacs; her heart was the heart of an insect" (PL, 296). From this position of smallness, Sophie views what she later speaks of with contempt as "white marble." "Off to the right Sophie saw Aubreyville spread out, and the white gash of the silica quarry." The sight makes her feel "the aftermath of disaster . . . as if they were all whisked off and cancelled, curled into dots, turned to atoms, but they didn't know it" (PL, 296). From this atomistic destruction, Sophie saves herself by an act of looking or reading. As she feels herself "shrinking, curled up into that sickening dot, but not vanishing, she held herself up there" by saying "Look here, look there, see the shapes on the earth" (PL, 296).

At the very moment that Sophie keeps herself thus precariously in existence while watching, her daughter-in-law is implicitly pictured as one of these atoms on the receding earth: "*Sitting by herself is my wife's greatest pleasure*" (PL, 297). This phrase, when it first appears, is a quotation but the antecedent of that quotation follows at a *later* point in this story (PL, 303). This dislocation allows us to feel just a trace of the impact of relativity. It is just about as much as can be borne. Isabel sitting safely on the ground, Sophie flying in the air, Denise reflected in the dark window – all these are fleeting images of survival. While Old Norse offers a glimpse of a woman's autonomy as a reader, it is not enough. Isabel's need, imaged in candy, commands our respect and compassion. When he beholds her body, the pilot briefly absolves her of the role of watcher and keeper. Kept and beheld, she does not have to be either Old Norse or an old nurse. "She felt rescued, lifted, beheld, and safe" (PL, 309). In this safety net the mother sways "back and forth" like a baby. Who can blame her for desiring such comfort? Even those readers who judge her will have to confront the shape of "White Dump" – which is the shape of our desires.

Chapter 12

Friend of My Youth
Making connections

"FRIEND OF MY YOUTH": GRIEVING THE MOTHER

The dedication page of *Friend of My Youth* reads: "To the memory of my mother" and the title story is a profoundly ironic reflection on the process of grieving a mother. In the opening paragraphs of the story, Munro refers once again to the "paralyzing disease" that claimed her mother's life. The thread of referentiality is becoming increasingly and self-consciously opaque. Instead of mimicking the mother (as did the daughter in "The Peace of Utrecht"), this daughter mocks her own obsession. In his recent review of this book, Peter Buitenhuis notes that the mother's "presence has been inescapable since Munro's earliest fiction." He refers back to the passage in "The Ottawa Valley," where the mother "looms too close" and notes: "She looms even more closely in this collection, although there is a sense that Munro has come to terms with her at last, as the title story, 'Friend of My Youth,' indicates" (*Books in Canada*, May 1990, 21–22). As Carol Shields observes, however, Alice Munro "overturns our expectations" just as we are "ready to be reassured, to be told that the daughter will come to an understanding of her mother." Instead of an archetypal reconciliation, we have a mother who refuses to be understood (*London Review of Books*, 7 February 1991, 22). The writing daughter's conscious failure to understand or represent the mother remains, then, at the heart of Munro's aesthetic.

The mother in the story teaches at "a one-room school, called Grieves School" and boards "with the Grieveses" (FY, 5). The sheer awkwardness of the proper noun draws us back to the verb and to the way this grieving transgresses literary proprieties, especially those that dictate closure. This education in grief refuses to stay within the confines of a one-room school. The story recalls Fame's description, in "The Progress of Love," of "something swelling out behind" the mother's stories, something like a

> cloud you couldn't see through, or get to the end of. There was a cloud,
> a poison, that had touched my mother's life. And when I grieved my

mother, I became part of it. Then I would beat my head against my mother's stomach and breasts, against her tall, firm front, demanding to be forgiven. My mother would tell me to ask God. But it wasn't God, it was my mother I had to get straight with.

(PL, 13)

The emphasis on religion in "Friend of My Youth" shows that it is not so easy to get around "God" when you are trying to get straight with your mother.

It was in "The Ottawa Valley" that the daughter first confronted the stark reality that she would never "get rid of" the mother. The Ottawa Valley in this story, even more than in the earlier one, is a place with almost supernatural qualities. "And when wood weathers in the Ottawa Valley, my mother said, I do not know why this is, but it never turns gray, it turns black. There must be something in the air, she said" (FY, 4). This "something in the air," like the poisonous milky fog, keeps taking the daughter back to old religions. When Munro wrote "Age of Faith" for *Lives of Girls and Women*, she may have thought she was finished with religion. To Hancock she explained: "That big section in *Lives* . . . [is] there because every child . . . in my generation went through some kind of religious crisis" (in Hancock, 1987, 215). Munro said of her characters: "I don't think religion is a big preoccupation of theirs, at all" (Hancock, 1987, 215). Although this is still true on the level of explicit theme, Munro's critique of patriarchal structures has led her deeper and deeper into the heart of the old religious stories. Ada's mother, in *Lives of Girls and Women*, was a religious fanatic kept in the background of the story. In "Friend of My Youth," by contrast, a religious fanatic is foregrounded not only as a mock mother but also as a friend of the mother's youth. Foreground and background in a Munro story, however, make up a palimpsest of densely layered images.

As she did in "The Ottawa Valley," the narrator notes that it "was not a valley at all, if by that you mean a cleft between hills" (FY, 5). This phrase picks up lines – almost quoting them – from the earlier story: "It was no valley. I looked for mountains, or at least hills, but in the morning all it was was fields and bush" (SIB, 229). This apparently casual self-allusion has, in fact, an oddly anti-referential effect. Since Munro detaches the word *valley* from our mental picture of a valley, it darkens and we become aware of the materiality of the sign. The passages from the two separate stories in fact share the exact opposite of what they appear to share. While they both refer to a specific region of Ontario, they also act like mirrors set up to question reality itself. A play on the word "reality" also surrounds the apparent references to Munro's "real" mother. The daughter asks forgiveness for having "kept a bugbear in [her] mind, instead of this reality" and the mother grants forgiveness. The phrase "this reality," however, does not refer to Munro's "real" mother but rather refers to the relative good health of the mother in the dream. These deliberate confusions, however, do not simply jettison the idea of referentiality. They are part of the method Munro uses to communicate the integrity of the "real" that is not contained in the daughter's constructions.

This dislocation of "reality" conditions our response to the picture of guilt with which the story concludes. Munro has recently observed to Lynne Truss that "guilt is generally a self-indulgent emotion" and she describes herself as working with "this extremely crazy Calvinism" in herself (*The Independent*, 14 October 1990, 33). She seems to agree with Austin, in "Pictures of the Ice": "'Guilt is a sin and a seduction. I've said that to many a poor soul that liked to wallow in it'" (FY, 146). In this story she reaches out for a historical context that helps her avoid the trap of self-indulgence. Her investigation of the crazy Calvinist context leads Munro to a retelling of stories told by her ancestor, James Hogg. Unlike Hogg, however, Munro places the mother figure at the centre of her investigation. The suffering mother is the mocking imitation of the scapegoat and an "incontestable crippled-mother power" (FY, 20) is felt all the more viscerally because it is so thoroughly domesticated. Guilt may be self-indulgent but it is also inescapable and the language becomes painfully plain as Munro cuts close to the bone: "This is a fancy way of saying that I was no comfort and poor company to her when she had almost nowhere else to turn" (FY, 20).

Munro's exploration of the daughter's guilt moves through levels of self-interrogation that are potentially paralyzing. If the daughter is not to be absurdly tangled up feeling guilty about the fact that she feels guilty, she must relate her investigation to the process of storytelling. The very phrase "fancy way of saying," in fact, refers back to mother and daughter's differing versions of the story of Flora. The title of the story is listed as one of several salutations written by the mother. The daughter in the story reads *"Friend of my Youth"* feeling an "impatience with the flowery language, the direct appeal for love and pity" (FY, 24). Munro's choice of that phrase for her title is a particularly poignant case of the strategy that I have associated with thrift-shop dressing. The mother's old flowery phrase, like the old name Flora, is carefully reinstated by the daughter and reinvested with a power that seeks to recover a matrilineal storytelling tradition.

Munro's continuing self-interrogation leads her repeatedly into a deepening exploration of the workings of our traditional notions about writing as these relate to the lives of our mothers. The references to her mother are a way of insisting on the fact of referentiality. It *has* to be Parkinson's Disease because that is what her mother really had but the line of referentiality leads, as it always does in Munro, to a conscious dead end. The mother's failed telling of Flora's story becomes a model for the daughter's failed telling of the mother's story. The thread of referentiality is deliberately blurred towards the end of the story, so that it becomes difficult to tell Flora and the mother apart. Either could be referred to in the following sentences: "she is weary of it, of me and my idea of her, my information, my notion that I can know anything about her" (FY, 26). This attitude to information from the past shapes the daughter's idea of history. All this was anticipated by the very title of "The Peace of Utrecht." The referentiality of that title might easily have triggered an avalanche of military historical information which would bury the bodies of all our mothers. The contrasting thread of referentiality leading to Munro's own mother in that story has been strong enough to sustain the high-wire act of a veritable parade of mock mothers.

I have been tracing what I see as an evolving and constantly revised aesthetic in Munro's fiction, one that takes this parade as an organizing image. "Friend of My Youth" sets up its own parade – the narrator's mother; Ellie; Flora; Nurse Atkinson; the narrator herself. Munro holds the parade still for a while so that we get in touch, once again, with the grief that generates these moving figures. Near the end of this story the daughter, looking as if down a historical corridor through this series of figures, confronts the changed mother in her dream and concludes that this mother

> changes more than herself. She changes the bitter lump of love I have carried all this time into a phantom – something useless and uncalled for, like a phantom pregnancy.
>
> (FY, 26)

This image brings to a kind of mock-fruition the aesthetic that has been developing in Munro's stories. The swelling bellies of the mock mothers in Munro's parade should have prepared us to see how the "bitter lump of love" renders maternity profoundly ambiguous.

Unlike the Munro who wrote "The Ottawa Valley," the Munro who wrote "Friend of my Youth" is not thinking out loud about giving up writing. This useless lump (like a jester's bauble) is now acknowledged as the heart of the storytelling process because it leads, repeatedly, to the staged failure of the clown. The daughter's *failures* to represent the mother, rather than representation itself, are seen as a series of filters through which the daughter views all the stories of the past. This view of history is rendered obliquely in the story's epilogue paragraph. In an abrupt non sequitur, Munro follows the image of the "phantom pregnancy" with a brief historical account about the Cameronians. The "Grieveses" are in the grip of a "freak religion from Scotland" (FY, 5) that does not look so freakish once Munro has domesticated it. In the creed of the Cameronians there is a rigidity that is reflected in the Protestant excesses with which Munro herself is familiar as a result of growing up in Ontario. The word *orange*, in Munro's stories, always comes with a cargo of religious history. As she traces the historical roots of these rigidities, Munro follows a path that leads her into a space shared with her ancestor, James Hogg.

Hogg's *The Brownie of Bodsbeck* questions the view of the Covenanters offered by Scott in *Old Mortality* and Hogg's reluctance to condemn is repeated in Munro. At the same time, however, Munro seems to test the limits of this tolerance. She describes a "monstrous old religion," containing a "configuration of the elect and the damned" (FY, 12) and thus picks up on the imagery of Hogg's classic: *The Private Memoirs and Confessions of a Justified Sinner*. This makes for a curious kind of intertextuality. When the daughter confesses that "the really mysterious person in the story, as my mother told it, was Robert" (FY, 21), those readers familiar with Hogg's classic might note that the name of his justified sinner is Robert. Although Robert Wringhim is accused of killing his own mother, however, Hogg's tale foregrounds the relationship of two brothers. Munro, by contrast, foregrounds the sisters and the mother and puts her Robert in the background. What is foregrounded, moreover, is the maternal storytelling process; this Robert appears "in the story, as my mother told it."

Munro isolates "a cloud, a poison" (PL, 13) that surrounds the symbol of Mother and she aligns it with the "poisonous book" read by Flora in her role as a "Presbyterian witch" (FY, 20–21). A "fog of platitudes and pieties" seems to the narrator to lurk about her mother's stories. The "incontestable crippled-mother power, which could capture and choke me" (FY, 20) is connected to the old ideology. Taking advantage of Hogg's earlier investigation of those horrors, Munro now adapts her exploration of them to the issue of maternity. The futility of getting rid of those ideologies is pictured as vividly as was the futility of trying to get rid of the mother. Flora, up on her ladders, in "kerchief and apron and Robert's baggy overalls that she donned for the climbing jobs," has the "air of a comedian – sportive, unpredictable" (FY, 7). Her method of survival commands respect, but she cannot purge the house of these poisons. The "great housecleaning" (FY, 7) only accentuates, for the reader, the fact that the outside of this house is black.

Flora is the most prominent of the maternal clowns in this parade against blackness. It takes "all her dignity and innocence to keep her from being a joke" (FY, 25) but she manages it. The jilted bride here, even more vehemently than in "The Ottawa Valley," takes upon herself the nurturing role. Her power, like that of Et in "Something I've Been Meaning to Tell You," cripples her sister. She treats Ellie like a child: "'Where's my little girl, then? Where's my Ellie? This isn't my Ellie, this is some crosspatch got in here in place of her!'" (FY, 11). The result is that Ellie is rendered voiceless and her body becomes the visible objectification of the scapegoat mother's body. Her first pregnancy is imaged as a "backup of blood" that threatens to choke her. "She would not take food, just whipped her head from side to side, howling. It looked as if she would die speechless" (FY, 10).

This is an image of what Flora decides to reject. She opts for the circumscribed power of a mock mother rather than succumbing to this kind of maternity. Ellie is seen, in the end, as nothing more than a "poor botched body, a failed childbearer, lying in bed" (FY, 22). She is punished for desire itself. "God dealt out punishment for hurry-up marriages . . . God rewarded lust with dead babies, idiots, harelips and withered limbs and clubfeet" (FY, 11). The "bloody detail" of Ellie's miscarriages relates these punishments to menstruation – an image that anticipates "Meneseteung." The wild howling of Ellie and her mangled body are images of a grotesque maternal body in this story. Flora's mock mothering, frenetic as it may be, is a contrasting ironic image of survival but her body is no more liberated. The term "whirling dervish" is used by the narrator's mother to describe Flora's housecleaning and it points usefully to a conflation of domestic hygiene and religious ideology. The term refers to Moslem friars whose vow is for poverty and austerity but whose practice demands the performance of a howling dance.

If Flora's dance is a mockery of the liberated body, then Audrey Atkinson's dance is surely another version of the same parody. In the ending contrived by the narrator, Flora "becomes crippled herself, with arthritis, hardly able to move" and Audrey Atkinson "comes into her full power" (FY, 21). With a "rival ruthlessness," Audrey out-mock-mothers Flora and it is Audrey who attempts to purge the house of the old religious poison. Audrey, as imagined by the narrator, takes out "a heap of old books" and burns them:

> Those smelly old books, as Audrey has called them. Words and pages, the ominous dark spines. The elect, the damned, the slim hopes, the mighty torments – up in smoke. There was the ending.
>
> (FY, 21)

The narrator is gleeful about this conclusion: "oh, this is it, this is it, I see the bare beauty of the ending I will contrive!" (FY, 21). This notion of the ending echoes Hogg's apocalyptic visions and at first appears to diminish them by acknowledging the contrivance. On another level, however, we see the tenacity of these rigidities and we see, certainly, the limits of Audrey Atkinson's victory. Book burning has never solved anything.

Like other nurses in Munro's fiction (beginning with Mary McQuade in "Images"), Audrey starts out as a sinister figure. Unlike Mary, Audrey gets her man but her dance is only apparently more liberating than was that of the mock mothers that preceded her. At her wedding, Audrey "danced with every man present except the groom, who sat scrunched into one of the school desks along the wall" (FY, 18). The bridegroom who is associated with Jesus Christ in other stories is here fixed as a permanent pupil with a lot left to learn. The body of the bride, meanwhile, in a dress of "satin with a sweetheart neckline" is seen as "idiotically youthful" (FY, 18). Nurse

Atkinson, with her "corsets as stiff as barrel hoops" and her "marcelled hair the color of brass candlesticks" and her "pinkish-orange eyebrows" (FY, 13) is a sadly failed clown. She tries and fails to separate her maternal behaviour from the Christian ideology that furnished the house before her arrival.

This story, then, examines the ideological basis of our notions of female power. It demonstrates how even women who explicitly repudiate religion and burn the books may be subject to the power in those old books. When Flora reads to Ellie "only short bits from the Bible," Ellie tries to cling to her and weeps. Sometimes "she made ridiculous complaints. She said there was a horned cow outside, trying to get into the room and kill her" (FY, 14–15). This phallic cow is like an image of the combined perversion of both male and female power in the ideology that motivates Flora. The potential for life itself turns into death within this ideology, a fact imaged in Ellie's terminal phantom pregnancy: "'My sister has a growth,' Flora said. Nobody then spoke of cancer" (FY, 8).

"Friend of My Youth" offers to Munro's readers an unusually explicit working out of the aesthetic I have been exploring in the preceding chapters. We can see here, as in so many other stories, how the power of the mother is projected into surrogate mother figures. Freed from the solemnity that surrounds our notions of maternity, the act of mothering may thus be explored as an expression of power. The woman that appears to be most powerless and helpless may wield the most sinister power if she manipulates the ideology so that the "crippled–mother" is identified with the crucified Jesus. On a more hopeful note, however, I note how the mother–daughter dialogue continues to subvert the old narrative structures that rush towards the wedding of bride and bridegroom. The mother herself was at the time blooming "in everybody's attention, about to set out on the deliciously solemn adventure of marriage" (FY, 15). The power of the story, however, is displaced from a focus on the solemnity of marriage and is relocated, instead, in Munro's ongoing masquerade of maternal clowns.

The oblique allusions to James Hogg make it possible for Munro to play out this masquerade against a background of religious history. The brutality in the last paragraph is consciously cavalier. The Cameronians "went into battle singing the seventy-fourth or seventy-eighth Psalms. They hacked the haughty Bishop of St Andrews to death on the highway and rode their horses over his body. One of their ministers, in a mood of firm rejoicing at his own hanging, excommunicated all the other preachers in the world" (FY, 26). This complete confidence, like that of Hogg's "justified sinner," derives from the preacher's conviction that he speaks as the very voice of the symbolic order predestined by God. Against this backdrop of faith, Munro places the "act of faith" (MJ, 31) that is involved in the writing of the salutation *Friend of my Youth*" (FY, 24). That maternal act is mimed by the daughter who narrates the story "Friend of My Youth."

It is mimed, in turn, by Munro who writes the book called *Friend of My Youth* and dedicates it to her mother.

"MENESETEUNG": FOOLING THE I

Claire Tomalin calls this "the finest and most intense" of the stories in this collection. Whether Almeda Joynt Roth is "partly real or wholly invented, she is a striking addition to Munro's gallery of odd, memorable women" (*The Independent*, 4 November 1990). I note with interest that Tomalin raises the question of Meda's reality, a question that seems to me central to Munro's method. This story is a mock-historical story resembling an elegant practical joke. From the first words, the specific details act as a consummate mimicry of the conventions of traditional histories: "In the front of the book is a photograph, with the photographer's name in one corner, and the date: 1865. The book was published later, in 1873" (FY, 50). Such conspicuous precision beguiles us into expecting conventional historical accuracy. Perhaps I can illustrate the joke best by confessing that I consulted various sources and got several librarians sleuthing for me in order to prove to myself that Almeda Joynt Roth is a fiction. I still have a lingering suspicion that there must really have been such a person and I would continue to suspect this even if Alice Munro herself assured me that she made the woman up.

The effect is like a literary version of *trompe-l'oeil* and it leaves the reader permanently but pleasantly wary. It seems, on reflection, to be the logical conclusion of Munro's "realism." As she writes in slow motion, setting up a float parade of tableaus that question our old views of narrative, the old images are taken out of their old story contexts. The result is similar to what Baudrillard terms the "enchanted simulation" of *trompe-l'oeil*. It leads from an ironic "excess of reality" to the "nullification of the real" and "contrasts completely with the representative space of the Renaissance" (Baudrillard, 1988, 154).

> The trompe-l'oeil does not attempt to confuse itself with the real. Fully aware of play and artifice, it produces a simulacrum by mimicking the third dimension, questioning the reality of the third dimension, and mimicking and surpassing the effect of the real, radically questioning the very principle of reality.
>
> (Baudrillard, 1988, 156)

Because the numbers 1865 and 1873 have been taken out of their contexts and put into play as imaginary times, Munro draws her reader into an experience of temporality that is oddly both estranged and domesticated. Munro's view of history, I have argued, is shaped by her efforts to pay tribute to the lives of our foremothers and this gives her mimicries an added dimension not included by Baudrillard. The opening description of a photograph pictures Meda for us as a comic artifact from the past:

> The poetess has a long face; a rather long nose; full, sombre dark eyes, which seem ready to roll down her cheeks like giant tears; a lot of dark hair gathered around her face in droopy rolls and curtains.
>
> (FY, 50)

This static picture forms a consciously histrionic tableau that will be brought to life as the story gathers its remarkable cumulative power. The giant tears are mocking, like those of the Mock Turtle in *Alice's Adventures in Wonderland*. If we notice that they are not in fact tears, we may begin the process of installing eyes in the rag-doll that Munro so often envisions.

This process of acquiring vision, however, easily becomes life-denying if we project too much power into the eyes of our foremothers. Like the blind Momma in "Walker Brothers Cowboy," this foremother will not see for us. By an exaggeration of feminine ornament in this story, Munro pictures the female artist as a grotesque so that we will not be tempted to worship. Wolfgang Kayser notes that among the "most persistent motifs of the grotesque we find human bodies reduced to puppets, marionettes, and automata, and their faces frozen into masks" (Kayser, 1966, 183). The frozen face of Meda acts as this kind of ornamental grotesque – almost as if it is a special kind of gargoyle. The imagination of the narrator, indeed, seems to be motivated by an effort to salvage some life from this brittle image. Like Anna, in "Providence," Meda threatens to turn into just another idol. In Rose's dream, Anna is

> covered with clay that seemed to have leaves or branches in it, so that the effect was of dead garlands. Decoration; ruination. And the clay or mud was not dry, it was still dripping off her, so that she looked crude and sad, a botched heavy-headed idol.
>
> (WDY, 133)

"Decoration; ruination." The challenge of these ornamental grotesques is clear: how to affirm the *lives* of our mothers and our daughters when the only means available to do so return us to the fact of artifice.

Munro's response to this challenge is multiple but she never takes the escape route of worshipping idols from the past. Her methods, instead, demonstrate that she takes on the challenge of being, herself, an artificer. By the time Munro is done, the decorated surface of this story and the multiplying slogans such as "Salt of the Earth" will be a disguising that allows us access to a grief more intense than what is felt in any other story by Alice Munro. Jarvis Poulter sees his salt as potential gold. When Almeda, however, asks him if it "does not mean . . . that there was once a great sea" (FY, 58), I imagine a sea of tears. Meaning, of course, cannot so easily be pinned down and the story does not dissolve into sentimentality.

Although I have a visceral response to this particular story it is, at the same time, one of the most decorative ever written by Munro. The word *decorate*, in fact, occurs often in this story. Meda gets "Honorable mention at the Fall Fair" for her "fancy iced cakes and decorated tarts" (FY, 58–59). In Munro's circus, her efforts get more than a mention. Meda sees her "efforts at composition" as a poor substitute for the "dazzling productions of embroidery" (FY, 51) that she is too clumsy to achieve.

Like Meda, Munro herself loves detail. W.J. Keith, in fact, cites her "excessive emphasis on details of dress and adornment" as evidence that Munro's impressive "reputation" may simply be due to the fact that she is offering "updated versions of the material that used to be called (in pre-feminist days) 'women's fiction'" (Keith, 1989, 172–173). Meda, a pre-feminist poetess, is a good figure to look at in responding to Keith's criticism. I have suggested that an application of Kaja Silverman's idea of "thrift-shop dressing" helps to account for Munro's recycling of vintage literary images (see Silverman, 1986, 139–151). "Meneseteung" is an astonishingly thrifty story. The details, in themselves, do not prove anything more than the excessive emphasis on guns and cars in the work of male authors. The focus has to be on Munro's technique, on her way of salvaging and updating the traditional decorations. This story offers one of the clearest examples of her strategy. Once again we experience the combination of irony and compassion with which Munro expresses (to adapt Silverman's terms) her "affection for objects which were once culturally cherished, but which have since been abandoned" (Silverman, 1986, 150). Munro avoids nostalgia, however, and she avoids also the "pitfalls of naive referentiality" and she does this by "putting quotation marks around the garments [she] revitalizes" (Silverman, 1986, 150).

Meda, in a pose of charmingly false modesty, apologizes for her "rude posies" (FY, 52) but Munro elevates her humble art so that it can act as a powerful challenge to the assumptions contained in the old symbols. She does this by giving us the ironic distance that allows us to see ourselves in the act of looking. The effect of her *trompe-l'oeil* is that we catch ourselves in the act of looking at a woman who is in the act of looking. Even if the eyes of Almeda Joynt Roth could roll down on us like giant tears and even if this Alice could swim in a sea of tears, we would still have to join the "giddy" school girls who recite: "*Tears, idle tears, I know not what they mean*" (SIB, 177). The awareness of surface, in other words, returns us to our role as beholders and readers. In this story Munro takes a giant step back from the grieving process, with the result that the tears themselves become mockingly decorative. Although the technique of enlargement is cinematic, I am also reminded of the tears of Saint Teresa as they look in the baroque poetry of Richard Crashaw. Munro's technique paradoxically draws us in by distancing us. The result is a sustained investigation of the relation of the body and life of the woman to female artifice. If literature can be seen as a house, Munro here examines the part played in it by the woman. "A man may keep his house decent, but he will never – if he is a proper man – do much to decorate it. Marriage forces him to live with more ornament" (FY, 57).

This story supports Naomi Schor's argument that a woman must learn to read ornamental detail in order to escape *being* an ornament. Baudrillard describes the "haunted and metaphysical objects" without referents, offensive in their insignificance (1988, 154). These are seen in a new way when they are the ghostly bodies of our foremothers. The word *alma*, I notice, can mean "soul; ghost; phantom" (*OED*). Munro's fiction, as I have been arguing, re-presences the absent mothers and shows that they can construct themselves as subjects with stories to tell. There is something chimeric about "Meneseteung" but there is also in it a frenzied crescendo of action – the pursuit, the beating, the cacophony of voices – that are like a literary version of Hieronymus Bosch or Pieter Bruegel. Pearl Street is very like any number of streets in Ontario towns and cities. At the same time it also resembles William Hogarth's "Gin Lane."

All this, of course, is grounded by Munro in the very act of narration. In "Meneseteung" the narrator is a kind of sleuth, scraping away at the earth to find the stone that contains the name *Meda*. This activity is like an absurdly literal acting out of her unearthing of Meda's voice. Since, however, the temporal setting is in fact imaginary, the result is that this mock historical distance collapses and makes us aware of Munro's own act of mock-mediation. Munro, so to speak, dissolves herself in the giant tears/eyes of Roth. This gives an unusual twist to the play with perspective that we know as *trompe-l'oeil*. Baudrillard comments on the inversion of depth:

> Instead of fleeing panoramically before the scrutinizing eye (the privilege of the panoptic eye), objects here "fool" the eye (*"trompent" l'oeil*) by some sort of internal depth: not by creating the illusion of a real world, but by eluding the privileged position of the gaze. The eye, instead of being the source of structured space, is merely the internal point of flight for the convergence of objects.
>
> (Baudrillard, 1988, 156)

In "Meneseteung" we can see clearly that Munro's fooling of the eye is also a fooling of the I. Baudrillard refers to the doubleness inherent in *trompe-l'oeil* that "recounts the subject's insane desire to grasp its own image, and then vanish. For reality is gripping only when we have lost our identity, or when it reappears as our hallucinated death" (1988, 156). This sense of hallucination is increasingly strong in Munro. Her stories sometimes read like the places where she hallucinates her own death. This may have to do with her own aging but it is also the organic extension of her developing aesthetic. The effort to seize the image fails invariably, leaving behind some surface detail, like the eyes of Orphan Annie in "Images" or the eyes of Meda in the picture. This "seizure rebounds," in Baudrillard's words, "on the surrounding world we call 'real,' revealing to us that 'reality' is nothing but a staged world, objectified according to rules of depth" (1988, 156). We become aware of these rules by virtue of the fact that they are undermined when a Valley is not a valley and when 1873 is not 1873. The context defined by Baudrillard goes a long way towards accounting for the eerie effect of Munro's fiction. I have tried several times to find Meneseteung in my historical atlas of Canada; always I fail and am returned to looking at the eyes of Almeda Joynt Roth. The overflow of those eyes/tears transgresses literary boundaries.

Political referentiality has been an implied problem in earlier stories by Munro and here the problem rises rather ominously up to the decorated surface. The grotesque, as Kayser notes, evokes "helplessness . . . before an increasingly absurd and fantastically estranged world" (Kayser, 1966, 78). In "Meneseteung" the woman who plays the part of artist watches helplessly as another woman is beaten. The story offers an unusually intense repetition of questions that haunt all of Munro's fiction. Who is the king of the royal beatings? Who is to blame for this suffering? Who has the power to stop it? As she did in "Royal Beatings," Munro encourages us to reflect on the way our response is conditioned by the fact that we live in an electronic culture. She also demonstrates, however, the aspects of human response that remain constant regardless of the fashions of a particular century. In the name Meda an attentive reader may hear both *Medea* and *media*; a nineteenth-century paper called *Vidette* will make many readers think of twentieth-century videos. When Meda reflects that "the word 'channelled' is appropriate" (FY, 70), the reader may think not only of the river and of a woman's body but also of television channelling. Such word-play signals Munro's continuing interest in how we see and in what Harold Innis (1951) called the "bias of communication." Readers of "Meneseteung" in 1990, as Munro well knows, are readers used to being watchers. "Today," as Baudrillard notes, "the trompe-l'oeil is no longer within the realm of painting. Like stucco, its contemporary, it can do anything, mimic anything, parody anything" (1988, 157). What he refers to as the "malevolent use of appearances" can be related, I think, to the violence in "Meneseteung." Since women have traditionally been deleted from the body of written history, it may be easier for a woman writer than for a man to challenge an "age of simulation" that "begins with the liquidation of all referentials" (Baudrillard, 1988, 167). This context helps to explain Munro's refusal to liquidate the most important of her referentials: the references to her own mother's illness and death.

I have argued that in every instance where Munro writes about violence, she also makes herself conscious of the violence of her own representation. It is an aspect of her aesthetic that is worked out in courageous detail in this story. In the story "Material," the writing woman whose pen makes "short jabbing sentences" on the paper (SIB, 44) denies her body ("pregnant with Clea") and projects her desires into the body of Dotty, the "harlot-in-residence" in the basement (SIB, 30). In this story Munro does a close-up examination of this process of projection. As she herself projects the writing process into the body of Roth and as Roth projects her voice into what happens to the nameless battered woman (whose mouth is "choked with blood;" FY, 63), we sense a consciously ironic passing on of moral responsibility and of desire. "The deepest desire is perhaps to give the responsibility for one's desire to someone else" (Baudrillard, 1988, 215).

The crucial element of Munro's fiction here is the self-consciousness of this act of projection. This is what distinguishes Meda's writing from the writing of Alice Munro. Unlike Meda, who is not aware of being *"sadly, a figure of fun,"* Munro is happily conscious of her own comic impulse. In the literary sense she has abandoned, as Meda does in a cosmetic sense, *"attention to decorum"* (FY, 71). When the body of the poet "walks upstairs leaving purple footprints and smelling her escaping blood and the sweat of her body" (FY, 71), we may be sure that we are not reading the writing of a lady. She does not walk "serenely like a *lady*" (DHS, 5). Munro's astonishing skill at "thrift-shop dressing" makes it possible for her to establish this ironic distance without viewing Meda with contempt. This is a special kind of self-parodic melodramatic comedy, one that comes with that double quality captured by Del as she quotes from "Mariana":

I was amazed to think that the person suffering was me, for it was not me at all: I was watching. I was watching, I was suffering. I said into the mirror a line from Tennyson. . . . I said it with absolute sincerity, absolute irony.

(LGW, 241)

This may be the most daringly innovative story that Munro has ever written. The bleeding edges of the self-consciously purple prose passages in this story seem to me to show that Munro is conscious of the enormous risks that a woman takes when she writes about menstruation. Barbara Walker has documented the "almost hysterical fear" evoked by menstrual blood because of the "central position" it occupied in "matriarchal theologies" (Walker, 1983, 641). A contemporary woman writer willing to violate the taboo against the subject, however, risks falling (as does Walker herself) into the trap of viewing menstrual blood as a sacred or immortal mystery (Walker, 1983, 637). In his 1987 interview with Alice Munro, Geoff Hancock referred to the "great blood mystery of women. . . . Menstrual blood; the bleeding that bleeds but doesn't cause death. And blood to milk. Blood to child. These are the three big transformations of blood in women" (Hancock, 1987, 216). In her response, Munro noted that she had never "written much about childbirth or any of that" and speculated that this might be "because so many people seemed to be dealing with it in ways that I didn't much like." She then added: "Maybe some day I'll find I have to do a story about something like that" (in Hancock, 1987, 216). "Meneseteung" may well be that story; certainly it shows how Munro's approach is different from that of "so many people." The main difference is that she firmly resists the temptation to claim for the woman writer a special mysterious power. There is something almost protestant about Munro's determined refusal to shirk the hard work of her craft. The lurid menstrual colours here, like the moon in the tin can in "The Moon in the Orange Street Skating Rink," do not represent Nature but are rather consciously artificial.

In *Mrs. Blood* and in *Intertidal Life*, Audrey Thomas (a Canadian writer who is also a friend of Alice Munro) struggles against the same temptation. It is therefore interesting to see that the names of her characters echo Munro's fiction. "The night of the first moon landing Peter and Alice and the two kids (not Flora, not yet) watched on a borrowed television" (Thomas, 1984, 16). Since this scene is reminiscent of "White Dump," the echo of the name Peter (also used by Munro in that story) is particularly resonant – as is the fact that Flora later reads a novel called *Nurse Prue* (Thomas, 1984, 16). Thomas's response to the challenge is very different from Munro's and she does not, in my view, completely succeed in resisting the temptation to essentialize. The almost teasingly obvious echoes, however, show us two women writers looking to each other for support.

The moon, blood, milk, eggs, cows – these are among the symbols that keep demanding to be reread. The challenge is to write from within a woman's body without trapping that body inside the old symbols. The flow of Meda's words starts with her menstrual flow: "her flow has started" (FY, 71). This is the most "natural" and yet the most daring conflation in the story. Munro positively dares us to think of Meda as dipping her pen in blood or milk – as if her pretty poems could be seen as just so many spontaneous abortions. Munro does not deny the power or importance of the natural process. Like Del Jordan, she is aware that

> anybody who will go into birth and death, who will undertake to see and deal with whatever is there – a hemorrhage, the meaty afterbirth, awful dissolution – anybody who does that will have to be listened to, no matter what news they bring.
>
> (LGW, 120)

Nor does Munro pretend that it is possible to escape the power of the old symbols that are based on this natural process. She does counter both levels – the biologic and the symbolic – with an exaggerated emphasis on interior decoration that puts the spotlight on the act of mediation. Instead of the symbol of a rose, Meda is confronted by roses in a tablecloth crocheted by her mother. Meda cannot mediate the dispute that she witnesses from her window, but it does make her a wary reader of the signs of invasion:

A lot of things to watch. For every one of these patterns, decorations seems charged with life, read to move and flow and alter. Or possibly to explode. Almeda Roth's occupation throughout the day is to keep an eye on them. Not to prevent their alteration so much as to catch them at it – to understand it, to be a part of it.

(FY, 69)

The poet in "Meneseteung" – her writing imaged both in the process of menstruation and in needlework – represents the latest development in Munro's way of seeing the woman's construction of herself as a subject in the face of the massive power of the old symbols. Munro's, however, in the words of Barbara Godard, is "an aesthetic of addition (as opposed to elimination)" (1984, 69). She does not deny the power in the hackneyed old symbols. "Almeda looks deep, deep into the river of her mind and into the tablecloth, and she sees the crocheted roses floating" (FY, 70). The "river of her mind" and the floating roses are conscious clichés that make us aware of the process of construction. Although they are viewed ironically, they are not treated as refuse. The story is simultaneously flowing and disrupted – like a float parade. Even as you feel yourself drawn into the workings of Almeda's mind, you find yourself comparing this picture with Monet's water lilies or with Keller's ornamental knots and joints – the *Knorpelgroteske* (see Kayser, 1966, Plate 6).

This self-conscious focus on the act of creating or framing keeps coming back to the creation of the self, as the opening portrait of Meda indicates. The name Almeda suggests Alma Mater, meaning bounteous mother, but when the name is abbreviated the maternal function is obscured. With her refusal to be a bounteous mother to Jarvis Poulter and his potential children, Almeda becomes Meda. The narrator refuses to allow her to be a phantom or an *alma* and re-presences her as a body. Since the narrative voice dwells on the name Meda, it becomes a kind of linguistic mirror for the writing I. Who da? You da? Yes, Me Da. This is foolish, of course, almost juvenile. It may not be much, as subject construction goes. It may be no more than the "bunchy and foolish" roses crocheted by her mother: "But their effort, their floating independence, their pleasure in their silly selves do seem to her so admirable. A hopeful sign. *Meneseteung*" (FY, 70).

Meneseteung is a sign, not a symbol, and this distinction seems to me crucial. Symbols are what you see when you stand outside the picture and recognize the labels attached within a symbolic order. Signs are what you see when you are inside the picture that you are observing. The "bunchy" roses are like the various lumps in Munro's fictions, signs of conscious and mocking impropriety, not places pregnant with symbolic meaning. Their beauty is subordinate to their "floating independence" and their pleasure in their "silly selves." In one sense, this image seems to embody the float parade that I have been seeing in Munro's fiction. The irony of this float parade of selves, however, is that you start to feel it as being beside the point when you allow yourself to take in the violence done to a woman's body. Meda's writing is a way of coping with a level of violence that is almost staggering. The phrase "A woman is being beaten" resonates in this story as does "A child is being beaten" in "Royal Beatings." "'There is the body of a woman'": this is what Meda announces to Jarvis Poulter. This body is like the text in a staged hermeneutic act that gives the story its intense focus.

> A woman's body heaped up there, turned on her side with her face squashed down into the earth. Almeda can't see her face. But there is a bare breast let loose, brown nipple pulled long like a cow's teat, and a bare haunch and leg, the haunch showing a bruise as big as a sunflower. The unbruised skin is grayish, like a plucked, raw drumstick.
>
> (FY, 65)

Like the body of the dead cow in "Heirs of the Living Body," this body is a parody of Mother Earth. Like Del, who cannot bring herself to touch the dead cow, Almeda reproaches herself: "If she had touched the woman, if she had forced herself to touch her, she would not have made such a mistake" (FY, 66). The big difference, however, is that this body is alive. When Jarvis Poulter "nudges the leg with the toe of his boot, just as you'd nudge a dog or a sow" (FY, 66), he acts out Meda's own fear and she "tastes bile at the back of her throat." The woman's rousing is seen as a farcical resurrection. "'There goes your dead body!'" Jarvis mocks (FY, 67) in what seems to be a parodic summing up of all the mock deaths that have been viewed in Munro's stories. Meda's subsequent rejection of Poulter is crucial to the fact that she finds her poetic voice but so is her distance from this living body. The questions that arise from this fact are deeply troubling – almost as if the reader must decide whether she is heir to a dead body or to a living body. If Almeda had brought herself to touch the woman, this whole story would not have existed. If she had stooped to act as a "keeper," she would not have taken up the position of "watcher" or writer. The question is like the one that seems to haunt Stella in "Lichen": am I my sister's keeper?

Never before has Munro dealt so explicitly with the way writing (like television) can be a channelling of violence:

> The changes of climate are often violent, and if you think about it there is no peace even in the stars. All this can be borne only if it is channelled into a poem, and the word "channelled" is appropriate, because the name of the poem will be – it *is* – "The Meneseteung."
>
> (FY, 70)

The passage echoes the one in "Age of Faith" where Del speculates that the "only way the world could be borne, *the only way it could be borne*" would be if "all those atoms, galaxies of atoms, were safe all the time, whirling away in God's mind" (LGW, 100). In this story, however, atomistic confusion is not only an epistemological problem but also (at least implicitly) a political one. The story does not lead to an easily defined political outrage, and yet there is an implied anger that shakes "Meneseteung" on its very foundations. If you listen carefully you can hear *wrath* in the name Roth.

Such a rhyme may seem far-fetched but the resulting absurdity is consistent with the effect of "Meneseteung." An exaggerated focus on rhyme for its own sake is, of course, a feature of bad poetry and Munro here displays a talent (never before used, as far as I know) for writing excellent bad poetry. Meda's poems are never unrhymed: "The rhyme used is what was once called 'masculine' ('shore'/'before'), though once in a while it is 'feminine' ('quiver'/'river')" (FY, 53). This heavy rhyme, verging on "feminine" excess, is a verbal grotesque that – however delicate – is a means of shaking "our confidence in language and the image of the world which it supplies" (Kayser, 1966, 154). The effect is like that in a poem by Morgenstern cited by Kayser in which the image of a seamstress (*Näherin*) is absurdly connected to the idea of proximity (*Nähe*), simply because of the accident of rhyme (Kayser, 1966, 154). Morgenstern noted, in 1896, how a word would suddenly strike him: "The total arbitrariness of language, which encompasses our world view – and, consequently, the arbitrariness of the world view – is revealed" (quoted by Kayser, 1966, 154).

Such an absurd arbitrariness is felt in the world of the seamstress in "Meneseteung." Does her accidental proximity to the beaten woman mean that the stitches of her feminine and masculine rhymes have any connection with the life of that woman? In response to the implied political urgencies in the story, Munro once again poses the process of reading and writing as it takes place in a woman's body. The window becomes a very important threshold image for this activity since it is the boundary between outside and inside, public and private.

The morning after the beating, Meda thinks she hears a crow on her windowsill, saying: "'Wake up and move the wheelbarrow!'" (FY, 64). The incident somewhat resembles one in a story by James Hogg entitled "Tibby Hyslop's Dream." Munro, however, uses the conscious absurdity to make the reading process visible. The word *wheelbarrow* is the miniature text within the text and Meda is the reader. The windowsill would traditionally be seen as a transparent threshold opening to the world out there; here it is an opaque and baffling text to be interpreted. Like Edgar Allan Poe's raven, Munro's crow speaks a word that takes us back to the person listening. Meda thinks the crow must mean "something else by 'wheelbarrow' – something foul and sorrowful" (FY, 64). The attentive reader may notice an earlier reference in the story to the drunken Queen

Aggie who is trundled around in a wheelbarrow by the town boys. Meda, however, does not make this connection. The failure of her reading is reflected back to us in the materiality of the word on the page since Munro uses italics: "Down against her fence there is a pale lump pressed – a body. / Wheelbarrow" (FY, 64).

I hear an ironic echo here of Robert Kroetsch's *What the Crow Said*. What the crow says in this story takes us back not only to the opacity of our own fictions but also to the materiality – the pale lumpishness – of the world. The male human body has historically been seen as an image of order that may be imitated in art. I think, for example, of Leonard Barkan's *Nature's Work of Art: The Human Body as Image of the World*. Munro's representation of the female body is much more problematic. Meda can make her rhymes work neatly but she cannot easily fit her own body or that of the beaten woman into the old order. Queen Aggie, the nameless battered woman, and the wheelbarrow remain disjointed. The connecting name Joynt emphasizes the structure of the human body. Meda complains that her joints ache (FY, 62). The word could also echo the verb "joined," however, thus contrasting with the "missed connection" in the "clumsy parody" on the street. The associations are automatic – almost surrealistic. They resist the logic of any given narrative order.

We might conclude that much depends on this wheelbarrow and think of the famous poem by William Carlos Williams. Like Williams, Munro moves to a discarding of symbolic associations as she works to focus on the materiality of the pale lump – both the object and the word. The technique, however, is closer to that used by Wallace Stevens in "The Man on the Dump." When everything is shed in that poem, then "the moon comes up as the moon / (All its images are in the dump)" (Stevens, 1967, 164). When all the symbols of Woman are shed (Moon, Mother Earth, etc.) the woman remains there as a woman – all the symbols are in the dump. "Of course the body is still there. Hunched up, half bare, the same as before" (FY, 66).

The body is still there. That sentence seems to embody the political dilemma that is consciously left over, something so powerful that it makes everything else seem slightly beside the point. The dilemma is focussed on the figure of Meda and on the conflict in her of the compassionate keeper and the ironic watcher. While she writes, Meda is "a long way now from human sympathies or fears" and she "doesn't think about what could be done for that woman" (FY, 70). Munro never offers solutions. She does, however, make us vividly conscious of the events that are going on even as Meda writes. As she writes, the basin of grape juice overflows, staining the kitchen floor: "and the stain will never come out" (FY, 70). The conscious exaggeration in the word *never* expresses guilt even as it mocks the temptation to wallow in guilt.

Meda rejects the traditional role of keeper or mother/wife, but as she watches the decorated and explosive surface of the old ideological patterns, does she acquire new responsibilities? "What is to be done, what is she to do?" (FY, 64). In the name "Meneseteung" there is the sound of *menace* as well as the sound of *tongue* and this conjunction directs us to Munro's reflections on the dangers surrounding the woman who finds her tongue. Throat, mouth, tongue – these are recurring images in the story. Almeda tastes bile at the back of her throat when Jarvis Poulter's toe nudges the woman's body. The woman's "mouth seems choked with blood" even as she cries theatrically "'Kill me! Kill me!'" (FY, 63). A man chases a woman and the woman is dispossessed, and yet the man too loses his voice. It is hard to distinguish the voices from each other and in the end the sound is "very confused," a "gagging" and "choking" sound of "self-abasement, self-abandonment" (FY, 64). While in Poulter's presence, Meda "can't open her mouth to speak to him. . . . If she opened her mouth, she would retch" (FY, 67).

The ironic focus of this story is on the image of a woman losing and finding her voice. When she does find her voice, what will she say? What the crow says stands in harsh contrast to what Meda says but both draw our attention to the process of mediation. The interpolated examples of Meda's poetry are the most subtle of Munro's many stagings of the reading act. They could be seen as a kind of practical joke on literary critics but it soon becomes difficult (as always in Munro) to tell who is the butt of the joke. The repetitive rhymes in Meda's poems encourage us to make other connections based on sound: Meda/media/Medea/mediate. . . . But where do these connections lead? I have indulged in enough wordplay to make it impossible to say that they lead to a dead end. I am very conscious, on the other hand, of the threat in the story – the threat of meaninglessness.

The story raises very difficult questions about the nature of art. When Poulter orders the woman to get up, she bangs her head on the fence: "As she bangs her head, she finds her voice and lets out an openmouthed yowl, full of strength and what sounds like an anguished pleasure" (FY, 66). To whom does it sound like pleasure? How does the yowl of this woman when she "finds her voice" relate to the poems Meda writes when she finds her voice? Meda may enjoy the sound of her own voice making rhymes, but what makes her voice come out for us as "art"? It is surely impossible for a reader to take conscious pleasure in her pretty rhymes (whether they be masculine or feminine) without noticing that art itself ends up acting as a kind of feminine escape from the brutality enacted on Pearl Street. These questions are so disturbing precisely because we are made conscious of how the act of beholding can change the world or the person that is beheld.

Almeda is a reluctant voyeur and her profound reluctance is duplicated in the writer and the reader. What else can a woman do as she watches the decorations and patterns of the past coming explosively to life? It may seem as if we have come a long way from the "ornate customs" of Del Jordan's aunts, but they – like Meda – live in a "tiny sealed-off country" (LGW, 59–60). The language Del learns from them is an "elegantly, ridiculously complicated language." Unlike Meda's, however, it incorporates irony. Meda sees no humour in the distinction between masculine and feminine rhymes and Munro positively dares us to see Meda as a joke. The aunts embody, as characters, the "Irish gift for rampaging mockery, embroidered with deference" (LGW, 37). In "Meneseteung" the mockery, by contrast, is something left out of the story itself. We may or may not choose to inject it – always at the risk of finding ourselves laughing at our own image in the mirror. Barbara Godard describes Del Jordan's aunts as speaking an ornate language that has become "ritual, emptied of meaning" and that "denies the physical or sexual body through which experience is gained" (Godard, 1984, 55). That denial is made explicit and visible in "Meneseteung."

This awareness of the denied body is what renders so ironic the project of "reclamation of literary foremothers" (Godard, 1984, 52) which is also made explicit in this story. Godard, writing before the publication of "Meneseteung," found an oblique reference in *Lives of Girls and Women* to Isabella Valancy Crawford, a poet who lived in Paisley, Ontario and who was known to contemporary readers only "through the ephemeral medium of the daily paper" (Godard, 1984, 57). Meda may well be another echo of that literary foremother but the fact that she is a fiction is crucial to this story. Meda finds her voice by losing it but we would never have heard that voice if the narrator had not found or salvaged it from the past. The act of mock-mediation or translation is crucial to the story's affirmation and it does define an explicit responsibility – that of the contemporary woman writer to the voices of the past. It is a responsibility, however, that is linked to the writer's responsibility to her craft by the fact that this is a mock-historical performance – a fiction. The writer's responsibility, in turn, is linked by Munro to our responsibilities in the real world that contains a river called the "Meneseteung."

Postscript: writing on a living author

It is now almost a decade since I first became obsessed with Munro's obsession with mothers. Since then, many readers have pointed out the "centrality of the mother in Munro's writing" (Irvine, 1983, 104). In an article entitled "Changing Is the Word I Want," Lorna Irvine argues that Munro's choice of fluid narratives that "refuse closure" can be attributed to "the difficulty experienced by a female writer in changing the mother into art" (Irvine, 1983, 101, 103). Irvine sees the mother in "The Ottawa Valley" whose "edges melt and flow" (SIB, 246) and the mother in "Mischief" who "sort of oozes over everything" (WDY, 103) as related to the "floating boundaries" and "open-endedness" that are characteristic of Munro's stories (Irvine, 1983, 109). "What I am arguing," writes Irvine, "is a different theory of narrative sequence" in which "texts may be imagined as being mothered and the different emphases that result from imagining writing in such a way" (Irvine, 1983, 110).

My own readings, like Irvine's, call for a new way of looking at sequence. I believe, however, that Munro's fiction shows more and more clearly that it is not possible for women to opt for a view of fiction as born rather than made. Irvine's own argument blurs in places where she, like the feminists cited by Domna Stanton, extolls "pre-oedipal unboundedness, relatedness, plurality, fluidity, tenderness, and nurturance" – all in the name of female difference (Stanton, 1986, 176). The call to see women's texts as mothered is not, by itself, adequate to do justice to Munro's achievement – her exquisite control of the craft of fiction. Nor does it account for the parade of often bizarre and sometimes grotesque surrogate mothers that marches, somersaults, and pirouettes across the pages of Munro's fiction. In the story "Memorial," there is a literary critic whose dilemma mirrors that of Munro's readers. "Eileen was gratified by the high incidence of crazy mothers in books, but failed to put this discovery to any use" (SIB, 212–213). In the writing of this book I have attempted to put this discovery to use in a way that would account for the hallucinatory quality of Munro's "realism." The spectacle of the float parade and the image of a family circus have been useful to me as I looked for alternatives to old ways of seeing narrative sequence. I have shamelessly mixed metaphors, adding to this the image of the writer as a thrift-shop dresser. Alice Munro's comic vision seems to allow for – even to invite – such unconventional methods.

Barbara Godard's dense reading of "Heirs of the Living Body" comes the closest to my own view of the woman's dilemma as posed by Munro. It is the "predicament of Rose," Godard argues, "to ape the fathers whom one resembles intellectually, or exist in limbo" (Godard, 1984, 48). This is the predicament that I have been tracing back to the earliest version in "Walker Brothers Cowboy." Although Godard claims that "Del gives birth to the text" (67), she steps back from the temptation to essentialize and emphasizes, instead, how Del's "aesthetic of camouflage and paradox" is "first learned from her mothers" (Godard, 1984, 68). Although Godard calls for a kind of "croneology" she does not pretend that it dispenses with chronology. She sees the power of an old woman who cast spells in "Spelling," but she does not pretend that we can forget about ordinary spelling. The argument of this book is consistent with Godard's description of Munro's aesthetic of camouflage. I began with the assumption that only careful response to Munro's crafty disguisings could do justice to her achievement. I ended with the conviction that the Mother is the most thoroughly disguised of all the figures in Munro's stories.

Like Irvine, I notice that the boundaries of Munro's stories are "floating" (Irvine, 1983, 109), but boundaries they remain, nonetheless. The image of the house is, after all, a commonplace that is positioned in the middle of Munro's fiction. I have taken up the stories one at a time because I could not otherwise resist the fluidity. Almost all the books and articles published on Munro seem to be considering all Munro's fiction at the same time. This, for me, is confusing. I learn more from the reading of a single detail – Smaro Kamboureli's isolation of the mother standing on her head, for example. I assume that Munro herself, having published the stories separately, does intend her house of fiction to have partitions. The rooms may be set up as a float parade that is part of one process but the parade does not turn into a pilgrimage that leads to the worship of an idol called Mother. This way of imaging narrative sequence begins to account, I hope, for the effect of simultaneous motion and stillness that is typical of a Munro story. I chose the image because it has the further advantage that it does not dissolve into a seraphic blur of maternal goodness.

Given the fact that so many critics have noticed Munro's obsession with mothers, I find it surprising that no full-length study has yet been published on the image. In an article published in 1976, Beverley Rasporich notes the high incidence in Munro's fiction of "Child-Women and Primitives." I therefore had hopes that her book, *Dance of the Sexes: Art and Gender in the Fiction of Alice Munro* (1990) might clarify the issue of maternity. That it does not is due primarily to the fact that Rasporich posits Mother as an essence that aborts questions before they can even be completely articulated. She sees Sophie in "White Dump," for example, as an "ironic reversal of the male interpretation of the goddess of love," only to reverse this reversal with the following statement: "At the same time, she is Munro's symbolic reinstatement and reinvestiture of the principle of the Mother-Goddess, of fertility, sexuality and power" (Rasporich, 1990, 37). If Sophie could be both, then we could have our cake and eat it too. Maybe we do. Maybe that is part of the pleasure of reading Alice Munro. I am not ready, however, to agree that she is "deified" by Munro "as the Roman goddess of love and fertility" (Rasporich, 1990, 37). Parody does tend to reinstate what it questions, as Linda Hutcheon has documented (Hutcheon, 1985), but this reinstatement is ironic. Munro takes a consistently ironic and wary approach to symbols and archetypes even as she makes it clear that there is no escape from them. Even when the metaphor is dead, like the "day-ud cow" in "Heirs of the Living Body," it still has to be read, however warily. Any effort to read Munro by subsuming the details of her stories into such patterns is doomed, in my view, to failure.

Readings of Munro may be hampered just as much, then, by a mis-guided feminist desire to worship matriarchal power as by more traditional approaches that diminish female power. It is, as Domna Stanton has argued, a temptation for feminists to "countervalorize the traditional antithesis that identifies man with culture and confines woman to instinctual nature" (Stanton, 1986, 170). We all do essentialize and the lust for metaphor (as "Bardon Bus" so dramatically proves) is not easily denied. Toril Moi describes Julia Kristeva's criticism, for example, as anti-biologic and anti-essentialist (Moi, 1985, 12), but Stanton argues persuasively that the mother, in Kristeva's writing, appears as "a passive instinctual force that does not speak, but is spoken by the male" (quoted by Stanton, 1986, 167). Munro does allude to the names of various pre-patriarchal goddesses but she never aligns herself with a simple version of the feminist agenda for recovering the power that is invested in those figures. The women in her stories are robust presences and they exercise power in more obvious ways: they tell stories; they read books; they have and voice opinions.

The major exception to this, of course, is the life of Alice Munro's own mother. Munro's mother clearly did have her own voice and her own presence. In Munro's fiction, however, the thread of referentiality leads to an absence that insistently refuses to be dissolved in any pattern, archetypal or carnivalesque. While the substitute mothers entertain us and while they exercise their power by deploying the old symbols, the "real" mother is dead. Images of her in the act of dying, moreover, bear a resemblance to Kristeva's image of abjection as associated with maternity. There is a wrenching pain in this conscious exclusion and Alice Munro touches my deepest sympathies at this point, a point at which I easily become inarticulate. As I confronted this fact, I began to wonder if consideration of the mother image in Munro has perhaps been blocked by the unresolved issues surrounding biography and autobiography. When I heard Munro on the CBC (Canadian Broadcasting Corporation), telling the interviewer that some time she would sit down and write her autobiography, I had two responses. I wondered to myself if she didn't realize that she has proved that autobiography in the old way is impossible. At the same time I wondered to myself if she didn't realize that everything she has already written is autobiography.

The issue of biography becomes a stumbling block for Rasporich, who falls into a temptation even as she defines that temptation: the "temptation to characterize the real Alice Munro" (Rasporich, 1990, 2). Of what use is it to know (assuming the description to be accurate) that Munro herself "has been, and still is, the traditional woman, used to nurturing, devoted to her children, her second husband and domestic routine" (Rasporich, 1990, 3)? Of what use is it to know the details of Munro's own relation to her mother? Of no use at all, says the voice of the New Critic in me, still demanding to be heard. But it is no longer possible to go back to the almost absolutist position of New Criticism. That position is compromised as soon as I introduce the extra-literary fact that Alice Munro's own mother died of Parkinson's Disease.

There remain many questions that I have not answered to my own satisfaction. I have noted with interest how often people assumed – when told that I was writing a book on mothering in Alice Munro's fiction – that I must be spending a good deal of my time in interviews with her. My astonishment that they would make this assumption was matched by their astonishment that I would not consult with Alice Munro herself. She is, after all, alive and well and living in Clinton, not too far from Toronto, where I live. I have offered assorted reasons for not doing so: I would be invading her privacy; I am not writing a biography; Munro does not like to talk about her fiction; she is not good at it; I would not think of wasting her time, and so on. I have many times revised my rationalizations. For example, I changed my mind and said yes, she *is* good at it, but to examine her way of protecting her space during interviews would take another book. (By comparison to the apparently guileless Alice Munro, Margaret Atwood is an open book.) I have never, however, revised my initial decision not to interview Alice Munro. I do not deny that I would enjoy talking to her about maternity, about jokes, about things Scottish, and about many other subjects. I have been scrupulous, however, about leaving her alone to do her writing. My most recent rationalization goes like this: if all of us wrote and telephoned the living authors we write about, they would soon have no time to write or to live.

I confess, however, that repeated questions about the real Alice Munro have got me thinking as have several startling instances of serendipity that disrupted my sense of detachment. The first of these, as I have already mentioned in the Preface, happened just after I began this book when a

Scottish friend told me he had heard that Munro was related to James Hogg, on whose work I had written my doctoral dissertation. I wrote to Munro asking if this could possibly be true and she promptly wrote back to confirm that she traces her ancestry to the Ettrick Shepherd. The second instance happened just before the publication of *Friend of My Youth*. I received a visit from Douglas Gibson who told me a story about Munro in which I made a startling appearance. After careful deliberation, Munro had settled on the painting by Mary Pratt ("Wedding Dress") that was to appear on the dustjacket of her new book. McClelland & Stewart approached Mary Pratt for copyright permission, only to be told that one Magdalene Redekop had already been granted copyright to use precisely the same painting on the cover of her book on Alice Munro. Readers may guess with what pleasure I gave up my plan to use the picture and with what feelings I viewed the book when it appeared in shop windows.

These incidents increase my desire to talk to Alice Munro. I do not consider myself or my book to be above a vulgar interest in the details of her life. I read, with avid interest, a journalistic account of how a telephone call interrupted her while in the act of making chutney and drinking sherry. I intend, indeed, to invite Alice Munro out to lunch when this manuscript is safely in the hands of my publisher. That I have not done so *before*, however, is a reflection of the fact that I am not sure what those conversations would do to my readings of her fiction – although it is true that I might acquire an excellent recipe for chutney. Like all scholars, I am conditioned to be wary of subjectivity. The painting, after all, *is* by Mary Pratt. James Hogg's poems and stories, after all, *are* his own creation. And what if I could say: "I was there. I went to Clinton to talk to Alice Munro"? Would that give my readings more authority and power? I think not and yet I am not absolutely sure. Writing on a living author has made me think about new ways of looking at the relation between writer and reader. Since writer and reader are exploring a shared imaginary space, it should not be so astonishing when their paths cross or when they suddenly find themselves standing, side by side, looking at the same painting. The fact that it *was* startling may reflect the rigidity of old expectations based on a view of art as existing in splendid isolation from life itself. It is just this view that is challenged by Munro's stories. In her stories, life itself consists of a series of overlapping stories that are constantly under revision.

Even as I say this, however, I am conscious of contradicting myself. This entire book has been an effort to pay tribute to Munro's achievement. It even implicitly assumes a hierarchy of artists and makes a claim that Munro should have a high place on that ladder. I have found myself, in fact, consciously resisting the desire to call her compassion Shakespearian. (There, now I *have* said it.) This contradiction itself was enough to prevent me from taking the bus to Clinton and from allowing my argument to be taken over either by a conventional or by an unconventional biographical bias. The Alice Munro I have been reading is one of the finest storytellers the world has ever seen. This book celebrates her achievement. But who does the Alice Munro in Clinton think she is? Munro's aesthetic involves, as I have argued throughout this book, a new attitude to identity and to autobiography. Barbara Godard observes that many "women have resorted to autobiography when taking up the pen: the plots of fiction have effectively reduced them to objects and in order to find new subjects they must work directly from their lives in 'personal fiction'" (Godard, 1984, 62). Munro, however, uses the idea of autobiography in a way that resists reductive reading. Godard, for example, concludes that "Uncle Craig is not uncle but father, Robert Laidlaw" (Godard, 1984, 57). This equation cannot be made to jive, however, with the fact that Munro's father, Robert Laidlaw, had not started writing (either history or fiction) when *Lives of Girls and Women* was published. Munro herself has expressed warm admiration for the book her father wrote just before he died. Even in the stories by Munro that do involve father figures, she invokes the *idea* of referentiality while, at the same time, presenting them as fictions.

The place where readings of Munro have been blocked – on the connection with autobiography – is the place of her greatest innovation. Literary theorists have been writing about women and autobiography, but as I read and reread Munro I concluded that they have more to learn from her than she has to learn from them. Over and over again, the reading of Munro's fiction has made me conscious of myself as a reader and it is precisely at these points that questions about autobiography arise. When Del reads a magazine article by an "author" who "was a famous New York psychiatrist, a disciple of Freud" an excerpted passage acts as a mirror for our own anxiety about authors and authority:

> For a woman, everything is personal; no idea is of any interest to her by itself, but must be translated into her own experience; in works of art she always sees her own life, or her daydreams.
>
> (LGW, 181)

I too see my own life in Munro's works of art. The death of my mother, my experience with infertility and adoption, the suicides of three friends – all these experiences have shaped my readings of Munro's fiction. To make such an admission is to take a calculated political risk. "She only says that because her experience has made her angry" is a common way of diminishing the political power of feminist polemics. More and more women, however, are taking that risk and appealing to the authority of their experience when it contradicts the old paradigms. In this book I have been conscious of trying to minimize that risk. The more visceral my subjective response to a particular image or story, the more I worked to find some objective context in literary history – the medieval festival of fools, the art history of the grotesque, etc.

I remain conscious, however, of many unanswered questions and these make themselves known to me in my dreams. There is an unwritten taboo, of course, that prevents scholars from admitting that they ever dream about the authors – living or dead – on whom they write. I violate this taboo in order to articulate the questions I cannot answer. In my dreams, Alice Munro usually appears as my sister. This is, in itself, an absurdity since I already have plenty of sisters – six, to be precise – and I don't really need another one. In one dream I try to interview her in a large kitchen during a typical Mennonite family gathering. The room is filled with the noise of all my sisters and my sisters-in-law talking so that I cannot hear Alice Munro. We move to a large gymnasium but there too I have trouble hearing because of the echoing sounds of men playing basketball. My dream fades out as I ask a man for advice on where to find a quiet space and he suggests the men's locker room.

In another dream, I am in a car with two versions of Alice Munro. I am sitting in the front passenger seat while one Alice Munro – a pregnant one – is driving the car through the Ottawa Valley. In my dream (and in my memory) it does have rolling hills. The other Alice Munro sits in the back seat of the car holding a tiny black box which could be either a tape recorder or a child's miniature coffin. In the dream I am asking Munro a question that I can reconstruct only with great difficulty when I wake up. Does she make a distinction, I ask, between autobiographical stories like "The Peace of Utrecht" or "The Ottawa Valley," and others which are more obviously invented?

Well, does she? During my years of writing this book, I have become intensely conscious of the reality of Alice Munro, always in the act of writing her next story. It's not that I feel "*at the mercy*" of what she might write next in the sense that it might contradict my reading. On the contrary, as new stories come out they appear to me to be astonishing confirmations of my earlier readings. I first read "Friend of My Youth" on the subway going home and found myself gasping audibly at the phrase "phantom pregnancy." I had been working with that image for so many years that I had almost come to think of myself as having created it. I see that image as the mock-fruition of Munro's aesthetic but who is it that is being mocked? It appears as a culmination to me, of course, because I am nearing the end of my book, but is it really a culmination of Munro's aesthetic?

My dreams set up signs pointing to the questions I have not answered – or perhaps even asked. Like many readers today, I have reconsidered the New Critical conditioning that goes into my assumptions about authors. Munro's stories, although well-wrought, are clearly questioning the view of art as an autonomous "well-wrought urn." The experience of writing this book, however, has convinced me that there are a lot of very important implications still to be worked out by readers who claim to have abandoned the New Critical assumptions about autonomy. I am writing this postscript because many of these questions do not get asked at all. The sense of closure as the place of an opening out of the questioning process is consistent with Munro's aesthetic. If a book or a story is any good at all, she seems to say, it should end by making you aware of its own limits, of the story that it has not told. As I finish this book I am very conscious of the books I have not written about Munro. This postscript, indeed, is a conscious mimicry of her own predilection for epilogues. The version of "Meneseteung" that was published in *The New Yorker*, for example, did not include the closing paragraph that Munro added when the story came out in *Friend of My Youth*:

> And they may get it wrong, after all. I may have got it wrong. I don't know if she ever took laudanum. Many ladies did. I don't know if she ever made grape jelly.
>
> (FY, 73)

I may have got it wrong too. My aim, however, was not to get it right but to delineate the space created by Alice Munro's stories. Her art is not a place where all the atoms are "safe all the time, whirling away in [the artist's] mind" (LGW, 100). It is, rather, like a series of overlapping circus rings within which we come to see the danger and where we learn to read the "signs of invasion." The effect of overlap or palimpsest is to make Munro an author who, like Jane Austen, is an intense pleasure to reread. Although she is committed to short stories for the reasons I have discussed, regular readers of Munro derive from her fiction a kind of pleasure that may not be so far from that offered by the serialized publication of novels in the nineteenth century. When the narrator of "Friend of My Youth," for example, expresses impatience with her mother's "flowery language" (FY, 24), reading pleasure is increased if we remember how the roots of Del's teeth ache with shame as she reads what her mother writes under the "nom de plume *Princess Ida*" (LGW, 81). In "Oranges and Apples" – to cite another example – "Barbara refused to ride on a float as the Downtown Merchants' contestant for the Queen of the Dominion Day Parade" (FY, 108). The astonishing density of that apparently simple sentence derives largely from the fact that we read into it from Munro's previous stories. Even the recycling of a name is effective: Barbara is the stranger you see in the mirror in "Tell Me Yes or No." The reader familiar with the larger body of Munro's fiction, will, furthermore, know very well that nobody can refuse to be in this float parade. Even the outcasts and the suicides (perhaps especially they) are a part of the performance.

Alice Munro's vision, like that of all comic writers, is one of the community rather than the individual. The people in her story are always in groups – part of a kinship structure, members of a town, residents in a nursing home. There is a breadth of compassion in her stories that also goes along with a comic vision. At the same time, however, Munro moves her narrative float parade against the grain of traditional comic structures that move helter-skelter towards weddings. In her comedy, by contrast, the woman is not, like the Rose, the object of a quest. The woman, rather, is a performer like any other member of the family circus. It becomes difficult, at the moments of most intense humour, to tell the women from the men, the fathers from the mothers. At this point Munro's comic vision reaches back (as does that of James Hogg) to make contact with a Socratic sense of mutual foolishness. The process of storytelling itself is a mimicking by a trickster who invariably makes a fool of herself. It is just here, then, that Munro's stories offer hope where many feminist fictions are despairing. Hope, however, is not the same as a solution. Like the narrator of "The Office," Munro obviously discovered early in her writing career that you cannot find "the solution" to your life. Domna Stanton concludes that "there is no final analysis, no solution" (Stanton, 1986, 177). Like many others, she argues that a constant deferral of meaning – a "putting off, however offputting it may seem" – is preferable to falling back into the desire to worship essential truths. Munro's fiction does contain something of this element of constant deferral to prevent a closure that ultimately denies the reality of the lives of girls and women. Stanton quotes a phrase by Kristeva: "that's not it, that's still not it" that captures Munro's revisionist style.

The comic affirmation, however, comes through in Munro's way of looking at failure. Her fiction is like that "constant critique that turns back on itself, in other words, an autocritique" (Kristeva quoted by Stanton, 1986, 173). It is also, however, a critique that laughs at itself. Munro's fiction takes up the challenge defined by Stanton – to interweave autocriticism "in the fabric of *l'écriture au maternel*" (Stanton, 1986, 173). In Munro's stories, however, this becomes a challenge that involves not only remembering but also laughter and forgetting. If there were only the "unceasing vigilance and self-interrogation" that Stanton describes (Stanton, 1986, 173), creative energy would be entirely taken up with the act of policing. Munro's fiction exposes the ironic loss of power that characterizes our pleasure in the reproduced images of popular culture. She does not judge or deny, however, that the pleasure is there.

False comforts are seen through in Munro's comic vision but there is no true comfort simply in debunking the false ones. The comfort, rather, comes from our sense of participation in a community that has mutual fears and desires. The backdrop of Munro's comic performances is black and the words of Bonaventura seem to capture something of her vision: "Life is only the fool's garb worn by the void, which proudly displays it, but in the end angrily tears it up" (quoted by Kayser, 1966, 60). I do not think, however, that Munro leaves her readers with so bleak a vision. The grotesque as she uses it is different from that defined by Kayser: "an unimpassioned view of life on earth as an empty meaningless puppet play or a caricatural marionette theatre. The divinity of poets and the shaping force of nature have altogether ceased to exist" (Kayser, 1966, 186). Alice Munro does not affirm the sacred power of the poet or of Mother Earth, but the life she so passionately affirms is in the play itself. Del Jordan's account of Miss Farris's view of art seems to me to describe Munro's own passion: "Devotion to the manufacture of what was not true, not plainly necessary, but more important, once belief had been granted to it, than anything else we had" (LGW, 131).

Like Del who plays the part of a puppet with a broken neck in *The Pied Piper*, Alice Munro's comic vision sees the human frailty and absurdity of the artist as the centre of the artistic process. Hers is not the comic vision of an artist who looks down and takes a jaded view of the world as an empty puppet show. Hers, rather, is the comic vision of an artist positioned within that show. The self-image of the female artist duplicates that of the mother, with the focus on the fact of choice. Marietta, the mother who performs the mock hanging in "The Progress of Love," for example, could be seen as a puppet whose neck is not broken. We laugh, Bergson says, when human behaviour is seen as mechanical (*Laughter*, 1900). Alice Munro's mirroring of herself, then, in the mechanical dancing of the puppet Alicia in "Something I've Been Meaning to Tell You," shows how central to her art is the willingness of the artist to make a fool of yourself.

The role of the traditional grotesque, according to Kayser, is to evoke and subdue the demonic.

> In spite of all the helplessness and horror inspired by the dark forces which lurk in and behind our world and have power to estrange it, the truly artistic portrayal effects a secret liberation. The darkness has been sighted, the ominous powers discovered, the incomprehensible forces challenged.
>
> (Kayser, 1966, 188)

Such a sense of liberation characterizes much of Munro's fiction. Her distortions lead, in the end, to a restored sense of proportion. When proportion is restored, however, Munro's stories always return us to the world we live in. There is no liberation from that world, only a revelation that we do not want to be liberated. We want to belong.

This sense that the interlocking and overlapping stories of a community include us is the greatest comfort of Munro's fiction. She herself has chosen to live in the kind of rural Ontario community that is pictured in her stories. This fact is consistent with her aesthetic. It is because Munro herself is always in the picture that she does not need to inhibit her ironic effects. The artist herself, far from being a remote circus-master, is the clown who is everywhere at once, taking breathtaking risks. The stories resemble the simulation of *trompe-l'oeil*. They clear an enchanted space within which the reader may experience the exhilaration of conscious growth. The questions multiply as you read a Munro story but what you question in the end is "reality" itself. During the whole time that I have been writing this book, the words of James Baldwin have been repeating themselves in my head. "Life is more important than art. That's why art is so important." Those words capture the aesthetic of Alice Munro. The questions in Munro's stories will keep multiplying for me even when I have finished my book. Like the conscious simulation of *trompe-l'oeil*, her stories clear an enchanted space within which, when you have finished reading, you can question the "reality" you live in.

Bibliography

Abrams, M.H. (1953) *The Mirror and the Lamp: Romantic Theory and the Critical Tradition*, New York: Oxford University Press.

Aitken, J.L. (1987) *Masques of Morality: Females in Fiction*, Toronto: The Women's Press.

Armstrong, N. and Tennenhouse, L. (eds) (1989) *The Violence of Representation and the History of Violence*, London: Routledge.

Atwood, M. (1976) *Lady Oracle*, Toronto: McClelland & Stewart.

——(1985) *The Handmaid's Tale*, Toronto: McClelland & Stewart.

Auerbach, N. (1985) "Engorging the Patriarchy," in *Historical Studies and Literary Criticism* (ed. J.J. McGann), Madison, Wis: University of Wisconsin Press.

——(1986) *Romantic Imprisonment: Women and Other Glorified Outcasts*, New York: Columbia University Press.

Bachofen, J.J. (1967) *Myth, Religion, and Mother Right*, Princeton, NJ: Princeton University Press.

Bailey, N. (1979) "The Masculine Image in *Lives of Girls and Women*," *Canadian Literature* 80: 113–120.

Bakhtin, M.M. (1968) *Rabelais and his World* (trans. H. Iswolsky), Bloomington, Ind: Indiana University Press.

——(1981) *The Dialogic Imagination: Four Essays* (trans. C. Emerson and M. Holquist), Austin, Tex: University of Texas Press.

Barkan, L. (1975) *Nature's Work of Art: The Human Body as Image of the World*, New Haven, Conn: Yale University Press.

Barthes, R. (1974) *S/Z* (trans. R. Miller), New York: Hill & Wang.

——(1975) *The Pleasure of the Text* (trans. R. Miller), New York: Hill & Wang.

——(1977) *Image, Music, Text: Essays Selected and Translated by Stephen Heath*, New York: Hill & Wang

Baudrillard, J. (1987) *The Ecstasy of Communication* (trans. 1988, B. Schutze and C. Schutze), New York: Semiotext(e).

——(1988) *Selected Writings* (ed. M. Poster, trans. J. Mourrain), Stanford, Calif: Stanford University Press.

Bellows, H.A., (ed.) (1923) *The Poetic Edda*, Princeton, NJ: Princeton University Press.

Benjamin, W. (1969) "The Work of Art in the Age of Mechanical Reproduction," in *Illuminations* (ed. H. Arendt, trans. H. Zahn), New York: Schocken Books.

Berger, J. (1972) *Ways of Seeing*, London: British Broadcasting Corporation.

Bergman, I. (1967) *A Film Trilogy* (trans. P. Britten Austin), London: Calders & Boyars.

Blake, W. (1969) *Complete Writings* (ed. G. Keynes), Oxford: Oxford University Press.

Blodgett, E.D. (1988) *Alice Munro*, Boston, Mass: Twayne.

Blonsky, M. (ed.) (1985) *On Signs*, Baltimore, Md: Johns Hopkins University Press.

Bloom, H. (1975) *A Map of Misreading*, New York: Oxford University Press.

Bouissac, P. (1985) *Circus and Culture: A Semiotic Approach* [1976], New York: University Press of America.

——(1990a) "Incidents, Accidents, Failures: the Representation of Negative Experience in Public Entertainment," in *Beyond Goffman: Studies on Communication, Institution, and Social Interaction* (ed. S.H. Riggins), Berlin: Mouton de Gruyter.

——(1990b) "The Profanation of the Sacred in Circus Clown Performance," in *By Means of Performance: Intercultural Studies of Theatre and Ritual* (ed. R. Schechner and W. Appel), Cambridge: Cambridge University Press.

Brodzki, B. (1988) "Mothers, Displacement, and Language in the Autobiographies of Nathalie Sarraute and Christa Wolf," in *Life/Lines: Theorizing Women's Autobiography* (ed. B. Brodzki and C. Schenck), Ithaca, NY: Cornell University Press.

Brodzki, B. and Schenck, C., (eds) (1988) *Life/Lines: Theorizing Women's Autobiography*, Ithaca, NY: Cornell University Press.

Brossard, N. (1983) *These Our Mothers; Or: The Disintegrating Chapter* (trans. B. Godard), Toronto: Coach House Press.

Browning, R. (1905) *Poetical Works*, London: Oxford University Press.

Brownstein, R. (1982) *Becoming a Heroine: Reading About Women in Novels*, New York: Viking Press.

Bruss, E. (1976) *Autobiographical Acts: The Changing Situation of a Literary Genre*, Baltimore, Md: Johns Hopkins University Press.

——(1980) "Eye for I: Making and Unmaking: Autobiography in Film," in *Autobiography: Essays Theoretical and Critical* (ed. J. Olney), Princeton, NJ: Princeton University Press.

Burton, K. (1956) *Sorrow Built a Bridge: The Life of Mother Alphonsa, Daughter of Nathaniel Hawthorne*, Garden City, NJ: Doubleday.

Bush, G. (1956) *Shakespeare and the Natural Condition*, Cambridge, Mass: Harvard University Press.

Carrington, I. de Papp (1989) *Controlling the Uncontrollable: The Fiction of Alice Munro*, DeKalb, IU: Northern Illinois University Press.

Carroll, L. (1960) *Alice's Adventures in Wonderland & Through the Looking-Glass*, New York: New American Library.

Carscallen, J. (1980) "Alice Munro," in *Profiles in Canadian Literature* no. 24 (ed. J.M. Heath), Toronto: Dundurn Press Limited.

——(1983) "Three Jokers: The Shape of Alice Munro's Stories," in *Centre and Labyrinth: Essays in Honour of Northrop Frye* (ed. E. Cook, C. Hošek, J. Macpherson, P. Parker and J. Patrick), Toronto: University of Toronto Press.

——(1984) "The Shining House: a Group of Stories," in *The Art of Alice Munro: Saying the Unsayable* (ed. J. Miller), Waterloo: University of Waterloo Press.

Chodorow, N. (1978) *The Reproduction of Mothering: Psychoanalysis and the Sociology of Gender*, Berkeley, Calif: University of California Press.

Cirlot, J.E. (1962) *A Dictionary of Symbols* (trans. J. Sage), New York: Routledge & Kegan Paul.

Cixous, H. and Clément, C. (1986) *The Newly Born Woman* (trans. B. Wing), Minneapolis, Minn: University of Minnesota Press.

Conrad, J. (1984) *Heart of Darkness*, Harmondsworth: Penguin.

Cook, E. (1988) *Poetry, Word-Play, and Word-War in Wallace Stevens*, Princeton, NJ: Princeton University Press.

Culler, J. (1982) *On Deconstruction: Theory and Criticism after Structuralism*, Ithaca, NY: Cornell University Press.

Cutler, E. (1967) *I Once Knew an Indian Woman*, Montreal: Tundra.

Dahlie, H. (1985) "Alice Munro and Her Works," in *Canadian Writers and their Works*, vol. 7 (ed. R. Lecker, J. David and E. Quigley), Toronto: ECW Press.

Daly, M. (1978) *Gyn/Ecology: The Metaethics of Radical Feminism*, Boston, Mass: Beacon Press.

Davies, Robertson (1970) *Fifth Business*, New York: Signet.

De Certeau, M. (1985) "Practices of Space," in *On Signs* (ed. M. Blonsky), Baltimore, Md: Johns Hopkins University Press.

De Lauretis, T. (1984) *Alice Doesn't: Feminism, Semiotics, Cinema*, Bloomington, Ind: Indiana University Press.

——(1987) "Gaudy Rose: Eco and Narcissism," in *Technologies of Gender: Essays on Theory, Film, Fiction* (ed. T. De Lauretis), Bloomington, Ind: Indiana University Press.

Derrida, J. (1974) *Of Grammatalogy* (trans. G. Chakravorty Spivak), Baltimore, Md: Johns Hopkins University Press.

——(1978) "Coming into One's Own" (trans. J. Hulbert), in *Psychoanalysis and the Question of the Text* (ed. G. H. Hartman), Baltimore, Md: Johns Hopkins University Press.

——(1985) *The Ear of the Other: Otobiography, Transference, Translation* (ed. C.V. McDonald, trans. P. Kamuf), New York: Schocken.

Dickens, C. (1965) *Great Expectations*, London: Macmillan.

Dinnerstein, D. (1976) *The Mermaid and the Minotaur: Sexual Arrangements and Human Malaise*, New York: Harper & Row.

Dombrowski, E. (1978) "'Down to Death': Alice Munro and Transience," *The University of Windsor Review* 14 (1): 21–29.

Duncan, S.J. (1984) "A Mother in India," in *Stories by Canadian Women* (ed. R. Sullivan), Toronto: Oxford University Press.

Durling, R.M. (1981) "Deceit and Digestion in the Belly of Hell," in *Allegory and Representation* (ed. S.J. Greenblatt), Baltimore, Md: Johns Hopkins University Press.

Eagleton, T. (1983) *Literary Theory: An Introduction*, Minneapolis, Minn: University of Minnesota Press.

Eldridge, L.M. (1984) "A Sense of Ending in *Lives of Girls and Women*," *Studies in Canadian Literature* 9 (1): 110–115.

Ellul, J. (1965) *On Propaganda: The Formation of Men's Attitudes*, New York: Random House.

Empson, W. (1951) *The Structure of Complex Worlds*, New York: New Directions.

Faulkner, W. (1929) *The Sound and the Fury and As I Lay Dying*, New York: Random House.

Fetterley, J. (1977) *The Resisting Reader: A Feminist Approach to American Fiction*, Bloomington, Ind: Indiana University Press.

Findley, T. (1986) *The Telling of Lies*, Harmondsworth: Penguin.

Fisher, E. (1979) *Woman's Creation: Sexual Evolution and the Shaping of Society*, Garden City, NY: Anchor Press.

Freud, S. (1953) "The Uncanny," in *The Standard Edition of the Complete Psychological Works of Sigmund Freud* (ed. J. Strachey) vol. 18, London: Hogarth Press.

——(1955) "Beyond the Pleasure Principle," in *The Standard Edition*, vol. 18.

——(1960) "Jokes and their Relation to the Unconscious," in *The Standard Edition*, vol. 8.

Freud, S. and Breuer, J. (1966) [1895] *Studies on Hysteria*, New York: Avon.
Frost, R. (1963) *Selected Poems*, New York: Holt, Rinehart & Winston.
Frye, N. (1976) *Spiritus Mundi: Essays on Literature, Myth, and Society*, Blooming-ton, Ind: Indiana University Press.
——(1980) *Creation and Recreation*, Toronto: University of Toronto Press.
——(1990) *Words With Power, Being a Second Study of "The Bible and Literature,"* London: Viking.
Gadpaille, M. (1988) *The Canadian Short Story*, Toronto: Oxford University Press.
Gibson, G. (1972) Interview with Alice Munro, in *Eleven Canadian Novelists*, Toronto: Anansi.
Gilbert, Sir W.S. and Sullivan, Sir A. (1938) *Princess Ida or Castle Adamant*, in *The Complete Plays of Gilbert and Sullivan* (ed. D.S. Klopfer), New York: Random House.
Gilman, C.P. (1989) *The Yellow Wallpaper and other Writing*, New York: Bantam.
Godard, B. (1984) "'Heirs of the Living Body': Alice Munro and the Question of the Female Aesthetic," in *The Art of Alice Munro: Saying the Unsayable* (ed. J. Miller), Waterloo: University of Waterloo Press.
Goffman, E. (1974) *Frame Analysis: An Essay on the Organization of Experience*, New York: Harper Colophon.
Gold, J. (1984) "Our Feeling Exactly: the Writing of Alice Munro," in *The Art of Alice Munro: Saying the Unsayable* (ed. J. Miller), Waterloo: University of Waterloo Press.
Gombrich, E.H. (1960) *Art and Illusion: A Study in the Psychology of Pictorial Representation*, Princeton, NJ: Princeton University Press.
Grant, D. (1970) *Realism*, London: Methuen.
Graves, R. (1960) *The White Goddess: A Historical Grammar of Poetic Myth*, London: Faber & Faber Ltd.
Hancock, G. (1987) Interview with Alice Munro, in *Canadian Writers At Work: Interviews with Geoff Hancock*, Toronto: Oxford University Press.
Harvey, Sir P. (ed.) (1967) *The Oxford Companion to English Literature*, Oxford: Clarendon Press.
Hawking, S. (1988) *A Brief History of Time: From the Big Bang to Black Holes*, New York: Bantam.
Heath, S. and Skirrow, G. (1986) "An Interview with Raymond Williams," in *Studies in Entertainment: Critical Approaches to Mass Culture* (ed. T. Modleski), Bloomington, Ind: Indiana University Press.
Hodgins, J. (1977) *The Invention of the World*, Toronto: Signet.
Hoggart, R. (1958) *The Uses of Literacy: Aspects of Working-Class Life with Special Reference to Publications and Entertainments*, Harmondsworth: Penguin.
Homans, M. (1986) *Bearing the Word: Language and Female Experience in Nineteenth-Century Women's Writing*, Chicago: University of Chicago Press.
Hopkins, G.M. (1953) *Poems and Prose* (ed. W.H. Gardner), Harmondsworth: Penguin.
Horwood, H. (1984) "Interview with Alice Munro," in *The Art of Alice Munro: Saying the Unsayable* (ed. J. Miller), Waterloo: University of Waterloo Press.
Howells, C.A. (1987) *Private and Fictional Words: Canadian Women Novelists of the 1970s and 1980s*, London: Methuen.
Hoy, H. (1980) "'Dull, Simple, Amazing and Unfathomable': Paradox and Double Vision in Alice Munro's Fiction," *Studies in Canadian Literature* 5: 100–115.
Hutcheon, L. (1985) *A Theory of Parody: The Teachings of Twentieth-Century Art Forms*, London: Methuen.
——(1988) *The Canadian Postmodern: A Study of Contemporary English-Canadian Fiction*, Toronto: Oxford University Press.

Huyssen, A. (1986) "Mass Culture as Woman: Modernism's Other," in *Studies in Entertainment: Critical Approaches to Mass Culture* (ed. T. Modleski), Bloomington, Ind: Indiana University Press.

Innis, H.A. (1951) *The Bias of Communication*, Toronto: University of Toronto Press.

Ions, V. (1965) *Egyptian Mythology*, London: Hamlyn.

Irigaray, L. (1985a) *Speculum of the Other Woman* (trans. G.C. Gill), Ithaca, NY: Cornell University Press.

——(1985b) *This Sex Which Is Not One* (trans. C. Porter with C. Burke), Ithaca, NY: Cornell University Press.

Irvine, L. (1983) "Changing Is the Word I Want," in *Probable Fictions: Alice Munro's Narrative Acts* (ed. L.K. MacKendrick), Toronto: ECW Press.

——(1986) *Sub/Version*, Toronto: ECW Press.

Jacobus, M. (1986) *Reading Woman: Essays in Feminist Criticism*, New York: Columbia University Press.

Jardine, A.A. (1985) *Gynesis: Configurations of Woman and Modernity*, Ithaca, NY: Cornell University Press.

Jarrell, R. (1941) "Graves and the White Goddess," in *The Third Book of Criticism*, New York: Farrar, Strauss & Giroux.

Joyce, J. (1916) *A Portrait of the Artist as a Young Man*, New York: Viking Press.

Kamboureli, S. (1986) "The Body as Audience and Performance in the Writing of Alice Munro," in *Amazing Space: Writing Canadian Women Writing* (ed. S. Neuman and S. Kamboureli), Edmonton, Alta: Longspoon/NeWest Press.

Kayser, W. (1966) *The Grotesque in Art and Literature* (trans. U. Weisstein), New York: McGraw-Hill.

Keith, W.J. (1989) *A Sense of Style: Studies in the Art of Fiction in English-Speaking Canada*, Toronto: ECW Press.

Kristeva, J. (1987) *Powers of Horror: An Essay on Abjection*, New York: Columbia University Press.

Lacan, J. (1977) *Ecrits: A Selection* (trans. A. Sheridan), New York: W.W. Norton.

——(1979) *The Four Fundamental Concepts of Psycho-Analysis* (ed. J.-A. Miller, trans. A. Sheridan), Harmondsworth: Penguin.

Laidlaw, R. (1979) *The McGregors: A Novel of an Ontario Pioneer Family*, Toronto: Macmillan of Canada.

Laplanche, J. (1976) *Life and Death in Psychoanalysis* (trans. J. Mehlman), Baltimore, Md: Johns Hopkins University Press.

Leisy, J.F. (1966) *A Folk Song Abecedary*, New York: Hawthorn.

Macdonald, R. McCarthy (1976) "A Madman Loose in the World: The Vision of Alice Munro," *Modern Fiction Studies* 22: 365–374.

——(1978) "Structure and Detail in *Lives of Girls and Women*," *Studies in Canadian Literature* 3: 199–210.

MacKendrick, L.K., (ed.) (1983) *Probable Fictions: Alice Munro's Narrative Acts*, Toronto: ECW Press.

Macpherson, J. (1981) *Poems Twice Told: The Boatman and Welcoming Disaster*, Toronto: Oxford University Press.

Martin, W.R. (1987) *Alice Munro: Paradox and Parallel*, Edmonton, Alta: University of Alberta Press.

Mellencamp, P. (1986) "Situation Comedy, Feminism, and Freud: Discourses of Gracie and Lucy," in *Studies in Entertainment: Critical Approaches to Mass Culture* (ed. T. Modleski), Bloomington, Ind: Indiana University Press.

Metcalf, J. (1972) "A Conversation with Alice Munro," *Journal of Canadian Fiction* 1 (4): 54–62.

Meyrowitz, J. (1985) *No Sense of Place: The Impact of Electronic Media on Social Behavior*, Oxford: Oxford University Press.

Michie, H. (1987) *The Flesh Made Word: Female Figures and Women's Bodies*, Oxford: Oxford University Press.

Miller, J. (ed.) (1984) *The Art of Alice Munro: Saying the Unsayable*, Waterloo: University of Waterloo Press.

Miller, N.K. (1986a) "Arachnologies: The Woman, The Text, and the Critic," in *The Poetics of Gender* (ed. N.K. Miller), New York: Columbia University Press.

——(1986b) "Changing the Subject: Authorship, Writing and the Reader," in *Feminist Studies/Critical Studies* (ed. T. de Lauretis), Bloomington, Ind: Indiana University Press.

Modleski, T. (1986) "The Terror of Pleasure: The Contemporary Horror Film and Postmodern Theory," in *Studies in Entertainment: Critical Approaches to Mass Culture* (ed. T. Modleski), Bloomington, Ind: Indiana University Press.

Moi, T. (1985) *Sexual/Textual Politics: Feminist Literary Theory*, London: Methuen.

Moss, J. (1977) "Alice in the Looking Glass: Munro's *Lives of Girls and Women*," in *Sex and Violence in the Canadian Novel: The Ancestral Present*, Toronto: McClelland & Stewart.

Mossberg, B. Clarke (1985) "A Rose in Context: The Daughter Construct," in *Historical Studies and Literary Criticism* (ed. J. McGann), Madison, Wis: University of Wisconsin Press.

Munro, A. (1968) *Dance of the Happy Shades* [DHS], Toronto: Ryerson Press.

——(1971) *Lives of Girls and Women* [LGW], Toronto: McGraw-Hill Ryerson.

——(1972) "The Colonel's Hash Resettled," in *The Narrative Voice: Short Stories and Reflections by Canadian Authors* (ed. J. Metcalf), Toronto: McGraw-Hill Ryerson.

——(1974a) *Something I've Been Meaning To Tell You* [SIB], Toronto: McGraw-Hill Ryerson.

——(1974b) "Home" [uncollected story], in *New Canadian Stories: 74* (ed. D. Helwig and J. Harcourt), Ottawa: Oberon.

——(1974c) "Everything Here is Touchable and Mysterious," in *Weekend Magazine* 11 May: 33.

——(1974d) "An Open Letter," *Jubilee* 1: 5–7.

——(1978a) *Who Do You Think You Are?* [WDY], Toronto: Macmillan [published in the United States in 1979 as *The Beggar Maid: Stories of Flo and Rose*, New York: A.A. Knopf].

——(1978b) "On Writing 'The Office,'" in *Transitions II: Short Fiction. A Source Book of Canadian Literature* (ed. E. Peck), Vancouver: Commcept.

——(1980) "Wood," *New Yorker* 24 November: 46–54.

——(1981) "Working for a Living," *Grand Street* 1 (1): 9–37.

——(1982a) *The Moons of Jupiter* [MJ], Toronto: Macmillan.

——(1982b) "What is Real?", in *Making it New: Contemporary Canadian Stories* (ed. J. Metcalf), Toronto: Methuen.

——(1986) *The Progress of Love* [PL], Toronto: McClelland & Stewart.

——(1990) *Friend of My Youth* [FY], Toronto: McClelland & Stewart.

Nabokov, V. (1969) *Ada or Ardor: A Family Chronicle*, New York: McGraw-Hill.

Neuman, S. and Kamboureli, S. (eds) (1986) *Amazing Space: Writing Canadian Women Writing*, Edmonton, Alta: Longspoon/NeWest Press.

Neumann, E. (1955) *The Great Mother: An Analysis of the Archetype* (trans. R. Mannheim), New York: Random House.

New, W.H. (1976) "Pronouns and Propositions: Alice Munro's Stories," *Open Letter* 3 (5): 40–49.

O'Connor, M. (1990) "Chronotopes for Women under Capital: An Investigation into the Relation of Women to Objects," in *Critical Studies* 2 (1–2): 1–15.

Ovid (1966) *Metamorphosis* (trans. F.J. Miller), Cambridge, Mass: Harvard University Press.

Palmer, P. (1989) *Contemporary Women's Fiction: Narrative Practice and Feminist Theory*, Jackson, Miss: University Press of Mississippi.

Parker, R. (1984) *The Subversive Stitch: Embroidery and the Making of the Feminine*, London: The Women's Press.

Perrakis, P.S. (1982) "Portrait of the Artist as a Young Girl," *Atlantis* 7 (2): 61–67.

Rasporich, B.J. (1976) "Child-Women and Primitives in the Fiction of Alice Munro," *Atlantis* 1 (2): 4–14.

——(1990) *Dance of the Sexes: Art and Gender in the Fiction of Alice Munro*, Edmonton, Alta: University of Alberta Press.

Redekop, M. (1985) "Beyond Closure: Buried Alive with Hogg's *Justified Sinner*," *ELH* 52 (1): 159–184.

——(1988) "Through the Mennonite Looking Glass," in *Why I Am A Mennonite* (ed. H. Loewen), Kitchener: Herald Press.

Rich, A. (1975) *Adrienne Rich's Poetry* (ed. B. Charlesworth Gelpi and A. Gelpi), New York: W.W. Norton.

——(1976) *Of Woman Born: Motherhood as Experience and Institution*, New York: W.W. Norton.

Riis, S. (1976) *The True Story of Ida Johnson*, Toronto: The Women's Press.

Rooke, C. (1989) "Munro's Food," in *Fear of the Open Heart: Essays on Contemporary Canadian Writing*, Toronto: Coach House Press.

Ross, C.S. (1983) "'At least part legend': The Fiction of Alice Munro," in *Probable Fictions: Alice Munro's Narrative Acts* (ed. L.K. MacKendrick), Toronto: ECW Press.

Schor, N. (1987) *Reading the Detail: Aesthetics and the Feminine*, London: Methuen.

Shelley, P.B. (1905) *The Complete Poetical Works*, London: Oxford University Press.

Silverman, K. (1986) "Fragments of a Fashionable Discourse," in *Studies in Entertainment: Critical Approaches to Mass Culture* (ed. T. Modleski), Bloomington, Ind: Indiana University Press.

Sparshott, F. (1982) *The Theory of the Arts*, Princeton, NJ: Princeton University Press.

——(1988) *Off the Ground: First Steps to a Philosophical Consideration of the Dance*, Princeton, NJ: Princeton University Press.

Stalleybrass, P. (1989) "'Drunk with the Cup of Liberty': Robin Hood, the Carnivalesque, and the Rhetoric of Violence in Early Modern England," in *The Violence of Representation and the History of Violence* (ed. N. Armstrong and L. Tennenhouse), London: Routledge.

Stanton, D. (ed.) (1984) *The Female Autograph*, Chicago: University of Chicago Press.

——(1986) "Difference on Trial: A Critique of the Maternal Metaphor in Cixous, Irigaray, and Kristeva," in *The Poetics of Gender* (ed. N. Miller), New York: Columbia University Press.

Stein, G. (1941) *Ida*, New York: Random House.

——(1967) *Look at Me Now and Here I Am: Writings and Lectures, 1909–45* (ed. P. Meyerowitz), London: P. Owen.

Stevens, W. (1967) *The Palm at the End of the Mind and other Poems*, New York: Random House.

Struthers, J.R. (1975) "Reality and Ordering: The Growth of a Young Artist in *Lives of Girls and Women*," *Essays on Canadian Writing* 3: 32–46.

——(1983) "The Real Material: An Interview with Alice Munro," in *Probable Fictions: Alice Munro's Narrative Acts* (ed. L.K. MacKendrick), Toronto: ECW Press.

Swift, J. (1967) *Poetical Works* (ed. H. Davis), London: Oxford University Press.

Tausky, T.E. (1986a) "'What Happened to Marion?': Art and Reality in *Lives of Girls and Women*," *Studies in Canadian Literature* 11 (1): 52–76.

——(1986b) "Biocritical Essay," *The Alice Munro First Accession: an Inventory of the Archive at the University of Calgary Libraries* (compiled by J.M. Moore and J.F. Tener, ed. A. Steele and J.F. Tener), Calgary: University of Calgary Press.

Tennyson, A. (1971) *Poems and Plays* (ed. T.H. Warren), Oxford: Oxford University Press.

Thacker, R. (1984) "Alice Munro: An Annotated Bibliography," in *The Annotated Bibliography of Canada's Major Authors*, vol. 5 (ed. R. Lecker and J. David), Toronto: ECW Press.

Thomas, A. (1984) *Intertidal Life*, Toronto: General Publishing.

Trebilcot, J. (ed.) (1983) *Mothering: Essays in Feminist Theory*, Totowa, NJ: Rowman & Allanheld.

Van Buren, J. Silverman, K. (1989) *The Modernist Madonna: Semiotics of the Maternal Metaphor*, Bloomington, Ind: Indiana University Press.

Walker, B.G. (1983) *The Woman's Encyclopedia of Myths and Secrets*, San Francisco: Harper & Row, Publishers.

——(1985) *The Crone: Woman of Age, Wisdom, and Power*, San Francisco: Harper & Row.

——(1988) *The Woman's Dictionary of Symbols and Sacred Objects*, San Francisco: Harper & Row.

Wallace, B. (1978) "Women's Lives: Alice Munro," in *The Human Element: Critical Essays* (ed. D. Helwig), Ottawa: Oberon.

Weaver, J. (1988) "Society and Culture in Rural and Small Town Ontario: Alice Munro's Testimony on the Last Forty Years," in *Patterns of the Past: Interpreting Ontario's History* (ed. R. Hall, W. Westfall and L. Sefton MacDowell), Toronto: Dundurn Press.

Welsford, E. (1935) *The Fool: His Social and Literary History*, Gloucester, Mass: Peter Smith, 1966 [first published by Faber & Faber in 1935].

White, A. (1989) "Hysteria and the End of Carnival: Festivity and Bourgeois Neurosis," in *The Violence of Representation and the History of Violence* (ed. N. Armstrong and L. Tennenhouse), London: Routledge.

Willeford, W. (1969) *The Fool and his Scepter: A Study in Clowns and Jesters and their Audience*, Evanston, Ill: Northwestern University Press.

Williams, R. (1974) *Television: Technology and Cultural Form*, New York: Schocken.

——(1989) *Raymond Williams on Television: Selected Writings* (ed. A. O'Connor), Toronto: Between the Lines.

Withycombe, E.G. (1977) *The Oxford Dictionary of English Christian Names*, Oxford: Oxford University Press.

Woolf, V. (1927) *To the Lighthouse*, London: Hogarth Press.

——(1931) *The Waves*, Harmondsworth: Penguin.

Yalom, M. (1985) *Maternity, Mortality, and the Literature of Madness*, University Park, Pa, and London: Pennsylvania State University Press.

Yeats, W.B. (1963) *Collected Poems*, London: Macmillan.

York, L. (1988) "The Delicate Moment of Exposure: Alice Munro and Photography," in *The Other Side of Dailiness: Photography in the Works of Alice Munro, Timothy Findley, and Margaret Laurence*, Toronto: ECW Press.

Index

"Images" 8, 20, 25, 39, 43–49, 65, 72, 97, 104–105, 164, 169, 171, 193, 220; "Labor Day Dinner" 31, 150, 152, 153; "Lichen" 27, 28, 40, 76, 92–93, 115, 148, 178, 182–191, 197, 204, 206; *Lives of Girls and Women* 44, 60–87, 88, 94, 115–116, 130, 137, 144, 149–150, 157, 185, 187, 203, 222, 234; "Lives of Girls and Women" 69–73, 109; "Marrakesh" 18–19, 135, 206; "Material" 14, 15, 31, 89, 107, 221; "Memorial" 229; "Meneseteung" xii, 28–9, 42, 62, 214, 216–228, 236; "Miles City, Montana" 3, 22, 178; "Mischief" 14, 131–132; "The Moon in the Orange Street Skating Rink" 29, 192–201, 222; *The Moons of Jupiter* 149–173; "The Moons of Jupiter" 149–50, 152–3, 156, 167–73, 177, 181, 203; "Mrs. Cross and Mrs. Kidd" 14, 151; "The Office" 49–50, 70, 75, 237; "Oranges and Apples" 236; "The Ottawa Valley" 32, 103–114, 115, 120–121, 128, 139, 152, 169, 185, 209, 210, 212, 213, 229, 235; "The Peace of Utrecht" 28, 50–7, 62, 77, 106, 107, 120, 168, 172, 178, 209, 212, 235; "Postcard" 125; "Princess Ida" 32, 60–5, 129, 176; "Privilege" 8, 15, 68–69, 131–134, 136; *The Progress of Love* 174–208; "The Progress of Love" 6, 8, 9, 29, 48, 69, 108, 172, 174–182, 177, 201, 209–210; "Providence" 56, 130, 217; "Prue" 151, 153, 158; "Red Dress 1946" 37; "Royal Beatings" 12–13, 33, 137, 168, 192, 220, 224; "Simon's Luck" 76; *Something I've Been Meaning to Tell You* 88–114, 151; "Something I've Been Meaning to Tell You" 14, 21–22, 33, 97–103, 183, 196, 213, 238; "Spelling" 139–142, 145, 230; "The Stone in the Field" 153, 155, 156, 161, 164–167, 172, 177; "Tell Me Yes or No" 96, 88–93, 158, 236; "The Turkey Season" 5, 152; "Walker Brothers Cowboy" 19, 29, 32, 37–43, 44, 48, 112, 149, 154, 177, 201, 217, 230; "White Dump" 26, 31, 176, 177, 201–208, 231; *Who Do You Think You Are?* 115–148,

150, 179; "Who Do You Think You Are?" 41, 142–148, 200; "Wild Swans" 20, 34, 72, 130, 134–139, 159, 192; "Winter Wind" 103–105

Nabokov, V. 64

orphans 17–20, 25, 47, 134–139, 162, 172, 220
Orpheus 58
Osiris 122

Palmer, P. 6
parades 24, 26, 63, 116, 121, 141–143, 145, 147–148, 148, 163, 175, 212, 216, 223, 229–230, 237
Parker, R. 196, 197
Penelope 97, 184
Pennington, B. 180–181
Persephone 122
photography 17–20, 73–76, 85, 190–191, 216
pied piper 58–59, 78–79, 102, 107, 111, 135, 138, 204, 238
Plato 19, 31, 47, 169, 193, 196
Poe, E.A. 12, 225
Poetic Edda, The 176, 205–206
popular culture 17–20, 115–148, 237; comic strips 26, 69; formula romances 196; get-well cards 196–197; magazines 24, 26, 67; movies 61, 134, 136, 186–188; newspapers 62, 82, 138, 158, 166, 187, 220; nursery rhymes 31, 87; pornography 115, 159; radio 116; songs 38, 111, 123, 124, 135, 163, 192, 204; stories 74–75, 101, 127–128, 193, 204; tabloids 169; television 23, 116–119, 162, 168, 200, 220, 224; video 220
Pratt, M. 7, 55, 233
Prometheus 201
prostitution 14–16, 69–73, 82, 131–134
Proust, M. 17, 63, 74
puppets 21–24, 76–79, 89, 98–99, 101, 110–111, 139–143, 174, 217, 237–238
Pygmalion 100, 129

quest romance 43–49, 50, 58, 71–72, 97–103, 106

Rabelais, F. 124